PRACTICAL GRAPH MINING WITH R

Chapman & Hall/CRC
Data Mining and Knowledge Discovery Series

SERIES EDITOR
Vipin Kumar
University of Minnesota
Department of Computer Science and Engineering
Minneapolis, Minnesota, U.S.A.

AIMS AND SCOPE

This series aims to capture new developments and applications in data mining and knowledge discovery, while summarizing the computational tools and techniques useful in data analysis. This series encourages the integration of mathematical, statistical, and computational methods and techniques through the publication of a broad range of textbooks, reference works, and handbooks. The inclusion of concrete examples and applications is highly encouraged. The scope of the series includes, but is not limited to, titles in the areas of data mining and knowledge discovery methods and applications, modeling, algorithms, theory and foundations, data and knowledge visualization, data mining systems and tools, and privacy and security issues.

PUBLISHED TITLES

INFORMATION DISCOVERY ON ELECTRONIC HEALTH RECORDS
Vagelis Hristidis

INTELLIGENT TECHNOLOGIES FOR WEB APPLICATIONS
Priti Srinivas Sajja and Rajendra Akerkar

INTRODUCTION TO PRIVACY-PRESERVING DATA PUBLISHING:
CONCEPTS AND TECHNIQUES
Benjamin C. M. Fung, Ke Wang, Ada Wai-Chee Fu, and Philip S. Yu

KNOWLEDGE DISCOVERY FOR COUNTERTERRORISM AND LAW ENFORCEMENT
David Skillicorn

KNOWLEDGE DISCOVERY FROM DATA STREAMS
João Gama

MACHINE LEARNING AND KNOWLEDGE DISCOVERY FOR
ENGINEERING SYSTEMS HEALTH MANAGEMENT
Ashok N. Srivastava and Jiawei Han

MINING SOFTWARE SPECIFICATIONS: METHODOLOGIES AND APPLICATIONS
David Lo, Siau-Cheng Khoo, Jiawei Han, and Chao Liu

MULTIMEDIA DATA MINING: A SYSTEMATIC INTRODUCTION TO CONCEPTS AND THEORY
Zhongfei Zhang and Ruofei Zhang

MUSIC DATA MINING
Tao Li, Mitsunori Ogihara, and George Tzanetakis

NEXT GENERATION OF DATA MINING
Hillol Kargupta, Jiawei Han, Philip S. Yu, Rajeev Motwani, and Vipin Kumar

PRACTICAL GRAPH MINING WITH R
Nagiza F. Samatova, William Hendrix, John Jenkins, Kanchana Padmanabhan,
and Arpan Chakraborty

RELATIONAL DATA CLUSTERING: MODELS, ALGORITHMS, AND APPLICATIONS
Bo Long, Zhongfei Zhang, and Philip S. Yu

SERVICE-ORIENTED DISTRIBUTED KNOWLEDGE DISCOVERY
Domenico Talia and Paolo Trunfio

SPECTRAL FEATURE SELECTION FOR DATA MINING
Zheng Alan Zhao and Huan Liu

STATISTICAL DATA MINING USING SAS APPLICATIONS, SECOND EDITION
George Fernandez

SUPPORT VECTOR MACHINES: OPTIMIZATION BASED THEORY, ALGORITHMS,
AND EXTENSIONS
Naiyang Deng, Yingjie Tian, and Chunhua Zhang

TEMPORAL DATA MINING
Theophano Mitsa

TEXT MINING: CLASSIFICATION, CLUSTERING, AND APPLICATIONS
Ashok N. Srivastava and Mehran Sahami

THE TOP TEN ALGORITHMS IN DATA MINING
Xindong Wu and Vipin Kumar

UNDERSTANDING COMPLEX DATASETS:
DATA MINING WITH MATRIX DECOMPOSITIONS
David Skillicorn

PRACTICAL GRAPH MINING WITH R

Edited by

Nagiza F. Samatova
William Hendrix
John Jenkins
Kanchana Padmanabhan
Arpan Chakraborty

CRC Press
Taylor & Francis Group
Boca Raton London New York

CRC Press is an imprint of the
Taylor & Francis Group, an **informa** business

A CHAPMAN & HALL BOOK

CRC Press
Taylor & Francis Group
6000 Broken Sound Parkway NW, Suite 300
Boca Raton, FL 33487-2742

Printed on acid-free paper
Version Date: 20130620

International Standard Book Number-13: 978-1-4398-6084-7 (Hardback)

Library of Congress Cataloging-in-Publication Data

Practical graph mining with R / editors, Nagiza F. Samatova, William Hendrix, John Jenkins, Kanchana Padmanabhan, Arpan Chakraborty.
     pages cm -- (Chapman & Hall/CRC data mining and knowledge discovery series)
    Includes bibliographical references and index.
    ISBN 978-1-4398-6084-7 (hardback)
    1. Data mining--Graphic methods. 2. Data visualization--Data processing. 3. R (Computer program language) I. Samatova, Nagiza F.

QA76.9.D343P725 2013
006.3'12--dc23
                                            2013019699

Visit the Taylor & Francis Web site at
http://www.taylorandfrancis.com

and the CRC Press Web site at
http://www.crcpress.com

Contents

List of Figures

List of Tables

Preface

Graph mining is a growing area of study that aims to discover novel and insightful knowledge from data that is represented as a graph. Graph data is ubiquitous in real-world science, government, and industry domains. Examples include social network graphs, Web graphs, cybersecurity networks, power grid networks, and protein-protein interaction networks. Graphs can model the data that takes many forms ranging from traditional vector data through time-series data, spatial data, sequence data to data with uncertainty. While graphs can represent the broad spectrum of data, they are often used when links, relationships, or interconnections are critical to the domain. For example, in the social science domain, the nodes in a graph are people and the links between them are friendship or professional collaboration relationships, such as those captured by Facebook and LinkedIn, respectively. Extraction of useful knowledge from collaboration graphs could facilitate more effective means of job searches.

The book provides a practical, "do-it-yourself" approach to extracting interesting patterns from graph data. It covers many basic and advanced techniques for graph mining, including but not limited to identification of anomalous or frequently recurring patterns in a graph, discovery of groups or clusters of nodes that share common patterns of attributes and relationships, as well as extraction of patterns that distinguish one category of graphs from another and use of those patterns to predict the category for new graphs.

This book is designed as a primary textbook for advanced undergraduates, graduate students, and researchers focused on computer, information, and computational science. It also provides a handy resource for data analytics practitioners. The book is self-contained, requiring no prerequisite knowledge of data mining, and may serve as a standalone textbook for graph mining or as a supplement to a standard data mining textbook.

Each chapter of the book focuses on a particular graph mining task, such as link analysis, cluster analysis, or classification, presents three representative computational techniques to guide and motivate the reader's study of the topic, and culminates in demonstrating how such techniques could be utilized to solve a real-world application problem(s) using real data sets. Applications include network intrusion detection, tumor cell diagnostics, face recognition, predictive toxicology, mining metabolic and protein-protein interaction networks, community detection in social networks, and others. These representative techniques and applications were chosen based on availability of open-source software and real data, as the book provides several libraries for the R statistical computing environment to "walk-through" the real use cases. The presented techniques are covered in sufficient mathematical depth. At the same time, chapters include a lot of explanatory examples. This makes the abstract principles of graph mining accessible to people of varying levels of expertise, while still providing a rigorous theoretical foundation that is grounded in reality. Though not every available technique is covered in depth, each chapter includes a brief survey of bibliographic references for those interested in further reading. By presenting a level of depth and breadth in each chapter with an ultimate focus on "hands-on" practical application, the book has something to offer to the student, the researcher, and the practitioner of graph data mining.

There are a number of excellent data mining textbooks available; however, there are a number of key features that set this book apart. First, the book focuses specifically on mining graph data. Mining graph data differs from traditional data mining in a number of critical ways. For example, the topic of classification in data mining is often introduced in relation to vector data; however, these techniques are often unsuitable when applied to graphs, which require an entirely different approach such as the use of graph kernels.

Second, the book grounds its study of graph mining in R, the open-source software environment for statistical computing and graphics (http://www.r-project.org/). R is an easy-to-learn open source software package for statistical data mining with capabilities for interactive, visual, and exploratory data analysis. By incorporating specifically designed R codes and examples directly into the book, we hope to encourage the intrepid reader to follow along and to see how the algorithmic techniques discussed in the book correspond to the process of graph data analysis. Each algorithm in the book is presented with its accompanying R code.

Third, the book is a self-contained, teach-yourself practical approach to graph mining. The book includes all source codes, many worked examples, exercises with solutions, and real-world applications. It develops intuition through the use of easy-to-follow examples, backed up with rigorous, yet accessible, mathematical foundations. All examples can easily be run using the included R packages. The underlying mathematics presented in the book is self-contained. Each algorithmic technique is accompanied by a rigorous and formal explanation of the underlying mathematics, but all math preliminaries are presented in the text; no prior mathematical knowledge is assumed. The level of mathematical complexity ranges from basic to advanced topics. The book comes with several resources for instructors, including exercises and complete, step-by-step solutions.

Finally, every algorithm and example in the book is accompanied with the snippet of the R code so that the readers could actually perform any of the graph mining techniques discussed in the book from (or while) reading it. Moreover, each chapter provides one or two real application examples, again with R codes and real data sets, that walk the reader through solving the real problem in an easy way.

We would like to acknowledge and thank the students of the CSC 422/522 Automated Learning and Data Analysis course taught in Fall 2009 at North Carolina State University, who wrote this book under the supervision and guidance of their instructor, Dr. Nagiza Samatova. Despite the contributed chapter format, a specific effort has been made to unify the presentation of the material across all the chapters, thus making it suitable as a textbook. We would also like to thank the students of the Fall 2011 batch of the same course, where the book was used as the primary textbook. The feedback provided by those students was extremely useful in improving the quality of the book. We would like to thank North Carolina State University, Department of Computer Science for their encouragement of this book; the anonymous reviewers for their insightful comments; the CRC Press editorial staff for their constant support and guidance during the publication process. Finally, we would like to thank the funding agencies National Science Foundation and the US Department of Energy for supporting the scientific activity of the various co-authors and co-editors of the book.

1

Introduction

Kanchana Padmanabhan, William Hendrix

North Carolina State University

Nagiza F. Samatova

North Carolina State University and Oak Ridge National Laboratory

CONTENTS

Recent years have been witnessing an explosion of graph data from a variety of scientific, social, economic, and technological domains. In its simplest form, a graph is a collection of individual objects interconnected in some way. Examples include electric power grids connecting power grids across geographically distributed locations, global financial systems connecting banks worldwide, and social networks linking individual users, businesses, or customers by friendship, collaboration, or transaction interactions.

Graph data analytics—extraction of insightful and actionable knowledge from graph data—shapes our daily life and the way we think and act. We often realize our dependence on graph data analytics only if failures occur in normal functioning of the systems that these graphs model and represent. A disruption in a local power grid can cause a cascade of failures in critical parts of the entire nation's energy infrastructure. Likewise, a computer virus, in a blink of an eye, can spread over the Internet causing the shutdown of important businesses or leakage of sensitive national security information.

Intrinsic properties of these diverse graphs, such as particular patterns of interactions, can affect the underlying system's behavior and function. Mining for such patterns can provide insights about the vulnerability of a nation's energy infrastructure to disturbances, the spread of disease, or the influence of people's opinions. Such insights can ultimately empower us with actionable knowledge on how to secure our nation, how to prevent epidemics, how to increase efficiency and robustness of information flow, how to prevent catastrophic events, or how to influence the way people think, form opinions, and act.

Graphs are ubiquitous. Graph data is growing at an exponential rate.

Graph data analytics can unquestionably be very powerful. Yet, our ability to extract useful patterns, or knowledge, from graph data, to characterize intrinsic properties of these diverse graphs, and to understand their behavior and function lags behind our dependence on them. To narrow this gap, a number of graph data mining techniques grounded in foundational graph-based theories and algorithms have been recently emerging. These techniques have been offering powerful means to manage, process, and analyze highly complex and large quantities of graph data from seemingly all corners of our daily life. The next section briefly discusses diverse graphs and graph mining tasks that can facilitate the search for solutions to a number of problems in various application domains.

1.1   Graph Mining Applications

Web Graphs: The world wide web (WWW) is a ubiquitous graph-structured source of information that is constantly changing. The sea of information captured by this graph impacts the way we communicate, conduct business, find useful information, etc. The exponentially growing rate of information and the complexity and richness of the information content presents a tremendous challenge to graph mining not only in terms of scaling graph algorithms to represent, index, and access enormous link structures such as citations, collaborations, or hyperlinks but also extraction of useful knowledge from these mountains of data.

A somewhat simplified model of the world wide web graph represents web pages as nodes and hyperlinks connecting one page to another as links. Mining the structure of such graphs can lead to identification of authorities and hubs, where authorities represent highly ranked pages and hubs represent pages linking to the most authoritative pages. Likewise, augmented with web page content evolving over time, more complex patterns could be discovered from such graphs including the emergence of hot topics or obsolete, or disappearing topics of interest. Further, structuring the content of web pages with semantic information about peoples, times, and locations such as whom, when, and where, and actions such as "visited," "is a friend of," "conducts business with," provides another means of more informative and yet more complex graphs. Mastering the art of searching such semantically rich graphs can turn the curse of this tsunami of data into the blessing—actionable knowledge.

Social Science Graphs: Social science graphs model relationships among groups of people and organizations. In these graphs, links between people/groups can represent friendship, political alliance, professional collaboration, and many other types of relationships. Among the largest and most popular social networking services are Facebook, LinkedIn, and Twitter. Mining such graphs can provide unprecedented opportunities for increasing revenues to businesses, advancing careers of employees, or conducting political campaigns. For example, Twitter is a platform where people can publicly communicate in short, text-based messages. A link in a Twitter graph is directed and connects a person called a "follower" to another person. Followers receive updates whenever any person they follow posts a message on Twitter. A follower can in turn restate the message to his/her followers. This way, the message of one person propagates through much of the social network. Mining such a graph can provide insights into identifying the most influential people or people whose opinions propagate the most in terms of reaching the largest number of people and in terms of the distance from the opinion origin. The ability to track the flow of information and reason about the network structure can then be exploited, for example to spread the word about emerging epidemics or influence the people's perception about an electoral candidate, etc.

Computer Networking Graphs: As opposed to graphs over Internet web pages, networking graphs typically represent interconnections (physical connections) among various routers (nodes) across the Internet. Due to the fact that there are billions of Internet users, managing such large and complex networks is a challenging task. To improve quality of services offered by Internet service providers to their customers, various graph mining tasks can provide valuable information pertaining to recurrent patterns on the Internet traffic, to detect routing instabilities, to suggest the placement of new routers, etc.

Homeland Security and Cybersecurity Graphs: Homeland security and cybersecurity graphs play a critical role in securing national infrastructure, protecting the privacy of people with personal information on Internet servers, and safeguarding networks and servers from intruders. Mining a cybersecurity graph with computers as its nodes and links encoding the message traffic among those computers can provide insightful knowledge of whether computer viruses induced in one part of the graph will propagate to other parts of the graph adversely affecting the functioning of critical infrastructure such as electric power grids, banks, and healthcare systems. Preventing or diminishing such adverse effects can take advantage of other graph mining tasks including identification of intruder machines, predicting which computers have been accessed without proper authorization, or which unauthorized users obtained root privileges.

Homeland security graphs capture important information from multiple sources in order to detect and monitor various national and international criminal activities. Criminal activity networks with nodes representing individuals suspected to be involved in violent crimes, narcotic crimes, or terrorist activity are linked to attributes about phone calls, emails, border-crossing records, etc. Mining such complex and often incomplete graphs presents a significant challenge. Graph-based algorithms can provide useful knowledge about missing links, anomalous trafficking activities, or predict target-critical infrastructure locations. It can also help reconstruct the potential criminal organizations or terrorist rings.

Biological Graphs: The functioning of a living cell is a fascinating set of molecular events that allows cells to grow, to survive in extreme environments, and to perform inter- and intra-cellular communication. Biomolecular machines act together to perform a wide repertoire of cellular functions including cellular respiration, transport of nutrients, or stress response. Such crosstalking biomolecular machines correspond to communities, or densely connected subgraphs, in an intracellular graph. Mining for communities that are frequent in unhealthy cells, such as cancer cells, but are missing in healthy cells, can provide informative knowledge for biomedical engineers and drug designers.

As a particularly important inter-cellular network, the human brain contains billions of neurons, trillions of synapses, forming an extraordinarily complex network that contains latent information about our decision making, cognition, adaptation, and behavior. Modern technologies such as functional neuroimaging provide a plethora of data about the structure, dynamics, and activities of such a graph. Mining such graphs for patterns specific to mentally disordered patients such as those affected by Alzheimer's and schizophrenia, provides biomarkers or discriminatory signatures that can be utilized by healthcare professionals to improve diagnostics and prognostics of mental disorders.

Chemical Graphs: The molecular structure of various chemical compounds can be naturally modeled as graphs, with individual atoms or molecules representing nodes and bonds between these elements representing links. These graphs can then be analyzed to determine a number of properties, such as toxicity or mutagenicity (the ability to cause structural alterations in DNA). The determination of properties such as these in a computational manner is extremely useful in a number of industrial contexts, as it allows a much higher-paced chemical research and design process. Mining for recurrent patterns in the database of mutagenic and non-mutagenic chemical compounds can improve our understanding of what distinguishes the two classes and facilitate more effective drug design methodologies.

Finance Graphs: The structure of stock markets and trading records can also be represented using graphs. As an example, the nodes can be brokers, banks, and customers, and the links can capture the financial trading information such as stocks that were bought or sold, when, by whom, and at what price. A sequence of such graphs over a period of time can be mined to detect people involved in financial frauds, to predict which stocks will be on the rise, and to distinguish stock purchasing patterns that may lead to profits or losses.

Healthcare Graphs: In healthcare graphs, nodes can represent people (lawyers, customers, doctors, car repair centers, etc.) and links can represent their names being present together in a claim. In such a graph, "fraud rings" can be detected, i.e. groups of people collaborating to submit fraudulent claims. Graph mining techniques can help uncover anomalous patterns in such graphs, for example, doctor A and lawyer B have a lot of claims or customers in common.

Software Engineering Graphs: Graphs can be used in software engineering to capture the data and control information present in a computer program. The nodes represent statements/operations/control points in a program and the edges represent the control and data dependencies among such operations. These graphs are mined for knowledge to help with the detection of replicated code, defect detection/debugging, fault localization, among other tasks. This knowledge can then be utilized to improve the quality, maintainability, and execution time of the code. For example, replicated code fragments that perform equivalent/similar functions can be analyzed for a change made to one replicated area of code in order to detect the changes that should be made to the other portions as well. Identifying these fragments would help us to either replace these clones with references to a single code fragment or to know beforehand how many code fragments to check in case of error.

Climatology: Climatic graphs model the state and the dynamically changing nature of a climate. Nodes can correspond to geographical locations that are linked together based on correlation or anti-correlation of their climatic factors such as temperature, pressure, and precipitation. The recurrent substructures over one set of graphs may provide insights about the key factors and the hotspots on the earth that affect the activity of hurricanes, the spread of droughts, or the long-term climate changes such as global warming.

Entertainment Graphs: An entertainment graph captures information about movies, such as actors, directors, producers, composers, writers, and their metrics, such as reviews, ratings, genres, and awards. In such graphs, the nodes could represent movies with links to attributes describing the movie. Likewise, such graphs may connect people such as actors or directors and movies. Mining such graphs can facilitate the prediction of upcoming movie popularity, distinguish popular movies from poorly ranked movies, and discover the key factors in determining whether a movie will be nominated for awards or receive awards.

Companies such as Netflix can benefit from mining such graphs by better organizing the business through predictive graph-based recommender algorithms that suggest customers to movies they will likely enjoy.

Another type of entertainment graph can be used to model the structure and dynamics of sport organizations and their members. For example, the NBA can mine sports graphs with coaches and players as nodes and link attributes describing their performance as well as outcomes of games. Mining the dynamics of such evolving sport graphs over time may suggest interesting sporting trends or predict which team will likely win the target championship.

1.2   Book Structure

The book is organized into three major sections. The introductory section of the book (Chapters 2–4) establishes a foundation of knowledge necessary for understanding many of the techniques presented in later chapters of the book. Chapter 2 details some of the basic concepts and notations of graph theory. The concepts introduced in this chapter are vital to understanding virtually any graph mining technique presented in the book, and it should be read before Chapters 5–11. Chapter 3 discusses some of the basic capabilities and commands in the open source software package R. While the graph mining concepts presented later in the book are not limited to being used in R, all of the hands-on examples and many of the exercises in the book depend on the use of R, so we do recommend reading this chapter before Chapters 5–12. Chapter 4 describes the general technique of kernel functions, which are functions that allow us to transform graphs or other data into forms more amenable to analysis. As kernels are an advanced mathematical topic, this chapter is optional; however, the chapter is written so that no mathematical background beyond algebra is assumed, and some of the advanced techniques presented in Chapters 6, 8, 9, and 10 are kernel-based methods.

The primary section of the book (Chapters 5–9) covers many of the classical data mining and graph mining problems. As each chapter is largely self-contained, these chapters may be read in any order once the reader is familiar with some basic graph theory (Chapter 2) and using R (Chapter 3). Chapter 5 covers several techniques for link analysis, which can be used to characterize a graph based on the structure of its connections. Chapter 6 introduces the reader to several proximity measures that can be applied to graphs. Proximity measures, which can be used to assess the similarity or difference between graphs or between nodes in the same graph, are useful for applying other data mining techniques, such as clustering or dimension reduction. Chapter 7 presents several techniques for mining frequent subgraphs, which are smaller sections of a larger graph that recur frequently. Chapter 8 describes several techniques for applying clustering to graphs. Clustering is a general data mining technique that is used to divide a dataset into coherent groups, where the data (graph nodes) in the same group are more closely related and nodes in different clusters are less related. Chapter 9 discusses the problem of classification in graphs, i.e., assigning objects into categories based on some number of previously categorized example, and presents several techniques that are effective in categorizing nodes or entire graphs.

The final section of the book (Chapters 10–12) represents a synthesis of the prior chapters, covering advanced techniques or aspects of graph mining that relate to one or more of the chapters in the primary section of the book. Chapter 10 deals with dimensionality reduction, which in general data mining, refers to the problem of reducing the amount of data while still preserving the essential or most salient characteristics of the data. In terms of graphs, though, dimensionality reduction refers to the problem of transforming graphs into low-dimensional vectors so that graph features and similarities are preserved. These transformed data can be analyzed using any number of general-purpose vector data mining techniques. Chapter 11 details basic concepts and techniques for detecting anomalies in graphs, which in the context of graphs, might represent unexpected patterns or connections or connections that are unexpectedly missing. As anomaly detection is related to both clustering and classification, Chapter 11 should be read after Chapters 8 and 9. Chapter 13 introduces several basic concepts of parallel computing in R, applying multiple computers to a problem in order to solve more or more complex problems in a reduced amount of time. Finally, Chapter 12 covers several basic and advanced topics related to evaluating the efficacy of various classification, clustering, and anomaly detection techniques. Due to its close relationship with these topics, Chapter 12 may optionally be read following Chapter 8, 9, or 11.

2

An Introduction to Graph Theory

Stephen Ware

North Carolina State University

CONTENTS

2.1 What Is a Graph?

When most people hear the word "graph," they think of an image with information plotted on an x and y axis. In mathematics and computer science, however, a graph is something quite different. A graph is a theoretical construct composed of points (called vertices) connected by lines (called edges). The concept is very simple, but graphs can have many interesting and important properties.

Graphs represent *structured data*. The vertices of a graph symbolize discrete pieces of information, while the edges of a graph symbolize the relationships between those pieces. Before we can discuss how to mine graphs for useful information, we need to understand their basic properties. In this section, we introduce some essential vocabulary and concepts from the field of graph theory.

2.2   Vertices and Edges

A **vertex** (also called a **node**) is a single point (or a connection point) in a graph. Vertices are usually labeled, and in this book we will use lower-case letters to name them. An **edge** can be thought of as a line segment that connects two vertices. Edges may have labels as well. Vertices and edges are the basic building blocks of graphs.

> **Definition 2.1** *Graph*
> A **graph** G is composed of two sets: a set of **vertices**, denoted $V(G)$, and a set of **edges**, denoted $E(G)$.

> **Definition 2.2** *Edge*
> An **edge** in a graph G is an unordered pair of two vertices (v_1, v_2) such that $v_1 \in V(G)$ and $v_2 \in V(G)$.

An edge is said to **join** its two vertices. Likewise, two vertices are said to be **adjacent** if and only if there is an edge between them. Two vertices are said to be **connected** if there is a path from one to the other via any number of edges.

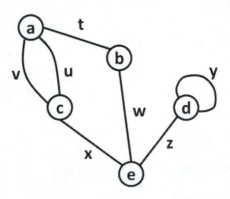

FIGURE 2.1: An example graph.

The example graph in Figure 2.1 has 5 labeled vertices and 7 labeled edges. Vertex a is connected to every vertex in the graph, but it is only adjacent to vertices c and b. Note that edges u and v, which can both be written (a,c), are multiple edges. Edge y, which can also be written (d,d) is a loop. Vertex b has degree 2 because 2 edges use it as an endpoint.

Some kinds of edges are special.

Definition 2.3 *Loop*
A **loop** is an edge that joins a vertex to itself.

Definition 2.4 *Multiple Edge*
In a graph G, an edge is a **multiple edge** if there is another edge in $E(G)$ which joins the same pair of vertices.

A multiple edge can be thought of as a copy of another edge—two line segments connecting the same two points.

Loops and multiple edges often make manipulating graphs difficult. Many proofs and algorithms in graph theory require them to be excluded.

Definition 2.5 *Simple Graph*
A **simple graph** is a graph with no loops or multiple edges.

An edge always has exactly two vertices, but a single vertex can be an endpoint for zero, one, or many edges. This property is often very important when analyzing a graph.

Definition 2.6 *Degree*
In a graph G, the **degree** of a vertex v, denoted $degree(v)$, is the number of times v occurs as an endpoint for the edges $E(G)$.

In other words, the degree of a vertex is the number of edges leading to it. However, loops are a special case. A loop adds 2 to the degree of a vertex since both of its endpoints are that same vertex. The degree of a vertex can also be thought of as the number of other vertices adjacent to it (with loops counting as 2).

2.3 Comparing Graphs

What does it mean to say that two graphs are the same or different? Since graphs represent structured data, we want to say that graphs are the same when they have the same structure. How do we know when that is the case? Before answering that question, we need to explore the idea that graphs can contain other graphs.

2.3.1 Subgraphs

Recall that a graph is simply defined as a set of vertices and edges. If we consider only a subset of those vertices and a subset of those edges, we are considering a *sub*graph. A **subgraph** fits the definition of a graph, so it is in turn a graph (which may in turn have its own subgraphs).

> **Definition 2.7** *Subgraph*
> A **subgraph** S of a graph G is:
>
> - A set of vertices $V(S) \subset V(G)$.
>
> - A set of edges $E(S) \subset E(G)$. Every edge in $E(S)$ must be an unordered pair of vertices (v_1, v_2) such that $v_1 \in V(S)$ and $v_2 \in V(S)$.

The last line of this definition tells us that an edge can only be part of a subgraph if both of its endpoints are also part of the subgraph.

2.3.2 Induced Subgraphs

The definition of a subgraph has two parts, but what if you were only given one of those parts and asked to make a subgraph? This is the notion of an **induced subgraph**. Subgraphs can be induced in two ways: by vertices or by edges.

> **Definition 2.8** *Induced Graph (Vertices)*
> In a graph G, the subgraph S **induced** by a set of vertices $N \subset V(G)$ is composed of:
>
> - $V(S) = N$
>
> - For all pairs of vertices $v_1 \in V(S)$ and $v_2 \in V(S)$, if $(v_1, v_2) \in E(G)$, then $(v_1, v_2) \in E(S)$.

You can think of a subgraph induced by a set of vertices like a puzzle. Given some set of vertices $N \subset V(G)$, find all the edges in G whose endpoints are both members of N. These edges make up the edges of the induced subgraph.

The darker part of the graph in Figure 2.2 is a subgraph of the whole. This subgraph is induced by the vertices $\{b, c, d\}$ or by the edges $\{w, x\}$.

Subgraphs can also be induced by edges.

> **Definition 2.9** *Induced Graph (Edges)*
> In a graph G, the subgraph S **induced** by a set of edges $M \subset E(G)$ is composed of:
>
> - $E(S) = M$
>
> - For each edge $(v_1, v_2) \in E(S)$, $v_1 \in V(S)$ and $v_2 \in V(S)$.

Again, think of an induced subgraph as a puzzle. Given some set of edges

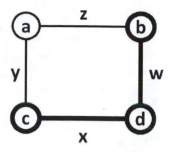

FIGURE 2.2: An induced subgraph.

$M \in E(G)$, find all the vertices in $V(G)$ that are endpoints of any edges in M. These vertices make up the vertices of the induced subgraph.

2.3.3 Isomorphic Graphs

It is helpful to think of graphs as points connected by lines. This allows us to draw them and visualize the information they contain. But the same set of points and lines can be drawn in many different ways. Graphs that have the same structure have the same properties and can be used in the same way, but it may be hard to recognize that two graphs have the same structure when they are drawn differently.

Definition 2.10 *Graph Isomorphism*
Two graphs G and H are **isomorphic** (denoted $G \simeq H$) if there exists a bijection f such that $f : V(G) \rightarrow V(H)$ such that an edge $(v_1, v_2) \in E(G)$ if and only if $(f(v_1), f(v_2)) \in E(H)$.

Informally, this means that two graphs are isomorphic if they can both be drawn in the same shape. If G and H are isomorphic, the bijection f is said to be an **isomorphism** between G and H and between H and G. The **isomorphism class** of G is all the graphs isomorphic to G.

Figure 2.3 shows three graphs: A, B, and C. All three graphs are isomorphic, but only A and B are automorphic. The first table shows one automorphism between A and B. The second table shows the isomorphism between A and C.

2.3.4 Automorphic Graphs

Note that when vertices and edges have labels, the notion of *sameness* and *isomorphism* are different. It is possible that two graphs have the same structure, and are thus isomorphic, but have different labels, and are thus not exactly the same.

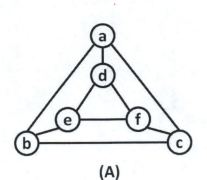 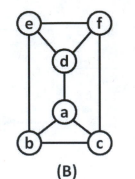 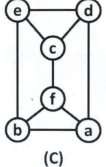

(A)   **(B)**   **(C)**

$V(A)$	$V(B)$
a	a
b	b
c	c
d	d
e	e
f	f
$V(A)$	$V(C)$
a	f
b	b
c	a
d	c
e	e
f	d

FIGURE 2.3: An example isomorphism and automorphism.

Labeled graphs are isomorphic if their underlying unlabeled graphs are isomorphic. In other words, if you can remove the labels and draw them in the same shape, they are isomorphic. But what if you can draw them in the same shape with the same labels in the same positions? This is the notion of **automorphic** graphs. Two automorphic graphs are considered to be the same graph.

Definition 2.11 *Graph Automorphism*
An **automorphism** between two graphs G and H is an isomorphism f that maps G onto itself.

When an automorphism exists between G and H they are said to be **automorphic**. The **automorphism class** of G is all graphs automorphic to G.

The distinction between isomorphism and automorphism may not be clear at first, so more explanation is required. Both an isomorphism and an automorphism can be thought of as a function f. This function takes as input a vertex from G and returns a vertex from H. Now suppose that G and H have both been drawn in the same shape. The function f is an isomorphism if, for every vertex in G, f returns a vertex from H that is in the same position. The function f is an automorphism if, for every vertex in G, f returns a vertex from H that is in the same location *and* has the same label. Note that all automorphisms are isomorphisms, but not all isomorphisms are automorphisms.

2.3.5 The Subgraph Isomorphism Problem

One common problem that is often encountered when mining graphs is the **subgraph isomorphism problem**. It is phrased like so:

> **Definition 2.12** *Subgraph Isomorphism Problem*
> The **subgraph isomorphism problem** asks if, given two graphs G and H, does G contain a subgraph isomorphic to H?

In other words, given a larger graph G and a smaller (or equal sized) graph H, can you find a subgraph in G that is the same shape as H?

This problem is known to be NP-complete, meaning that it is computationally expensive. Algorithms that require us to solve the subgraph isomorphism problem will run slowly on large graphs—perhaps so slowly that it is not practical to wait for them to finish.

2.4 Directed Graphs

Edges have so far been defined as unordered pairs, but what if they were made into ordered pairs? This is the idea behind a **directed graph** or **digraph**. In these kinds of graphs, edges work one way only.

> **Definition 2.13** *Directed Graph*
> A **directed graph** D is composed of two sets: a set of vertices $V(D)$ and a set of edges $E(D)$ such that each edge is an ordered pair of vertices (t, h). The first vertex t is called the **tail**, and the second vertex h is called the **head**.

An edge in a directed graph is usually drawn as an arrow with the arrowhead pointing toward the head vertex. In a directed graph, you can follow an edge from the tail to the head but *not* back again. Directed graphs require us to redefine some of the terms we established earlier.

Figure 2.4 shows a directed graph. If you start at vertex a, you can travel to any other vertex; however, you cannot reach a from any vertex except itself. This is because a has indegree 0. Vertex e has outdegree 2.

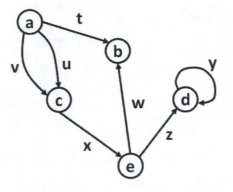

FIGURE 2.4: An example directed graph.

Definition 2.14 *Indegree*
In a digraph D, the **indegree** of a vertex v is the number of edges in $E(D)$ which have v as the head.

Definition 2.15 *Outdegree*
In a digraph D, the **outdegree** of a vertex v is the number of edges in $E(D)$ which have v as the tail.

Definition 2.16 *Digraph Isomorphism*
Two digraphs J and K are **isomorphic** if and only if their underlying undirected graphs are isomorphic.

Note that, like labeled graphs, we ignore the direction of the edges when considering isomorphism. Two digraphs are isomorphic if you can change all the directed edges to undirected edges and then draw them in the same shape.

2.5   Families of Graphs

Some kinds of graphs that obey certain rules are known to have helpful properties. We now discuss some common families of graphs that you will encounter in this book.

2.5.1   Cliques

A **clique** is a set of vertices which are all connected to each other by edges.

Definition 2.17 *Clique*

A set of vertices C is a **clique** in the graph G if, for all pairs of vertices $v_1 \in C$ and $v_2 \in C$, there exists an edge $(v_1, v_2) \in E(G)$.

If you begin at one vertex in a clique, you can get to any other member of that clique by following only one edge.

A clique is very similar to the idea of a **complete graph**. In fact, a clique is exactly the same as a complete subgraph.

Definition 2.18 *Complete Graph*

A **complete graph** with n vertices, denoted K_n, is a graph such that $V(K_n)$ is a clique.

A complete simple graph has all the edges it can possibly contain, but just how many edges is that? Consider the fact that every vertex is adjacent to every other vertex. That means each vertex in a complete graph with n vertices will have degree $n-1$. To find the number of edges, we simply multiply the degree of each vertex by the number of vertices and divide by 2. We need to divide by 2 because each edge gets counted twice (since it connects two vertices). Thus, the total number of edges in a complete graph is $\frac{n(n-1)}{2}$.

In Figure 2.5, graph A contains a clique of size 5. If we remove vertex f, graph A is a complete graph. Graph B shows a path of length 4 between vertices a and e. Graph C shows a cycle of length 5.

2.5.2 Paths

If you think of the vertices of a graph as cities and the edges of a graph as roads between those cities, a **path** is just what it sounds like: a route from one city to another. Like a set of driving directions, it is a set of roads which you must follow in order to arrive at your destination. Obviously, the next step in a path is limited to the roads leading out of your current city.

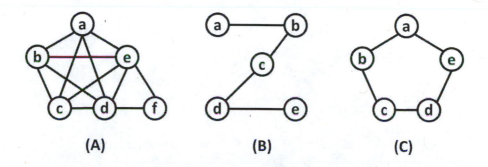

(A)   (B)   (C)

FIGURE 2.5: An example directed graph.

Definition 2.19 *Path (Edges)*
A **path** of length n, denoted P_n, in a graph G is an ordered set of edges $\{(v_0, v_1), (v_1, v_2), (v_2, v_3), \ldots, (v_{n-1}, v_n)\}$ such that each edge $e \in E(G)$.

A path can also be defined in terms of vertices, but the concept is the same.

Definition 2.20 *Path (Vertices)*
A **path** of length n, denoted P_n, in a graph G is a set of $n + 1$ vertices $\{v_1, v_2, \ldots, v_n, v_{n+1}\}$ such that for i from 1 to n, there exists an edge $(v_i, v_{i+1}) \in E(G)$.

A path is sometimes called a **walk**. Note that there may be more than one path between the same two vertices in a graph.

Now that we have defined a path, we can revisit an earlier concept from the beginning of this chapter and define it more precisely.

Definition 2.21 *Connected Vertices*
Two vertices are **connected** if and only if there exists a path from one to the other.

Definition 2.22 *Connected Graph*
A graph G is a **connected graph** if, for every vertex v, there is a path to every other vertex in $V(G)$.

In other words a connected graph cannot have any parts which are unreachable, such as a vertex that is not an endpoint for any edge. In future chapters of this book, when we use the term **graph**, we mean a **simple connected graph** by default.

A path is **simple** if it never visits the same vertex twice. A path is **open** if its first and last vertices are different. A path is **closed** if its first and last vertices are the same.

2.5.3   Cycles

There is another name used to describe a closed path.

Definition 2.23 *Cycle*
A **cycle** of length n, denoted C_n, in a graph G is a closed path of length n.

A **simple cycle** is the same as a simple closed path, with the exception that it may visit one vertex exactly twice: the vertex which is both the start and end of the cycle.

Note that, like K_n above, P_n and C_n name graphs (which may be subgraphs of other graphs). If a graph contains a cycle of length 5, it is said to contain C_5. P_n, or the "path graph" can be drawn as a line. C_n, or the "cycle graph" can be drawn as a ring.

2.5.4 Trees

Trees are graphs that obey certain structural rules and have many appealing mathematical properties. Like trees in nature, a **tree** graph has exactly one vertex called the **root**. This root, or **parent**, can have any number of **children** vertices adjacent to it. Those children can, in turn, be parents of their own children vertices, and so on. A vertex which has no children is called a **leaf**.

> **Definition 2.24** *Tree*
> A graph G is a **tree** if and only if there is exactly one simple path from each vertex to every other vertex.

Trees are sometimes defined in a different but equivalent way:

> **Definition 2.25** *Tree*
> A graph G is a **tree** if and only if it is a connected graph with no cycles.

The graph in Figure 2.6 is a tree, and vertex a is the root. The root has 3 children: b, c, and d. Vertices d, e, f, h, and i are leaves. Vertex c is the parent of g. Vertex a is an ancestor of g and, likewise, vertex g is the descendant of a.

Trees are often modeled as directed graphs. If this is the case, the root vertex must have indegree 0. It will have outdegree equal to the number of its children. All vertices other than the root have indegree exactly 1. That one incoming edge must be coming from the parent vertex. Leaf vertices have outdegree 0.

Similar to a human family tree, we can define that vertex d is a **descendant** of vertex a if there is a path from a to d. All of a vertex's children are its descendants, but not all of its descendants are its children; they might be its grandchildren or great grandchildren.

Likewise, we can define that vertex a is an **ancestor** of vertex d if there is a path from a to d. A vertex's parent is its ancestor, but a vertex can have

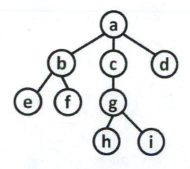

FIGURE 2.6: An example tree.

ancestors which are not its parent (i.e., grandparents, great grandparents, etc.).

Note that trees are defined recursively. If you consider only a child vertex and all of its descendants as a subgraph, it is also a tree that has that vertex as the root.

2.6 Weighted Graphs

Many kinds of graphs have edges labeled with numbers, or weights. The weight of an edge often represents the cost of crossing that edge.

Definition 2.26 *Weighted Graph*
A **weighted graph** W is composed of two sets: a set of vertices $V(W)$ and a set of edges $E(W)$ such that each edge is a pair of vertices v_1 and v_2 and a numeric weight w.

Weighted graphs are often used in path-finding problems. Consider Figure 2.7. There are many shortest paths from vertex a to vertex d, because there are many ways to reach d by only crossing 3 edges. The path $\{a, b, e, d\}$ and the path $\{a, c, e, d\}$ are both shortest paths.

However, when we consider the *cost* of a path, there is only one lowest cost path. The path $\{a, b, e, d\}$ costs $5 + 9 + 2 = 16$. The path $\{a, b, e, d\}$ only costs $-3 + 15 + 2 = 14$, so it is the lowest cost path.

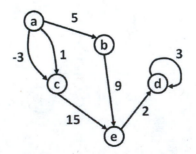

FIGURE 2.7: A directed, weighted graph.

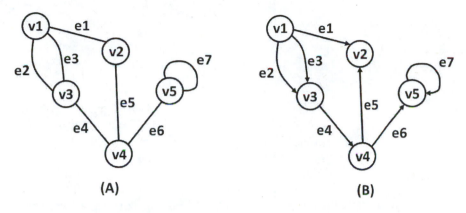

FIGURE 2.8: Two example graphs, an undirected version (A) and a directed version (B), each with its vertices and edges numbered.

2.7   Graph Representations

There are several different ways to represent a graph, each with its own advantages and disadvantages. For each example, we will refer to the graphs in Figure 2.8. For the definitions below, let $n = |V(G)|$, the number of vertices in the graph. Let $m = |E(G)|$, the number of edges in the graph. In both graphs in Figure 2.8, $n = 5$ and $m = 7$.

2.7.1   Adjacency List

The adjacency list is the simplest and most compact way to represent a graph.

> **Definition 2.27** *Adjacency List*
> Given a graph G such that $V(G) = \{v_1, v_2, \ldots, v_n\}$, the **adjacency list** representation of G is a list of length n such that the ith element of the list is a list that contains one element for each vertex adjacent to v_i.

The adjacency list for graph A is:

```
Graph A:
[1] [2, 3, 3]
[2] [1, 4]
[3] [1, 1, 4]
[4] [2, 3, 5]
[5] [4, 5]
```

The adjacency list for graph B is:

```
Graph B:
```

```
[1] [2, 3, 3]
[2] []
[3] [4]
[4] [2, 5]
[5] [5]
```

If you have the adjacency list of a graph, you can easily answer the question, "Which vertices are adjacent to the ith vertex?" To find which vertices are adjacent to v_2 in graph A, look at the second element of graph A's adjacency list. It contains a list of the vertices that have edges leading to or from v_2. In this case, we see that v_2 is adjacent to v_1 and v_4.

This representation requires the least amount of memory to represent on a computer, so it is ideal for very fast algorithms. Specifically, an adjacency list requires about $n + 2m$ bytes for an undirected graph and about $n + m$ bytes for a directed graph. Algorithms exist for finding a path between two vertices that can run in $O(n + m)$ time, so this representation would be ideal in that case.

2.7.2 Adjacency Matrix

An adjacency matrix is similar to an adjacency list.

Definition 2.28 *Adjacency Matrix*
Given a graph G such that $V(G) = \{v_1, v_2, \ldots, v_n\}$, the **adjacency matrix** representation of G is a $n \times n$ matrix. If $a_{r,c}$ is the value in the matrix at row r and column c, then $a_{r,c} = 1$ if v_r is adjacent to v_c; otherwise, $a_{r,c} = 0$.

The adjacency matrix for graph A is:

$$\begin{pmatrix} 0 & 1 & 1 & 0 & 0 \\ 1 & 0 & 0 & 1 & 0 \\ 1 & 0 & 0 & 1 & 0 \\ 0 & 1 & 1 & 0 & 1 \\ 0 & 0 & 0 & 1 & 1 \end{pmatrix}$$

The adjacency matrix for graph B is:

$$\begin{pmatrix} 0 & 1 & 1 & 0 & 0 \\ 0 & 0 & 0 & 0 & 0 \\ 0 & 0 & 0 & 1 & 0 \\ 0 & 1 & 0 & 0 & 1 \\ 0 & 0 & 0 & 0 & 1 \end{pmatrix}$$

If you have the adjacency matrix of a graph, you can easily answer the question, "Are v_r and v_c adjacent?" To determine if there is an edge between v_2 and v_4 in graph A, we can check the adjacency matrix for graph A at row 2, column 4. The value at that location is 1, so an edge does exist.

An adjacency matrix requires about n^2 bytes to represent on a computer, but many graph algorithms (like the ones discussed in this book) require $\Omega(n^2)$ time. In other words, the amount of time it takes to set up an adjacency matrix is not very much when compared to how long the algorithm will take to run.

2.7.3 Incidence Matrix

The incidence matrix representation is less popular than the adjacency matrix, but it can still be helpful in certain situations.

Definition 2.29 *Incidence Matrix*
Given a graph G such that $V(G) = \{v_1, v_2, \ldots, v_n\}$ and $E(G) = \{e_1, e_2, \ldots, e_m\}$ the **incidence matrix** representation of G is an $n \times m$ matrix. Let $a_{r,c}$ be the value in the matrix at row r and column c.

- If G is undirected, $a_{r,c} = 1$ if v_r is the head or the tail of e_c; otherwise, $a_{r,c} = 0$.

- If G is directed, $a_{r,c} = -1$ if v_r is the tail of e_c; $a_{r,c} = 1$ if v_r is the head of e_c; $a_{r,c} = 0$ if e_c is a loop; otherwise, $a_{r,c} = 0$.

The incidence matrix for graph A is:

$$
\begin{pmatrix}
1 & 1 & 1 & 0 & 0 & 0 & 0 \\
1 & 0 & 0 & 0 & 1 & 0 & 0 \\
0 & 1 & 1 & 1 & 0 & 0 & 0 \\
0 & 0 & 0 & 1 & 1 & 1 & 0 \\
0 & 0 & 0 & 0 & 1 & 1 & 1
\end{pmatrix}
$$

The incidence matrix for graph B is:

$$
\begin{pmatrix}
-1 & -1 & -1 & 0 & 0 & 0 & 0 \\
1 & 0 & 0 & 0 & 1 & 0 & 0 \\
0 & 1 & 1 & -1 & 0 & 0 & 0 \\
0 & 0 & 0 & 1 & -1 & -1 & 0 \\
0 & 0 & 0 & 0 & 0 & 1 & 0
\end{pmatrix}
$$

If you have the incidence matrix of a graph, you can easily answer the question, "Which vertices make up an edge?" Consider edge e_4 in graph B. To find out which vertex is the tail, we can look through the 4th column on the incidence matrix until we find the value -1 at row 3. This means that vertex v_3 is the tail of edge e_4. Likewise, we see that vertex v_4 is the head of e_4 because the value of the matrix af column 4 and row 4 is 1.

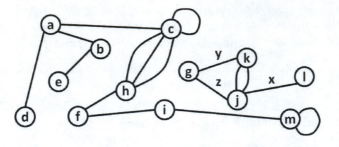

FIGURE 2.9: Problems 1 and 2 refer to this graph.

2.8   Exercises

1. Count the number of the following in Figure 2.9:

   (a) Vertices
   (b) Edges
   (c) Multiple edges
   (d) Loops
   (e) Vertices adjacent to vertex a
   (f) Vertices connected to vertex a

2. Draw the subgraph induced by the following in Figure 2.9:

   (a) Induced by the vertices $\{a, b, c, d, e\}$
   (b) Induced by the edges $\{x, y, z\}$

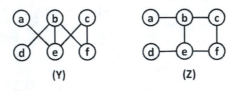

FIGURE 2.10: Problem 3 refers to these graphs.

3. In Figure 2.10, are graphs Y and Z isomorphic? If so, give an isomorphism. Are they automorphic? If so, given an automorphism.

4. A planar graph is a graph that can be drawn on a plane (such as a sheet of paper) so that none of its edges cross. Attempt to draw the following, and conjecture which of these tasks are possible and which are impossible:

    (a) Draw a planar clique of size 4.

    (b) Draw a planar clique of size 5.

    (c) Draw a planar clique of size 6.

5. Draw an undirected tree and then attempt to do the following tasks. Conjecture which of these tasks are possible and which are impossible:

    (a) Draw a directed tree with the same number of vertices and edges.

    (b) Draw a new undirected tree with the same number of vertices but a different number of edges.

    (c) Add an edge to the tree without creating a cycle.

    (d) Remove an edge from the tree without disconnecting any pair of vertices.

3

An Introduction to R

Neil Shah

North Carolina State University

CONTENTS

3.1 What Is R?

R is a language for statistical computing and graphics. The R environment provides a multitude of built-in functions in the "base" package, many of which are commonly required for elementary data analysis (e.g., linear modeling, graph plotting, basic statistics). However, the beauty of R lies in its almost infinite expandability and versatility. Approximately 2,500 (and counting) packages have been developed for R by the active R community. These packages serve to augment R's natural capabilities in data analysis and often focus on developments in various scientific fields, as well as techniques used in highly specialized data analyses.

3.1.1 A Brief History

R is a GNU implementation of the *S* language, a popular statistical language developed at Bell Laboratories by John Chambers and his colleagues. While R is not *S* itself, much *S* code can run in R without any change. R itself was developed as an open-source alternative to the *S* environment. It was developed by Robert Gentlement and Ross Ihaka. The name R is partially a reference to the main authors of R as well as a play on the name *S*.

3.1.2 Common Uses of R

R is a uniting tool between all types of application scientists who deal with data management and analysis. It is used commonly in disciplines such as business modeling and projection, stock performance, biology, biochemistry, high-performance computing, parallel computing, statistics, and many more. Within each of these disciplines, R can also be applied to many different domain-specific tasks. Because of R's ease-of-use and simplicity, it has become a staple tool for many scientists to interface their work with software and augment possibilities and speed-up tasks. The R useR! conference is held each year to unite application scientists and industry representatives who work with R as a medium to enable them to perform tasks integral to their work and research.

If you have R installed on your system already, you can continue with this chapter as it is. However, if you have not yet installed R you should skip to the last section of this chapter, which covers installation routines, before continuing.

3.2   What Can R Do?

As a flexible language, R inherently provides many statistical functions involving inference tests, clustering, and curve fitting. Additionally, R can be put to use in many disciplines with the employment of various packages and libraries contributed by the R community. R is also equipped with excellent graphing and plotting methods to generate publication-quality images.

3.2.1   Data Manipulation

R provides many methods to work with data in a variety of ways. As a scripting language, R also has support for reading and writing data from files, creating data sequences, performing operations on data, summarizing data, and also casting data to other types. In the next few sections, we will address these various operations.

3.2.1.1   Reading from files

The most common R function for reading data from files is the **read.table** command. This command reads data of a matrix or table type and reads the data (including any headers) into R as a data frame type. Later in this chapter, we will see how to cast this data-frame into other, more commonly used types (such as matrices). The syntax of the **read.table** function is as follows:

```
 1 > students = read.table(''students.txt'',header=TRUE)
 2 > students
 3     Name Age ID
 4 1  Alex   16   1
 5 2 Jacob   15   2
 6 3   Sue   17   3
 7 > students[1]
 8     Name
 9 1  Alex
10 2 Jacob
11 3   Sue
12 > students[''Name'']
13     Name
14 1  Alex
15 2 Jacob
16 3   Sue
```

Here we have a tab-delimited file "students.txt" containing the records of several high-school students. We use the **read.table** function to read the records from the file and store them as a data-frame type into the variable

students. We use the "header=TRUE" (optional) argument to specify that
we wish to keep the headings of the columns upon importing the data into R.
We can refer to the imported data set by typing the name of the variable that
references the data at the R prompt. As you can see, we can refer to a column
in R by either referencing its index (here we use index 1 as the first column)
or by its name (in this case, the name of the column containing student names
is "Name").

The `scan` function can also be used to read data from files, but is far less
common. However, you can read about `scan` in the R help pages, by typing
in R's prompt:

```
1 > help(scan)
```

3.2.1.2   Writing to Files

It is useful to occasionally save your R session's output to a file. The best way
to do this is to access the "Save to File" functionality from R's "File" menu.
You may also look into the `sink` and `capture.output` functions to automate
these processes, but these are not commonly used.

3.2.1.3   Creating Data

Generating sequences of data is considerably straightforward in R. The most
frequently used data types in R are vectors, matrices, lists, and data frames.
One important fact to note is that in R, indexing of elements is done from array
index 1—to those of you who have studied other programming or scripting
languages, this will take some getting used to. However, the first element of
any data type in R is accessed as `element[1]`, and not `element[0]`. This
information will help you understand the examples presented in this section.
We will cover the most frequently used data types in R with some depth in
the next paragraphs.

Vectors are used in R as the most basic of data types, often used to store
single-dimensional data. They can be of various sub-types, but most frequently
are of type "numeric" in order to store integers or decimal numbers. Vectors
can also store string data ("character" type vectors). The following code shows
some rudimentary numeric and character data vector generation techniques:

```
1 > a = 1:10
2 > b = c(1:10)
3 > c = c(1,4,2,11,19)
4 > d = seq(0,10,by=2)
5 > a
6 [1]  1  2  3  4  5  6  7  8  9 10
7 > b
8 [1]  1  2  3  4  5  6  7  8  9 10
9 > c
```

```
10 [1]   1   4   2  11  19
11 > d
12 [1]   0   2   4   6   8  10
13 > e = 10:1
14 > f = c(10:1)
15 > g = seq(10,0,by=-2)
16 > e
17 [1] 10   9   8   7   6   5   4   3   2   1
18 > f
19 [1] 10   9   8   7   6   5   4   3   2   1
20 > g
21 [1] 10   8   6   4   2   0
22 > h = ''hello''
23 > h
24 [1] ''hello''
```

The first operator used here creates a vector consisting of the numbers from 1 to 10. The colon operator denotes a range, or series of values. The c function creates an identical vector, but is a cleaner and more acceptable way of performing the same operation. The c function also allows us to specify whichever numbers we want to put in a vector. In most cases, you should use c to create vectors or sequences of values. The seq function generates a sequence (and returns a value of type vector). In this case, we generate a sequence of numbers from 0 to 10 in steps of 2. In the next three examples, we can see that by specifying a range from a larger number to a smaller number, we can also create sequences in a decreasing fashion. We can also use negative values as step increments in the seq function. The last example involves creation of a character vector, or a string.

In contrast with vectors, matrices are frequently used to hold multidimensional data. The following code shows how to create matrices using R:

```
1 > m1 = matrix(c(1:10),nrow=2,ncol=5,byrow=FALSE)
2 > m1
3      [,1] [,2] [,3] [,4] [,5]
4 [1,]    1    3    5    7    9
5 [2,]    2    4    6    8   10
6 > m2 = matrix(c(1:10),nrow=2,ncol=5,byrow=TRUE)
7 > m2
8      [,1] [,2] [,3] [,4] [,5]
9 [1,]    1    2    3    4    5
10 [2,]    6    7    8    9   10
```

Matrices are created using the matrix function. The arguments most commonly passed include the vector of values to be used, the number of rows, and the number of columns. The "byrow" argument takes a boolean value to determine whether the matrix should be created in a row-by-row or column-by-column fashion. Additionally, the functions nrow and ncol can be passed as an

argument to return a single length vector respectively containing the number
of rows or columns the matrix has. Matrix multiplication can be done using
the %*% operator; for example, A %*% B will return the matrix multiplication
of two compatible matrices, *A* and *B*.

Lists in R are collections of other objects, known as *components*. These
components need not be of the same type, so a single list can contain a character vector (string), numeric vector, and a matrix all at once as three separate
components. The following code shows a simple example of how to create a
list object:

```
1 > list1 = list(name=''Jacob'',age=22, luckynumbers=c(3,7,9))
2 > list1
3 $name
4 [1] "Jacob"

5 $age
6 [1] 22

7 $luckynumbers
8 [1] 3 7 9
```

Lists are created using the list function. The arguments passed to the
function are the components that are to be added to the list. Components
can be accessed from the list by name or by numerical index; for example, the
age component can be accessed as either list1$age or as list1[2]. Unlike
vectors, lists have two indexing operators: '[]' and '[[]]'. The former operator
is the general indexing operator—using this operator with a list will result in
selecting a sublist from the parent list. For example, the code list1[2] will
return a list with a single component called *age*. The latter operator, '[[]]' is a
list-specific indexing operator that allows specific selection of list components
outside of list context. For example, the code list1[[2]] will simply return
a numeric vector with the value of *age*.

Data frames are essentially lists with the class *data.frame*. The components
of data frames must be vectors, matrices, lists, or other data frames. Each
component added to the data frame must be "compatible" in having an equal
number of rows, or elements (in case of a vector). The data frame will have as
many individual elements as the sum of all its individual components. Since
data frames are still of type list, they have the characteristic of being able to
hold multiple data types together. A simple example of creating a data frame
is given below.

```
1 > a = c(1,2,3)
2 > b = matrix(c(4:15),nrow=3,ncol=4)
3 > p = c(''R'',''is'',''awesome'')
4 > df = data.frame(a,b,p)
5 > a
```

```
6  [1]  1  2  3
7  > b
8          [,1] [,2] [,3] [,4]
9  [1,]     4    7   10   13
10 [2,]     5    8   11   14
11 [3,]     6    9   12   15
12 > p
13 [1]  ''R''         ''is''         ''awesome''
14 > df
15   a X1 X2 X3 X4          p
16 1 1  4  7 10 13          R
17 2 2  5  8 11 14         is
18 3 3  6  9 12 15    awesome
```

Data frames are created using the `data.frame` function. The arguments passed to the function, like a list, are the components that are to be added to the data frame. A data frame for purposes of accessing data can be considered a matrix with columns of different attributes. As you can see in the above example, it is generally displayed in a similar fashion to a matrix. Data frames have a similar indexing scheme to lists. The code `df[1]` returns a data frame with data from vector *a*. However, the code `df[[1]]` returns the first component of the data frame (vector *a*) outside of the data frame context.

3.2.1.4 Operating on data

R provides very convenient methods to modify existing data. Common operations on vectors and matrices are all built into R. These operations are fairly intuitive, some of which are shown in the following code segment:

```
1  > a = c(1:10)
2  > a
3  [1]  1  2  3  4  5  6  7  8  9 10
4  > a*2
5  [1]  2  4  6  8 10 12 14 16 18 20
6  > a/2
7  [1] 0.5 1.0 1.5 2.0 2.5 3.0 3.5 4.0 4.5 5.0
8  > a^3
9  [1]    1    8   27   64  125  216  343  512  729 1000
10 > a/a
11 [1] 1 1 1 1 1 1 1 1 1 1
12 > sum(a)
13 [1] 55
14 > b = matrix(c(1:4),nrow=2,ncol=2,byrow=TRUE)
15 > b
16        [,1] [,2]
17 [1,]     1    2
```

```
18 [2,]      3     4
19 > b*2
20         [,1] [,2]
21 [1,]      2     4
22 [2,]      6     8
23 > b/2
24         [,1] [,2]
25 [1,]    0.5     1
26 [2,]    1.5     2
27 > b/b
28         [,1] [,2]
29 [1,]      1     1
30 [2,]      1     1
31 > b %*% b
32         [,1] [,2]
33 [1,]      7    10
34 [2,]     15    22
```

In the above code block, we can see that R allows all sorts of operations on vectors, including scalar multiplication and division, as well as vector multiplication. In regards to matrices, scalar multiplication and division are also allowed, in addition to the useful matrix multiplication operation (denoted by operator "%*%").

Additionally, R provides very convenient logical row, column and subset selections from data objects. This capacity allows easy access to "slices" or samples of large data sets. The indexing operator '[]' can be used for selecting not only individual elements from vectors, lists, matrices, or data frames but also a wealth of tasks. The following examples will highlight some of these tasks and their means of use. While the examples here deal with numeric vectors and matrices, the uses of the indexing operator can be extended to other data types effectively as well.

```
 1 > a = c(1,2,3,4,5)
 2 > b = matrix(c(1:9),nrow=3,ncol=3)
 3 > a
 4 [1] 1 2 3 4 5
 5 > b
 6         [,1] [,2] [,3]
 7 [1,]      1     4     7
 8 [2,]      2     5     8
 9 [3,]      3     6     9
10 > a[3]
11 [1] 3
12 > a[-3]
13 [1] 1 2 4 5
14 > a[2:4]
```

```
15 [1] 2 3 4
16 > b[2,]
17 [1] 2 5 8
18 > b[,2]
19 [1] 4 5 6
20 > b[2,2]
21 [1] 5
```

In the first example shown, `a[3]` simply showcases what you have learned thus far about the indexing operator—it can be used to select individual elements. In this example, the third element in vector a is returned to the user. The next example is a bit more intriguing—when a minus is used in front of an index in the context of '[]', the element is *excluded* from the selection. The result of `a[-3]` is all the elements of vector a, with the exception of the element at index 3. The next example outlines the concept of range selection—R does not require you select only a single index, but allows you to select a series of indices just as easily. In this example, the 2nd through 4th elements of vector a are selected, as denoted by the range `2:4`.

The next few examples are applied to matrices, in order to outline the use of the indexing operator on multidimensional data objects. The first of the matrix examples shows that selections can be done row-wise; in this example specifically, the second row-vector of matrix b is selected. The next example is similar, but done column-wise; the second column-vector is selected. The last example shows how to access individual elements from a matrix by specifying the row and column indices (first and second, respectively).

The last important means to operate on data which we will discuss in this introductory chapter is the use of control statements in R. Control statements primarily encompass conditional execution (the `if` expressions) and repetitive execution (`for` and `while` loops). Additionally, we will broach the topic of using the `apply` family of functions to emulate repetitive execution.

Conditional execution is essential in writing many useful R scripts. Consider the (commonly encountered) case in which one desires his or her code to perform different tasks depending on the value of a variable. `if` expressions aim to address this problem of conditional execution. `if` statements have the form `if (cond) snippet1 else snippet2`, where the condition `cond` evaluates to a logical value. In the case that `cond` evaluates to be *TRUE*, then `snippet1` is executed; conversely, in the case that `cond` is *FALSE*, then `snippet2` is executed. `snippet2` can also be a group of statements, if surrounded by the left and right curly bracket symbols ({ and }) and separated with semicolons. A `condition` can be created using any of the logical operators introduced later in this chapter. The following example highlights the use of the `if` conditional.

```
1 > a = 2
2 > if(a < 5) x=1 else x=2
3 > x
4 [1] 1
```

```
5 > a = 7
6 > if(a < 5) x=1 else x=2
7 > x
8 [1] 2
```

Here, we run the same conditional if statement two times with the same conditions, except the difference in the value of the input. This difference causes the conditional to evaluate to *TRUE* in the first case and *FALSE* in the second. As a result, the value of the variable x differs after the execution of both conditional statements.

Repetitive execution is typically done using the for and while statements. Both of these statements simply repeat the nested code as long as their conditions hold true. The for loop is constructed like so: for(name in expr1) expr2, where name is a temporary naming convention for each item produced by the expression expr1. expr2 is the code that is run for each of the items. Two examples of how to use the for loop are given below.

```
 1 > for(i in c(1:10))
 2 + print(i)
 3 [1] 1
 4 [1] 2
 5 [1] 3
 6 [1] 4
 7 [1] 5
 8 [1] 6
 9 [1] 7
10 [1] 8
11 [1] 9
12 [1] 10
13 > x = list(c(1:3),c(4:6),c(7:9))
14 > x
15 [[1]]
16 [1] 1 2 3
17 [[2]]
18 [1] 4 5 6
19 [[3]]
20 [1] 7 8 9
21 > for(i in x)
22 + print(mean(i))
23 [1] 2
24 [1] 5
25 [1] 8
```

The first example simply iterates over a numeric vector spanning from 1 to 10. For each of the items in this vector (numbers 1 through 10), a `print` command is issued to display the item. The numbers from 1 to 10 are printed as a result. The second example shows a slightly more complicated `for` loop which iterates over each item from a list of vectors and prints its mean. The result is the sequential output of the average values from the first, second and third vectors that composed the list object *x*.

The `while` loop is similar to the `for` loop. A `while` statement is constructed as `while(cond) expr1`, where the expression `expr1` executes as long as the condition `cond` holds true. An example of using the `while` statement is given below.

```
> a = 0
> while(a < 10)
+ + a = a+1+ print(a)+
[1]  1
[1]  2
[1]  3
[1]  4
[1]  5
[1]  6
[1]  7
[1]  8
[1]  9
[1]  10
```

In this example, the `while` construct is executed as long as the condition that $a < 10$ holds true. For as long as the condition is true, the value of a is incremented and printed. As a result, the values of a in each iteration of the `while` loop are printed sequentially.

In many cases, frequent loop usage can cause code to appear messy or perform poorly in terms of speed. The R `apply` family of functions serves to address these concerns by simplifying (and in many cases improving performance of) for repetitive execution.

While there are many `apply` functions, the most frequently used are `apply` and `lapply` (as well as its close neighbor, `sapply`). These functions allow one to perform repetitive execution of a function over elements of a matrix and a list, respectively. These functions (along with the rest of the family) each have varying arguments, so it is suggested that the user run the `help` command on each variant individually to read the detailed specifics on how to use each. Examples concerning the use of `apply` and `lapply` are given below.

```
> x = matrix(c(1:16),nrow=4,ncol=4,byrow=TRUE)
> x
       [,1] [,2] [,3] [,4]
[1,]    1    2    3    4
```

```
 5 [2,]    5    6    7    8
 6 [3,]    9   10   11   12
 7 [4,]   13   14   15   16
 8 > apply(x,1,max)
 9 [1]   4   8  12  16
10 > apply(x,2,max)
11 [1]  13  14  15  16
12 > y = list(c(1:4),c(5:8),c(9:12),c(13:16))
13 > y
14 [[1]]
15 [1] 1 2 3 4

16 [[2]]
17 [1] 5 6 7 8

18 [[3]]
19 [1]   9  10  11  12

20 [[4]]
21 [1]  13  14  15  16

22 > lapply(y,max)
23 [[1]]
24 [1]  4

25 [[2]]
26 [1]  8

27 [[3]]
28 [1]  12

29 [[4]]
30 [1]  16
```

The first example shows two simple uses of the `apply` function. The `apply` function is used to apply a function (in this case, the `max` function) to the rows or columns of a matrix. The first arguments passed are input matrices. The second arguments passed to the `apply` functions are identifiers; 1 signifies that the function should be applied to each row of the matrix, whereas 2 signifies that the function should be applied to each column. Lastly, the third arguments are the functions to be executed on each of the rows or columns. The results of the two `apply` calls are two vectors containing the results of applying the `max` function to each of the "items" (rows and columns) from the matrix x.

The second example shows the use of the `lapply` function. The `lapply` function is used to apply a function (in this case, the `max` function) to each element of a list. The first argument passed to `lapply` is the input list. The second argument is the function to be executed on each element of the list. The result of the `lapply` call is a list containing the results of applying the `max` function to each of the "items" (in this case, vectors) from the list *y*. `sapply` does exactly the same thing as `lapply`, but returns a vector containing the results instead of a list.

3.2.1.5   Summarizing data

Summarizing a series of values is a common operation in a variety of disciplines. Computing basic statistics is useful in working with any large data set. R provides summary functions for common statistical operations. For the slightly more advanced operations concerning standard deviation, variance, and more, we may import the stats package that comes preinstalled with the conventional R installation. The following functions show the proper usage of these summary functions. Additionally, note that we use the `library` function to load an installed library.

```
 1 > data = c(3,17,4,13,91,55,10)
 2 > min(data)
 3 [1] 3
 4 > max(data)
 5 [1] 91
 6 > mean(data)
 7 [1] 27.57143
 8 > median(data)
 9 [1] 13
10 > summary(data)
11    Min. 1st Qu.  Median    Mean 3rd Qu.    Max.
12    3.00    7.00   13.00   27.57   36.00   91.00
13 > library(stats)
14 > sd(data)
15 [1] 33.08503
16 > var(data)
17 [1] 1094.619
```

3.2.1.6   Typecasting data

R provides an entire suite of functions that serve to effectively (and usually very accurately) cast data to other (compatible types). The functions create a new variable that is a forced version of the input variable. The following R code shows some of these functions:

```
 1 > b = matrix(c(1:4),nrow=2,ncol=2,byrow=TRUE)
 2 > b
 3      [,1] [,2]
```

```
4  [1,]    1    2
5  [2,]    3    4
6  > as.data.frame(b)
7    V1 V2
8  1  1  2
9  2  3  4
10 > as.matrix(b)
11       [,1] [,2]
12 [1,]    1    2
13 [2,]    3    4
14 > as.vector(b)
15 [1] 1 3 2 4
16 > as.list(b)
17 [[1]]
18 [1] 1

19 [[2]]
20 [1] 3

21 [[3]]
22 [1] 2

23 [[4]]
24 [1] 4
```

3.2.2   Calculation

R makes for a great calculator. It provides an easy pathway to simple tasks such as scalar, vector, and matrix addition and subtraction, multiplication, division, exponentiation, cumulative sums, and much more. Upon learning to use R, it becomes an exceptionally handy and easy-to-use tool for crunching numbers. For more advanced operations such as matrix multiplication, and finding matrix inverses, eigenvalues, and eigenvectors, there are a multitude of functions that are more than willing to do work for you at only a fraction of the time it would take for you to solve them yourself!

3.2.3   Graphical Display

R has a powerful ability to graph and plot data and generate publication-quality images. The most common graphical function you will likely use in R is the `plot` function, which simply plots a vector of y values against a vector of x values. The following is an example of the conventional use of this function:

```
1 > x = c(1,3,4,5,8)
2 > y = c(2,4,7,3,9)
```

```
3 > plot(x,y,type=''l'',col=''black'',
4 + xlab=''Values from X'',ylab=''Values from Y'',
5 + main=''Plot of Y vs. X'',font.main=2,font.lab=1,pch=19)
```

The `plot` command accepts several parameters, the most basic of which are the two value vectors that are to be plotted (x and y, in this case). Additionally, we have specified type="l" for a graph using lines. It is common practice to specify a graph color, and also specify the x-label, y-label, and main title. There are many more options to customize plotting. Type `help(plot)` at the R prompt to learn about these.

3.3   R Packages

In this textbook, we will be using a variety of packages that allow us to more easily perform certain tasks. It is critical to understand how to download and import packages in R. In the following sections, you will learn how to do both of these things.

3.3.1   Downloading a Package

You can download and install packages using both graphical and text-based interfaces. The means by which you can do so are explained in the next few sections.

3.3.1.1   Graphical user interfaces

If you are using the R GUI in a Windows or OSX environment, the easiest way to download a package is to click on the "Packages" menu in R. From this menu, you should select the "Install package(s)..." item. You will be presented with a menu asking you to select the location of the mirror closest to you to download the package from. Upon selecting a mirror, you will be shown a list of all packages available for download on CRAN. By simply selecting and double-clicking any of these, the package will be downloaded to your hard drive. Additionally, package dependencies will also be downloaded and installed for you. For this reason, downloading packages using the inbuilt functionalities is very user-friendly. Downloaded packages are automatically unpacked and installed for you.

Another way to download packages involves downloading the R package from a browser-accessible webpage (most commonly a CRAN mirror). If you download a package to your local disk, you can select the "Install package(s) from local zip files...", and browse to the location of the downloaded zip file. Upon selecting this file, the package will be installed for you.

3.3.1.2 Command-line interfaces

If you are using R in a command-line OSX or *NIX environment, then you can install packages using CLI-accessible methods. To install packages from local .tar.gz files, you can use the command $R_HOME/bin/R CMD INSTALL *filename* from within your terminal environment (not within the R environment). The package will be installed to the default R directory for packages.

If you wish to install a package directly from a CRAN mirror, you can start the R environment with $R_HOME/bin/R, and from within the R CLI, enter the following:

```
1 > install.packages(''packagename'');
```

3.3.2 Importing a Package

To import a package into your R session, you can simply enter the following:

```
1 > library(packagename);
```

3.3.3 Getting Help

To learn more about a package (version, title, author, etc.), you can use:

```
1 > library(help = packagename);
```

To find out which functions are inside a package, you can use:

```
1 > ls(package:packagename);
```

Lastly, to find information on how to use a function (which arguments to provide to the function, what type the function returns, etc.), you can use:

```
1 > help(functionname);
```

As a helpful note, press the "q" key to quit out of the help screens and get back to R.

3.4 Why Use R?

You may be wondering whether R is indeed the best tool for this type of work. Rather, why not *SAS* or *S+* or even some other scripting environment with packages, such at *MATLAB*? R has many benefits which make it the ideal candidate for our use. We will highlight these benefits briefly in the following sections.

3.4.1   Expansive Capabilities

The CRAN (Comprehensive R Archive Network) package repository currently features 2,482 packages for download. Almost all of these have functional versions for Windows, *NIX, and OSX. You may do some browsing on the R website *http://www.r-project.org/* to find the download mirror nearest to you, but *http://cran.revolution-computing.com/web/packages/index.html* shows a full list of the packages available on CRAN. The majority of these packages have excellent documentation and can be understood and employed with minimal user effort.

To install any of these packages, simply click on its name and download the archive corresponding to your operating system. Then, in your R environment, click on the "Packages" drop-down menu, and select the option to install a package from local files. Next, browse to and select the downloaded package, and R will do the rest. Additionally, you may employ the use of a library in an R session by typing library(*libname*) once installed. All libraries come with references, so be sure to use those to understand how to work with the library.

In addition to using packages that others have developed, R lets anyone and everyone develop packages for personal or public use! You can submit packages to CRAN (provided that they meet specified guidelines) and have them featured as well!

3.4.2   Proactive Community

R is all about the community. With more than 2 million users and thousands of contributors around the world, chances are you can find someone to answer your questions. Do a quick search online for "R help" and you'll find an assortment of mailing lists and forums where you can find answers to the most common questions, or ask your own. Check out *http://www.inside-R.org/*, a new community site for R sponsored by Revolution Analytics. It provides a great language reference, as well as a lot of promotional information about R. Every so often, it has tips and tricks on how to perform certain tasks.

3.5   Common R functions

In the next few sections, you will find short descriptions and information about functions that you may commonly use when working with R. For a full reference, you should run the `help` command on any of these functions.

3.5.1   Data Manipulation

`read.table`
The `read.table` command commonly accepts an input file and reads the data from the file into a variable. It accepts a number of other arguments, the most common of which denotes whether the file has a header line or not (header=TRUE or header=FALSE).

`c`
The c command accepts a range or comma-delimited list of values and creates a vector with them.

`matrix`
The `matrix` command accepts a vector or range of values, as well as several other arguments. The most common of these are the "nrow," "ncol," and "byrow" arguments. "nrow" specifies the number of rows in the matrix, whereas "ncol" specifies the number of columns. The "byrow" argument is TRUE when the data should be read in row-by-row, and false when the data is meant to be read column-by-column.

`seq`
The `seq` command accepts a start and end value, as well as the "by" argument, which denotes step-size in the sequence. The `seq` command can also accept a start value larger than the end value, in which case it will create a decreasing sequence.

`as.data.frame`
The `as.data.frame` command accepts an input and forces the values to take the composition of a data-frame.

`as.vector`
The `as.vector` command accepts an input and forces the values to take the composition of a vector.

`as.list`
The `as.list` command accepts an input and forces the values to take the composition of a list.

`as.matrix`
The `as.matrix` command accepts an input and forces the values to take the composition of a matrix.

`apply` family
The `apply` family of functions are used to execute a function repeatedly on items of a particular data type (list, matrix, etc.) The `apply` family is composed of `apply`, `lapply`, `sapply`, `vapply`, `mapply`, `rapply`, and `tapply`. Run `help` on each of these to learn their specific use-cases.

3.5.2   Calculation

While there are no real functions for calculation, there are some common operators that one should know how to use in R.

3.5.2.1   Mathematical operators

+

The "+," or plus sign in R functions the same way as it would elsewhere. It is used to add numbers, vectors, or matrices.

-

The "-," or minus sign in R functions the same way as it would elsewhere. It is used to subtract numbers, vectors, or matrices.

*

The "*," or multiplication sign in R functions the same way it would elsewhere. It is used to multiply numbers, vectors, or matrices (component multiplication, not matrix multiplication).

/

The "/," or division sign in R functions the same way it would elsewhere. It is used to divide numbers, vectors, or matrices (component division).

**

The "**" operator in R functions as exponentiation. The value preceding the operator is the base, whereas the value succeeding the operator is the power.

%%

The "%%" sign is the modulus operator in R which returns the remainder of the division of two values. The value preceding the operator is divided by the value succeeding the operator, and the remainder is returned.

%*%

This is the matrix multiplication sign. It should be preceded and succeeded by a matrix. This operation will return a resultant matrix which is the product of the matrix multiplication action.

~

The "~" operator is used to define a relational "model" in R. The general format for a model is $y \sim x$. This model is a simple linear regression of y on x. More complex models can also be built; for example, $y \sim x + z$ creates the multiple regression model of y on x and z. Polynomial models can also be built as follows: $y \sim poly(x,3)$ for polynomial regression of y on x of degree 3. In order to find the coefficients of such a model object, one can use function `lm` with the model as the argument.

3.5.2.2   Logical operators

< or >
The "<" and ">" operators function as less than and greater than signs. These are used in logical calculations (with numbers) and return TRUE or FALSE values.

<= or >=
The "<=" and ">=" operators function as less than or equal to and greater than or equal to signs. They are used in logical calculations (with numbers) and return TRUE or FALSE values.

!=
The "!=" operators function as a 'not equal to' sign. It tests for equality between two numbers or variables and returns TRUE or FALSE values.

!
The "!" operator functions as a 'not' sign. It negates the value of the variable it precedes.

3.5.3   Graphical Display

plot
The plot function accepts vectors for x and y coordinates and plots them in a graphics window. The function accepts many more arguments (far too many to list here): the most commonly used arguments are the *xlab* and *ylab* arguments that are assigned strings for axis labels, the *main* and *sub* arguments that are assigned strings for main and secondary plot titles, and the *type* argument that is assigned a single letter controlling the type of plot produced (the most commonly used are "p" for plotting individual points (default), "l" for plotting lines, and "b" for a combination of both "p" and "l").

title
The title function adds a title(s) to the currently active plot. It accepts a single required argument for main plot title, and an optional secondary argument for a sub-title.

pairs
The pairs function accepts a numeric matrix or data frame and produces a series of pairwise plots where every column of the input is plotted against every other column of the input.

points
The points function accepts vectors for x and y coordinates and plots the specified points in a graphics window.

abline

The `abline` function accepts the slope and intercept of the line to be drawn (a and b, respectively) and draws the line on a graphics window. The function $abline(lm(y \sim x))$ can be used to draw a regression line between vectors y and x (containing the y and x coordinates of concern).

text

The `text` function adds text to a plot. It accepts arguments x, y, and a third argument for the text to be placed at point (x, y) of the active plot.

hist

The `hist` function accepts a vector of values and plots a histogram with the values on the x-axis and their frequencies on the y-axis.

x11

The `x11` function creates a new graphics window so multiple plots are not overwritten in the same window. It is used commonly between generating plots.

3.5.4   Probability Distributions

summary

The `summary` function summarizes some of the basic statistics of various fitting models provided as arguments. Most commonly, it is used on univariate data (vectors), and returns the global minimum, 1st quartile, median, mean, 3rd quartile, and maximum of the data.

fivenum

The `fivenum` function accepts numerical data as the input argument and returns the minimum, 1st quartile, median, 3rd quartile, and maximum of the data.

density

The `density` function is commonly used in conjunction with the `plot` function to produce density plots of univariate data. It can be used as $plot(density(x))$, where x is some univariate vector of data.

ecdf

The `ecdf` function is commonly used in conjunction with the `plot` function to produce the empirical cumulative distribution plot of univariate data. It can be used as $plot(ecdf(x))$, where x is some univariate vector of data.

boxplot

The `boxplot` function generates comparative boxplots of as many input vectors as are provided. This is especially useful for comparing multiple samples of data.

t.test

The **t.test** function performs the classical Student's *t*-test on two samples of data. It accepts many arguments, the most basic of which are the two vectors of data samples, and the *var.equal* boolean variable that specifies equal variances or unequal variances of the samples. In case of unequal variances, Welch's *t*-test is used instead of the classical *t*-test.

var.test

The **var.test** function performs the *F*-test to compare variances of two samples of data. It accepts the sample vectors as input arguments.

3.5.5   Writing Your Own R Functions

Like most other programming languages, R provides users the capacity to create their own functions. In R, functions have their own object type (called "function"). Functions are typically blocks of code that allow performing a certain task repeatedly on multiple data *inputs* that yield varying data *outputs*; these outputs are typically called "return values." Learning how to write functions will drastically increase your productivity while working in R.

Functions are defined in the following manner: *fnname ← function(arg1, arg2, ...)* {*code here* }. Then, calling a function is as simple as entering its name and corresponding valid arguments into the R prompt. For example, entering *fnname(a,b)* in the R prompt would result in R running function *fnname* with variables *a* and *b*. Furthermore, in R, function arguments need not be restricted to a certain data type; this means that your functions can accept any type of arguments, as long as the arguments have compatibility with the code/expressions used inside the function. Consider the following example:

```
 1 > add2 <- function(x,y)
 2 + + x + y+
 3 > a = c(1,2,3,4,5)
 4 > b = c(2,3,4,5,6)
 5 > a
 6 [1] 1 2 3 4 5
 7 > b
 8 [1] 2 3 4 5 6
 9 > add2(a,b)
10 [1]   3  5  7  9 11
11 > d = matrix(c(1:9),nrow=3,ncol=3)
12 > f = matrix(c(10:18),nrow=3,ncol=3)
13 > d
14        [,1] [,2] [,3]
15 [1,]    1    4    7
16 [2,]    2    5    8
```

```
17 [3,]     3     6     9
18 > f
19          [,1] [,2] [,3]
20 [1,]     10    13    16
21 [2,]     11    14    17
22 [3,]     12    15    18
23 > add2(d,f)
24          [,1] [,2] [,3]
25 [1,]     11    17    23
26 [2,]     13    19    25
27 [3,]     15    21    27
```

In this example, we defined a function *add2* that took two arguments and returned the sum of the arguments as defined by the "+" operator. In both usecases of the function, we used arguments of different data types: the first usecase involved vectors, whereas the second usecase involved matrices. Since both vectors and matrices can be summed using the "+" operator, R happily accepted the function calls without complaints. However, had we used a third usecase where we tried to call *add2(a,d)*, we would have received an error, since the "+" operator does not allow summation of a vector with a matrix.

Lastly, this example also shows how R deals with function returns. Essentially, the result of the last statement of code in the function is used as the return value of the overall function. In order to group multiple objects into the return value of a single function, the most straightforward solution is to package the objects together appropriately using a vector or list object.

Additionally, functions can call other functions provided that the inner function calls use arguments or variables visible to the parent function. Consider the following example:

```
1 > statcalc <- function(x)
2 + {
3 + me = mean(x);
4 + med = median(x);
5 + stdv = sd(x);
6 + va = var(x);
7 + c(me,med,stdv,va);
8 + }
9 > a = c(1,2,3,4,5)
10 > a
11 [1] 1 2 3 4 5
12 > statcalc(a)
13 [1] 3.000000 3.000000 1.581139 2.500000
```

In this example, we created a function *statcalc* designed to compute the mean, median, standard deviation, and variance of an input. Specifically, *statcalc* creates 4 local variables, *me, med, stdv,* and *va* inside the function, and assigns them the values of the respective *mean, median, sd,* and *var* inbuilt R functions. Finally, *statcalc* creates a 4-element vector containing these values. Since the last statement of code here is the creation of the vector containing statistics of *a*, the return value of function *statcalc* is this vector. We provided *statcalc* with the input vector *a*, and received the return value of a vector containing the statistics we specified in *statcalc*. By specifying the creation of this vector as the last line of our function, we were able to package together these 4 individual statistic variables into a single object for the function to return.

3.6   R Installation

You can run R on Windows, *NIX, and OSX environments. The installation processes for all of these are slightly different, but not very difficult.

3.6.1   Windows Systems

Installation of R on Windows systems is simple with a graphical interface. To install R on your Windows machine, go to *http://cran.revolution-computing.com/bin/windows/base/* and select the download appropriate for your system. Most users will likely want the 32-bit version of R (if you don't know whether your machine is 32-bit or 64-bit, be safe and use the 32-bit). Note that there is a link on the page to select a 64-bit version as well, so if your machine is running a 64-bit Windows OS, feel free to download that one as well and utilize all of your memory.

Upon downloading the executable installer file, run it, and follow the instructions to get your R installation up and running!

3.6.2   *NIX Systems

Installing R on a *NIX system is not as easy, but can be done without too much effort. You will want to navigate to *http://cran.revolution-computing.com/* and download the .tgz archive that contains the R installation files. Upon downloading the archive, you will want to start up a terminal session and navigate to the directory your archive was downloaded to. Next, you should untar your archive (by using "tar zxf *.tgz"). Upon navigating to the directory in which all your files were untarred, you can now enter the "configure," "make," and "make install" commands to fully install your R environment.

3.6.3 Mac OSX Systems

If you use OSX, then you will want to navigate to *http://cran.revolution-computing.com/bin/macosx/*, and download the .pkg file displayed on the webpage. You can then simply install that .pkg file and follow any instructions along the way. Upon doing so, you will have your R environment ready to go!

3.7 Exercises

1.  ```
    1 > year=seq(1790,1950,10)
    2 > m.age=c(15.9,15.7,15.9,16.5,17.2,17.9,19.5,20.2,
    3 +20.6,21.6,22.9,23.8,24.9,26.1,27.1,29.5,30.4)
    ```

    The above code creates a vector named year with the sequence of years between 1790 and 1950 (with a step-size of 10) and another vector named m.age with the median age of residents of the United States.

    Calculate the mean, standard deviation, and variance of the data in m.age using R functions. Additionally, calculate the minimum, maximum, first, and third quartile values of age.

2. Using the data from Exercise 1, create a plot which has an x-label of "Year", y-label of "Median Age", plot *title* of "Plot of U.S. Resident Median Age by Decade from 1790-1950", and lines between points.

    HINT: Use help(plot) to find detailed information about the plot function and its arguments.

3.  ```
    1 > x = c(1:10)
    2 > y=x^2
    ```

    The R code above simply creates 2 vectors, x and y, corresponding to values of the function $y = x^2$ in the domain [1,10]. Use R expressions to write the following:

    (a) Four plus the square of x.
    (b) The difference of y and x.
    (c) The sum of all elements in y.
    (d) A vector containing the product of each entry of x with the corresponding entry of y.
    (e) The first 5 elements of y (use the facts that a range of values can be written as a:b, and you can access elements of a vector with a call such as $v[a:b]$, where a and b are indices).

4. Use the R seq function to write the following:

(a) A sequence of odd numbers between 1 and 10.

(b) A sequence of even numbers between 1 and 10.

(c) A sequence of decreasing numbers from 10 to 1.

(d) A sequence of cubes of odd numbers between 1 and 10.

5. $(A) = \begin{pmatrix} 2 & 5 \\ 8 & 4 \end{pmatrix} (B) = \begin{pmatrix} 7 & 6 \\ 2 & 3 \end{pmatrix}$

Given the matrices above, use R to calculate the following (and provide the code used to do so):

(a) The matrix sum.

(b) The sum of the first matrix with 3 times the second matrix.

(c) The determinant of **A**.

(d) The matrix multiplication of **A** with **B**.

(e) The transpose of **B** (use the t function).

6.
```
1 > addfour = function(x){x+4}
```

This is an R function. Functions accept arguments and return values in accordance with their purpose. In this example, we consider a function addfour, which accepts any data type x which supports addition with a scalar in R. This includes matrices, vectors, etc. Write your own simple function to find the cube of its input.

7. Download the random package and use a function in the package to create a 10x10 data frame with 100 random numbers between 1 and 25.

4

An Introduction to Kernel Functions

John Jenkins

North Carolina State University

CONTENTS

4.1   Kernel Methods on Vector Data

There are a myriad number of data mining tasks that can be performed on sets of *vectors* with continuous vector components, i.e., whose values are real numbers. For wide vectors corresponding to high-dimensional spaces, it might be useful to filter out individual vector components that do not contribute to the data patterns being studied to make the problem easier to work with and to reduce noise (see Chapter 10 on *dimension reduction*). Perhaps the vectors are each assigned a discrete property, and we want to predict properties of new, unseen vectors (see Chapter 9 on *classification*).

In these and other cases, the continuous nature of vector data allows us to perform data mining algorithms in a *geometric context*. The most well-known example of this is in classification, where *support-vector machines* construct linear separators (hyperplanes) between classes of vector data based on various

53

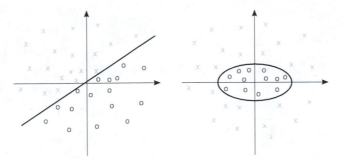

FIGURE 4.1: An example dataset. On the left, a class assignment where the data can be separated by a line. On the right, a class assignment where the data can be separated by an ellipse.

criteria, such as maximum separating distance [3, 4, 18, 19, 21, 22]. Other well-known data mining algorithms that perform on vector data include *k-means clustering*, a method of separating a vector dataset into groups of spatially colocated vectors, as well as *principle component analysis* (PCA), a method of reducing the dimensionality of vectors by projecting them into a lower-dimensional space that maintains the relationships in the data. k-means is discussed in Chapter 8, while PCA is discussed in Chapter 10.

An example vector dataset that support vector machines could be used on is shown in Figure 4.1. Two sets of two-dimensional vectors are shown, one that can be easily separated by a linear boundary, and one that cannot. Trying to define the non-linear boundary without seeing the exact layout of the data is extremely difficult, whereas defining a linear boundary for the other dataset is much simpler. More importantly, separating hyperplanes, in general, aren't as difficult to compute in higher-dimensional spaces than non-linear boundaries in the original space.

The example in Figure 4.1 is an illustration of the *curse of complexity*: simple learning rules (e.g. linear classifiers) are easier to apply than complex ones (e.g. non-linear classifiers) [21]. In fact, for data mining this "curse" tends to be more important than the corresponding *curse of dimensionality*, which refers to the difficulty in performing statistical methods (such as sufficiently sampling a space) in higher-dimensional spaces. In other words, it is more beneficial to increase the dimensionality of the data to allow the use of simpler data mining algorithms than to reduce the dimensionality of the data and perform more complex data mining.

Using this insight, what if we transformed the data from its original space into some higher-dimensional space so that we can use simple data mining algorithms using linear relationships in the transformed data? This strategy of mapping the data prior to performing analyses is referred to as a *kernel method*, shown in Figure 4.2, and the space the data is transformed into is called the *feature space*, named because each dimension in the space can be

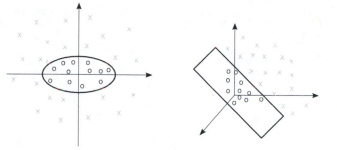

FIGURE 4.2: The example non-linear dataset from Figure 4.1, mapped into a three-dimensional space where it is separable by a two-dimensional plane.

thought of as a "feature" of the original data. More specifically, the space is a *Hilbert space*, which is a generalization of two- and three-dimensional Euclidean spaces. Given an appropriate transformation, we can make the mining process vastly simpler by using a simpler mining algorithm in the more complex space.

Definition 4.1 *Kernel Method*
The transformation of data in a problem's input space into a high-dimensional feature space, allowing the performing of analysis algorithms on the transformed space.

However, providing an *explicit* transformation of the entire data set is limiting in a number of ways. For instance, the transformation can be computationally intensive. Each feature may require non-constant time to compute (such as computing a feature as a linear combination of the input space) and there can be an arbitrarily large number of dimensions to project into. In the worst case, the explicit feature space transformation could be more expensive than the actual analysis function! Furthermore, perhaps we wish to generalize a kernel to vectors of any number of dimensions. An explicit transformation would be ill-suited for this, and would require an increasing computational time on the order of the input dimension times the feature space dimension. Finally, many feature spaces could be infinite, which is the case for many types of kernels, some of which are featured in this book.

To remove these limitations, an *implicit* transformation can be used by replacing operations in the analysis algorithm itself with operations corresponding to a different feature space. Consider the following feature space transformation for two-dimensional vectors $\mathbf{x} = (x_1, x_2)$:

$$\phi(\mathbf{x}) = (x_1^2, \sqrt{2}x_1x_2, x_2^2)$$

This new space can be used to separate the data in Figure 4.1 using a hyperplane. This is shown in Figure 4.2. Recall that the *inner product*, or dot product, of vectors $\mathbf{x} = (x_1, x_2, \dots)$ and $\mathbf{y} = (y_1, y_2, \dots)$ is equal to

TABLE 4.1: Some common kernel functions, for input vectors x and y

Polynomial	$(\mathbf{x} \cdot \mathbf{y} + \theta)^d$
Gaussian RBF	$e^{|\mathbf{x}-\mathbf{y}|^2/c}$
Sigmoidal	$\tanh(\alpha(\mathbf{x} \cdot \mathbf{y}) + \theta)$

$\mathbf{x} \cdot \mathbf{y} = x_1 y_1 + x_2 y_2 + \dots.$ Consider the inner product of vectors in this new space:

$$\langle \phi(\mathbf{u}), \phi(\mathbf{v}) \rangle = (u_1^2 v_1^2 + 2u_1 u_2 v_1 v_2 + u_2^2 v_2^2)$$
$$= (u_1 v_1 + u_2 v_2)^2$$
$$= (\mathbf{u} \cdot \mathbf{v})^2$$

As shown, we can represent the inner product of vectors in the feature space solely by using the inner product of the original space. Thus, if we can represent the algorithm using inner products (as SVMs, PCA, and k-means clustering all can), then we can avoid computing the feature space at all. This strategy is known as the *kernel trick*, and the function that computes the inner product in the feature space is known as a *kernel function* [1, 17]. As it turns out, there are a huge number of kernel functions that we can use, allowing the use of higher-dimensional feature spaces without changing the underlying mining algorithm and with little additional computation. In fact, we might not even know the exact definition of the feature space, only that the kernel function encapsulates some high-dimensional feature space, increasing the generality of the trick.

Definition 4.2 *Kernel Function*
A symmetric, positive semi-definite function which represents the inner product of vectors in some feature space.

Definition 4.3 *Kernel Trick*
The use of kernel functions to allow linear analysis algorithms based on inner products to model nonlinear relationships in the input space.

Table 4.1 shows some of the more common kernel functions, including the polynomial kernel we just showed for $\theta = 0$ and $d = 2$. If you were having trouble thinking of an infinite feature space, the Gaussian radial basis function (RBF) kernel represents an infinite *Hilbert space*, as do the graph kernels discussed in this book. Note that many of these kernels are *parameterized*, which means that the choice of parameter could have a dramatic effect on the effectiveness of the function on a particular problem instance. Methods to find the best pairings of kernel functions and parameters range from simple guess-and-check, to grid searches of various complexity [9], to stochastic methods (involving a random element) that iteratively find local optima or even build new kernel functions [8].

To summarize the flow of operations that occur when incorporating kernel

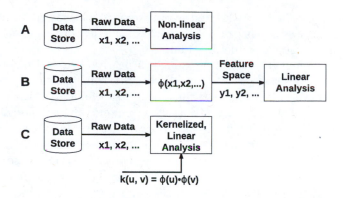

FIGURE 4.3: A: Analysis on some unmodified vector data. B: Analysis on an explicit feature space, using the transformation ϕ. C: Analysis on an implicit feature space, using the kernel function k, with the analysis modified to use only inner products.

functions, refer to Figure 4.3. Once again, the benefits of the kernel trick (part C of the Figure) is that we can use a simpler analysis function based on linear relationships, while avoiding working directly in some feature space (as in part B), which is beneficial both when we cannot simply express the feature space nor explicitly compute it in an efficient manner. However, a "kernelized" analysis algorithm must be used that performs only inner products on input data pairs.

Mathematically, there are a few important restrictions on kernel functions. First, kernel functions must be *symmetric*. That is, if K is a kernel function and d_i and d_j are input data points, then:

$$K(d_i, d_j) = K(d_j, d_i) \tag{4.1}$$

This makes sense intuitively because one would expect the same inner product from a pair of data points regardless of order. Second, kernel functions must be *positive semi-definite*. Formally, for a kernel function K, any set of points $d_1, d_2, \ldots, d_n$ and any set of real number constants $x_1, x_2, \ldots, x_n$, the following inequality must hold:

$$\sum_{i=1}^{n} \sum_{j=1}^{n} K(d_i, d_j) x_i x_j \geq 0. \tag{4.2}$$

This ensures that K actually represents some feature space. Another mathematical way to express this is, given a *kernel matrix* $\mathbf{M}$ that contains the value of the kernel function applied to all pairs of input points, for any vector $\hat{\mathbf{x}}$,

$$\hat{\mathbf{x}}^T \mathbf{M} \hat{\mathbf{x}} \geq 0. \tag{4.3}$$

From the theoretic point of view, the second restriction represents a special case of Mercer's Theorem [12] and allows kernel functions to serve as valid similarity measures by ensuring that there is some feature space whose inner product is given by the kernel function.

While the symmetry condition is held in nearly all kernel functions used in practice, the positive semi-definite condition is sometimes either extremely difficult to prove or doesn't hold for all inputs. Thankfully, as long as the function approximates a similarity measure, empirically, the kernel function can perform well, though not without its problems [10]. For instance, a commonly used kernel, the sigmoid kernel in Table 4.1, performs well in a number of scenarios despite not being positive semi-definite in certain cases [21]. Another consideration is that the kernel function can be valid within the context of a problem through constraints on the input, while actually not being a valid kernel function otherwise. That is, a kernel function may not be positive semi-definite over some sets of input data, but it can serve as a valid kernel function if the range of data being worked on ensures the property.

4.1.1   Utilizing Kernel Functions in R

The overarching goal for allowing kernel functions to be used in R is to be able to swap different kernel functions for use in data mining algorithms without requiring changes to the data mining method. Hence, the two activities are separated in code. That is, the *kernel matrix* is first computed for the data set, and then the matrix (rather than the raw data) is passed into the data mining algorithm. This decomposition allows for minimal code changes to use different kernel functions.

The following R snippet shows an example kernel function computation followed by a data mining algorithm, using the kernelized support vector machines algorithm ksvm, provided in the kernlab package:

```
 1 > #[Example use of ksvm, on arbitrary data]
 2 > # load arbitrary dataset and corresponding class labels
 3 > data <- ...
 4 > labels <- ...
 5 > # generate kernel matrix on data
 6 > trainMatrix <- myKernelFunctionMatrix(data, ...)
 7 > # run kernelized support vector machines
 8 > #   note that many kernels are built in that can be
 9 > #   accessed through the 'kernel' argument, but we
10 > #   have already "kernelized" the data, so ksvm is
11 > #   told to treat the input as a kernel matrix
12 > model <- ksvm(trainMatrix, labels, kernel='matrix')
```

The kernel function myKernelFunctionMatrix merely creates an $n \times n$ kernel matrix, where n is the number of elements and entry i, j represents the kernel function applied to all pairs of data i and j. Kernel functions may also be parameterized, so additional parameters need to be set as necessary. Thanks to the decomposition of the kernel data mining methods, this line is the only one that needs changing based on the kernel used. The resulting matrix is then sent into the `ksvm` function, which has no idea what the original data is, because it only depends on the inner products provided in the kernel matrix. For the process of *model selection*, which selects the kernel function and necessary parameters, a loop could be put over `myKernelFunctionMatrix`, testing different kernel parameters and choosing the one that leads to the best results when running the `ksvm` routine.

4.2   Extending Kernel Methods to Graphs

While kernel functions enable data mining in a geometric context, we can interpret kernel functions as a measurement of similarity between pairs of input data. Furthermore, if we can prove that a function on an arbitrary pair of input data is positive semi-definite, then the function represents the inner product in some feature space. Therefore, it is possible to define kernel functions for structured data, such as graphs, strings, etc., for which a vector-based representation of the raw data is simply not possible. The primary advantage of doing this is that it allows a rich class of vector-based data mining algorithms to be performed on datasets consisting of graphs, alongside algorithms working directly on graphs.

For graphs, two simple questions to ask from a data mining perspective are "How similar are two graphs?" and "How similar are two vertices within a graph?" (*between-graph* and *within-graph* similarity, respectively). Both problems have wide-reaching applicability in many areas, such as biology, where proteins and interactions between them are commonly represented in graph form, and chemistry, where compounds can be represented as labeled graphs. In both examples, being able to compare two graphs and compare individual vertices within a graph are important problems to consider. For instance, chemical compounds can be classified into different groups dependent on their chemical properties, and classifiers can evaluate possible properties of new chemicals by comparing their similarity to other, known graphs or estimating them via a model built by comparing graphs in a training set of known compounds.

Naïve methods of comparing graphs, such as by size or by vertex degree, are poor graph similarity metrics. The size of a graph says very little about its underlying *structure*. For instance, the graphs in Figure 4.4 have the same size with very different structures. In terms of between-graph similarity, graphs B and C in Figure 4.4 are more similar to each other than to graph A, sharing more common edges. In terms of within-graph similarity, vertices 1 and 2 in graph C could be said to be more similar than vertices 1 and 3, which share

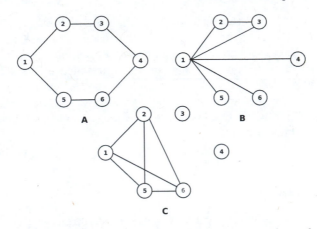

FIGURE 4.4: Three undirected graphs of the same number of vertices and edges. How similar are they?

no common neighbors. So, a method is needed that captures structural characteristics of graphs that are comparable between graphs or between vertices.

One such method of comparing structural characteristics is by performing graph and subgraph isomorphism tests. This is the subject of Chapter 7 on frequent subgraph mining and is an important comparison metric between graphs. If parts of some graph are isomorphic to parts of another graph, then those graphs could be said to be more similar than a pair that shares less isomorphic subgraphs. In fact, graph mining techniques exist that efficiently define and enumerate subgraphs as features, using them for classification (such as gBoost [16]). However, subgraph isomorphism is known to be an intractable problem (that is, algorithms performing subgraph isomorphism have exponential run-time in the size of the graphs). Thus, a major problem in graph analytics is how to perform these comparisons in a more efficient manner, or that at least have a polynomial run-time.

4.3   Choosing Suitable Graph Kernel Functions

A significant problem lies in the choice of a graph kernel function to use. Without making assumptions about the data we are working with, there are no provably better kernel functions, as the underlying distribution of a sampling of the data cannot be known, and we can always provide a distribution such that one kernel method performs better than another and vice versa. This inability to determine data-independent "better" functions is referred to as *no free lunch* [24]. Thankfully, in most application contexts, there is almost always expert knowledge about the domain being studied, which drives the kernel selection process. For graphs, there are a number of structural characteristics one may wish to capture in a kernel function, typically based on operations on the graph's adjacency matrix representation. The following kernels attempt to capture these, but first, an important result in collapsing series of matrices is needed for these kernels to be able to be computed within a reasonable amount of time.

4.3.1 Geometric Series of Matrices

A *geometric series* is an infinite sum of the form:

$$s = \sum_{i=0}^{\infty} a^i = 1 + a + a^2 + \dots \tag{4.4}$$

Ideally, we would like a closed form solution to this quantity if one exists, as it allows us to use it in calculation (an important concept when extending to graph kernels). To see if a closed form is possible, let's start with the finite series:

$$s_n = \sum_{i=0}^{n} a^i = 1 + a + a^2 + \dots + a^n \tag{4.5}$$

A useful strategy is to consider the relation between sums of different values of n and solve for the series. For this problem, we make use of the property that s_{n+1} is equivalent to multiplying s_n by a and adding 1:

$$s_{n+1} = 1 + a s_n \tag{4.6}$$

Next, let's simplify the difference between the quantities s_n and s_{n+1} to get rid of the s_{n+1} term:

$$s_n - s_{n+1} = s_n - 1 - a s_n$$
$$= -a^{n+1}$$

Finally, solve the latter two quantities for s_n:

$$s_n - 1 - a s_n = -a^{n+1}$$
$$(1 - a)s_n = 1 - a^{n+1}$$
$$s_n = \frac{1 - a^{n+1}}{1 - a} \tag{4.7}$$

If we consider the limit as $n \to \infty$, then $s_{n \to \infty} = 1/(1-a)$, for $0 < a < 1$. For instance, the geometric series where $a = \frac{1}{2}$ converges to 2.

Now, consider the following series for some matrix $\mathbf{A}$:

$$s_n = \sum_{i=0}^{n} \mathbf{A}^i \tag{4.8}$$

Using a similar strategy, compute the difference between consecutive terms and simplify:

$$s_n - s_{n+1} = s_n - I - \mathbf{A}s_n \qquad (4.9)$$

$$= -\mathbf{A}^{n+1} \qquad (4.10)$$

Now, solve for s_n:

$$s_n - I - \mathbf{A}s_n = -\mathbf{A}^{n+1}$$

$$(I - \mathbf{A})s_n = I - \mathbf{A}^{n+1}$$

$$s_n = (I - \mathbf{A}^{n+1})(I - \mathbf{A})^{-1} \qquad (4.11)$$

The conditions for Equation 4.11 to converge as $n \to \infty$ are much more involved than the geometric series involving a single constant. However, for the purposes of graph kernels, we can use a *decay factor* γ, producing a matrix series of the form:

$$s_n = \sum_{i=0}^{\infty} \gamma^i \mathbf{A}^i \qquad (4.12)$$

This equation has a similar closed form:

$$s_n = (I - \gamma^{n+1}\mathbf{A}^{n+1})(I - \gamma\mathbf{A})^{-1} \qquad (4.13)$$

To "force" the quantity to converge as $n \to \infty$, for our purposes we can take advantage of the fact that $\mathbf{A}$ is an adjacency matrix. Consider $\mathbf{A}^2$, the set of walks of length two. Since $\mathbf{A}$ is an adjacency matrix, the maximum entry in $\mathbf{A}^2$ is no greater than the smaller of the maximum indegree Δ^+ and maximum outdegree Δ^- of the matrix. In undirected graphs, these quantities are the same. Therefore, let

$$\gamma < \frac{1}{\min(\Delta^+(\mathbf{A}), \Delta^-(\mathbf{A}))} \qquad (4.14)$$

Under this condition, Equation 4.13, as $n \to \infty$, reduces to

$$s_n = (I - \gamma\mathbf{A})^{-1} \qquad (4.15)$$

This result allows us to compute similarity between pairs of vertices directly (within-graph similarity) or construct graphs containing structural information on a pair of graphs and sum the entries to compute similarity.

In R, the formula in Equation 4.15 can be simply represented as follows (gamma and $n \times n$ adjacency matrix A):

```
1 # [Computation of collapsed geometric sum of matrices,
2 #  using decay factor]
3 geoSeriesSum <- solve(diag(n)-(gamma*A))
```

The solve function, when presented with a single matrix argument $\mathbf{M}$, returns $\mathbf{M}^{-1}$.

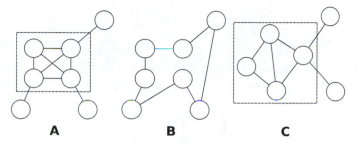

FIGURE 4.5: Three graphs to be compared through walk-based measures. The boxed in regions represent vertices more likely to be visited in random walks.

4.3.2   Between-graph Similarity

4.3.2.1   Walk-based metrics

The simplest and most intuitive method of comparing structural properties of graphs, without considering graph isomorphism, is to compare walks between a pair of graphs. If two graphs have similar random-walk sequences, then they can be considered similar with regards to their structure. For example, Figure 4.5 shows three graphs that we want to compare for similarity. Starting from a random vertex, graph A is heavily skewed towards landing in the 4-clique, regardless of starting vertex and walk length, while B is equally likely to land in any of its vertices. Therefore, we would want to conclude that graphs A and B are dissimilar. On the other hand, comparing graphs A and C would conclude in a somewhat higher degree of similarity than between A and B, as both have a grouping of nodes that are more likely to be part of random walks than others.

However, how would we quantitatively compare an arbitrary pair of graphs in a kernel function? We could use some complicated metrics to compare a pair of graphs directly, but a more elegant method is to combine the two graphs into a common structure, and performing analysis on the new structure. The simplest way of combining the structural properties of a pair of graphs is by using the *direct product* of two graphs, which allows analysis of a single graph that contains properties of both graphs (see Figure 4.6).

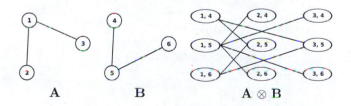

FIGURE 4.6: Two graphs and their direct product.

Definition 4.4 *Direct Product*

The graph $G_1 \otimes G_2 = (V_x, E_x)$, for $G_1 = (V_1, E_1)$ and $G_2 = (V_2, E_2)$, where $V_x = V_1 \times V_2$ and $((v_i, v_h), (v_j, v_k)) \in E_x$ if and only if $(v_i, v_j) \in E_1$ and $(v_h, v_k) \in E_2$.

In other words, each vertex of the direct product graph is a pair of vertices, one from each graph, and an edge exists between each pair of vertex pairs if and only if an edge is between each pair of vertices in their respective original graphs. The adjacency matrix of the direct product graph can be obtained from the adjacency matrices of two graphs $\mathbf{A}_{m \times n}$ and $\mathbf{B}_{p \times q}$ as follows:

$$\begin{bmatrix} a_{1,1}\mathbf{B} & \cdots & a_{1,n}\mathbf{B} \\ \vdots & \ddots & \vdots \\ a_{m,1}\mathbf{B} & \cdots & a_{m,n}\mathbf{B} \end{bmatrix}$$

where $a\mathbf{B}$ represents the multiplication between the scalar a, which is an element of a matrix, by the entire matrix $\mathbf{B}$. The following R code shows the calculation of the direct product for the two graphs shown in Figure 4.6. The function `directProduct` is available in the GraphKernelFunctions package, which requires the `spam` and `fBasics` functions internally.

```
1  library(GraphKernelFunctions)
2  library(spam)
3  library(fBasics)
4  data(GraphA)
5  data(GraphB)
6  GraphA
7     1 2 3
8  1 0 1 1
9  2 1 0 0
10 3 1 0 0
11 GraphB
12    4 5 6
13 4 0 1 0
14 5 1 0 1
15 6 0 1 0
16 directProduct(GraphA,GraphB)
17     1:4 1:5 1:6 2:4 2:5 2:6 3:4 3:5 3:6
18 1:4  0   0   0   0   1   0   0   1   0
19 1:5  0   0   0   1   0   1   1   0   1
20 1:6  0   0   0   0   1   0   0   1   0
21 2:4  0   1   0   0   0   0   0   0   0
22 2:5  1   0   1   0   0   0   0   0   0
23 2:6  0   1   0   0   0   0   0   0   0
24 3:4  0   1   0   0   0   0   0   0   0
25 3:5  1   0   1   0   0   0   0   0   0
26 3:6  0   1   0   0   0   0   0   0   0
```

However, if the algorithm used permits, we can avoid explicit computation of the direct product matrix. Given the direct product definition, we can map any index of the direct product matrix back into the respective indices of the input matrices. This is captured in the function `implicitDPAdjacencyTest` from the GraphKernelFunctions package.

```
1 library(GraphKernelFunctions)
2 implicitDPAdjacencyTest(GraphA,GraphB,2,3)
3 [1] 0
4 implicitDPAdjacencyTest(GraphA,GraphB,2,4)
5 [1] 1
```

The direct product graph is suitable for comparing the walks between graphs in a kernel function [6]. The intuition behind this measure is that, given two graphs, the all-pairs information in the direct product captures walks that are similar in number and length. Thus, the walks of similar graphs will "transfer" onto the direct product graph. This idea is used in Chapter 9 for chemical compound classification. To compute the number of walks given an adjacency matrix $\mathbf{A}$ of a graph, we can compute $\mathbf{A}^n$, where n is the walk length; each element $\mathbf{A}_{i,j}$ represents the number of walks of length n from vertex i to vertex j. The proof of this is left as an exercise.

For a more accurate measure of similarity, we wish to capture walks of multiple lengths, which suggests a summation of the direct product graph adjacency matrices. However, a direct summation is both biased towards longer walks (in a strictly numerical fashion) and extremely expensive to compute, especially for increasingly large walk lengths. Therefore, using a decay factor allows us to count shorter walks as more significant while providing a closed-form summation. Equation 4.15, using the decay factor in Equation 4.14, allows us to provide this closed-form solution using the direct product graph as the adjacency matrix. Given the resulting matrix, we can perform a number of operations to arrive at a final answer, such as merely summing the elements of the resulting matrix. This process, along with more real-world examples, is described in more detail in Algorithms 23 and 22 of Chapter 9.

4.3.2.2 Pitfalls of walk-based kernels and potential solutions

While walk-based kernels are an elegant method of comparing graph structures, there are still numerous problems to contend with. First, while the method avoids subgraph isomorphism testing, it is still computationally expensive. Naïvely, if both graphs have N vertices, building the direct product graph and taking the inverse leads to a $O(N^6)$ time complexity, which is infeasible for graphs with a large number of vertices (the direct product graph is an $N^2 \times N^2$ matrix, and the inverse operation is of roughly cubic time with respect to the matrix dimension). Huge improvements on the time can be made by using alternate representations and sets of equations, which reduces the time to $O(N^3)$ [23]. In both cases, short cycles and undirected edges can lead to arbitrarily high similarity of vertices in the direct product graph,

skewing the resulting similarity values and ultimately reducing accuracy. This
phenomenon is known as *tottering*.

Definition 4.5 *Tottering*
The tendency of walk-based graph analysis measures to be significantly biased
towards undirected edges and short cycles.

There have been a number of attempts to reduce the problem of tottering and in general make walk-based kernel functions more robust. The most
straightforward way to avoid tottering is to explicitly prevent tottering between two vertices by modifying the graph structure [11]. Let $G = (V, E)$ be
a directed graph (undirected graphs can also be used, with two directed edges
replacing each undirected edge). Let G_t be a *2-totter-free graph*, a directed
graph such that:

$$G_t = (V \cup E, E'), \tag{4.16}$$

where

$$E' = \{(v, (v, t)) \mid v \in V, (v, t) \in E\}$$
$$\cup \{((u, v), (v, t)) \mid (u, v), (v, t) \in E, u \neq t\}. \tag{4.17}$$

See Figure 4.7. Each edge in the original graph is now a vertex in the new
graph. Each edge in the new graph connects vertices in the original graph
with their corresponding outgoing edges. Finally, edges are placed between
vertices representing edges in the original graph only if they do not form
a 2-cycle. The resulting graph is then used in graph kernels, and prevents
tottering between two vertices. However, does the same hold for more than
two vertices (Exercise 8)? In any case, the R implementation of performing this
transformation on the graph is provided by the function `TotterTransform`,
an example of which is shown below (based on Figure 4.7).

```
1 # [Example usage and output of the "Totter-free Transform"]
2 library(GraphKernelFunctions)
3 library(combinat)
4 library(multicore)
5 GraphC
6           e1 e2 e3 e4
7 edge-from  1  1  2  2
8 edge-to    2  3  1  3
9 TotterTransform(GraphC)
10    edge-from edge-to
11 1         1     1-2
12 2         1     1-3
13 3         2     2-1
14 4         2     2-3
15 5       1-2     2-3
16 6       2-1     1-3
```

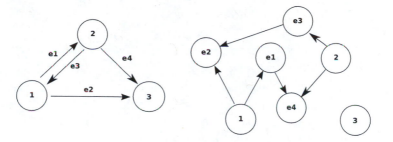

FIGURE 4.7: A graph and its 2-totter-free transformation.

Other methods work to reduce the size of the direct product graph to allow more efficient computation. For instance, *label enrichment* [11] is used to label vertices based on structural properties. For instance, the nth-order *Morgan Index* of a vertex defines the number of neighbors at most n hops away [13]. By only putting together vertices in the direct product graph with similar n^{th}-order Morgan indices, the direct product size can be substantially reduced. However, structural information is lost, as similarity becomes more strongly dependent on vertex degree.

A second method is to remove the vertex/edge redundancy when performing random walks, instead of moving towards *paths*. Recall that simple paths are walks in which no vertex is visited more than once. Finding all paths in a graph is computationally intensive (NP-complete), as is finding the longest path in a graph. However, finding the shortest paths between each vertex pair is much easier to compute. Shortest path kernels exploit the structural characteristics of shortest paths.

One way of incorporating shortest path information into kernel functions uses a similar strategy as the tottering prevention and label enrichment schemes: pre-process the graph and use existing kernel functions on the result. To incorporate shortest paths into graph kernels, the *Floyd transformation* is used [2], named after the underlying use of the Floyd-Warshall all-pairs shortest path algorithm [5]. First, the Floyd-Warshall algorithm is used to obtain the all-pairs shortest path matrix, where each (i, j) entry denotes the shortest path length between vertices i and j. From there, the weighted Floyd-transformed graph S is constructed. Let $G = (V, E)$ be an input graph, $\mathbf{M}$ the Floyd-Warshall matrix, and $w(x, y)$ be the weight of some edge (x, y). Then,

$$\mathbf{S} = (V, E'),$$
$$E' = \{(u, v) \mid u \neq v, \mathbf{M}_{u,v} \neq \infty\},$$
$$w(i, j) \in E' = \mathbf{M}_{i,j}. \tag{4.18}$$

Note that a weight of ∞ signifies that no path exists between the two vertices.

The resulting kernel is then defined as a sum of kernel functions on edge pairs. For Floyd-transformed graphs $S_1 = (V_1, E_1)$ and $S_2 = (V_2, E_2)$,

$$k_{shortest\_path}(S_1, S_2) = \sum_{e_1 \in E_1} \sum_{e_2 \in E_2} k_{walk}^{(1)}(e_1, e_2), \qquad (4.19)$$

where k_{walk}^1 is a walk-based kernel only considering single-hop walks. The walk-based kernel can simply check for edge weight equality or perform some operation on the edge weights, such as multiplication. Unfortunately, the run-time of the overall method is $O(n^4)$, making it very expensive for large graphs.

4.3.2.3   Other between-graph metrics

Aside from walk- and path-based kernels, there is a wealth of other between-graph kernels. For instance, kernel functions have been developed based on *graph edit distances* [14]. This metric provides a count for the number of "modifications" needed to change one graph to an isomorphism of another. Possible modifications include the addition and removal of nodes, as well as the addition and removal of edges. Not only does this capture structural similarity (a low graph edit distance implies highly similar graphs), but costs can be added to each operation to weight one (edge addition/removal) over another (vertex addition/removal) and the comparison does not change drastically under noisy or imperfect input data. Unfortunately, the kernel itself is not always positive-definite.

Another example pivots on the idea of walks as a similarity metric. The *cyclic pattern kernel* defines graph similarity in terms of simple cycles, rather than walks/paths [7]. By labeling and giving a canonical ordering to possible cycles, the cycles in different graphs can be compared quantitatively. However, the number of cycles is exponential in size and kernels based on cyclic patterns are NP-hard (exponential run-time) in general, though this worst case is rarely seen.

Many kernels have been proposed based on subgraph isomorphism, comparisons of graph substructures, etc. Chapter 7 on frequent subgraph mining discusses the relative concepts in greater depth, but a few pertinent subgraph-based kernels are worth mentioning here. One utilizes a *subtree-like pattern*, similar to random walks but rather with rooted tree structures [15]. The general algorithm compares a pair of vertices with a kernel function, then recursively compares all sets of neighbors of each via kernel functions. Of course, this is an extremely expensive operation, but allows for a very rich structural comparison of graph pairs. Another kernel, in order to prevent the exponential runtime of subgraph isomorphism, restricts the subgraphs to a fixed number of nodes. These are called *graphlets*, and the kernel function counts the number of isomorphic graphlets that two graphs share [20]. While this necessitates model selection by parameterizing the kernel and reduces the amount of structural information gleaned compared to pure subgraph isomorphism testing, it is nevertheless effective at reducing the computation necessary.

4.3.3 Within-Graph Similarity

When the goal is to compare individual vertices in a graph, many of the concepts used in the between-graph kernels apply here; rather than taking the direct product graph and then performing some operation, take the original graph and perform a similar operation. The simplest and most intuitive similarity metric between vertices is comparing the neighborhood of each vertex. Two vertices that have similar neighbors, neighbors of neighbors, etc. can be said to be more similar with respect to the graph, or in general, when they share *outgoing* paths to other vertices. Similarly, two vertices can be considered more similar when common neighboring vertices connect to it, or in general, when there are common *incoming* paths to them. When a graph is undirected, these two measures are the same. This concept, though not encapsulated in a kernel function, is discussed to a large degree in Chapter 8, using the similarity metric of *shared nearest neighbors*. However, how do we encode neighborhood information suitable for kernel function computation?

Given an adjacency matrix $\mathbf{A}$ for a directed graph, similarity using outgoing paths can be computed as $\mathbf{A}\mathbf{A}^T$, where $\mathbf{A}^T$ is the transpose of $\mathbf{A}$, and similarity using incoming paths can be computed as $\mathbf{A}^T\mathbf{A}$. For unweighted graphs, each entry i, j in $\mathbf{A}\mathbf{A}^T$ represents the number of common single-hop neighbors that vertices i and j link to. In $\mathbf{A}^T\mathbf{A}$, each entry i, j represents the number of vertices that link to both vertex i and j. To account for paths of length greater than one, $(\mathbf{A}\mathbf{A}^T)^n$ and $(\mathbf{A}^T\mathbf{A})^n$ can be computed, and a similar summation as Equation 4.15 can be used to converge the resulting series.

Tottering is also a problem with this approach, though with vertex degrees rather than short, cyclic walks. For $n > 1$, the vertex degree introduces a significant bias into the resulting matrix; vertices with larger degrees are artificially more "similar" to other vertices than low degree vertices. One way to handle this is to use the results of computing both series corresponding to $\mathbf{A}\mathbf{A}^T$ and $\mathbf{A}^T\mathbf{A}$ to determine relationships. This is used by Neumann Kernels in Chapter 6. Another way to handle this is to *normalize* the matrix, usually by scaling the matrix by some combination of vertex degrees. This is used in the Laplacian Kernel in Chapter 9.

4.4 Kernels In This Book

In this chapter we have presented only a very small sampling of kernel functions, as well as some preliminary ideas about how to use graph properties to devise kernel functions. Here, we have tried to give a more intuitive understanding of kernel methods and their use in both vector and graph data. The remainder of the book explores various aspects of kernel methods further and in context of real-world problems:

1. Chapter 6 uses the Neumann Kernel, based on the within-graph computations described in Section 4.3.3, to model *relatedness* between vertices and *importance* of vertices, with use-cases in filtering web page searches and calculating co-citation correlations in academic publications. Chapter 6 shares much more commonality than the use of a kernel function, however. The kernels in this chapter, and indeed throughout most of the book, depend on comparing local structural properties of graphs to other graphs (or vertices to other vertices). Measuring the degree of proximity between vertices in a graph underlies a large swath of graph analysis techniques, even if the exact methods used aren't the same.

2. Chapter 8 does not define a particular kernel function; rather, it discusses how to perform k-means clustering, a spatial organization of input data in some Hilbert space into k partitions, or clusters, using kernel functions rather than direct computation on vector data. As an exemplar, they discuss the clustering of individuals with like interests in a social network, represented as a graph.

3. Chapter 9 discusses aspects of both between-graph and within-graph classification using graph kernels, discussing the direct product kernel we introduced in Section 4.3.2 as well as the Laplacian kernel, based on the matrix operations used to compute vertex similarity with respect to outgoing edges discussed in Section 4.3.3. They additionally use a *regularization operation* to avoid the problems with vertex degrees discussed. Finally, they link their graph classification methods to classifying web pages based on desired properties as well as classifying chemical compounds based on discrete chemical properties of known compounds.

4. Chapter 10 discusses dimension reduction, describing the Principle Component Analysis (PCA) algorithm and the modification of it to use kernel functions, using the applications of tumor diagnosis and facial recognition.

4.5   Exercises

1. Recall that a *kernel matrix* for a set of input data is a matrix where each i, j entry is the value of the kernel function computed on datum i and datum j. Given kernel matrices **A** and **B** in Figure 4.8 representing different kernel functions on a set of data, is it possible for the underlying kernel function to be:

   (a) Symmetric?

(b) Positive semi-definite? (Hint: compute symbolically, then think about vectors that could possibly make the sum negative)

(c) Valid kernel functions?

$$A = \begin{bmatrix} 1 & 0 & -1 \\ 0 & 1 & 2 \\ -1 & 2 & 1 \end{bmatrix} \quad B = \begin{bmatrix} 2 & -1 & 1 \\ -1 & 3 & 0 \\ 1 & 2 & 2 \end{bmatrix}$$

FIGURE 4.8: Kernel matrices for problem 1.

2. Many algorithms, such as k-means clustering (see Chapter 8), rely on the *Euclidean distance function* between vectors $u = (u_1, u_2, \ldots, u_n)$ and $v = (v_1, v_2, \ldots, v_n)$:

$$d(u, v) = d(v, u) = \sqrt{(v_1 - u_1)^2 + (v_2 - u_2)^2 \ldots + (v_n - u_n)^2}.$$

Show that the distance function can be kernelized, that is, can be written in terms of inner products between vectors u and v. This shows that analysis algorithms based on distance metrics can also use kernel functions.

3. Given kernel functions k_1 and k_2, define k' to be $k'(x, y) = \alpha k_1(x, y) + \beta k_2(x, y)$, for $\alpha, \beta \geq 0$. Is k' a valid kernel function?

4. How many different undirected, simple, labeled, 4-vertex, 3-edge graphs can one construct? How about for an n-vertex, m-edge undirected simple labeled graph? What does this say about using metrics such as size for computing similarity between graphs?

5. Given some $n \times m$ matrix $\mathbf{A}$, is the matrix $\mathbf{A}\mathbf{A}^T$ symmetric ($\mathbf{A}\mathbf{A}^T_{i,j} = \mathbf{A}\mathbf{A}^T_{j,i}$ for all i, j)? Is the matrix $\mathbf{A}^T\mathbf{A}$ symmetric?

6. In Section 4.3.2, it was noted that, for an $m \times m$ adjacency matrix $\mathbf{A}$, $\mathbf{A}^n$ represents a matrix where each entry (i, j) is the number of walks of length n from vertex i to vertex j. Prove by induction that this is the case. (Hint: What does the definition of matrix multiplication mean in this context?)

7. Let G_1 be an n-vertex, m-edge undirected graph, and G_2 be an h-vertex, k-edge undirected graph. Consider the direct product graph $G_x = G_1 \otimes G_2$

   (a) How many vertices are in G_x?

   (b) How many edges are in G_x?

   (c) How large is the adjacency matrix for G_x? What does this say about performing the direct product kernel on large graphs?

8. In Section 4.3.2.2, the 2-totter-free graph was introduced. Answer the following:

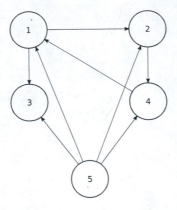

FIGURE 4.9: Graph used in Problem 9

(a) Can there exist any cycles in the 2-totter-free graph that contain vertices of the original graph?

(b) Can there exist any cycles in the 2-totter-free graph that contain vertices representing edges of the original graph?

9. Given the graph in Figure 4.9, perform the following:

   (a) Compute the adjacency matrix $\mathbf{A}$ corresponding to the graph.

   (b) Compute $\mathbf{AA}^T$, the similarity measure of vertices with respect to outgoing edges.

   (c) Compute $\mathbf{A}^T\mathbf{A}$, the similarity measure of vertices with respect to incoming edges.

   (d) Compute the squares of each. For $(\mathbf{AA}^T)^2$, how similar is each vertex to vertex 5 compared to each other? For $(\mathbf{A}^T\mathbf{A})^2$, how are the relative similarity scores affected by vertex 5?

10. A *hypergraph* is a graph where an edge (called a hyperedge or link) may connect multiple vertices (a subset of the vertex set, to be exact). A matrix representation for such a graph is an $v \times e$ matrix, where v is the number of vertices, e is the number of links, and an entry (i, j) corresponds to edge j being incident on vertex i.

   (a) Given a hypergraph with n vertices, m edges and with matrix representation $\mathbf{M}$, what are the dimensions of $\mathbf{MM}^T$? What about $\mathbf{M}^T\mathbf{M}$?

   (b) What does this say about using neighborhood-based kernels on vertices of hypergraphs? Is there anything to be worried about?

Bibliography

[1] M. Aizerman, E. Braverman, and L. Rozonoer. Theoretical foundations of the potential function method in pattern recognition learning. *Automation and Remote Control*, 25:821–837, 1964.

[2] K.M. Borgwardt and H.P. Kriegel. Shortest-path kernels on graphs. In *Proceedings of the Fifth IEEE International Conference on Data Mining*, ICDM '05, pages 74–81, Washington, DC, USA, 2005. IEEE Computer Society.

[3] B.E. Boser, I.M. Guyon, and V.N. Vapnik. A training algorithm for optimal margin classifiers. *Proceedings of the 5th Annual ACM Workshop on Computational Learning Theory*, pages 144–152, 1992.

[4] C. Cortes and V.N. Vapnik. Support vector networks. *Machine Learning*, 20:273–297, 1995.

[5] R.W. Floyd. Algorithm 97: Shortest path. *Communications of the ACM*, 5(6):345, 1962.

[6] T. Gartner, P. Flach, and S. Wrobel. On graph kernels: Hardness results and efficient alternatives. In *Conference on Learning Theory*, pages 129–143, 2003.

[7] T. Horváth, T. Gärtner, and S. Wrobel. Cyclic pattern kernels for predictive graph mining. In *Proceedings of the Tenth ACM SIGKDD International Conference on Knowledge Discovery and Data Mining*, KDD '04, pages 158–167, New York, NY, USA, 2004.

[8] T. Howley and M.G. Madden. The genetic kernel support vector machine: Description and evaluation. *Artificial Intelligence Review*, 24:379–395, 2005.

[9] C.-W. Hsu, C.-C. Chang, and C.-J. Lin. A practical guide to support vector classification. *Technical Report, Department of Computer Science, National Taiwan University, 2003, 2003.* http://www.csie.ntu.edu.tw/~cjlin/papers/guide/guide.pdf.

[10] H.-T. Lin and C.-J. Lin. A study on sigmoid kernels for SVM and the training of non-PSD kernels by SMO-type methods. *Technical Report, Department of Computer Science and Information Engineering, National Taiwan University*, Taipei, Taiwan, 2003.

[11] P. Mahe, N. Ueda, T. Akutsu, J.-L. Perret, and J.-P. Vert. Extensions of marginalized graph kernels. *International Conference on Machine Learning (ICML)*, pages 552–559, 2004.

[12] J. Mercer. Functions of positive and negative type and their connection with the theory of integral equations. *Philosophical Transactions of the Royal Society*, 209:441–458, 1909.

[13] H.L. Morgan. The generation of a unique machine description for chemical structures: A technique developed at chemical abstracts service. *Journal of Chemical Documentation*, pages 107–113, 1965.

[14] M. Neuhaus and H. Bunke. A random walk kernel derived from graph edit distance. In Dit-Yan Yeung, James Kwok, Ana Fred, Fabio Roli, and Dick de Ridder, editors, *Structural, Syntactic, and Statistical Pattern Recognition*, volume 4109 of *Lecture Notes in Computer Science*, pages 191–199. Springer Berlin / Heidelberg, 2006.

[15] J. Ramon and T. Gärtner. Expressivity versus efficiency of graph kernels. *Science*, pages 65–74, 2003.

[16] H. Saigo, S. Nowozin, T. Kadowaki, T. Kudo, and K. Tsuda. gBoost: a mathematical programming approach to graph classification and regression. *Machine Learning*, 75:69–89, 2009.

[17] S. Saitoh. *Theory of Reproducing Kernels and its Applications*. Longman Scientific and Technical, Harlow, England, 1988.

[18] B. Scholkopf. *Support Vector Learning*. Oldenbourg Verlag, Munich, 1997.

[19] B. Scholkopf, C.J.C. Burges, and A.J. Smola. *Advances in Kernel Methods: Support Vector Learning*. MIT Press, Cambridge, MA, 1999.

[20] N. Shervashidze, S.V.N. Vishwanathan, T.H. Petri, K. Mehlhorn, and K.M. Borgwardt. Efficient graphlet kernels for large graph comparison. *Proceedings of the International Workshop on Artificial Intelligence and Statistics Society for Artificial Intelligence and Statistics*, 5:488–495, 2008.

[21] V.N. Vapnik. *The Nature of Statistical Learning Theory*. Springer-Verlag, New York, 1995.

[22] V.N. Vapnik. *Statistical Learning Theory*. Wiley, New York, 1998.

[23] S.V.N. Vishwanathan, K.M. Borgwardt, and N.N. Schraudolph. Fast computation of graph kernels. In *Advances in Neural Information Processing Systems 19 (NIPS 2006)*, pages 1–2. MIT Press, 2006.

[24] D.H. Wolpert. The supervised learning no-free-lunch theorems. In *Proc. 6th Online World Conference on Soft Computing in Industrial Applications*, pages 25–42, 2001.

5

Link Analysis

Arpan Chakraborty, Kevin Wilson, Nathan Green, Shravan Kumar Alur, Fatih Ergin, Karthik Gurumurthy, Romulo Manzano, and Deepti Chinta

North Carolina State University

CONTENTS

5.1 Introduction

Link Analysis deals with mining useful information from linked structures
like graphs. Graphs have vertices representing objects and links among those
vertices representing relationships among those objects. Data mining covers
a diverse set of activities that deal with independent sets of data that may
be numerical or otherwise. Link mining works with graph structures that
have nodes with defined set of properties. These nodes may be of the same
type (homogeneous) or different (heterogeneous). The World Wide Web can
be considered a homogeneous network (all nodes are web URLs), while a
network of bibliographic links and citations is a heterogeneous multi-mode
network (nodes may be papers, books, magazine articles, etc.) [15]. We first
take a very generic look at links, and establish what kind of information and
benefits can be obtained by studying links.

5.1.1 Links in Daily Life

The most common interpretation of the word *link* today is *hyperlink*—a means
of connecting two web documents wherein activating a special element embedded in one document takes you to the other. What other kinds of 'links'
can you think of that we see around us?

Think about the more abstract case of social links. You are *connected*
to your parents via a parent-child relation, while you are connected to your
next-door neighbor via a neighbor-neighbor link. You and your friends are
connected to each other through the friendship relation. We can also think
of you and your car being linked to each other as well. Thus, we see that in

reality, the term tends to have a very broad meaning. Also, there are several different kinds of relations that exist among people, and even between people and other objects.

5.1.2 How to Define a Link?

What is common among these different meanings of *link*? Well, the fundamental observation is that a link *connects* two objects. Note that there are instances where a link connects more than two objects, for example, the sentence "Bruce gifted Jane an expensive necklace," relates Bruce, Jane and the expensive necklace within an act of gifting. For simplicity, we will only consider simple links that deal with only two objects. Any complex link can always be broken down into such simple links by introducing new intermediate objects.

A link represents a relationship and connects two objects that are related to each other in that specific way. A collection of links representing the same kind of relationship form a network, or graph, where the objects being related correspond to the graph vertices and the links themselves are the edges. When two objects being related by a link are of the same kind, then the network formed by such links is termed a *homogeneous* network. The friendship relation, for instance, forms a homogeneous network of friends, whereas the car-owner relation defines a *heterogeneous* network. When a network consists of several kinds of links, it is said to be *multi-relational*, or sometimes *multi-mode*. An example could be a family tree that connects people using relationships, such as parent-child, sibling, spouse, etc.

5.1.3 What to Learn from Links?

After getting an idea of what link analysis enables us to know, we may want to figure out how to use that information. With more and more information becoming available today in databases, structured documents, plain texts, transcribed conversations, and sometimes even in non-verbal form, such as images and videos, the possibilities for link analysis, as well as the associated challenges, are growing by leaps and bounds. There is a multitude of practical scenarios in which link analysis techniques are currently in use.

The most common examples are from the domain of computer networks. You may want to know which servers are likely to get the most load? Or which communication nodes may get disconnected easily? You may want to reason about how *reliable* a network is, or find out which nodes form a critical backbone of a network. A number of pure graph-theoretic techniques do exist to answer some of these questions, but they easily become intractable with increasing network size. On the other hand, though graph mining approaches also consume a considerable amount of processing resources, they can employ heuristics to estimate results, and therefore be made to sacrifice accuracy for timely performance. Moreover, learning methods usually become more accurate with larger amounts of data, making them further suitable for most real-world problems.

Link analysis can also give us some interesting insight into the world around us. In the World Wide Web, if web pages are considered as nodes and hyperlinks as edges, then the average distance between any two pages is about 19 [1]. The famous collaboration graph centered on mathematician Paul Erdős gives a surprisingly low average Erdős number of about 5 (the Erdős number of an author is the minimum number of links in the collaboration graph that need to be traversed starting at that author to reach Paul Erdős; here only connected authors are considered) [16]. We now use similar information in our daily lives, for instance, when establishing new professional acquaintances on networks, such as LinkedIn®, we sometimes check their number of connections, or what networks they are connected to.

5.2   Analyzing Links

As mentioned before, we can learn a number of things about a network and its nodes by studying links. In this section, we discuss the different ways in which link information can be used, and the associated end results. Before we define these different Link Analysis tasks, we must establish a clear interpretation of what kind of links we will be talking about.

5.2.1   Links as Edges in a Graph

Simply put, links are like edges in a graph. Correspondingly, the objects that links connect are like nodes or vertices in a graph. Therefore, any network of links can be represented as a graph $G = (V, E)$, where V denotes the set of vertices (nodes) and E denotes the set of edges (links). This abstraction enables us to directly reason about links using concepts from graph theory. Henceforth, in our discussion, we will treat networks of links as graphs.

Note that this abstraction may not accurately represent some of the relationships that real-world links represent, like a ternary relation mentioned earlier. In that case, further simplification may be required to model a real-world network as an abstract graph. In addition, we sometimes require labels or weights to be associated with links (or even nodes). Appropriate modifications and enhancements made to our graph model can take care of these issues.

5.2.2   Kinds of Link Analysis Tasks

The domain of Link Analysis encompasses several distinct tasks. These are essentially determined by the different possible outcomes of analyzing link

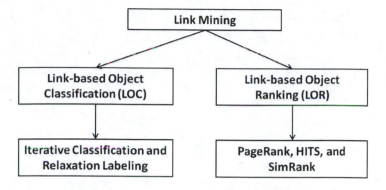

FIGURE 5.1: Link-based mining activities.

data. Link Analysis tasks can usually be grouped into a small set of overall categories. We take a look at these categories below.

5.2.2.1 Link-based Object Classification (LOC)

LOC (Link-based Object Classification) is a technique used to assign class labels to nodes according to their link characteristics. One very simplified example is to classify nodes as strongly connected and weakly connected depending solely on their degree (i.e., the number of edges they have incident on them).

A slightly more complex process would be to find the average distance of each node to all the other nodes, and classify them according to that quantity. The distance of one node to another is the number of edges that need to be traversed along the shortest path between them. Assuming that all nodes are connected to each other (in the graph theory sense), this average distance would be an indicator of how *central* a node is within a network. Thus, nodes can be classified as belonging to the core of a network or not, based on a suitable threshold.

LOC can also incorporate information about a node's properties for classification. For instance, if your task is to create compatible teams from a pool of personnel, and you have generic preference data from everyone, then you can build up a graph, where each node represents a person and each edge represents a common preference between two persons. You can then manually assign different group labels to a select set of individuals (who may have been designated as team leaders), and then assign groups to everyone else based on the number of edges they share with people who have already been labeled. A few iterations of this process should result in an amicable classification of team members. Such classification efforts that create groups of nodes are sometimes referred to as Group Detection tasks.

5.2.2.2   Link-based Object Ranking (LOR)

LOR (Link-based Object Ranking) ranks objects in a graph based on several factors affecting their importance in the graph structure, whereas LOC assigns labels specifically belonging to a closed set of finite values to an object [15]. The purpose of LOR is not to assign distinctive labels to the nodes—usually, all nodes in such networks are understood to be of the same type—the goal is to associate a relative quantitative assessment with each node.

LOR can sometimes be a more fine-grained version of LOC, such as in our strongly/weakly connected example above, if we desire to mark each node with the precise number representing its degree of connectivity, then it can be one form of ranking the nodes. Ranking tasks are usually much more complex than that, and take into account a large part of the graph when coming up with a figure for each node.

One of the most well-known ranking tasks is ranking web pages according to their relevance to a search query. Research and practical use have shown that the relevance of a search result not only depends upon the content of the document but also on how it is linked to other similar documents. There are algorithms that try to identify research papers that have the most comprehensive knowledge about a given topic by analyzing how many other relevant papers have cited them. Some social network games include a notion of popularity that is defined by how well-connected each person is with others and what this person's respective popularity figure is.

5.2.2.3   Link prediction

Being able to see the future is usually a nice capability, although it is quite hard. Predicting how things may turn out, within some proven bounds of approximation, is not bad either. Prediction has always been a basis for development of many artificial intelligence techniques. In the field of Link Analysis as well, prediction plays an important role.

Imagine being able to look at data regarding the growth of a company's internal network over the past five years, and being able to tell what kind of infrastructure development may be necessary to meet the demands over the next year or two. Wouldn't that be an empowering tool for corporate planners and managing bodies? At a larger scale, governments can use such techniques, for instance, to design roadways to relieve future congestion by strategically connecting towns and cities. Scientists can use predictive models of molecular bonding that have been derived from carefully studied experiments, to simulate formation of interesting biomolecular structures.

Note that while LOC and LOR use analysis of links to talk about the nodes in a network, Link Prediction actually deals with links themselves. A common example of prediction is trying to guess which authors will co-author a paper in the future, given a current collaboration graph. Here, we try to infer new collaboration links, but do not say anything new about the authors themselves.

5.2.3 Some Link Analysis Techniques

In the following sections we take a detailed look at some representative techniques that illustrate Link Analysis tasks. First, we discuss some metrics that are commonly used for analyzing social networks in Section 5.3. Several key concepts are explained with examples and snippets of R code that can be used to analyze other kinds of networks as well. We then introduce PageRank in Section 5.4 as an example of LOR algorithm that provides a numerical rank to web pages by studying the quality of the references or backlinks to that page. The second main algorithm presented is used for Link Prediction based on the proximity of vertices in a network, in Section 5.6. The theory behind the algorithms, mathematical preliminaries, and their usage in R are discussed.

5.3 Metrics for Analyzing Networks

This section discusses the social network analysis (SNA) metrics available in R. The role of social networking in today's world is presented, followed by a discussion of SNA metrics available in R. The intuition behind each of the SNA metrics is discussed using a random sample graph representing a social network (the nodes of the graph being the members of the social network and the edges of the graph being the links/relations between the members). The SNA package in R is used to calculate metrics like density, extract, betweenness centrality, etc.

The data in Table 5.1 and the following headlines[1] give an idea of the popularity of social networks:

- *Social Networks and Blogs Now 4th Most Popular Online Activity, Ahead of Personal Email, Nielsen Reports*, March 9, 2009

- *Nielsen Reports 17 Percent of Time Spent on the Internet in August Devoted to Social Networking and Blog Sites, up from 6 Percent a Year Ago*, September 23, 2009

Table 5.1 illustrates that millions of minutes are spent in browsing social networking sites every year, and the numbers are clearly increasing. Thus, the popularity of social networking seems to be on the rise. The important question is, "Why does the analysis of the behavior of members of such sites and the overall site's properties attract interest?" The budget share of online marketing and advertisement in social networking sites increases proportionally with their popularity and ratings. As per `socialnetworkingwatch.com`,

---

[1]`http://en-us.nielsen.com/dropdown/news/news_releases`

TABLE 5.1: Top 10 social networking and blog sites: Total minutes spent by surfers in April 2008 and April 2009 (Source: Nielsen NetView)

Site	Apr '08 Minutes	Apr '09 Minutes	% Growth
Facebook	1,735,698	13,872,640	699
Myspace.com	7,254,645	4,973,919	-31
Blogger	448,710	582,683	30
Tagged.com	29,858	327,871	998
Twitter.com	7,865	299,836	3712
MyYearbook	131,105	268,565	105
LiveJournal	54,671	204,121	273
LinkedIn	119,636	202,407	69
SlashKey	-	187,687	-
Gaia Online	173,115	143,909	-17

Facebook stands first in hit-wise rankings as per September 2009 of social networking sites in the U.S. MySpace is the second followed by YouTube, Tagged, and Twitter. LinkedIn is ranked 15 with Hi5 at 24.

A more detailed study of social networks concentrates only on a particular section of the social network (based on features like age, country, community, etc.) and the study extends to the level of the individual members of the network for more specific marketing needs. A company trying to advertise its products related to a specific age group is likely to research those social networking sites that are popular among the targeted consumers. The advertisements might also be targeted at those particular members who are most likely to be interested in the products/services promoted [7]. Many characteristics are of interest including the number of targeted users in the network, how far or near the targeted users are in the network, how active each of them is, how connected a given member is to the set of the targeted users, etc.

Apart from the marketing research prospective, social network analysis is also relevant to other fields like national security against terrorist attacks (to visualize and quantify terrorist networks), medicine (to study propagation of a specific disease in a community/network), geography (to understand the interactions between users of different states and countries), politics (to campaign for elections), social psychology (to study the nature of specific user/users in the network), etc.

Irrespective of the ultimate goal, social network analysis studies the information flow and interactions between the members of a given network. Graphical representation of a social network is a popular way to understand and analyze the behavior of both the individuals and the overall network. The nodes/vertices in the graph represent the members of the network and the relationship between them is represented as edges/links.

To summarize, social network analysis (SNA) is the representation and analysis of relationships/information flow between individuals, groups, organizations, servers, and other connected entities [21] [10]. In this section, we discuss the most common SNA metrics and the intuition behind each metric. We will use a simple random graph of 10 nodes to demonstrate the use of these metrics in R.

The R code below can be used to generate this test graph. The package sna (line 2) is used to generate a random graph with 10 nodes. This generated graph (shown in Figure 5.2) will be our sample social networking site graph for further analysis [37].

```
1 > # Load the sna (social network analysis) library
2 > library(sna)
3 > # plink(probability of a link between any 2 vertices)
4 > N=10
5 > plink=0.2
6 > # sna::rgraph()
7 > # 5th argument in rgraph decides if loops
8 > # are allowed in the generated graph
9 > graph_adj=rgraph(N,1,plink,"graph",FALSE)
```

An undirected Bernoulli random graph of 10 vertices is generated using the function **rgraph** (line 9). The adjacency matrix representation of the resultant graph is shown below. A value of 1 represents the presence of a link and the value of 0 represents the absence of the link between the nodes (column and row numbers in the matrix) of the graph.

```
10 > # generated graph in a matrix format
11 > graph_adj
12        [,1] [,2] [,3] [,4] [,5] [,6] [,7] [,8] [,9] [,10]
13 [1,]  0    1    1    1    0    0    0    0    0    0
14 [2,]  1    0    0    0    0    0    0    0    0    0
15 [3,]  1.   0    0    0    0    0    0    0    1    0
16 [4,]  1    0    0    0    1    1    0    0    0    0
17 [5,]  0    0    0    1    0    0    1    0    0    0
18 [6,]  0    0    0    1    0    0    0    0    1    0
19 [7,]  0    0    0    0    1    0    0    0    0    0
20 [8,]  0    0    0    0    0    0    0    0    1    0
21 [9,]  0    0    1    0    0    1    0    1    0    0
22 [10,] 0    0    0    0    0    0    0    0    0    0
23 > # convert to igraph object
24 > graph <- graph.adjacency(graph_adj, mode="undirected")
25 > # plot the graph
26 > plot(graph)
```

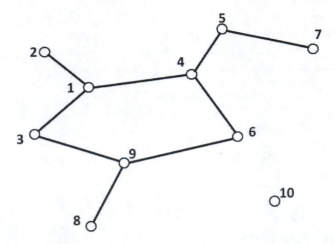

FIGURE 5.2: A randomly generated 10-node graph representing a synthetic social network.

Different Social Network Analysis Metrics in R

Given a graph represented by a matrix in R, we can now compute various SNA metrics. Let us look at some of the functions available in R. Note that we will be referring to the graph in Figure 5.2.

5.3.1   Degree

Definition 5.1 *Degree*
The degree of a vertex is the number of edges incident to it.

So, the degree of a node is the number of direct connections the node has in a network. A vertex with higher degree is more connected compared to a vertex with lower degree, and thus the graph can in general resist more link/vertex failures. In Figure 5.2, nodes 1, 4, and 9 have the higher degree, and so these nodes play the role of connectors in the network.

An example that uses the function `degree` to calculate the degree of vertices in the given graph is presented below:

```
1 > degree(graph)
2 [1] 3 1 2 3 2 2 1 1 3 0
```

Here, as expected, node 10 has a degree of 0. Node 1 is connected to nodes 2, 3, and 5, hence, leading to a degree of 3.

In a real-world scenario, the connectors could be the foreign relationship representatives of different countries of the world. Each connector has links to its country's population, on the one hand, and links to the foreign relation-ship representatives of other countries, on the other hand. The countries not involved in the network would be isolated like node 10 in our graph.

5.3.2 Density

> **Definition 5.2** *Density*
> The density of a graph is the number of existing edges over the number of possible ones.

A graph with higher density is more connected compared to a graph with lower density, and thus the graph can, in general, resist more link failures.

Now, compare the graph in Figure 5.2 with a fully connected graph of 10 nodes (a graph having 10 nodes and each node connected to every other node in the network). Obviously, the fully connected graph has the highest density, equal to 1.

Now, suppose our *network1* is the network of all the students in a given class at school and our *network2* is all the students in the school. In this sce-nario, we can assume that every student in a given class knows every other student in the class, whereas every student in the school may or may not know every other student in the school. This makes *network1* denser than *network2*. If a student drops out of a class, *network1*'s density is not affected, but *net-work2*'s density might depend on the students' betweenness and closeness in *network2*, defined later in the chapter.

A higher value of density corresponds to a highly connected graph and a lower value indicates a sparsely connected graph. The R code for calculating graph density using the function gden is given below.

```
1 > #gden is used to find the density of a graph
2 > gden(graph,mode="graph")
3 [1] 0.4
```

Here, the total number of possible edges is 45 (for 10 nodes), whereas the graph has 18 edges (18 ones in the matrix representation). Therefore, the density is 0.4 for the given graph.

5.3.3 Connectedness

> **Definition 5.3** *Connectedness*
> Krackhardt's connectedness for a digraph G is equal to the fraction of all dyads (a group of two nodes), u and v, such that there exists an undirected path from u to v in G.

The corresponding R function connectedness takes one or more graphs and returns the Krackhardt connectedness scores. A graph with higher connectedness is more connected compared to a graph with lower connectedness, thus the graph can, in general, resist more link failures.

When the value of `connectedness` is 1, then the graph given is fully connected and so results in a TRUE output for the function `is.connected`. Whereas, if the value of `connectedness` is 0, then the vertices in the graph are completely isolated.

Consider a 10-node graph, where node 1 is connected to 8 nodes (excluding itself and node 10), and so are nodes 2 through 9. Node 10 is not connected to any of the other nodes. So, summing up the actual degrees and dividing by the maximum possible degrees of all nodes, we have:

$$\text{connectedness} = \frac{8+8+8+8+8+8+8+8+8+0}{9+9+9+9+9+9+9+9+9+9} = 0.8$$

```
1 > #is.connected is used for strict connectedness
2 > is.connected(graph)
3 [1] FALSE
4 > connectedness(graph)
5 [1] 0.8
```

Similarly, the function `is.isolate` is used to check if a node is isolated in the given graph.

```
1 > is.isolate(graph,1)
2 [1] FALSE
3 > is.isolate(graph,10)
4 [1] TRUE
```

5.3.4 Betweenness Centrality

Betweenness centrality is a measure of the degree to which a given node lies on the shortest paths (geodesics) between the other nodes in the graph.

> **Definition 5.4** *Betweenness Centrality*
>
> Betweenness centrality (C_b) of a node $v \in V(G)$ in the graph G is defined as
>
> $$C_b(v) = \sum_{s,t \neq v} \frac{\Omega_v(s,t)}{\Omega(s,t)} \tag{5.1}$$
>
> where $\Omega(s,t)$ is the number of distinct geodesics from node $s \in V(G)$ to node $t \in V(G)$ and $\Omega_v(s,t)$ is the number of geodesics from s to t that pass through v.

To explain the intuition behind the betweenness centrality metric, we introduce the terms *distance* and *geodesics*. Distance between two nodes in a graph is the minimum number of hops or edge traversals required to reach the destination node from the starting node. For example, the number of hops between the nodes 1 and 9 via the path 1-3-9 is 2 and via the path 1-4-6-9 is 3 (Figure 5.2). Thereby, the distance between nodes 1 and 9 is 2 considering all the possible paths.

In some social networks, accessibility to certain features of a node (e.g., profile, pictures, scrapbook/wall) are restricted by the distance to that node from a given node (the number of hops present in the shortest path between the two nodes). For example, in LinkedIn, suppose that the graph in Figure 5.2 is a subgraph of 10 nodes representing 10 users. Here user 8 has one friend, user 9. Below is a list of hops interpreted in terms of "Friends" in a social network:

- 0th hop = User under consideration (user 8)

- 1st hop = Friend (user 9)

- 2nd hop = Friend of a Friend (users 3 and 6)

- 3rd hop = Friend of a Friend of a Friend (users 1 and 4)

Given that any user in LinkedIn can access profiles up to a distance of 3, user 8 can access information of users 9, 3, 6, 1 and 4.

Consider this situation: If user 10's account is disabled, user 8 or any other user in the given network has no change in his/her neighborhood. Whereas, if user 9 is missing from the graph, user 8 is completely isolated from the other users in the network. Betweenness is a measure that represents the influence a node has over the connectivity of all the other nodes in a given network.

A geodesic is the shortest path between any two nodes in a network. For instance, in Figure 5.2, the path 1-4-6 is a geodesic representing the shortest path between nodes 1 and 6. A node has high betweenness if the shortest paths (geodesics) between many pairs of the other nodes in the graph pass through that node. A node has low betweenness if most of the geodesics in the graph do not pass through that node. Thus, a node with high betweenness, when it fails, has higher influence on the connectivity of the network [10]. Consider the following example:

```
1 > #Here node 4 has the highest betweenness
2 > betweenness(graph)
3   [1] 20 0 8 28 14 12 0 0 16 0
```

From Figure 5.2, it can be observed that nodes 2, 7, 8, and 10 are not in any of the geodesics. Also, node 4 has the highest betweenness.

The path lengths, or geodesic distances, are calculated using the function geodist in R.

```
1 > geo=geodist(graph)
2 > geo$gdist
3      [,1] [,2] [,3] [,4] [,5] [,6] [,7] [,8] [,9] [,10]
```

4	[1,]	0	1	1	1	2	2	3	3	2	Inf
5	[2,]	1	0	2	2	3	3	4	4	3	Inf
6	[3,]	1	2	0	2	3	2	4	2	1	Inf
7	[4,]	1	2	2	0	1	1	2	3	2	Inf
8	[5,]	2	3	3	1	0	2	1	4	3	Inf
9	[6,]	2	3	2	1	2	0	3	2	1	Inf
10	[7,]	3	4	4	2	1	3	0	5	4	Inf
11	[8,]	3	4	2	3	4	2	5	0	1	Inf
12	[9,]	2	3	1	2	3	1	4	1	0	Inf
13	[10,]	Inf	Inf	Inf	Inf	Inf	Inf	Inf	Inf	Inf	0

From the result of `geodist`, it could be inferred that node 5 requires two hops to reach node 1 and node 10 is not reachable by any other node (i.e., it is at infinite distance).

5.3.5   Egocentricity

Definition 5.5 *Egocentric network*
The egocentric network (or "ego net") of vertex v in graph G is the subgraph of G consisting of v and its neighbors.

The function `ego.extract` is useful for finding local properties associated with particular vertices. In Figure 5.3, the egocentric networks of nodes 9 and 7 are marked. The egocentric network of vertex 9 has nodes 3, 6, and 8. Similarly, an egocentric network of vertex 7 has node 5. Figure 5.4 shows the egocentric network of node 1.

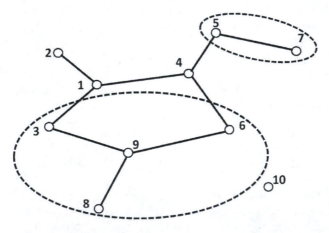

FIGURE 5.3: The egocentric networks for nodes 9 and 7.

In the example below, the function `ego.extract` is given a graph as its input (Figure 5.2) and is used to generate the egocentric network of the vertex 6.

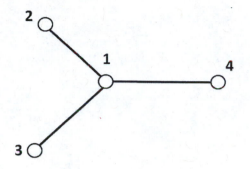

FIGURE 5.4: The egocentric network of node 1.

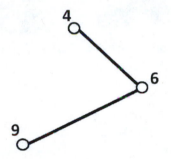

FIGURE 5.5: The egocentric network of node 6.

```
1 > ego.extract(graph,6)
2 $'6'
3       [,1] [,2] [,3]
4 [1,] 0    1    1
5 [2,] 1    0    0
6 [3,] 1    0    0
```

Here, the egocentric network of node 6 has nodes 6, 4, and 9. Note that the extract above (in matrix form) numbers nodes 6, 4, and 9 as 1, 2, and 3, respectively. Thus, it can be inferred from the extract that node 6 is connected to both nodes 4 and 9, whereas nodes 4 and 9 are not directly connected to each other. This is easily verified in the visual representation of the sub-graph (Figure 5.5).

An egocentric network can be further used to compute SNA metrics within local neighborhoods. This is especially useful when we have very large networks and would like to focus on its subset for a particular application.

5.3.6   Closeness Centrality

Closeness Centrality (CLC) is a measure defined for nodes of a given graph. The higher the value of CLC for a node is, the *closer* the node is to the other nodes in the graph.

Definition 5.6 *Closeness Centrality*
For a node v, CLC is defined as the ratio of the total number of nodes in the graph minus one to the sum of the shortest distances (geodesics) of the node v to every other node in the graph [10].

So,

$$CLC(v) = \frac{|V| - 1}{\sum_{i, v \neq v_i} \text{distance}(v, v_i)} \tag{5.2}$$

where $|V|$ is the number of nodes in the given graph, and v_i is the node i of the given graph.

If a node v is connected to all the other nodes in the graph directly (i.e., if all other nodes in the graph are a hop away from v, then the CLC for the node v is 1). As the number of direct links decreases, the CLC also decreases. Thereby, CLC represents how reachable the nodes of the graph are from any given node under consideration.

Consider node 10 in the graph of Figure 5.2. Since it is isolated (not connected to any other node in the network), the closeness of the vertices from this node is 0 and the distance is infinite. Now, consider a sub-graph of the graph (egocentric network of node 6 shown in Figure 5.5) for better understanding of `closeness`. The closeness of node 6 is $(3-1)/(1+1) = 1$. So, node 6 can reach all the other nodes in `graph1` in one hop. Now, considering node 4,

$CLC(4)$ is $(3-1)/(1+2)=2/3=0.667$.

Similarly, $CLC(9)$ in `graph1` is 0.667. So, it can be inferred that nodes 4 and 9 are equally close to the other respective nodes in the graph and node 6 is superior to nodes 4 and 9 in this aspect.

```
1 > graph1=ego.extract(graph,6)
2 > closeness(graph1)
3                 6
4 [1,]  1.0000000
5 [2,]  0.6666667
6 [3,]  0.6666667
```

A number of complex properties of nodes can be obtained by combining and/or building upon these metrics. In fact, one very popular kind of metric used to order webpages is PageRank, which is primarily based on degree measures. We will discuss PageRank in the following section.

5.4 The PageRank Algorithm

Contrary to popular belief, PageRank is not named after the fact that the algorithm ranks pages, rather it is named after Larry Page, its inventor. Ranks are not assigned to subject domains, but to specific web pages. According to the creators, the rank of each web page averages at about 1. It is usually depicted as an integer in the range $[0, 10]$ by most estimation tools, 0 being the least ranked. Ranks of some websites, for example, are:

- www.ncsu.edu—Rank 8

- www.google.com—Rank 10

- www.elquinegocios.cl/tag/naturales—Rank 0

PageRank is an algorithm that addresses the Link-based Object Ranking (LOR) problem. The objective is to assign a numerical rank or priority to each web page by exploiting the "link" structure of the web [15]. We will work with a model in which a user starts at a web page and performs a "random walk" by randomly following links from the page he/she is currently in. PageRank of a web page is the probability of that web page being visited on a particular random walk [8].

The fundamentals of this algorithm are based on the count and quality of 'backlinks' or 'inlinks' to a web page. A backlink of a page P_u is a citation to P_u from another page.

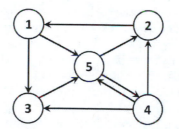

FIGURE 5.6: A five web page network.

Figure 5.6 shows a network consisting of 5 web pages. The links coming into page 5 are backlinks for that page and links going out from page 5 are called outlinks. Page 4 and page 1 have a single backlink each, pages 2 and 3 have two backlinks each, and page 5 has three backlinks. Accordingly, page 5 is the most important. PageRank considers the quality of ranks as well, thereby making the ranks more reliable. Hence, a backlink from page 5 holds more value than a backlink from page 1. Page 3 has a higher rank than page 2, since page 3 has backlinks from page 4 and page 1, whereas page 2 has backlinks from pages 4 and 5.

5.4.1 Challenges and Issues

It is a challenge to rank web pages in the order of their significance, both overall as well as pertaining to a particular query. There are many aspects of a web page that make it relevant such as:

- Web page changes;

- The frequency of Web page changes;

- Keyword changes and keyword count changes;

- The number of new backlinks; and

- Data availability and stability.

The above features are quite replicable. Competing profit-seeking ventures may manipulate their web pages' properties in order to project a false importance within the web, thus skewing search results enormously. Any evaluation strategy that counts replicable features of web pages is prone to manipulation. Hence, PageRank tries to approximate the overall relative importance of web pages based on the link structure of the web. The importance of a web page can be rated based on the number of backlinks to that page and the importance of the web pages that provide these backlinks, i.e., a web page referred to by important and reliable web pages, is important and reliable.

5.4.2 Algorithmic Intuition

A simple approach to calculate the rank of a page would be to consider only the count of its backlinks. The drawback with this approach is that the credibility of the backlinks cannot be trusted. It is fairly simple for anyone to spam links to a page and thereby increase its backlink count, thus increasing the rank. To avoid such spamming, PageRank also considers the rank of the web pages that provide the backlinks. This iterative procedure makes the ranking process more accurate and reliable.

The algorithm associates a numerical value to every web page, representing its relative importance within the Internet. This number is used by Google to index the web pages while displaying the search results. The Web has about a trillion unique URLs. Considering each of these web pages as a vertex and the links between pages as edges, the Web can be modeled as a directed graph. The relative importance of the web pages that provide the backlink in addition to the number of backlinks for a given page are used to rank web pages. The computational and mathematical backbone of PageRank is the *power method*, which computes an eigenvector of a matrix. It is a recursive procedure that can run for days in case of bigger matrices representing the Web. This technique is explained in Section 5.4.3.1.

5.4.3   Mathematical Formulation

Before we proceed, we define some important terminology and notation summarized in Table 5.2.

TABLE 5.2: PageRank Notation

Symbol	Meaning
P	A web page
d	Damping factor—the probability that a user opens a new web page to begin a new random walk
$PR(P)$	PageRank of page P
$deg(P)^-$	The number of links coming into a page P (in-degree of P)
$deg(P)^+$	The number of links going out of a page P (out-degree of P)
$N(P)^-$	The set of pages that point to P (the in-neighborhood of P)
$N(P)^+$	The set of pages a web page P points to (the out-neighborhood of P)
W	A hyperlink matrix representing the network, whose entries constitute the fractional PageRank contributions
x	Eigenvector containing the ranks for each vertex in the network.

In order to compute the rank of a page, say P_1, we need to look at all the pages that link to it, i.e., they have backlinks to P_1. Assume that one such page P_2 also has three other outlinks (to other pages) in addition to the link to P_1. Now, the score contributed by P_2 to P_1 is only $\frac{1}{4}$th of its own PageRank. To get to the total for P_1, we need to sum up such values for all pages that link to it. Generally, if the page P_v has n links to other pages $\{P_u \mid u \in 1, \ldots, n\}$, then the page P_v contributes only $\frac{1}{deg(P_v)^+}$th of its links to the PageRank of a page P_u:

$$PR(P_u) = \sum \frac{PR(P_v)}{deg(P_v)^+} \qquad (5.3)$$

Applying Equation 5.3 to Figure 5.6, the PageRank of the web page 2 is given in Equation 5.4:

$$PR(2) = \frac{PR(5)}{2} + \frac{PR(4)}{3} \qquad (5.4)$$

Similarly, we can find the ranks for all the other pages in the network. For every page P_v, find the number of outlinks of P_v (i.e., $deg(P_v)^+$) and its

PageRank $PR(P_v)$. Now, for each P_v, we first find the ratio of its PageRank to the corresponding outlink count and compute the sum over all pages that link to a particular page of interest. More formally, the PageRank of a page P is defined as [8]:

$$PR(P) = (1 - d) + d(\frac{PR(P_1)}{deg(P_1)^+} + \frac{PR(P_2)}{deg(P_2)^+} + \ldots + \frac{PR(P_n)}{deg(P_n)^+}) \qquad (5.5)$$

The damping factor d is used to take into account the probability of a user getting bored and opening a new page to start another session. A typical value for d is 0.85. Conversely, $(1 - d)$ is the probability that a user will not get bored and stay on the current web page.

5.4.3.1   The power method

The power method is a recursive method used to compute an eigenvector of the eigenvalue 1 of a square matrix $\mathbf{W}$. This matrix is similar to an adjacency matrix representation of a graph, except that instead of using Boolean values to indicate presence of links, we indicate the fraction of rank contribution for a link connecting two vertices in the graph. For a web page pair (P_u, P_v), the corresponding entry in $\mathbf{W}$ is,

$$\mathbf{W}_{u,v} = (\frac{1}{deg(P_v)^+}) \qquad (5.6)$$

This value denotes the fraction of $PR(P_v)$ contributed towards $PR(P_u)$ [9]. Each column in $\mathbf{W}$ must sum to a total PageRank value of 1, since the sum of all fractional PageRank contributions to a page must sum to 1. The matrix $\mathbf{W}$ for the network in Figure 5.6 is,

$$\mathbf{W} = \begin{pmatrix} 0 & 1 & 0 & 0 & 0 \\ 0 & 0 & 0 & \frac{1}{3} & \frac{1}{2} \\ \frac{1}{2} & 0 & 0 & \frac{1}{3} & 0 \\ 0 & 0 & 0 & 0 & \frac{1}{2} \\ \frac{1}{2} & 0 & 1 & \frac{1}{3} & 0 \end{pmatrix} \qquad (5.7)$$

The following linear equations can be derived from Equation 5.7:

$$PR(1) = \frac{PR(2)}{1} \qquad (5.8)$$

$$PR(2) = \frac{PR(4)}{3} + \frac{PR(5)}{2} \qquad (5.9)$$

$$PR(3) = \frac{PR(1)}{2} + \frac{PR(4)}{3} \qquad (5.10)$$

$$PR(4) = \frac{PR(5)}{2} \qquad (5.11)$$

$$PR(5) = \frac{PR(1)}{2} + \frac{PR(3)}{1} + \frac{PR(4)}{3} \tag{5.12}$$

We can write these in the form, $\mathbf{W} \cdot \mathbf{x} = \mathbf{x}$, where $\mathbf{x}$ is defined in Equation 5.13:

$$\mathbf{x} = \begin{bmatrix} PR(1) & PR(2) & PR(3) & PR(4) & PR(5) \end{bmatrix}^T \tag{5.13}$$

If λ is the eigenvalue of the eigenvector $\mathbf{x}$, then it can be found using Equation 5.14,

$$\mathbf{W} \cdot \mathbf{x} = \lambda \mathbf{x} \tag{5.14}$$

For an eigenvalue of 1 ($\lambda = 1$), we find the eigenvector to be:

$$\mathbf{x} = \begin{bmatrix} 0.4313 & 0.4313 & 0.3235 & 0.3235 & 0.6470 \end{bmatrix}^T \tag{5.15}$$

This ranking differs from what we interpreted while ranking pages based on just the backlinks. For example, page 5 was ranked the highest, since it had backlinks from more pages, but in this case, pages 1, 2 and 4, 5 are ranked the same. The rank for page 5 is the highest and understandably so, since it possesses more backlinks.

While ranking the entire web, each web page is a vertex in the graph and we can imagine the size of the square matrix $\mathbf{W}$, which could contain a billion rows and columns. In such cases, computing this eigenvector is impossible, and we will have to resort to computing it in a recursive fashion. It is calculated repetitively until the values in the matrix converge. We start by considering a vector $\mathbf{x}^0$ as the base case and then working up to find the value of $\mathbf{x}^k$. This recursive process can then be denoted [3] as in Equation 5.16:

$$\mathbf{W} \cdot \mathbf{x}^k = \mathbf{x}^{k+1} \tag{5.16}$$

This does not, however, solve our problem entirely, since we have to deal with the problem of dangling vertices [3]. A network containing a dangling vertex is characterized by a matrix with 0's in a column of the matrix. The value of the matrix rank may not converge if the network has dangling vertices. Some modifications need to be made to the method we have described to find the completely converged values of $\mathbf{x}$, in case of networks with dangling vertices. For a network without any dangling vertices, and a damping factor of 0.85, it is reported that 50-100 iterations are necessary for this matrix to converge, and the computation process could take days to complete.

5.4.4 Algorithm Description

The line numbers at the end of each step correspond to the line numbers of that step in Algorithm 1.

1. The PageRank algorithm has two input parameters, the graph G and a damping factor d and produces a list of PageRank values as output corresponding to each vertex on the graph.

2. It maintains an auxiliary storage, $(PP[P_i])$, to store results from the computation of PageRank (Line 2).

3. Initially, for each page in G, PageRank initializes that page to the value $\frac{1}{N}$, where N is the total number of pages (Lines 5-8).

4. The PageRank algorithm runs until the values of consecutive runs of the PageRank algorithm converge. The converged values are the final PageRank values (Line 9).

5. For every page in the graph P_i, consider all its outlinks, say P_j and for each such outlink, add to its auxiliary storage the value $\frac{PR[P_i]}{deg(P_i)+}$ (Lines 10-14).

6. For every page P_i in the graph, set its PageRank to the sum of $\frac{d}{N}$ and $(1-d) \times (PP[P_i])$ and reset the value of auxiliary storage to 0 for the next iteration (Lines 15-18).

7. Normalize values to ensure that the sum of the PageRank values of all pages in G is 1 (Line 19).

5.4.5   PageRank in R

The igraph package contains graph manipulation functions that operate on a graph object. Functions are available to generate graphs from adjacency lists or matrices, to find various graph parameters like density, to find subgraphs, or to plot graphs in 2D/3D. The function `page.rank` in igraph computes the PageRank of the vertices in the graph object passed as parameter. The function returns the ranks of the vertices selected to be considered for ranking in the graph. This section will illustrate details about the algorithm's usage in R. We will look at basic syntax and usage of the function.

Install the igraph package and use `library(igraph)` to make use of its functions. [The syntax of the function is summarized in Table 5.3.] Use the following example R code to generate a random graph and calculate its PageRank vector.

```
1 > library(igraph)
2 > g <- random.graph.game(20, 5/20, directed=TRUE)
3 > page.rank(g)$vector
4 [1] 0.03686596 0.02552204 0.05456715 0.03623592
5 0.03608888 0.01366011 0.04652149 0.04414025
6 0.08562624 0.06189504 0.01751444 0.08791547
7 0.05319910 [14] 0.05706331 0.04290224 0.06482654
8 0.05538546 0.06322104 0.04124198 0.07560734
9 > plot(g)
```

---

1 Algorithm: PageRank calculation of a single graph

Input: G—Directed graph of N web pages
d—Damping factor
Output: $PR[1 \ldots N]$, where $PR[P_i]$ is the PageRank of page P_i

2 Let $PP[1 \ldots N]$ denote a spare array of size N

3 Let d denote the probability of reaching a particular node by a random jump either from a vertex with no outlinks or with probability $(1 - d)$

4 Let $N(P_u)^+$ denote the set of pages with at least one outlink

5 foreach P_i in N pages of G **do**

6 $PR[P_i] = \frac{1}{N}$

7 $PP[i] = 0$

8 end

9 while PR not converging **do**

10   **foreach** P_i in N pages of G **do**

11   **foreach** P_j in $N(P_i)^+$ **do**

12 $PP[P_j] = PP[P_j] + \frac{PR[P_i]}{deg(P_i)^+}$

13   **end**

14   **end**

15   **foreach** P_i in N pages of G **do**

16 $PR[P_i] = \frac{d}{N} + (1 - d)(PP[P_i])$

17 $PP[P_i] = 0$

18   **end**

19   Normalize $PR[P_i]$ so that $\sum_{P_i \in N} PR[P_i] = 1$

20 end

Algorithm 1: PageRank calculation of a single graph

TABLE 5.3: Parameters for `page.rank`

Parameter	Use
graph	The input graph object.
vertices_of_interest	Vertices for which rank needs to be calculated (note that rank need not be computed for all vertices).
directed	Boolean value to indicate directed graphs.
damping_factor_val	Damping factor—probability of a user starting a new random web page.
weights	Assign weights to edges in the graph to calculate a weighted PageRank.

The `random.graph.game` is an alias of the `erdos.renyi.game` function that can be used to create random graphs. The first parameter of this function is the number of vertices in the graph followed by the number of edges in the

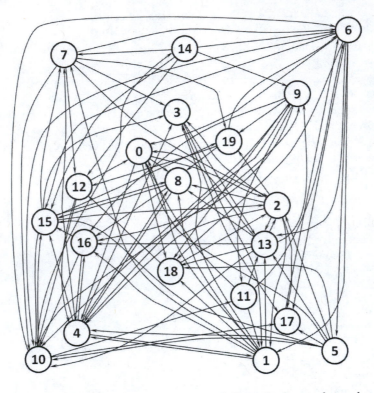

FIGURE 5.7: A randomly generated 20-node directed graph.

second parameter. In our usage, we have specified this as a probability of an edge between any two nodes.

The above function call creates a directed random graph with 20 vertices, stored in the graph object *g* with an edge between two vertices occurring with probability of 5/20. This results in a graph as depicted in Figure 5.7.

```
10 > g2 <- graph.star(10)
11 > page.rank(g2)$vector
12 [1] 0.68005764 0.03554915 0.03554915 0.03554915
13 0.03554915 0.03554915 0.03554915 0.03554915
14 0.03554915 0.03554915
15 > plot(g2)
```

Likewise, the `graph.star` function is one of several methods that can be used to generate several types of graphs, such as citation graphs, ring graphs, and star graphs. In the example above, `graph.star` creates a star graph *g2*. In a star graph, every vertex is connected to a center vertex and no other vertex. This is used to depict the vertex that has the highest PageRank in our simulation. This results in a graph as depicted in Figure 5.8.

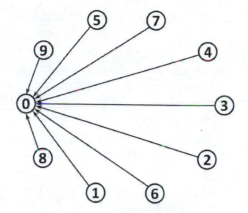

FIGURE 5.8: Depiction of nodes with their PageRank in the star graph $g2$.

5.5   Hyperlink-Induced Topic Search (HITS)

In Section 5.4, we discussed the PageRank method for determining the importance of a node in a graph via essentially performing a random walk on the Web. There are many other algorithms for this task of ranking the importance of the node in the graph. One such technique is the HITS algorithm [8] to identify authority and hub nodes, as discussed in this section.

The Hyperlink-Induced Topic Search algorithm was originally proposed by Kleinberg (1999) [20] as a method of filtering results from web page search engines in order to identify results most relevant to a user query. The algorithm models links between web pages as a directed graph and is generalizable to other problems that can be modeled in the same way. The HITS algorithm has also been successfully applied to the identification of email spamming machines [12]. In this context, email servers and recipients are modeled as a bipartite graph and hub/authority scores are used to identify spam machines (which are considered to be machines that send email but are not email servers).

HITS' original application was in web page searching and filtering. It is considered a "runtime" algorithm because it is applied only when a user actually submits a query to a search engine—i.e., the results of HITS are *not* precomputed. HITS is an iterative algorithm that is repeated a specified number of times, typically indicated by a variable, k_{max}. During the k_{max} iterations, the algorithm will typically converge towards a solution. It is important to note that Kleinberg does not specify any convergence criteria; however, in the paper, he notes that in practice, a value of $k_{max} = 20$ is a commonly used upper bound for the number of iterations. HITS returns two vectors, each of which contains a score for each vertex in the graph. A high-level overview of HITS is as follows:

1. **Select initial set of web pages relevant to the user's query.**
   An initial set of web pages relevant to the user's query are selected
   in order to reduce the problem to a manageable size.

2. **Initialize vectors.** HITS returns two vectors: one that scores each
   vertex's importance as a *hub* and the other that scores each vertex's
   importance as an *authority*. These terms are defined in Section 5.5.1.
   Each element of these vectors is initialized to 1.

3. **Iteratively update vectors.** The algorithm iterates, k_{max} times,
   updating the two score vectors during each iteration.

4. **Normalize vector scores.** In order to ensure vectors are scaled
   appropriately and also reach convergence, they are normalized after
   each iteration of the algorithm.

5. **Output vectors.** The final step of the algorithm is to output the
   final vectors after k_{max} iterations.

Figure 5.9 gives a high-level overview of the HITS algorithm.

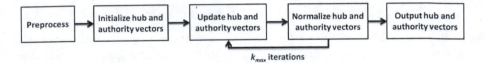

FIGURE 5.9: HITS algorithm flow: web pages are preprocessed before hub
and authority vectors are iteratively updated and normalized.

In Section 5.5.1, we discuss a vertex's role as a hub and authority and the
initial selection of web pages from a user's query. In Section 5.5.3, we describe
in detail how the Hub and Authority vectors are updated and normalized. Finally, in Section 5.5.4, we describe how the algorithm converges. The complete
algorithm is described in full by pseudocode in Algorithm 2.

5.5.1 Vertices as Hubs and Authorities

Given a dataset that can be modeled as a directed graph, where the vertices of
the graph represent data items and the edges represent relationships between
data items, we would like to identify which items are most closely related.
In the context of web page searching, the goal is to filter an existing set of
search results to identify those web pages most closely related to a user's
query. In order to identify the most relevant pages we calculate two measures
of importance for each vertex:

Definition 5.7 *Authority*
A vertex is considered an authority if it has many pages that link to it (i.e.,
it has a high indegree).

Definition 5.8 *Hub*
A vertex is considered a hub if it points to many other vertices (i.e., it has a high outdegree).

These concepts are illustrated in Figure 5.10.

FIGURE 5.10: (a) A web page that points to many other web pages is known as a hub. (b) A web page that is pointed to by many other web pages is an authority.

In order to identify the most relevant pages for a user's query, we aim to find pages that are considered authoritative on the subject. Authority pages are pointed to by many hubs, and hubs point to many authority pages. Thus, finding the most relevant pages is reduced to the problem of finding dense subgraphs of hubs and authorities where the most relevant results are obtained from a bipartite graph. This type of subgraph is illustrated in Figure 5.11.

The HITS algorithm requires web data to be preprocessed to limit the set of web pages under consideration. Typically, a set of pages most relevant ($\sim$200) to the user's initial query is retrieved from the World Wide Web. This initial set is known as the *root set*. The root set is then "grown" by including additional pages relevant to the user's query. These pages are obtained by including any pages that link to a page in the root set, up to a pre-determined maximum ($\sim$50). This is known as the *base set* and is subsequently encoded as an adjacency matrix which is used as the input to the HITS algorithm. The overall process is illustrated in Figure 5.12.

5.5.2 Constructing an Adjacency Matrix from Web Data

Figure 5.13 represents the base set of web pages derived from a particular user's query. In order to process these data using HITS to generate hub and authority scores, we must first represent the graph as an adjacency matrix.

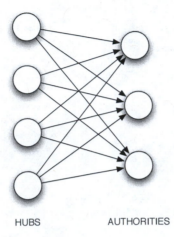

HUBS   AUTHORITIES

FIGURE 5.11: A bipartite graph represents the most strongly connected group of vertices in a graph. Hubs and Authorities exhibit a mutually reinforcing relationship.

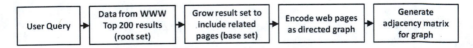

FIGURE 5.12: HITS preprocessing: an initial selection of web pages is grown to include additional related pages, encoded as a graph, and an adjacency matrix is generated.

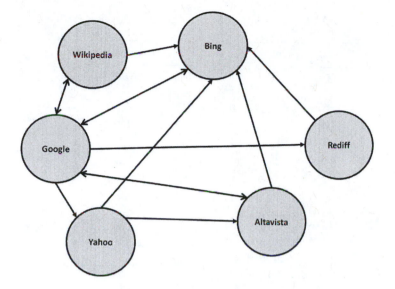

FIGURE 5.13: Graph for the query "search engine," run on the web. For illustrative purposes, we consider six web pages, namely Bing.com, Google.com, Wikipedia.org, Yahoo.com, Altavista.com, and Rediffmail.com.

Definition 5.9 *Adjacency matrix*
The adjacency matrix is defined as:

$$\mathbf{A}_{\{ij\}} = \begin{cases} 1, & \text{if } e_{\{ij\}} \in E \\ 0, & \text{otherwise} \end{cases}$$

Entries in the adjacency matrix are 1 if there is a hyperlink from one page to another.

For example, there exists a hyperlink from Google to Yahoo, so $\mathbf{A}_{\{Google,Yahoo\}} = 1$. Conversely, there is no hyperlink from Yahoo to Google, so $\mathbf{A}_{\{Yahoo,Google\}} = 0$. We remove any self-loops and consider $\mathbf{A}_{\{ii\}} = 0$ (e.g., $\mathbf{A}_{\{Google,Google\}} = 0$). The complete adjacency matrix for Figure 5.13 is shown in Table 5.4.

The adjacency matrix can be converted to a graph in R, as shown below.

```
1 #Get all required packages
2 library(igraph)
3 library(LinkAnalysis)

4 # Adjacency matrix for web page graph
5 A<-matrix(c(0, 1, 1, 0, 0, 0,
6             1, 0, 1, 1, 1, 1,
7             0, 1, 0, 0, 0, 0,
```

TABLE 5.4: Adjacency matrix for web link data

	Wiki	Google	Bing	Yahoo	Altavista	Rediff
Wikipedia	0	1	1	0	0	0
Google	1	0	1	1	1	1
Bing	0	1	0	0	0	0
Yahoo	0	0	1	0	1	0
Altavista	0	1	1	0	0	0
Rediffmail	0	0	1	0	0	0

```
8       0, 0, 1, 0, 1, 0,
9       0, 1, 1, 0, 0, 0,
10      0, 0, 1, 0, 0, 0),
11      nrow=6,ncol=6,
12      byrow=TRUE);

13 #Get a directed unweighted graph from adjacency matrix
14 G<-graph.adjacency(A,mode=c("directed"),
15                    weighted=NULL);

16 #labeling each vertex of graph
17 G$label<-c("Wikipedia","Google",
18      "Bing","Yahoo","Altavista,"Rediffmail");
```

The adjacency matrix **A** forms the input to the R implementation of HITS. Given an adjacency matrix and a parameter k_{max}, the algorithm proceeds iteratively, computing hub and authority scores for each vertex. The calculation of hub and authority scores and the updating process are discussed in the next section.

5.5.3   Updating Hub and Authority Scores

During each iteration of the algorithm, both hub and authority scores for each vertex are updated. We define two vectors to store the authority and hub scores for each vertex. The authority scores form a column vector $\mathbf{a} = (a_1, a_2, \ldots, a_n)^{\mathbf{T}}$, and hub scores form a column vector $\mathbf{h} = (h_1, h_2, \ldots, h_n)^{\mathbf{T}}$, where n is the number of vertices in the graph. The authority and hub scores are initialized to 1 for each web page:

$$\mathbf{a}^{(0)} = \begin{bmatrix} 1 \\ 1 \\ \vdots \\ 1 \end{bmatrix}, \ \mathbf{h}^{(0)} = \begin{bmatrix} 1 \\ 1 \\ \vdots \\ 1 \end{bmatrix},$$

and are updated according to operations $\mathcal{I}$ and $\mathcal{O}$, respectively. Note that the initial hub and authority vectors are not normalized to length one.

Definition 5.10 *Update authority scores ($\mathcal{I}$).*
We use the previous iteration hub score to calculate the current iteration of the authority scores. An individual authority score for vertex $i \in V(G)$ is updated as follows:

$$a_j^{(k)} \leftarrow \sum_{(i,j) \in E} h_i^{(k-1)}, \tag{5.17}$$

where k represents the current iteration and $k-1$ is the previous iteration. Using the adjacency matrix $\mathbf{A}$, the authority vector update operation $\mathcal{I}$ can be defined as:

$$\mathbf{a}^{(k)} \leftarrow \mathbf{A}^{\mathbf{T}} \cdot \mathbf{h}^{(k-1)}. \tag{5.18}$$

Definition 5.11 *Update hub scores ($\mathcal{O}$).*
We use the current iteration's authority scores to calculate the current iteration of the hub scores. An individual hub score for vertex $i \in V(G)$ is updated as follows:

$$h_i^{(k)} \leftarrow \sum_{(i,j) \in E} a_j^{(k)}, \tag{5.19}$$

where k represents the current iteration. Using the adjacency matrix $\mathbf{A}$, the hub vector update operation $\mathcal{O}$ is defined as:

$$\mathbf{h}^{(k)} \leftarrow \mathbf{A} \cdot \mathbf{a}^{(k)}. \tag{5.20}$$

Below, we illustrate one iteration of $\mathcal{I}$ to update the authority vector $\mathbf{a}$.

$$\mathbf{a}^{(1)} = \mathbf{A}^{\mathbf{T}} \cdot \mathbf{h}^{(0)} \tag{5.21}$$

$$= \begin{bmatrix} 0 & 1 & 1 & 0 & 0 & 0 \\ 1 & 0 & 1 & 1 & 1 & 1 \\ 0 & 1 & 0 & 0 & 0 & 0 \\ 0 & 0 & 1 & 0 & 1 & 0 \\ 0 & 1 & 1 & 0 & 0 & 0 \\ 0 & 0 & 1 & 0 & 0 & 0 \end{bmatrix}^{\mathbf{T}} \cdot \begin{bmatrix} 1 \\ 1 \\ 1 \\ 1 \\ 1 \\ 1 \end{bmatrix} \tag{5.22}$$

$$= \begin{bmatrix} 0 & 1 & 0 & 0 & 0 & 0 \\ 1 & 0 & 1 & 0 & 1 & 0 \\ 1 & 1 & 0 & 1 & 1 & 1 \\ 0 & 1 & 0 & 0 & 0 & 0 \\ 0 & 1 & 0 & 1 & 0 & 0 \\ 0 & 1 & 0 & 0 & 0 & 0 \end{bmatrix} \cdot \begin{bmatrix} 1 \\ 1 \\ 1 \\ 1 \\ 1 \\ 1 \end{bmatrix} \qquad (5.23)$$

$$= \begin{bmatrix} 1 \\ 3 \\ 5 \\ 1 \\ 2 \\ 1 \end{bmatrix} \qquad (5.24)$$

We normalize the vector after each iteration by dividing each element by the square root of the sum of squares of the elements.

$$\mathbf{a}^{(1)} = \begin{bmatrix} \frac{1}{\sqrt{1^2+3^2+5^2+1^2+2^2+1^2}} \\ \frac{3}{\sqrt{1^2+3^2+5^2+1^2+2^2+1^2}} \\ \frac{5}{\sqrt{1^2+3^2+5^2+1^2+2^2+1^2}} \\ \frac{1}{\sqrt{1^2+3^2+5^2+1^2+2^2+1^2}} \\ \frac{2}{\sqrt{1^2+3^2+5^2+1^2+2^2+1^2}} \\ \frac{1}{\sqrt{1^2+3^2+5^2+1^2+2^2+1^2}} \end{bmatrix} \qquad (5.25)$$

$$= \begin{bmatrix} \frac{1}{\sqrt{41}} \\ \frac{3}{\sqrt{41}} \\ \frac{5}{\sqrt{41}} \\ \frac{1}{\sqrt{41}} \\ \frac{2}{\sqrt{41}} \\ \frac{1}{\sqrt{41}} \end{bmatrix} \qquad (5.26)$$

$$= \begin{bmatrix} 0.15617 \\ 0.46852 \\ 0.78087 \\ 0.15617 \\ 0.312348 \\ 0.15617 \end{bmatrix} \qquad (5.27)$$

Formally, the normalization operations are defined below.

Definition 5.12 *Normalize hub and authority scores.*
We normalize weights of the hub scores to ensure:

$$\sum_{a \in \mathbf{a}} a^2 = \sum_{h \in \mathbf{h}} h^2 = 1.$$

To do this, we divide each component of the vectors **a** and **h** by the sum of squares of their respective components. Formally,

$$\mathbf{a} = \frac{\mathbf{a}}{||\mathbf{a}||} \text{ and} \qquad (5.28)$$

$$\mathbf{h} = \frac{\mathbf{h}}{||\mathbf{h}||}, \qquad (5.29)$$

where

$$||\mathbf{a}|| = \sum_{a \in \mathbf{a}} a^2 \qquad (5.30)$$

5.5.4 Convergence of the HITS Algorithm

While Kleinberg's original paper discusses convergence of the algorithm, we should note that no formal convergence criteria are integrated into the algorithm. In practice, a common upper bound for k_{max} is 20. Generally, after a number of iterations, the authority and hub scores do not vary much and can be considered to have "converged" [20].

To illustrate this concept we run the algorithm with $k = 1, 2, 3, \ldots, 6$ and observe the output scores. The complete algorithm can be run in R as shown below. In this case, we use $k_{max} = 6$.

```
1  library(igraph)
2  library(ProximityMeasure)
3  A<-matrix(c(0, 1, 1, 0, 0, 0,
4              1, 0, 1, 1, 1, 1,
5              0, 1, 0, 0, 0, 0,
6              0, 0, 1, 0, 1, 0,
7              0, 1, 1, 0, 0, 0,
8              0, 0, 1, 0, 0, 0),
9              nrow=6,ncol=6,
10             byrow=TRUE);
11 G<-graph.adjacency(A,mode=c("directed"),weighted=NULL);

12 kmax<-6;
13 op<-HITS(G,kmax);
14 op;
```

Table 5.5 shows the convergence of the authority scores for the web search

TABLE 5.5: Convergence of authority scores, **a**, over k_{max} iterations. Decimals have been rounded to three places.

Iteration (k)	0	1	2	3	4	5	6
Wikipedia	1	0.156	0.204	0.224	0.232	0.236	0.237
Google	1	0.469	0.388	0.350	0.332	0.324	0.320
Bing	1	0.781	0.777	0.769	0.765	0.762	**0.761**
Yahoo	1	0.156	0.204	0.224	0.232	0.236	0.238
Altavista	1	0.312	0.347	0.369	0.378	0.383	0.385
Rediffmail	1	0.156	0.204	0.224	0.232	0.236	0.238

TABLE 5.6: Convergence of hub scores, **h**, over k_{max} iterations. Decimals have been rounded to three places.

Iteration (k)	0	1	2	3	4	5	6
Wikipedia	1	0.454	0.418	0.401	0.393	0.389	0.378
Google	1	0.567	0.624	0.648	0.659	0.664	**0.666**
Bing	1	0.170	0.139	0.126	0.119	0.116	0.115
Yahoo	1	0.397	0.404	0.408	0.409	0.410	0.411
Altavista	1	0.454	0.418	0.401	0.393	0.389	0.387
Rediffmail	1	0.284	0.279	0.276	0.274	0.273	0.273

graph over $k = 1, 2, 3, \ldots, 6$ iterations. Table 5.6 shows the hub score convergence.

We can see from Tables 5.5 and 5.6 that after the fifth iteration, the authority and the hub scores do not vary much. A high authority score of 0.671 for Bing indicates that Bing is an informative page. Similarly, a high hub score (0.761) for Google indicates that Bing contains links to highly informative pages like Google.

Having discussed encoding the graph as an adjacency matrix, updating hub and authority scores, normalizing of hub and authority scores, and iterating until convergence, we are now in a position to present pseudocode for the complete algorithm, which appears in Algorithm 2.

The algorithm requires an adjacency matrix **A** and parameter k_{max} as input. Let n be the number of vertices V of graph G (represented by the adjacency matrix **A**). Lines 1 and 2 initialize the hub and authority vectors, respectively. Line 4, the $\mathcal{I}$ operation, transposes the adjacency matrix and performs matrix multiplication. Similarly, line 5, the $\mathcal{O}$ operation, performs matrix multiplication. Line 6 normalizes the authority vector by dividing each authority value by the sum of all squared authority values. Line 7 normalizes the hub matrix by dividing each hub value by the sum of all squared hub values, which takes $O(n)$ time. Line 9 returns the authority and hub vectors.

Input: A—An adjacency matrix representing a collection of items (e.g. web pages)

k_{max}—A natural number (number of iterations)

Output: $\mathbf{a}^{(k_{max})}, \mathbf{h}^{(k_{max})}$—Vectors of hub and authority scores for each vertex in the graph

1 $\mathbf{a}^{(0)} \leftarrow (1, 1, 1, \ldots, 1) \in \mathbb{R}^n$

2 $\mathbf{h}^{(0)} \leftarrow (1, 1, 1, \ldots, 1) \in \mathbb{R}^n$

3 **for** $k = 1$ **to** k_{max} **do**

4   Apply the $\mathcal{I}$ operation to $(\mathbf{A}^T, \mathbf{h}^{(k-1)})$, to obtain new authority scores, $\mathbf{a}^{(k)}$ (Dfn. 5.10)

5   Apply the $\mathcal{O}$ operation to $(\mathbf{A}, \mathbf{a}^{(k)})$, to obtain new hub scores, $\mathbf{h}^{(k)}$ (Dfn. 5.11)

6   Normalize $\mathbf{a}^{(k)}$ (Eqn. 5.28)

7   Normalize $\mathbf{h}^{(k)}$ (Eqn. 5.29)

8 **end**

9 **return** $(\mathbf{a}^{(k_{max})}, \mathbf{h}^{(k_{max})})$

Algorithm 2: HITS Algorithm

Using the Coppersmith Winograd matrix multiplication algorithm [11], the total complexity of Algorithm 2 is approximately $O(k_{max} \cdot n^{2.376})$.

5.5.5 Strengths and Weaknesses

The most obvious strength of HITS is the two separate vectors it returns, which allow the application to decide on which score it is most interested in. In terms of resources, HITS is very efficient, since a dense subgraph may be relatively small compared to the whole graph. For example, the set of relevant documents returned from a query is much smaller than all URLs on the Web.

The query-based use of HITS has some weaknesses, since in certain applications, such as in web searches, the graph must be regenerated dynamically each time.

Using a query-based system can also lead to manipulation of the algorithm. For example, if a web page creator wanted his web page to appear higher in a search query, the creator could make "spam" pages that link to the original site to give it an artificially high authority score [22].

One more weakness is that of "topic drift." Imagine that, for a particular query, there is a web page that remotely pertains to the query but is primarily about a different topic. This web page, although it is loosely related, may have a very high authority score in its own area, which may "overpower" more relevant web pages with lower authority scores [28]. This weakness can sometimes be handled by adding another relevancy factor to judge how well a document relates to the original query [22].

Another weakness that is also cited is the poor performance of HITS versus other algorithms [24], primarily because of a poor selection of k_{max}, the number of iterations. Studies have shown that, in the worst case scenario, HITS requires a k_{max} that is super-exponential to the graph size in order to converge [31]. Alternatively, some researchers, rather than using a fixed value for k_{max}, run HITS until the change in the hub and authority scores drops below a certain level.

5.6   Link Prediction

Imagine a graph-based friendship structure. One of the basic operations on such a network is to search for new friends and connections. Link prediction methods are a set of methods that can be used to predict new links in a graph. Link prediction can be used to identify new connections in a friendship network. A co-authorship network contains links among authors if they have collaborated at work. It might be interesting to find newer links among the same set of authors at a later point of time, disregarding newer authors who have published material in this time interval.

Link prediction is performed in several ways, such as the use of Relational Markov Networks (RMN) in cases where the data is relational. A relational database consists of data that are related using associations and is-a hierarchies [36]. Some link predictors use this relational data to generate some candidates of features and consequently select from this set using the statistical model selection criteria [32].

In this section, we concentrate on the approaches to link prediction based on measures for analyzing the 'proximity' of vertices in a network [29]. The notion of closeness is defined by a value called the 'proximity measure.' Several distance or proximity measures like Jaccard, Euclidean, and Minkowski can be used to compute proximity measures. For example, the Euclidean distance looks at the Root Mean Square difference between the numeric attributes of two nodes and outputs a physical distance similar to real-world distance measurements. *Single linkage*-based measures depend on the distance between two instances, whereas *group linkage* measurements are the average of linkage measurements among several nodes in two different groups or clusters.

5.6.1   What Is Link Prediction?

Given a snapshot of a social network in a time interval t_0 to t_0', it is possible to accurately predict the edges that will be added to the network during the future interval from time t_1 to t_1' [29]. The training set and the testing set are the graphs in the interval t_0 to t_0' and t_1 to t_1', respectively. While predicting links based on distance metrics, we do not use external properties but make best use of features intrinsic to the graph to make judgments. From an SNA standpoint, chances of a person making a new friend in the future are high if the new person happens to be an existing friend's friend, thereby making him/her a mutual friend. This notion of 'closeness' is what needs to be searched for in a graph.

Consider a social network $G(V, E)$, a graph with V vertices and E edges. If $G(t_0, t_0')$ is a graph containing all such interactions among verticles that take place in the time interval (t_0, t_0'), and (t_1, t_1') is a time interval occurring after (t_0, t_0'), then the task of link prediction is to provide a list of edges that are present in $G(t_1, t_1')$ but absent in $G(t_0, t_0')$. The timestamps indicate that $G(t_0, t_0')$ is the training set and the one to be predicted is the subgraph $G(t_1, t_1')$.

TABLE 5.7: Link prediction notation

Symbol	Meaning
$G(t_i, t_j)$	Snapshot of graph G between time t_i and t_j
core	Set of vertices with at least a threshold number of edges
$k_{training}$	Number of edges a vertex in the training set must have in order to be in the core set
k_{test}	Number of edges a vertex in the test set must have in order to be in the core set
E_{old}	Set of edges in the training set
E_{new}	Set of edges in the test set
$|E_{new}^*|$	Set of edges common to the sets E_{new} and $core \times core$
$score(u, v)$	Negative value of the shortest path length between vertices u and v
$J(A, B)$	Jaccard coefficient for sets A and B
$H(u, v)$	Number of steps in the walk from the start vertex u to destination vertex v, also known as 'hitting time'
$c(u, v)$	The commute time is the sum of hitting times in both directions, $H(u, v)$ and $H(v, u)$

5.6.2 How to Predict Links

The algorithm explained in this section performs link prediction using proximity measures. Proximity measures are used to find similarity between a pair of objects (see also Chapter 6 on different proximity measures). In the link prediction problem, we look at what measure would best find points that are close to each other in terms of proximity, and how this proximity would most likely turn into a future collaboration or interaction. We need to disregard all those vertices that got added after the training period, (t_0, t_0'), because we want only edges that have been added between the same set of vertices that were present in the training set.

A 'threshold' on the number of edges a vertex needs to be adjacent to (in the training set and test set) is defined so that the prediction process is performed on a subset of the graph. The *core* set contains vertices that are adjacent to 3 or more edges in the graph. $k_{training}$ is the number of edges a vertex in the training set has to be adjacent to in order to enter the core set. In the graph depicted in Figure 5.14, we have the training set containing vertices A to H, in which the vertices A, B, C, and F have more than 3 edges adjacent to them, we will say that these edges belong to *core*. This graph assumes the value of $k_{training}$ to be 3. The following edges are all part of another set called E_{old}: $A \rightarrow C$; $A \rightarrow G$; $A \rightarrow D$; $C \rightarrow E$; $C \rightarrow G$; $B \rightarrow D$; $B \rightarrow H$; $B \rightarrow F$; $E \rightarrow F$; and $F \rightarrow H$.

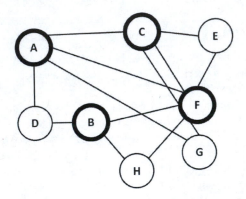

FIGURE 5.14: A graph with the core vertices in bold.

Given the training set, $G(V, E_{old})$ as in Figure 5.14, we would like to predict the new edges among the vertices in *core*, in the test set. We do not want to predict edges between vertices other than the ones in *core*, and we do not want to predict the edges that are already present in the training set. These new interactions are labeled E_{new}. $V \times V - E_{old}$ would result in the set E_{new}. In Figure 5.15, we depict the test set containing all the vertices including a new vertex I. The edges in the figure are the ones that we would like to predict. Note that these edges are only among A, B, C, and F. Since we would like to find out the accuracy of our link prediction, we define E_{new}^* as $E_{new} \cap (core \times core)$. We are interested only in newly predicted interactions that are also in the neighborhood defined by *core*. Once we have found a ranked list L sorted as per decreasing confidence, we pick the first n pairs in the set $core \times core$, where n is the count of E_{new}^*, given by $|E_{new}^*|$. The size of the intersection of this set with that of E_{new}^* is finally determined.

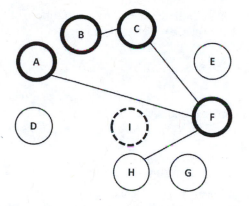

FIGURE 5.15: Diagram depicting the test set and the newly predicted edges among the vertices A, B, C, and F (core vertices).

5.6.3 Link Prediction Methods

The proximity measures used to perform link prediction are explained in this section. The proximity measures assign a numerical value $score(u, v)$ to the edge connecting a pair of nodes u and v. A list L is produced by ranking all such pairs in decreasing order of their $score(u, v)$. The score is defined as a negative value of the shortest path length [29]. All the proximity metrics in this section must be adapted so that they can be used to predict links. We will consider the proximity measures under three different categories:

- Node neighborhood-based methods;

- Methods based on the ensemble of paths; and

- Higher-level approaches.

5.6.3.1 Node Neighborhood-Based Methods

In the SNA scenario, it is highly likely that two people will become friends in the future if they happen to share a friend when the analysis is conducted. The more the number of common friends is, the higher the probability of future interaction is. This is the principle behind node neighborhood-based methods. If the intersection set of the neighbors of the two vertices u and v happens to be a null set, we can deduce that they do not share any common neighbors, and thus the probability of the two vertices to share an edge at any time in the future is near zero. On the other hand, if this set happens to be a union of the neighbors of the two vertices, we know that they share a lot of neighbors.

1. **Common neighbors**
   The common neighbors method is a simple measure that takes into account the intersection set of the neighbors of the vertices u and v.

This set would contain all the common neighbors of the two vertices. The value of $score(u,v)$ is given in Equation 5.31:

$$score(u, v) = |N(u) \cap N(v)| \qquad (5.31)$$

Newman [25] has computed the probability of a future collaboration using common neighbors. In this, the probability of collaboration between vertices in two collaboration networks is measured as a function of:

- The number of mutual neighbors in the network;
- The number of previous interactions; and
- The number of previous interacting vertices.

The observation is that a future interaction is strongly linked to all the above factors. The neighboring vertices of u and v are compared and all matching vertices are designated as common neighbors.

2. **Jaccard coefficient**
   The Jaccard coefficient is a proximity measure based on the node neighborhood principle. Mathematically, the Jaccard coefficient for two sets A and B can be represented as a ratio of the size of their intersection to the size of their union. The Jaccard coefficient of A and B is calculated as in Equation 5.32:

$$J(A, B) = \frac{|A \cap B|}{|A \cup B|} \qquad (5.32)$$

   To measure dissimilarity, we would subtract $J(A, B)$ from 1. Given values, $A = (1, 0, 0, 0, 0, 0, 0, 0, 0, 0)$ and $B = (0, 0, 0, 0, 0, 0, 1, 0, 0, 1)$, the $J(A, B)$ value can be calculated as 0 using Equation 5.33:

$$\frac{f_{11}}{f_{01} + f_{10} + f_{11}}, \qquad (5.33)$$

   where f_{ij} is the frequency of simultaneous occurrence of i and j in A and B, respectively.

   Notice, however, that this version of the Jaccard coefficient would make sense only in case of multi-dimensional vector data. For the vertices u and v, we modify the Jaccard coefficient and define it as Equation 5.34 for the link prediction problem:

$$score(u, v) = \frac{|N(u) \cap N(v)|}{|N(u) \cup N(v)|} \qquad (5.34)$$

3. **Adamic-Adar**

    Another measure based on common neighbors for measuring proximity is Adamic-Adar [2]. This method computes the similarity between any two vertices u and v using a common feature of the two, namely z. The similarity measure is defined in Equation 5.35:

    $$\Sigma_z \frac{1}{log(freq(z))}, \tag{5.35}$$

    where $freq(z)$ is the frequency of occurrence of the common feature between u and v.

    Using this measure we would then estimate the score as follows,

    $$score(u, v) = \Sigma_{z \in N(u) \cap N(v)} \frac{1}{log(|N(z)|)} \tag{5.36}$$

5.6.3.2 Ensemble of All Path-Based Methodologies

In machine learning, 'ensemble' refers to a method which utilizes a collection of models to perform a prediction instead of using a single or a constituent model. Learners select the best hypotheses for a given prediction problem based on a best fit. There maybe cases where some hypotheses may not provide the required prediction accuracy levels, in such cases an ensemble combines weak learners to form a single strong learner.

1. **PageRank**

    PageRank has been explained in detail in the previous section. For the PageRank algorithm, we need to consider two important terms before defining the score. In a graph G, for two vertices u and v, the hitting time in a random walk is the number of steps in the walk to reach the destination vertex v from the start vertex u and is denoted as $H(u, v)$. If we consider the hitting time with source vertex v and destination vertex u, then the hitting time $H(v, u)$ does not need to be the same as the hitting time $H(u, v)$. To describe this, we need to understand the term commute time, which is the sum of the hitting times in both directions, $H(u, v) + H(v, u)$ denoted as, $c(u, v)$. The score $s(u, v)$ is thus defined as,

    $$s(u, v) = -H(u, v) \tag{5.37}$$

    Using commute time instead, we could negate $c(u, v)$ to get the score.

    The previous section dealt in depth with the workings of PageRank and its implementation.

2. **SimRank**

   SimRank is a link analysis algorithm that works on a graph G to measure the similarity between two vertices u and v in the graph. For the nodes u and v, it is denoted by $s(u, v) \in [0, 1]$. If $u = v$, then $s(u, v) = 1$. The definition iterates on the similarity index of the neighbors of u and v itself. We can denote SimRank mathematically as,

$$s(u, v) = \frac{C}{|N(u)||N(v)|} \sum_{x \in N(u)} \sum_{y \in N(v)} s(x, y) \qquad (5.38)$$

   where $C \in [0, 1]$ is a constant factor. The similarity score for two nodes is taken to be the final SimRank value obtained. Thus, $score(u, v) = s(u, v)$.

5.6.3.3   Higher Level Methodologies

Higher level proximity measures are meta approaches that can be used along with other approaches discussed above in the other two categories.

1. **Unseen bigrams**

   A bigram is any two letter or two word group, and a specific instance of an N-gram. Some common examples of bigrams are TH, AN, IN, etc. If such a bigram is not present in the training set but is found to be present in the test set, it is termed an unseen bigram. This approach can be used to fortify the scores we have already calculated using the other methods described above. Once we have the $score(x, y)$ using any of the methods we already detailed, we look at other nodes that are similar to x. Consider s to be the set of nodes that are similar to x; if we use S_δ^x to depict δ similar nodes to x [29], where $\delta \in \mathbb{Z}^+$, then the update calculation of unweighted $score(x, y)$ will be done as in Equation 5.39:

$$score^*_{unweighted}(x, y) = |z : z \in N(y) \cap S_\delta^x|, \qquad (5.39)$$

   where, z is a vertex similar to x.
   Weighted score for the same is calculated as follows:

$$score^*_{weighted}(x, y) = \Sigma_{z \in N(y) \cap S_\delta^x} score(x, z) \qquad (5.40)$$

2. **Clustering**

   Getting rid of edges that are tentative and vague is one way of making sure that prediction accuracy increases. If link prediction is attempted on such a graph containing only edges that are appropriate to the prediction process, we can be assured of better results. Jon Kleinberg *et al.* [29] suggest that in order to calculate the

$score(x, y)$, we can initially find the $score(u, v)$, where $u, v \in E_{old}$. From this list, we then remove $(1 - \rho)$ edges, where the calculated score is found to be low. This way we arrive at a subgraph lacking edges that are not of much interest to the prediction process. $score(x, y)$ must then be calculated on the new subgraph that we recently formed.

5.6.4   Link Prediction Algorithm

A high level abstraction of the process of predicting links is given in Figure 5.16. We follow this by developing an algorithm for pre-processing the graph data for link prediction. Then we describe how to use this processed graph data to compute most probable links.

Graph Data Processing

The line numbers at the end of each step correspond to the line numbers of that step in Algorithm 3.

1. Accept raw data representation of a collaboration or co-authorship network, in the form of an edge list and a year attribute for each edge at the least.
2. Split this data into training and test sets (the training and test durations are decided by a parameter to the function) (Lines 3-4).
3. For maximum accuracy, the prediction process should depend only on attributes intrinsic to the network. Hence, the newer vertices in the test graph that are not in the training graph are pruned (Lines 5-6).

The pruned test graph may still contain newer edges not present in the training graph. These are the edges we seek to predict.

Next, we will go over the key steps of graph data processing:

- Create a data frame from a given file

```
1 > rawdataframe <- read.table(path,sep=" ",fill=TRUE)
```

- Get the year range

```
2 > begin_year <- min(rawdataframe$V3)
3 > end_year <- max(rawdataframe$V3)
```

- Based on test duration given, split data into training and test sets

```
4 > trainingdataframe <- rawdataframe[!rawdataframe$V3
5 %in% c((end_year-testduration+1):end_year),]
6 > testdataframe <- rawdataframe[rawdataframe$V3
7 %in% c((end_year-testduration+1):end_year),]
```

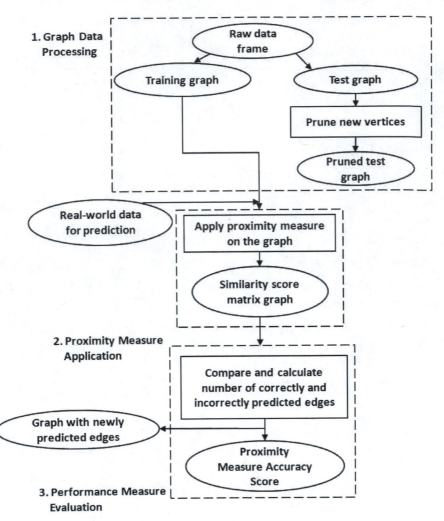

FIGURE 5.16: High-level abstraction of the link prediction process.

- Convert data frames into graphs

```
 8 > rawgraphdata <- graph.data.frame(rawdataframe,
 9 directed=isDirected, vertices = NULL)
10 > traininggraphdata <- graph.data.frame(trainingdataframe,
11 directed=isDirected, vertices = NULL)
12 > testgraphdata <- graph.data.frame(testdataframe,
13 directed=isDirected, vertices = NULL)
```

- Remove newly added vertices and edges from test graph

---

1 **Algorithm:** Graph Data Processing

Input: D—Duration of test data
G—Input graph
Output: $G_{training}$—The training graph
G_{test}—The test graph
G'_{test}—The pruned test graph
```
/* Let year_begin denote begin year of data        */
/* Let year_end denote end year of data             */
/* Let pruned denote vertices to be pruned from the test
   data                                             */
/* Let V(G) denote vertices of graph G              */
```
2 Extract the $year_{begin}$ and $year_{end}$ from the year attribute of the edges.
```
/* Split the data into G_training and G_test        */
```
3 $G_{test} = G[year_{end} - D + 1 : year_{end}]$
4 $G_{training} = G - G_{test}$
5 $pruned = V(G_{test}) - V(G_{training})$
6 $G'_{test} = V(G_{test}) - pruned$
7 **return** $G_{training}$, G_{test}, G'_{test}

Algorithm 3: Processing of input data

```
14 > testgraphdata_cleaned <- delete.vertices(testgraphdata,
15 V(testgraphdata)[!V(testgraphdata)$name
16   %in% V(traininggraphdata)$name])
```

- Return the created graphs

```
17 return(graphlist)
```

Link Prediction: Computing Most Probable Links

After having processed the graph data, the steps involved in computing probable links are quite straightforward. Using the training graph generated in Section 5.6.4:

1. Compute the score of all possible edges using the chosen proximity measure (Line 2, Algorithm 4).

2. Select the proximity values above the threshold and return the edges associated with these values as a graph (Lines 3-5).

To predict probable links in R, follow the following steps:

- Compute pairwise link prediction values

```
1 predval <- measure(g)
```

---

1 **Algorithm:** Compute Most Probable Links

Input: G—Input graph
T—Threshold for prediction
m—Proximity measure to be used in link prediction (a function that
takes a graph as input)
Output: $G_{predicted}$—A graph containing predicted scores
```
/* Let Predicted denote a matrix of proximity values for
   each pair of vertices                                        */
/* Let Output denote a matrix of boolean values
   corresponding to the proximity values that satisfy
   threshold T                                                  */
/* Compute the proximity values by applying the measure on
   G                                                            */
```
2 $Predicted := m(G)$
3 $Output := (Predicted >= T)$
4 Generate graph $G_{predicted}$ from adjacency matrix represented by
$Output$
5 **return** $G_{predicted}$

Algorithm 4: Computing most probable links by applying a proximity
measure

- Select links with the predicted value above the threshold

  ```
  2 adjmatrix <- (predval >= threshold)
  ```

- Prevent self-links

  ```
  3 diag(adjmatrix) <- FALSE
  ```

- Convert TRUE's to 1's

  ```
  4 adjmatrix[adjmatrix == TRUE] <- 1
  ```

- Return predicted edges

  ```
  5 return(graph.adjacency(adjmatrix))
  ```

Performance Evaluation

We have seen several different proximity measures that can be used for link
prediction; some additional ones are also presented in Chapter 6. One may
wish to compare the performance of these measures. In this section, we present
one approach for comparing different performance measures. Chapter 12 describes a set of different performance evaluation approaches, and discusses the
pros and cons of each.

We assume that enough data is available so that we can obtain training and test datasets. Algorithm 5 presents some of the key performance metrics, called True Positives (TP), True Negatives (TN), False Positives (FP), and False Negatives (FN).

---

1 **Algorithm:** Performance Measure

Input: $G_{predicted}$—A graph containing predicted scores
G_{test}—Input graph
Output: TP—True Positive value
TN—True Negative value
FP—False Positive value
FN—False Negative value

2 TP = Number of edges present in $G_{predicted}$ AND present in G_{test}

3 TN = Number of edges not present in $G_{predicted}$ AND present in G_{test}

4 FP = Number of edges present in $G_{predicted}$ AND not present in G_{test}

5 FN = Number of edges not present in $G_{predicted}$ AND not present in G_{test}

6 **return** TP, FP, TN, FN

Algorithm 5: Computing the performance measure

To calculate these performance metrics, you may use the following R code:

- Compare adjacency matrices row by row

```
6 testmatrix <- get.adjacency(testgraph)
7 predictedmatrix <- get.adjacency(predictedgraph)
```

- Compute the values of true and false positives and true and false negatives

```
8  > tp <- ((predictedmatrix == 1)
9         & (predictedmatrix == testmatrix) )
10 > tn <- ((predictedmatrix == 0)
11         & (predictedmatrix == testmatrix) )
12 > fp <- ((predictedmatrix == 1)
13         & (predictedmatrix != testmatrix) )
14 > fn <- ((predictedmatrix == 0)
15         & (predictedmatrix != testmatrix) )
```

- Number of correctly predicted edges

```
16 > Outputlist <- list(truepositive = tp,
17     truenegative = tn, falsepositive = fp, falsenegative = fn)
```

5.7   Applications

5.7.1   Citation Ranking in Collaboration Networks

M.J. Newman [26] describes collaboration networks as 'small worlds,' where any two authors in the network have a 'small path' through other authors in the network. Citation ranking is the process of ranking authors in a collaboration network, according to the number of references each author has scored. While the number of references is a key parameter in judging an author and also assigning a numerical rank, it is not a very reliable parameter. The ranking scheme of the PageRank algorithm as explained in Section 5.4 considers the rank of the page that provides rank to another page while ranking. Similarly, if the citation is from an author who himself has a high rank, the citation holds more value than another from an author who himself has none. Using such a ranking scheme, we will be able to identify and separate high quality publications form others since

- A high quality publication is cited more often,

- The probability of the publication being cited by another high quality publication is high, and

- A numerical ranking provides an easy form of reference for quality.

In this section, we analyze the PageRank algorithm using a collaboration network data set. This data set is a weighted co-authorship network of authors who posted preprints in the Astrophysics e-print archive between the dates January 1st, 1995 and December 31st, 1999 [26]. The data set has been pruned and consists of 101 vertices representing 101 unique authors with 125 edges denoting the collaborations among these authors. A sample snapshot of the edgelist of the data is as follows:

```
1 [26]    21 --   22
2 [27]     6 --   23
3 [28]    23 --   24
4 [29]     6 --   24
5 [30]    25 --   26
6 [31]    25 --   27
7 [32]    26 --   27
```

The resultant graph for the pruned data is as shown in Figure 5.17.

Next, we shall perform a walkthrough of the steps necessary to apply PageRank on our data.

1. Initially, the data set needs to be downloaded from the URL `http:`

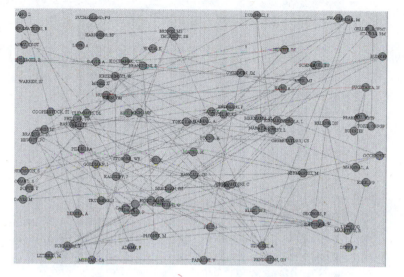

FIGURE 5.17: Pruned co-authorship network.

//www-personal.umich.edu/~mejn/netdata/. Among the different network datasets provided there, choose "Astrophysics collaborations." From the downloaded archive, extract the "astro-ph.gml" file.

2. Next, the data needs to be read and plotted into a graph. `astrogr` is an `igraph` object that stores the graph structure represented by the downloaded file.

```
1 astrogr <- read.graph('astro-ph.gml', 'gml')
```

3. The data set as obtained is very huge and for our analysis we will prune the data set to consist only of vertices whose id values are less than 100 using the command here:

```
2 astrogr_sub <- delete.vertices(astrogr, V(astrogr)
3 $id[V(astrogr)$id > 100])
```

4. The `delete.vertices` function is present in the igraph package and can be used to prune vertices from the graph. The first argument to this function is the `igraph` object and the second is the argument specifying the vertices to be removed. In our case this is the set of vertices with id greater than 100. The resultant graph is stored in the `astrogr_sub` variable.

5. We mentioned the fact that in this graph, the edges are weighted. To view the edge weights, use this command in R:

₄ E(astrogr_sub)$value

6. Now we use the `page.rank` function to compute the Page Rank values for each of the 101 vertices using the following command:

   ₅ page.rank(astrogr_sub, V(astrogr_sub),
   ₆ directed = FALSE,
   ₇ weights = E(astrogr_sub)$value)$vector

7. Note here that in the example in Section 5.4.5, we did not make use of this parameter since we were only dealing with unweighted graphs. Here, we make use of the edge weights by specifying `weights = E(astrogr_sub)$value` in the function.

8. The PageRank values are printed as a probability distribution for all vertices in the graph. The `V(astrogr_sub)$label` command can be used to print the labels of the vertices, which contain the corresponding PageRank values. Here's a subset from the end of the list of vertices:

   ₁ > V(astrogr_sub)$label[91:101]
   ₂ [91] 0.010399650 0.001492724 0.007271856
   ₃ [94] 0.010372191 0.010247723 0.010247723
   ₄ [97] 0.008114594 0.008114594 0.012486225
   ₅ [100] 0.005663178 0.009763029

We can make some useful observations from the assignment of PageRank values to all the vertices. For example, consider vertex id 92, whose PageRank assignment is 0.001492724. If we look at the edge list carefully, we can see that this vertex does not have any backlinks at all. This is definitely a candidate for a low citation score and hence this author must be assigned a low rank. On the edge list of 92, we have 93, whose value is also low but greater than 92 since 93 has one link more than 92. One important fact to be noted here is that the rank of the entire network adds up to 1.

5.7.2 Web Page Link Analysis with HITS

To illustrate how HITS is used in real applications, we have used data extracted from http://matalon.org/search-algorithms on 100 web pages. This data was obtained by running a web crawler on the web and traversing the hyperlinks available on each web page. This data set, though, is limited to just 100 web pages. We extracted the adjacency matrix for these 100 web pages from the website and put this matrix into the file `webPageLinks.txt`. This text file contains a 100×100 matrix, where each element represents the links from one URL to another.

To apply HITS to this data set, we need to run the following R code:

```
1  #load libraries
2  library(igraph)
3  library(ProximityMeasure)
4  #webPageLinks data is loaded
5  data(webPageLinks)
6  #data is converted to undirected graph
7  g<-graph.adjacency(webPageLinks)
8  #HITS function is called for hitsdata and
9  # number of iterations are set to 20
10 #output stores authority and hub scores of
11 # all 100 nodes
12 output<-HITS(g,20)
13 #To get the best authority node
14 max.col(matrix(output[1:100],nrow=1))
15 #To get the best hub node
16 max.col(matrix(output[101:200],nrow=1))
```

The above code returns vertex number 23 (http://www.google.com/intl/iw/options/index.html) as the best authority, with an authority score of 0.701, and vertex number 38 (http://images.google.com/) as the best hub, with a hub score of 0.200. The high authority score for http://www.google.com/intl/iw/options/index.html indicates that this site is an informative page. Similarly, the high hub score for http://mages.google.com/ indicates that this site contains links to highly informative pages, like http://www.google.com/intl/iw/options/index.html.

5.8 Bibliographic Notes

Link Analysis techniques provide tools for classifying inferred entities that can be used in disciplines that rely on relational databases, such as direct marketing, customer relationship management, and financial decision making [40]. Its applications also include learning models of domains, such as counterterrorism detection, drug and other law enforcement, money laundering, and stock fraud [33]. Link mining techniques are useful when predicting the numbers and type of links between two objects, inferring the existence or the identity of an object by discovering subgraph patterns [14].

PageRank is used to provide a numerical importance ranking to every page by considering the incoming links to that page. PageRank originated with the idea of a random surfer starting at a page and then following outlinks from every page he visits. The 'Random Surfer' model is elucidated by L. Page *et al.* [30]. While computing the PageRank, we need to find a vector **r** with the PageRanks as components. We use another square matrix, **L**, where the fraction of incoming links from every other page is indicated. **r** is an eigenvector of **L** with eigenvalue $\lambda = 1$ and the power method uses this fact to compute this eigenvector, until it converges [5]. T. Haveliwala *et al.* [18] provide three different algorithms based on extrapolation methods to compute the eigenvectors. These are principally based on the techniques for extrapolation that are explained originally in [19].

The damping factor accounts for random selection of new random walk surfs. While the damping factor d is a value in the range [0,1], 0.85 is usually chosen as a standard value. Values closer to one are generally considered to be the best choice. P. Boldi *et al.* explain the effects of PageRank at the boundary values and how to select the right value of d [6]. The same issue is also explored in [13]. At a $d = 1$, the PageRank becomes linearly dependent on the backlink degree of vertices. Improvements for PageRank are possible and attempts have been made to make PageRank better using the popularity measure of a link between objects. Ranking lists that are calculated based on these popularities are used to produce popularity propagation factors, which are also used while ranking objects [27]. PageRank has become one of the most widely used object ranking algorithms on a daily basis thanks to the Google™ search engine, but it is still an open challenge that will continue being worked upon.

Given a graph, the problem of predicting newer links among the same set of vertices at a future point of time is called link prediction. Some practical illustrations of the problem are predicting possible friends in a friendship network and predicting collaborations among authors in a co-authorship network. Semantics is generally used to perform such activities, and a good background reading is provided in [34]. Data is generally relational in nature consisting of objects and links among them representing some useful relationship between the objects. Relational Markov Network is a solution to the problem of working with large relational data sets [35]. Using this concept, we can train models that when used in experiments have performed link prediction with acceptable levels of performance and accuracy [36].

Proximity measures like Euclidean distance are often used to enumerate and quantify the distance between clusters to roughly estimate the similarity between clusters in a physical distance perspective. Our chapter has explained link prediction from the point of view of proximity measures where we consider how various proximity measures can form scores, and proceed to predict based on such scores [29]. Tsuyoshi Murata *et al.* [23] take into account the weights of links, thereby taking the structure of the graph into consideration during link prediction. Although this is only a marginal deviation from what we have done, it has benefits over considering only proximity for link prediction. Co-authorship network-specific measures are author-keyword analysis and word-counts. A summary of prediction using supervised learning methods has been experimented with by Mohammed Al Hasan *et al.* [17]. Link prediction has exciting applications, especially considering the rapid growth of social network structures and the size of these networks.

Techniques such as classification, clustering, and association analysis rely on the data being represented in a single table or file [14]. Often, single table data limits the usability of the information and derives to uncertain and directly observed inferences that do not necessarily reach the data's full potential. The need for mining semi-structured data has thus increased, and the use of graphs as a data structure that represents symbolic sequences, trees and relations has been implemented. Graphs are the most generic topological structures, and their use in Link Mining is indispensable because structures, such as ordered and unordered trees, text tags, sequences and relational structures are sub-classes of general graphs [39].

Social networking sites account for a major market share in advertising in today's online world. Analysis of social networking sites, the interactions between different users, the information flow, the rate of the information flow, role played by each member in a social network, and comparisons between different social networks available are some of the issues gaining a lot of importance [7, 38]. The analysis results are used to determine how important a member of a social networking community is and, in general, how popular the given social network is. A lot of research is also taking place in protecting the privacy of the users during the release of the social networking site data for analysis. Factors like the identity of the members [4], the relationship between the members, implementing the privacy rules, automation of the rule-implementation process, etc., are being studied. Also, the reasons for the high usage of social networks are researched both to study the general user trend and to predict links in such networks.

5.9 Exercises

1. Why do you think PageRank was conceptualized? What would have happened had we just considered the number of backlinks to a page to rank a page high or low?

2. Let the adjacency matrix for a graph of four vertices (n_1 to n_4) be as follows:

$$A = \begin{bmatrix} 0 & 1 & 1 & 1 \\ 0 & 0 & 1 & 1 \\ 1 & 0 & 0 & 1 \\ 0 & 0 & 0 & 1 \end{bmatrix}.$$

Calculate the authority and hub scores for this graph using the HITS algorithm with $k = 6$, and identify the best authority and hub nodes.

3. Now that you know how the PageRank function in R works, try to

find the effect of changing the value of the damping factor in the example in Section 5.4.5 to the value 0.65 and note the changes.

4. Can you give any two advantages/disadvantages of the PageRank algorithm?

5. What is the complexity of the PageRank algorithm? Can you make an argument about why that is the complexity of this algorithm?

6. Is there a possibility that a website's PageRank would increase? What about the chances of it decreasing?

7. Given the HITS scoring vector

$$
\mathbf{x} = \begin{bmatrix} 3.12 \\ 4.38 \\ 6.93 \\ 3.41 \\ 1.88 \\ 4.53 \end{bmatrix},
$$

normalize $\mathbf{x}$ for the next iteration of the algorithm.

8. After reading Section 5.3 answer the following:

   (a) Define the density of a graph.
   (b) What does a TRUE for `is.isolate(graph,5)` indicate?
   (c) Given a graph variable 'graph' what is the difference between '`is.connected(graph)`' and '`connectedness(graph)`' in R?
   (d) Define the degree of a vertex in a graph.

9. (a) Explain the differences between the hub and authority scores in the HITS algorithm.
   (b) How could someone use the definitions to exploit the HITS algorithm?
   (c) Is it reasonable to use static (i.e., unchanging) data over the k iterations of HITS? Justify your answer.

10. Consider the graph (Figure 5.18) with 6 pages (A, B, C, D, E and F) where:
    $A \rightarrow B, C$
    $B \rightarrow A, D, E$
    $C \rightarrow A, F$
    $F \rightarrow B$

    Assume that the PageRank values for any page m at iteration 0 is $PR(m) = 1$ and that the damping factor for iterations is $d = 0.85$. Perform the PageRank algorithm and determine the rank for every page at iteration 2.

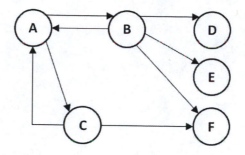

FIGURE 5.18: A simple graph for Question 10.

11. Consider the undirected graph (Figure 5.19) with 7 nodes (A, B, C, D, E, F and G) with the following edges:
    $A \rightarrow B, D$
    $B \rightarrow C, E, G$
    $C \rightarrow D, E$
    $D \rightarrow F$
    $E \rightarrow G$

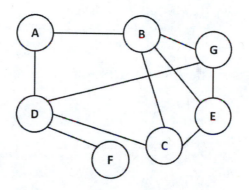

FIGURE 5.19: A simple graph for Question 11.

Using the Common Neighbors and the Jaccard's Coefficient methods, provide the ranked list in decreasing order of scores calculated by each proximity measure. Remember, the score values provided by the proximity measures are used to predict future links.

12. Consider the graph (Figure 5.20) with 7 pages (A, B, C, D, E, F and G) where:
    $A \rightarrow B$
    $B \rightarrow A, C, D, E$
    $C \rightarrow A, E$

$$D \rightarrow C$$
$$E \rightarrow G$$
$$F \rightarrow E, G$$
$$G \rightarrow A, F$$

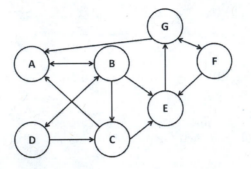

FIGURE 5.20: A graph for Question 12.

Assume that the PageRank values for any page m at iteration 0 is $PR(m) = 1$ and that the damping factor for iterations is $d = 0.85$. An additional page H is added to the graph, where the page has a single outlink to one (and only one) of the previous existing pages. The PageRank values for this new graph on iteration 2 are the following.

$PR(A) = 1.4834375$ $PR(B) = 1.180625$
$PR(C) = 1.393125$
$PR(D) = 0.49$
$PR(E) = 1.1221875$
$PR(F) = 0.755625$
$PR(G) = 1.425$
$PR(H) = 0.15$

(a) Determine to what page H outlinks.

(b) Would the change in the graph dramatically affect the PageRank values for every node if more iterations are performed? Why/Why not? Justify?

13. Consider Figure 5.21. It depicts pages A, B and C with no inlinks, and with initial PageRank = 1. Initially, none of the pages link to any other pages and none link to them.

Answer the following questions, and calculate the PageRank for each question.

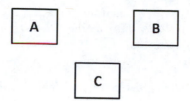

FIGURE 5.21: A graph for Question 13.

(a) Link page A to page B.
(b) Link all pages to each other.
(c) Link page A to both B and C, and link pages B and C to A.
(d) Use the previous links and add a link from page C to page B.

Bibliography

[1] L. Adamic. The small world web. In *Proceedings of the 3rd European Conference on Research and Advanced Technology for Digital Libraries*, pages 443–452, 1999.

[2] L. Adamic and E. Adar. Friends and neighbors on the Web. *Social Networks*, 25:211–230, 2001.

[3] D. Austin. How Google finds your needle in the Web's haystack. *American Mathematical Society Feature Column*, 2006.

[4] L. Backstrom, C. Dwork, and J.M. Kleinberg. Wherefore art thou R3579X?: Anonymized social networks, hidden patterns, and structural steganography. In *Proceedings of the 16th International Conference on World Wide Web*, pages 181–190, 2007.

[5] P. Berkhin. A survey on PageRank computing. *Internet Mathematics*, 2:73–120, 2005.

[6] P. Boldi, M. Santini, and S. Vigna. PageRank as a function of the damping factor. In *Proceedings of the 14th International Conference on World Wide Web*, pages 557–566, 2005.

[7] D. Boyd. Why youth (heart) social network sites: The role of networked publics in teenage social life. In *MacArthur Foundation Series on Digital Learning: Youth, Identity, and Digital Media Volume*. MIT Press, 2007.

[8] S. Brin and L. Page. The anatomy of a large-scale hypertextual Web search engine. In *Proceedings of the 7th International Conference on World Wide Web*, pages 107–117, 1998.

[9] K. Bryan and T. Leise. The $25,000,000,000 eigenvector: The linear algebra behind Google. *SIAM Review*, 48:569–581, 2006.

[10] D.J. Cook and L.B. Holder. *Mining Graph Data*. John Wiley & Sons, 2006.

[11] D. Coppersmith and S. Winograd. Matrix multiplication via arithmetic progression. *Journal of Symbolic Computation*, 9:251–290, 1990.

[12] P. Desikan and J. Srivastava. Analyzing network traffic to detect e-mail spamming machines. In *Proceedings of the ICDM Workshop on Privacy and Security Aspects of Data Mining*, pages 67–76, 2004.

[13] S. Fortunato and A. Flammini. Random walks on directed networks: The case of PageRank. *International Journal of Bifurcation and Chaos*, 17:2343–2353, 2007.

[14] L. Getoor. Link mining: A new data mining challenge. *ACM SIGKDD Explorations Newsletter*, 5:84–89, 2003.

[15] L. Getoor and Christopher P. Diehl. Link mining: A survey. *ACM SIGKDD Explorations Newsletter*, 7:3–12, 2005.

[16] J.W. Grossman. The evolution of the mathematical research collaboration graph. *Congressus Numerantium*, pages 201–212, 2002.

[17] M.A Hasan, V. Chaoji, S. Salem, and M.J. Zaki. Link prediction using supervised learning. In *Proceedings of the 4th Workshop on Link Analysis, Counter-terrorism and Security*, 2006.

[18] T. Haveliwala, S. Kamvar, D. Klein, C. Manning, and G. Golub. Computing PageRank using power extrapolation. *Technical Report, Stanford InfoLab*, 2003.

[19] S.D. Kamvar, T.H. Haveliwala, C.D. Manning, and G.H. Golub. Extrapolation methods for accelerating PageRank computations. In *Proceedings of the 12th International Conference on World Wide Web*, pages 261–270, 2003.

[20] J.M. Kleinberg. Authoritative sources in a hyperlinked environment. *Journal of the ACM*, 46:668–677, 1999.

[21] D. Knoke and S. Yang. *Social Network Analysis*. Sage Publications, 2008.

[22] Amy N. Langville and Carl D. Meyer. A survey of eigenvector methods for web information retrieval. *SIAM Review*, 47:135–161, 2005.

[23] T. Murata and S. Moriyasu. Link prediction of social networks based on weighted proximity measures. In *Proceedings of the IEEE/WIC/ACM International Conference on Web Intelligence*, pages 85–88, 2007.

[24] M.A. Najork. Comparing the effectiveness of HITS and SALSA. In *Proceedings of the 16th ACM Conference on Information and Knowledge Management*, pages 157–164, 2007.

[25] M.E J. Newman. Clustering and preferential attachment in growing networks. *Physical Review E*, 64:025102, 2001.

[26] M.E.J. Newman. The structure of scientific collaboration networks. *Proceedings of the National Academy of Sciences of the United States of America*, 98:404–409, 2001.

[27] Z. Nie, Y. Zhang, J. R. Wen, and W. Y. Ma. Object-level ranking: Bringing order to web objects. In *Proceedings of the 14th International Conference on World Wide Web*, pages 567–574, 2005.

[28] S. Nomura, S. Oyama, T. Hayamizu, and T. Ishida. Analysis and improvement of hits algorithm for detecting web communities. *Systems and Computers in Japan*, 35:32–42, 2004.

[29] D.L. Nowell and J. Kleinberg. The link prediction problem for social networks. In *Proceedings of the 12th International Conference on Information and Knowledge Management*, pages 556–559, 2003.

[30] L. Page, S. Brin, R. Motwani, and T. Winograd. The PageRank citation ranking: Bringing order to the Web. *Technical Report, Stanford InfoLab*, 1998.

[31] E. Peserico and L. Pretto. Score and rank convergence of HITS. In *Proceedings of the 32nd International ACM SIGIR Conference on Research and Development in Information Retrieval*, pages 770–771, 2009.

[32] A. Popescul and L.H. Ungar. Statistical relational learning for link prediction. In *Proceedings of the 2nd Workshop on Learning Statistical Models from Relational Data*, pages 109–115, 2003.

[33] T. Senator. Link mining applications: Progress and challenges. *ACM SIGKDD Explorations Newsletter*, 7:76–83, 2005.

[34] S. Staab, P. Domingos, P. Mike, J. Golbeck, Li Ding, T. Finin, A. Joshi, A. Nowak, and R. R. Vallacher. Social networks applied. *IEEE Intelligent Systems*, 20:80–93, 2005.

[35] B. Taskar, P. Abbeel, and D. Koller. Discriminative probabilistic models for relational data. In *Proceedings of the 18th Conference on Uncertainty in Artificial Intelligence*, pages 895–902, 2002.

[36] B. Taskar, M. Wong, P. Abbeel, and D. Koller. Link prediction in rela-
     tional data. In *Proceedings of 17th Annual Conference on Neural Infor-
     mation Processing Systems*, 2004.

[37] Carter T.B. Social network analysis with sna. *Journal of Statistical
     Software*, 24:1–51, 2008.

[38] A.L. Traud, E.D. Kelsic, P.J. Mucha, and M.A. Porter. Comparing com-
     munity structure to characteristics in online collegiate social networks.
     SIAM Review, 53:526–543, 2011.

[39] T. Washio and H. Motoda. State of the art of graph-based data mining.
     ACM SIGKDD Explorations Newsletter, 5:59–68, 2003.

[40] X. Yin. Scalable mining and link analysis across multiple database rela-
     tions. *ACM SIGKDD Explorations Newsletter*, 10:26–27, 2008.

6

Graph-based Proximity Measures

Kevin A. Wilson, Nathan D. Green, Laxmikant Agrawal, Xibin Gao, Dinesh Madhusoodanan, Brian Riley, and James P. Sigmon

North Carolina State University

CONTENTS

6.1 Defining the Proximity of Vertices in Graphs

In order to apply several different graph-based data mining techniques like classification and clustering (discussed further in Chapter 9 Classification, and Chapter 8, Cluster Analysis, respectively), it is necessary to first define proximity measures between vertices in a single graph. This chapter focuses on within-graph proximity measures that will be used in the application of several data mining techniques later in the book. We introduce two different algorithms for measuring proximity between vertices in a graph:

1. **Shared Nearest Neighbor (SNN).** Shared Nearest Neighbor defines proximity, or *similarity*, between two vertices in terms of the number of neighbors (i.e., directly connected vertices) they have in common. SNN is described in detail in Section 6.2.3.

2. **The Neumann Kernel.** The Neumann Kernel is a generalization of HITS described in Chapter 5 that models the *relatedness* of vertices within a graph based on the number of immediate and more distant connections between vertices. It uses a tunable parameter to control how much weight is given to the more distant connections, which can produce results based entirely on the immediate neighbors or results that take the full structure of the graph into consideration, like HITS. Section 6.3 discusses Neumann Kernels.

Before we proceed it is important to define some common terminology and notation. Table 6.1 defines the key terms in this chapter with which the reader should be familiar. To ensure consistency, Table 6.2 defines the notation that will be used throughout the chapter.

TABLE 6.1: Glossary of terms used in this chapter

Term	Description
Citation graph	A citation graph is a representation that shows the citation relationships (cited references and citing articles) between two objects (e.g., articles, documents or papers).
Co-citation matrix	A matrix that connects vertices cited by the same source
Bibliographic coupling matrix	A matrix that connects vertices with one or more shared bibliographic references
Diffusion factor	A tunable parameter that controls the balance between relatedness and importance
Term-document matrix	A matrix in which the rows represent terms, columns represent documents, and entries represent a function of their relationship (e.g., frequency of a given term in a document)
Document correlation matrix	A matrix in which the rows and the columns represent documents, and entries represent the semantic similarity between two documents
Term correlation matrix	A matrix in which the rows and the columns represent terms, and entries represent the semantic similarity between two terms
Neumann Kernel	A specific kernel function applied to computing term-document similarity

TABLE 6.2: Description of notation used in this chapter

General notation	Meaning
G	A directed, unweighted, simple graph
$V(G)$	Vertex set of graph G
$E(G)$	Edge set of graph G
$|V(G)|$	Number of vertices in graph G
$\mathbf{A}$	Adjacency matrix derived from graph G
$\mathbf{A}^{-1}$	Inverse of matrix $\mathbf{A}$
$\mathbf{I}$	Identity matrix
$|\delta^+(v)|$	Outdegree of vertex v
$|\delta^-(v)|$	Indegree of vertex v
$\Delta^+(G)$	Maximum outdegree of graph G
$\Delta^-(G)$	Maximum indegree of graph G

HITS notation	Meaning
$\mathbf{x}$	Column vector containing the authority weights
$\mathbf{y}$	Column vector containing the hub weights
$\mathcal{I}$	Operation that updates the set of authority weights ($\mathbf{x}$)
$\mathcal{O}$	Operation that updates the set of hub weights ($\mathbf{y}$)
k	Number of iterations to run the algorithm
$\mathbf{x}^{(i)}$	Authority weight vector after the ith iteration
$\mathbf{y}^{(i)}$	Hub weight vector after the ith iteration
$\mathbf{x}^{(0)}$	Initial authority weight vector
$\mathbf{y}^{(0)}$	Initial hub weight vector
x_j	Hub weight for vertex j
y_j	Authority weight for vertex j

Neumann Kernel notation	Meaning
$\mathbf{X}$	Term-document matrix
$\mathbf{K}$	Document correlation matrix
$\mathbf{T}$	Term correlation matrix
$\mathbf{C}$	Citation matrix
$\mathbf{B}$	Bibliographic coupling matrix
$\mathbf{P}$	Co-citation coupling matrix
λ_m	Maximum eigenvalue of matrix
γ	Diffusion/Decay factor

SNN notation	Meaning
k	Number of nearest neighbors to include in proximity calculation

6.2 Shared Nearest Neighbor

In Shared Nearest Neighbor (SNN), vertices are characterized by their neighbors. The underlying assumption is that if two vertices have several neighbors in common, then they are more likely to be similar. Figure 6.1 provides a high-level overview of the SNN algorithm.

   This section begins with an introduction to proximity graphs, illustrated through an example of similar web pages. We then discuss the concept of nearest neighbors, a proximity measure based on the number of neighbors of a given vertex. Finally, we discuss the SNN proximity measure in detail.

6.2.1 Proximity Graphs

A proximity, or similarity, graph on a set of objects is a graph obtained by connecting two objects in the set by an edge if the two objects are similar to each other in some sense. Proximity measures are used to determine the extent to which the two vertices are connected or belong to a common group. The specific definition of proximity depends on the specific application for which it is used. For example, in a co-authorship network, authors might be connected if they publish in the same field or in the same journals. In other cases, proximity can estimate the likelihood that a missing link will exist in the future, as we discussed in Chapter 5, Link Analysis. For instance, on social networking sites, the missing link might represent the communities a user would like to join. Proximity measures can also be used to track the propagation of a product or an idea within a social network setting.

   Consider the graphs shown in Figures 6.2 and 6.3. If we define two vertices to be similar if they are connected by an edge, then vertex s_1 in Figure 6.2 is similar to a_1 and vertex a_1 is similar to t_1. If we define two vertices to be similar if they share common neighbors, then vertices s_2 and t_2 in Figure 6.3

FIGURE 6.1: A high-level overview of the SNN algorithm described in detail in Algorithm 6.

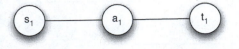

FIGURE 6.2: Example proximity graph in which vertices are similar only if they are connected by an edge.

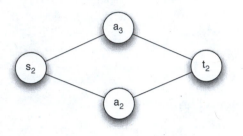

FIGURE 6.3: Proximity graph to show proximity based on vertices sharing neighbors.

can be considered similar because they share a_2 and a_3 as common neighbors. This definition of proximity forms the basis of the SNN proximity measure. Though vertices s_2 and t_2 are considered similar for sharing two neighbors, we can generalize this concept, so that only vertices that share *at least* k neighbors are considered similar, for some integer k.

Before discussing SNN similarity, it is important to understand the concept of the k-Nearest Neighbor (KNN) graph. The KNN graph is a proximity graph created by connecting each vertex in an edge-weighted graph to its k nearest vertices. The result is a graph such that each vertex $v \in V(G)$ is linked with k of its nearest neighbors, where k is between 0 and $|V(G)|$.

A naïve approach for constructing the KNN graph would compare every pair of vertices in the graph and run in $O(|V(G)|^2)$ time; however, the KNN graph can be calculated in $O(k|V(G)|log(|V(G)|))$ [6]. The KNN graph has applications in cluster analysis and outlier detection.

For example, consider the proximity graph described in Table 6.3. This table gives pairwise proximity values among six objects. For a value of $k = 2$, the KNN graph appears in Figure 6.4.

In the rest of this chapter, we focus on creating an SNN graph.

TABLE 6.3: An example of a proximity matrix

points	x_1	x_2	x_3	x_4	x_5	x_6
x_1	0	1.5	1.6	2.8	1.7	2.1
x_2	1.5	0	2	3	4	4.5
x_3	1.6	2	0	1.1	1.2	2.6
x_4	2.8	3	1.1	0	3	2
x_5	1.7	4	1.2	3	0	1.1
x_6	2	4.5	2.6	2	1.1	0

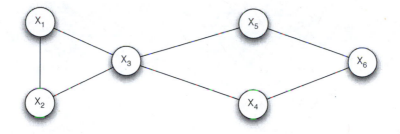

FIGURE 6.4: The KNN graph obtained from the proximity matrix in Table 6.3 and $k = 2$.

6.2.2 Computing the Similarity of Web Pages

This section introduces an alternative to direct similarity measures [6], Shared Nearest Neighbor. SNN is an indirect approach to similarity based on the principle that if two vertices have more than k neighbors in common, then they can be considered similar to one another, even if a direct edge between them does not exist.

We illustrate the concept of an SNN using the undirected graph of web pages in Figure 6.5. In the figure, the vertices of the graph represent web pages, and the edges represent hyperlinks between the web pages. The adjacency matrix appears in Table 6.4. In R, this graph can be constructed as follows.

```
1 #Get all required packages
2 library(igraph)
3 library(ProximityMeasure)
4 #Adjacency matrix for web pages graph
5 A<-matrix(c(0, 1, 0, 0, 1, 0,
6             1, 0, 1, 0, 1, 0,
7             0, 1, 0, 1, 0, 0,
8             0, 0, 1, 0, 1, 1,
```

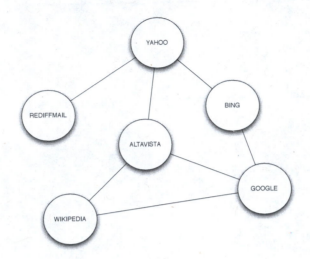

FIGURE 6.5: Undirected graph of web page links for SNN proximity measure.

TABLE 6.4: Adjacency matrix for the undirected proximity graph illustrated in Figure 6.5

	Wiki	Google	Bing	Yahoo	Altavista	Rediff
Wikipedia	0	1	0	0	1	0
Google	1	0	1	0	1	0
Bing	0	1	0	1	0	0
Yahoo	0	0	1	0	1	1
Altavista	1	1	0	1	0	0
Rediffmail	0	0	0	1	0	0

```
 9                  1, 1, 0, 1, 0, 0,
10                  0, 0, 0, 1, 0, 0),
11                  nrow=6,ncol=6,FALSE);
12 #Labeling all vertices of graph by respective web pages
13 G = graph.adjacency(A)
14 V(G)$label<-c("Wikipedia","Google",
15                  "Bing","Yahoo","Altavista","Rediffmail");
```

We first load the required packages, igraph and ProximityMeasure, then define the adjacency matrix for the graph. Finally, we label the vertices to match the graph shown in Figure 6.5. We can observe from the graph that the vertices representing Altavista and Bing have two shared vertices, namely Yahoo and Google, whereas Yahoo and Google share Altavista and Bing as neighbors. We can identify these "shared nearest neighbors" in R by using the SNN_GRAPH function to identify all the vertices that have two shared neighbors:

```
 1 #Converting adjacency matrix to graph
 2 G<-graph.adjacency(A,mode=
 3                          c("undirected"),weighted=NULL);
 4 #Set minimum number of shared neighbors in SNN graph
 5 k<-2;
 6 #Calling SNN function
 7 G2<-SNN_GRAPH(A , k);
 8 #Plot the SNN graph returned by SNN_GRAPH function.
 9 tkplot(G2,vertex.label.color="black",
10                          vertex.size=29);
```

Prior to running the algorithm we convert the adjacency matrix to an R graph and set the number of shared neighbors, $k = 2$. We then run the SNN algorithm and plot the result, which is shown in Figure 6.6. Thus, the SNN_GRAPH function returns a graph of connected vertices that have at least k shared neighbors, where k is an input parameter that can be changed as required by the application.

In Figure 6.6, the vertices that have at least two common neighbors are connected by an edge. At a value of $k = 2$, "Altavisa" and "Bing" are similar to each other, as are "Google" and "Yahoo." Having worked through an example, we are now in a position to formally define the Shared Nearest Neighbor proximity measure.

6.2.3 Shared Nearest Neighbor Definition

This section formally introduces the Shared Nearest Neighbor graph.

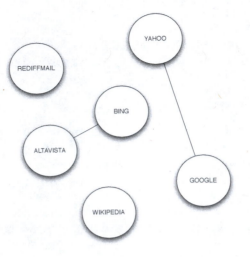

FIGURE 6.6: Graph illustrating the results of the SNN Algorithm applied to the graph shown in Figure 6.5, with $k = 2$.

An SNN graph is a special type of KNN graph in which an edge exists between two vertices v_i and v_j if there are at least k vertices adjacent to both v_i and v_j. The formal definition of the SNN graph appears below.

Definition 6.1 *Shared Nearest Neighbor graph*
Let $V = \{v_1, v_2, v_3, \ldots, v_n\}$ be the set of nodes in a KNN graph G. In the SNN graph derived from G, the neighbors of v_i are the nodes $v_j, j \neq i$, such that v_i and v_j have at least k neighbors in common or, equivalently, if there exist at least k distinct paths of length two between v_i and v_j in G.

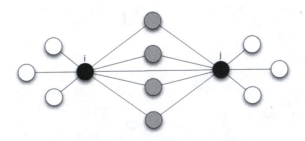

FIGURE 6.7: A KNN graph.

In Figure 6.7, each of the two black vertices i and j have eight near-

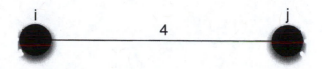

FIGURE 6.8: An SNN graph derived from the KNN graph of Figure 6.7, where $k = 4$.

est neighbors, including each other. Four of those nearest neighbors are shared, shown in gray. Thus, the two black vertices are similar when $k = 4$ because vertices v_i and v_j share four common neighbors. This similarity is indicated by an edge between them in the SNN graph in Figure 6.8.

Algorithm 6 illustrates how the SNN graph can be calculated for an unweighted KNN graph G. Since there are three nested loops in the algorithm, the computational complexity for Algorithm 6 is $O(n^3)$. Note that if G is a weighted graph, we can apply this algorithm to the KNN graph of G.

Input: G—an undirected graph
Input: k—a natural number (number of shared neighbors)
Output: G'—Shared Nearest Neighbor graph.

1 Initialize the SNN graph G' with $|V(G)|$ vertices and no edges
2 **foreach** $i = 1$ to $V(G)$ **do**
3   **foreach** $j = i + 1$ to $V(G)$ **do**
4   *counter* = 0
5   **foreach** $m = 1$ to $V(G)$ **do**
6   **if** vertex i and vertex j both have an edge with vertex m **then**
7   *counter* = *counter* + 1
8   **end**
9   **if** *counter* $\geq k$ **then**
10   Connect an edge between vertex i and vertex j in G'
11   **end**
12 **end**
13 **return** G'

Algorithm 6: SNN Algorithm

A more efficient way to calculate the SNN graph is to use the fact that the number of common neighbors between two different vertices equals the number of paths of length two between them. If $\mathbf{A}$ is the adjacency matrix of graph G, then $\mathbf{A}^2$ counts the number of paths of length two between every pair

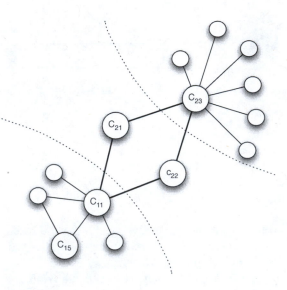

FIGURE 6.9: Figure indicating the ability of shared nearest neighbor to form links between nodes in different clusters.

of vertices, and if we are using efficient matrix multiplication, this calculation requires less than $O(n^3)$ time.

6.2.4 Strengths and Weaknesses

One of the main advantages of SNN is that it considers not only direct associations between vertices, but also indirect connections. This ability can be used to find similarities between vertices that are not adjacent.

Another advantage of SNN in the context of clustering (see Chapter 8, Clustering) is its ability to handle clusters of varying size, shape, and density. One situation that SNN handles well is when two nodes are relatively close, but the nodes belong to different clusters, illustrated in Figure 6.9.

However, SNN does not take into account the weight of the links between the vertices in a graph. For example, SNN could establish a link between two vertices with common neighbors that are not very strongly related to the vertices, which may represent poor similarity.

6.3 Evaluating Relatedness Using Neumann Kernels

With SNN, we dealt with undirected but possibly edge-weighted graphs. In this section, we introduce a concept of proximity that works for both directed and undirected graphs. As an example of a directed graph, if nodes correspond to journal articles, then directed edges may correspond to a citation of one article by another.

Ito *et al.* [10] and Shimbo *et al.* [16] developed a kernel-based framework for calculating both *importance* and *relatedness*. They show that the HITS algorithm (described in Chapter 5, Link Analysis) can be generalized using a Neumann Kernel, resulting in an efficient and powerful mechanism for determining "relatedness" between vertices.

When considering relatedness, we emphasize two techniques: co-citations and bibliographic couplings. Co-citation is calculated between a pair of documents and is a measure of how many documents cite both documents in this pair. Bibliographic coupling is a measure of how many common citations exist in both of the documents. Each of these can be easily obtained from the adjacency matrix of the graph; however, unlike with web hyperlink data, both of these graphs are undirected (there is no order to citations, etc.).

6.3.1 Calculating Co-citation and Bibliographic Coupling

To illustrate how the Neumann Kernel represents relatedness and importance, we consider an example of citations in journal articles [10]. Figure 6.10 represents eight journal articles and the citations that exist between them. In this graph, each vertex represents a journal article, and each directed edge represents a citation of one article by another. We can define the adjacency matrix for this graph using R.

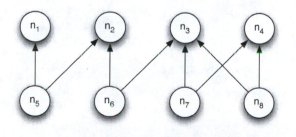

FIGURE 6.10: Directed graph to model journal article citations, where each edge indicates citations of one article by another. For example, article n_5 cites both articles n_1 and n_2.

```
1  #Adjacency matrix for citation graph
2  C<-matrix(c(0,0, 0, 0, 0, 0, 0, 0,
3             0, 0, 0, 0, 0, 0, 0, 0,
4             0, 0, 0, 0, 0, 0, 0, 0,
5             0, 0, 0, 0, 0, 0, 0, 0,
6             1, 1, 0, 0, 0, 0, 0, 0,
7             0, 1, 1, 0, 0, 0, 0, 0,
8             0, 0, 1, 1, 0, 0, 0, 0,
9             0, 0, 1, 1, 0, 0, 0, 0),
10            nrow=8,ncol=8,
11            byrow=TRUE)
```

As stated above, co-citation and bibliographic coupling are two measures of vertex relatedness. Figure 6.11 illustrates the co-citation graph and bibliographic coupling graph for the citation graph shown in Figure 6.10. In the bibliographic coupling graph, two journal articles (vertices) are connected if both of them cite at least one common journal article. In Figure 6.11 (A), nodes n_5 and n_6 are connected by an edge of weight 1 because they cite only one common node, n_2. Similarly, in Figure 6.11 (B), nodes n_3 and n_4 are connected by an edge of weight 2 because they are both cited by nodes n_7 and n_8.

Both of these graphs can be generated directly from the adjacency matrix of the citation graph. The formal definitions for the bibliographic coupling and co-citation matrices are as follows.

Definition 6.2 *Bibliographic coupling matrix*
The bibliographic coupling matrix, **B**, is defined as:

$$\mathbf{B} = \mathbf{CC}^{\mathbf{T}},$$

where **C** is the adjacency matrix of the citation graph.

Definition 6.3 *Co-citation matrix*
The co-citation matrix, **P**, is defined as:

$$\mathbf{P} = \mathbf{C}^{\mathbf{T}}\mathbf{C},$$

where **C** is the adjacency matrix of the citation graph.

We can calculate the co-citation matrix **P** as follows:

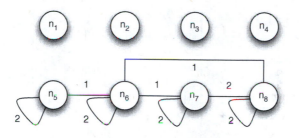

(A) Bibliographic coupling graph.

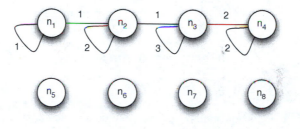

(B) Co-citation graph.

FIGURE 6.11: Bibliographic coupling graph (A) and co-citation graph (B) for the citation graph in Figure 6.10.

$$\mathbf{P} = \mathbf{C}^T\mathbf{C} \tag{6.1}$$

$$
= \begin{bmatrix}
0 & 0 & 0 & 0 & 1 & 0 & 0 & 0 \\
0 & 0 & 0 & 0 & 1 & 1 & 0 & 0 \\
0 & 0 & 0 & 0 & 0 & 1 & 1 & 1 \\
0 & 0 & 0 & 0 & 0 & 0 & 1 & 1 \\
0 & 0 & 0 & 0 & 0 & 0 & 0 & 0 \\
0 & 0 & 0 & 0 & 0 & 0 & 0 & 0 \\
0 & 0 & 0 & 0 & 0 & 0 & 0 & 0 \\
0 & 0 & 0 & 0 & 0 & 0 & 0 & 0
\end{bmatrix}
\tag{6.2}
$$

$$
\times \begin{bmatrix}
0 & 0 & 0 & 0 & 0 & 0 & 0 & 0 \\
0 & 0 & 0 & 0 & 0 & 0 & 0 & 0 \\
0 & 0 & 0 & 0 & 0 & 0 & 0 & 0 \\
0 & 0 & 0 & 0 & 0 & 0 & 0 & 0 \\
1 & 1 & 0 & 0 & 0 & 0 & 0 & 0 \\
0 & 1 & 1 & 0 & 0 & 0 & 0 & 0 \\
0 & 0 & 1 & 1 & 0 & 0 & 0 & 0 \\
0 & 0 & 1 & 1 & 0 & 0 & 0 & 0
\end{bmatrix}
\tag{6.3}
$$

$$
= \begin{bmatrix}
1 & 1 & 0 & 0 & 0 & 0 & 0 & 0 \\
1 & 2 & 1 & 0 & 0 & 0 & 0 & 0 \\
0 & 1 & 3 & 2 & 0 & 0 & 0 & 0 \\
0 & 0 & 2 & 2 & 0 & 0 & 0 & 0 \\
0 & 0 & 0 & 0 & 0 & 0 & 0 & 0 \\
0 & 0 & 0 & 0 & 0 & 0 & 0 & 0 \\
0 & 0 & 0 & 0 & 0 & 0 & 0 & 0 \\
0 & 0 & 0 & 0 & 0 & 0 & 0 & 0
\end{bmatrix}
\tag{6.4}
$$

In R, this calculation can be performed using the matrix multiplication and matrix transpose functions:

```
1 t(C) %*% C
```

Similarly, we can calculate the bibliographic coupling matrix as $\mathbf{B} = \mathbf{C} \cdot \mathbf{C}^T$. In R, we calculate this matrix using:

```
1 C %*% t(C)
```

Co-citation and bibliographic coupling can be applied as a measure of relatedness to a domain such as journal article citations. Although the application appears limited, this technique is generalizable to many different domains through the use of Neumann Kernels. In the next section, we will show that the concepts of co-citation and bibliographic coupling are analogous to the concepts of "document correlation matrix" and "term correlation matrix" from the information retrieval field. We leverage this equivalence to provide a formal definition for the Neumann Kernel.

TABLE 6.5: Term-document matrix for the sentences "I like this book" and "We wrote this book"

	D_1	D_2
I	1	0
like	1	0
this	1	1
book	1	1
We	0	1
wrote	0	1

6.3.2 Document and Term Correlation

The Neumann Kernel method was originally developed by Kandola, Shawe-Taylor and Cristianini [12] for information retrieval, and it can be applied to documents, papers, articles, journals, and other types of data. Shimbo *et al.* [16] describe the algorithm in terms of matrix operations on a term-document matrix.

Definition 6.4 *Term-document matrix*
The term-document matrix $\mathbf{X}$ represents a relationship between documents and terms in those documents, where documents are represented as columns, terms are represented as rows, and entries in the matrix are the number of times a given term appears in a given document. A term-document matrix can be viewed as a bipartite graph where one partite set corresponds to the documents and the other corresponds to terms contained in the documents.

Consider the two short documents:

$D_1 = $ "I like this book," and
$D_2 = $ "We wrote this book."

The term-document matrix $\mathbf{X}$ for the above example is shown in Table 6.5. For example, in the given documents, the term 'book' appears once in each of the documents, so the corresponding entries in the matrix are both one.

Given a term-document matrix, we can generate a document correlation matrix, which is a matrix that summarizes the common terms between a series of documents. In the previous example, documents D_1 and D_2 have two terms in common, 'this' and 'book.' The document correlation matrix for this example appears in Table 6.6. We formally define the document correlation matrix below.

TABLE 6.6: Document correlation matrix for the sentences "I like this book" and "We wrote this book"

	D_1	D_2
D_1	4	2
D_2	2	4

TABLE 6.7: Term correlation matrix for the sentences "I like this book" and "We wrote this book"

	I	like	this	book	We	wrote
I	1	1	1	1	0	0
like	1	1	1	1	0	0
this	1	1	2	2	1	1
book	1	1	2	2	1	1
We	0	0	1	1	1	1
wrote	0	0	1	1	1	1

Definition 6.5 *Document correlation matrix*
The document correlation matrix $\mathbf{K}$ is defined by:

$$\mathbf{K} = \mathbf{X}^{\mathbf{T}}\mathbf{X},$$

where $\mathbf{X}$ is the original term-document matrix.

We can also define a term correlation matrix $\mathbf{T}$, which represents the co-occurrence of terms in a set of documents. The term correlation matrix for our earlier example is shown in Table 6.7. For example, the term 'this' appears twice with the term 'book' (once in each of the documents). Hence, the corresponding value in the term correlation matrix is 2. We formally define the term correlation matrix below.

Definition 6.6 *Term correlation matrix*
The term correlation matrix $\mathbf{T}$ is defined by:

$$\mathbf{T} = \mathbf{X}\mathbf{X}^{\mathbf{T}},$$

where $\mathbf{X}$ is the original term-document matrix.

6.3.3 Neumann Kernels in Practice

Neumann Kernels provide a generalized framework for scoring vertices in terms of importance (similar to HITS) or relatedness (similar to co-citation and bibliographic coupling) based on the value of a configurable parameter,

TABLE 6.8: Adjacency matrix for the directed graph in Figure 6.10

	n_1	n_2	n_3	n_4	n_5	n_6	n_7	n_8
n_1	0	0	0	0	0	0	0	0
n_2	0	0	0	0	0	0	0	0
n_3	0	0	0	0	0	0	0	0
n_4	0	0	0	0	0	0	0	0
n_5	1	1	0	0	0	0	0	0
n_6	0	1	1	0	0	0	0	0
n_7	0	0	1	1	0	0	0	0
n_8	0	0	1	1	0	0	0	0

the *decay factor*, denoted by γ. We discuss how to choose a value for γ and the implications of different values for γ in the next two sections. First, though, we illustrate the general operation of the Neumann Kernel algorithm, followed by its formal derivation. This section links together the previous sections on the co-citation and bibliographic coupling relatedness measures and term and document correlation matrices.

Table 6.8 defines the adjacency matrix for the graph shown in Figure 6.10. Given the citation matrix in Table 6.8, we can use R to calculate the Neumann Kernel:

```
1  #Get all required packages
2  library(igraph)
3  library(ProximityMeasure)
4  #Encode graph as adjacency matrix
5  C<-matrix(c(0, 0, 0, 0, 0, 0, 0, 0,
6             0, 0, 0, 0, 0, 0, 0, 0,
7             0, 0, 0, 0, 0, 0, 0, 0,
8             0, 0, 0, 0, 0, 0, 0, 0,
9             1, 1, 0, 0, 0, 0, 0, 0,
10            0, 1, 1, 0, 0, 0, 0, 0,
11            0, 0, 1, 1, 0, 0, 0, 0,
12            0, 0, 1, 1, 0, 0, 0, 0),
13            nrow=8,ncol=8,
14            byrow=TRUE)
15 #Create graph from adjacency matrix
16 G<-graph.adjacency(C,mode=c("directed"),weighted=NULL)
17 #Call to Neumann Kernel function for graph G.
18 Neumann_Kernel(G)
```

6.3.4   Derivation of Neumann Kernels

The Neumann Kernel in its original form is defined in terms of the term-document matrix $\mathbf{X}$. In preparation for computing the Neumann Kernels, we first compute the document correlation matrix $\mathbf{K} = \mathbf{X^T X}$ and term correlation matrix $\mathbf{T} = \mathbf{X X^T}$ [10]. The Neumann Kernel defines two matrices, $\widehat{\mathbf{K}}_\gamma$ and $\widehat{\mathbf{T}}_\gamma$, with γ as a decay factor. These matrices are defined mathematically as follows:

$$N_\gamma(\mathbf{K}) = \quad \widehat{\mathbf{K}}_\gamma = \quad N_\gamma(\mathbf{X^T X}) = \quad \mathbf{X^T X} + \gamma(\mathbf{X^T X})^2 + \dots \quad (6.5)$$

$$N_\gamma(\mathbf{T}) = \quad \widehat{\mathbf{T}}_\gamma = \quad N_\gamma(\mathbf{X X^T}) = \quad \mathbf{X X^T} + \gamma(\mathbf{X X^T})^2 + \dots \quad (6.6)$$

Equation 6.5 computes a weighted sum of $(\mathbf{X^T X})^n$ over every natural number n. Since the (i, j)-element of $(\mathbf{X^T X})^n$ represents the number of paths of length n between vertices i and j in the matrix $\mathbf{X^T X}$, each element in the kernel matrix represents a weighted sum of the number of paths between vertices. In other words, these equations relate not just documents or terms that share an edge, but also documents or terms that are more distantly connected [10].

In the above equations, $\widehat{\mathbf{K}}_\gamma$ gives the similarity between documents and $\widehat{\mathbf{T}}_\gamma$ gives the similarity between terms, as $\mathbf{X^T X}$ (which is equal to the document correlation matrix $\mathbf{K}$) appears in Equation 6.5 and $\mathbf{X X^T}$ (which is equal to the term correlation matrix $\mathbf{T}$) appears in Equation 6.6. Each of these equations uses γ to control the balance between importance and relatedness.

Now, we will try to simplify the equations so that we can compute the values of $\widehat{\mathbf{K}}_\gamma$ and $\widehat{\mathbf{T}}_\gamma$ more easily. Equations 6.5 and 6.6 can be rewritten as:

$$\widehat{\mathbf{K}}_\gamma = \mathbf{X^T X} \sum_{n=0}^{\infty} \gamma^n (\mathbf{X^T X})^n \qquad (6.7)$$

$$\widehat{\mathbf{T}}_\gamma = \mathbf{X X^T} \sum_{n=0}^{\infty} \gamma^n (\mathbf{X X^T})^n \qquad (6.8)$$

Since $\mathbf{K} = \mathbf{X^T X}$ and $\mathbf{T} = \mathbf{X X^T}$, Equations 6.7 and 6.8 become:

$$\widehat{\mathbf{K}}_\gamma = \mathbf{K} \sum_{n=0}^{\infty} \gamma^n \mathbf{K}^n \qquad (6.9)$$

$$\widehat{\mathbf{T}}_\gamma = \mathbf{T} \sum_{n=0}^{\infty} \gamma^n \mathbf{T}^n \qquad (6.10)$$

These equations still need to calculate $\mathbf{K}^n$ and $\mathbf{T}^n$, though, which is computationally expensive. So, we use the idea of a convergent geometric series to reduce the time complexity of the algorithm. A well-known mathematical fact is that the geometric series

$$\sum_{n=0}^{\infty} a^n,$$

where a is a scalar, converges to $\frac{1}{1-a}$ under the condition that $|a| < 1$. Similarly, the geometric series

$$\sum_{n=0}^{\infty} \mathbf{A}^n,$$

where $\mathbf{A}$ is a matrix, converges to $(\mathbf{I} - \mathbf{A})^{-1}$ under the condition that $|\lambda_m| < 1$, where λ_m is the maximum eigenvalue of $\mathbf{A}$. From the Perron-Frobenius theorem [1], the maximum eigenvalue λ_m of a matrix lies between the *maximum indegree* and *maximum outdegree* of the matrix.

Using the notations $\Delta^-(G)$ and $\Delta^+(G)$ to represent the maximum indegree and outdegree of G, respectively, we can write the lower bound for the maximum eigenvalue as:

$$\lambda_m \geq \min\{\Delta^-(G), \Delta^+(G)\}. \tag{6.11}$$

If γ is chosen such that $\gamma < \frac{1}{\lambda_m}$, Equations 6.9 and 6.10, respectively, converge to:

$$\widehat{\mathbf{K}}_\gamma = \mathbf{K}(I - \gamma\mathbf{K})^{-1} \tag{6.12}$$

$$\widehat{\mathbf{T}}_\gamma = \mathbf{T}(I - \gamma\mathbf{T})^{-1} \tag{6.13}$$

When $\gamma = 0$, the above two equations become:

$$\widehat{\mathbf{K}}_\gamma = \mathbf{K}, \tag{6.14}$$

$$\widehat{\mathbf{T}}_\gamma = \mathbf{T}, \tag{6.15}$$

which are the document correlation matrix and the term correlation matrix, respectively. In this case, the Neumann Kernel gives the relatedness between documents and between terms when $\gamma = 0$. Similarly, when γ is larger, then the kernel output matches with HITS.

In Equations 6.12 and 6.13, there are two matrix multiplications, one inverse calculation, and one matrix subtraction, for a reduction in the computational complexity of the kernel calculation relative to Equations 6.9 and 6.10.

Figure 6.12 provides a high-level overview of the Neumann Kernel algorithm.

We give a pseudocode description of the Neumann Kernel technique in Algorithm 7. The input to this algorithm is a directed graph G. Line 3 calculates

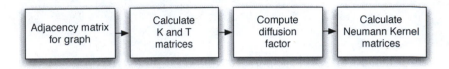

FIGURE 6.12: A high-level overview of the Neumann Kernel algorithm described in detail in Algorithm 7.

Input: G—a directed graph representing a collection of items (e.g., web pages)

Output: $\widehat{\mathbf{K}}_\gamma$ and $\widehat{\mathbf{T}}_\gamma$, Neumann Kernel matrices

1 $\mathbf{A} \leftarrow$ adjacency matrix of G

2 Compute $\mathbf{A^T}$

3 $\mathbf{K} \leftarrow \mathbf{A^T A}$

4 $\mathbf{T} \leftarrow \mathbf{A A^T}$

5 Compute $\Delta^+(G)$ and $\Delta^-(G)$

6 Choose γ between 0 and $\frac{1}{\min\{\Delta^+(G),\Delta^-(G)\}}$

7 Compute $\widehat{\mathbf{K}}_\gamma \leftarrow \mathbf{K}(\mathbf{I} - \gamma\mathbf{K})^{-1}$

8 Compute $\widehat{\mathbf{T}}_\gamma \leftarrow \mathbf{T}(\mathbf{I} - \gamma\mathbf{T})^{-1}$

9 **return** $\widehat{\mathbf{K}}_\gamma, \widehat{\mathbf{T}}_\gamma$

Algorithm 7: A pseudocode description of the Neumann Kernel algorithm

the transpose of the adjacency matrix of G, and lines 4 and 5 multiply the adjacency matrix and its transpose to get matrices $\mathbf{K}$ and $\mathbf{T}$. Line 6 computes the maximum indegree and outdegree of G, and line 7 uses these values to choose a value for the decay factor γ. How best to choose this value for γ is discussed in Section 6.3.5. Finally, lines 8 and 9 apply Equations 6.12 and 6.13 to calculate $\widehat{\mathbf{K}}_\gamma$ and $\widehat{\mathbf{T}}_\gamma$, and line 10 returns these two values.

6.3.5 Choosing the Decay Factor

The decay factor γ is a mechanism for controlling how much relative weight is given to vertices farther away in the graph when calculating relatedness. The underlying assumption is that vertices closer to the vertex in question are more strongly related than those farther away, and our choice of γ allows us to balance the contributions of vertices that are closer and more distant.

Choosing a value of $\gamma = 0$ allows us to give no weight at all to vertices outside of the immediate neighbors. For this choice of γ, the output of the Neumann Kernel will simply be relatedness among the vertices, i.e., the document correlation matrix $\mathbf{K}$ and the term correlation matrix $\mathbf{T}$, as noted in Equations 6.14 and 6.15.

Larger values of γ increase the contribution of the vertices farther away in the graph, giving us a value that scores the importance of each node, like HITS. As discussed previously, the value of γ must be less than $\frac{1}{\lambda_m}$ so that the geometric sequences in Equations 6.5 and 6.6 can converge to Equations 6.12 and 6.13. Since we know that λ_m must lie between $\Delta^+(G)$ and $\Delta^-(G)$, we need to choose γ to be less than

$$\frac{1}{\min\{\Delta^+(G), \Delta^-(G)\}}.$$

In the next section, we will discuss more concrete examples on how the Neumann Kernel, document and term correlation matrices, and HITS compare.

6.3.6 Relationships among Neumann Kernels, HITS, and Co-citation/Bibliographic Coupling

As we have discussed previously, Neumann Kernels provide a framework for calculating the importance and relatedness of vertices within a graph. This technique is a generalization of both the HITS algorithm and the co-citation/bibliographic coupling matrix technique. We illustrate this concept using the graph shown in Figure 6.10 and the associated adjacency (citation) matrix in Table 6.8. In order to provide a comparison between these techniques, we first apply the Neumann Kernel using different values of γ to calculate relatedness between the vertices of the graph. We can then assess the importance of each node by taking the sum of the relatedness values to the other vertices.

Choosing a value of $\gamma = 0$ results in the co-citation matrix $\mathbf{K}$ (see Figure 6.9 (B)):

$$\hat{\mathbf{K}}_0 = \mathbf{P} \tag{6.16}$$

$$= \mathbf{C}^T \mathbf{C} \tag{6.17}$$

$$= \begin{bmatrix} 1 & 1 & 0 & 0 & 0 & 0 & 0 & 0 \\ 1 & 2 & 1 & 0 & 0 & 0 & 0 & 0 \\ 0 & 1 & 3 & 2 & 0 & 0 & 0 & 0 \\ 0 & 0 & 2 & 2 & 0 & 0 & 0 & 0 \\ 0 & 0 & 0 & 0 & 0 & 0 & 0 & 0 \\ 0 & 0 & 0 & 0 & 0 & 0 & 0 & 0 \\ 0 & 0 & 0 & 0 & 0 & 0 & 0 & 0 \\ 0 & 0 & 0 & 0 & 0 & 0 & 0 & 0 \end{bmatrix} \tag{6.18}$$

If we compare the sum of the rows in this matrix, we see that using $\gamma = 0$ (or the technique of constructing the co-citation matrix) would rank the authority of the papers as:

$$n_3 > n_2 = n_4 > n_1 > n_5 = n_6 = n_7 = n_8.$$

However, if we increase the decay factor to $\gamma = 0.207$, we get the following matrix for $\mathbf{K}$:

$$\hat{\mathbf{K}}_{0.207} = \begin{bmatrix} 10 & 34 & 82 & 58 & 0 & 0 & 0 & 0 \\ 34 & 127 & 315 & 223 & 0 & 0 & 0 & 0 \\ 82 & 315 & 805 & 572 & 0 & 0 & 0 & 0 \\ 58 & 223 & 572 & 408 & 0 & 0 & 0 & 0 \\ 0 & 0 & 0 & 0 & 0 & 0 & 0 & 0 \\ 0 & 0 & 0 & 0 & 0 & 0 & 0 & 0 \\ 0 & 0 & 0 & 0 & 0 & 0 & 0 & 0 \\ 0 & 0 & 0 & 0 & 0 & 0 & 0 & 0 \end{bmatrix}, \tag{6.19}$$

which gives a ranking of:

$$n_3 > n_4 > n_2 > n_1 > n_5 = n_6 = n_7 = n_8.$$

We now compare these results to the HITS algorithm. We can run HITS on our example graph using the following R code:

```
1 #Get all required packages
2 library(igraph)
3 library(ProximityMeasure)
4 #Adjacency matrix for citation graph
5 C<-matrix(c(0, 0, 0, 0, 0, 0, 0, 0,
6             0, 0, 0, 0, 0, 0, 0, 0,
```

TABLE 6.9: Authority and hub scores (from the HITS algorithm) for citation data example in Figure 6.10

Article	Authority	Hub
n_1	0.08466727	0.00000000
n_2	0.31116868	0.00000000
n_3	0.77293020	0.00000000
n_4	0.54642878	0.00000000
n_5	0.00000000	0.18042241
n_6	0.00000000	0.49413333
n_7	0.00000000	0.60136512
n_8	0.00000000	0.60136512

```
7     0, 0, 0, 0, 0, 0, 0, 0,
8     0, 0, 0, 0, 0, 0, 0, 0,
9     1, 1, 0, 0, 0, 0, 0, 0,
10    0, 1, 1, 0, 0, 0, 0, 0,
11    0, 0, 1, 1, 0, 0, 0, 0,
12    0, 0, 1, 1, 0, 0, 0, 0),
13    nrow=8,ncol=8,
14    byrow=TRUE)
15 #Create graph from adjacency matrix
16 G<-graph.adjacency(C,mode=c("directed"),weighted=NULL)
17 #Number of iterations
18 k<-10
19 #Call to HITS function for graph G and iterations k=10.
20 output<-HITS(G,k)
21 #Authority & Hub Vector for nodes
22 output
```

The hub and authority scores produced by HITS appear in Table 6.9. Notably, the authority scores from HITS rank the vertices as

$$n_3 > n_4 > n_2 > n_1 > n_5 = n_6 = n_7 = n_8,$$

which matches the Neumann Kernel authority ranking using $\gamma = 0.207$ [10].

As the parameter γ increases, the measures induced by the kernel assume the character of global importance rather than relatedness. At $\gamma = 0.207$, the authority ranking produced by the Neumann Kernel matches the authority ranking of HITS. Thus, by varying the value of the decay factor γ, the Neumann Kernel can calculate authority and hub scores that include only local information, like in the co-citation matrix, or scores that depend on the global structure of the graph, like the HITS algorithm.

6.3.7   Strengths and Weaknesses

The weaknesses of the Neumann Kernel are similar to those of HITS described in Chapter 5, Link Analysis. Its primary weakness, like HITS, is topic drift [5]. A new weakness appears when comparing Neumann Kernels with other kernel methods, such as the Laplacian diffusion (see Chapter 4, An Introduction to Kernels). Unlike Neumann Kernels, Laplacian matrices penalize loops, which was shown to be detrimental in a study comparing graph kernel methods for collaborative recommendation systems [7]. These same types of errors may appear in a co-citation graph structure [10].

The main strength of the Neumann Kernel is its ability to balance relatedness and importance, much like a generalized version of HITS. By tuning the parameters of the kernel, one can find a harmony between relatedness and importance. Also, the Neumann Kernel technique subsumes other known algorithms, such as co-citation coupling and bibliographic coupling [16], which is a very useful feature for link analysis.

6.4   Applications

In this section, we discuss a co-citation analysis example using Shared Nearest Neighbor with a real-world data set. The data set can be downloaded from the book website, along with the associated R code.

6.4.1   Co-citation Analysis with Shared Nearest Neighbor

To illustrate the Shared Nearest Neighbor (SNN) algorithm, we apply the SNN algorithm to a subset of the citation data set obtained from `http://vlado.fmf.uni-lj.si/pub/networks/data/`. The graph is a paper citation network [2] from the 2001 Graph Drawing Conference proceedings. It contains a vertex for every paper in the proceedings for every Graph Drawing conference between the years 1994 and 2000, where the edges represent the citation of one paper by another. The dataset consists of 311 papers and 646 citation relationships. We can use the following R code to load the citation data and construct the SNN graph.

```
1 #Load libraries
2 library(igraph)
3 library(ProximityMeasure)
4 #Load the Citations data using
5 data(citation)
6 #Convert the data to an undirected graph
7 m<-as.matrix(citation[,1:2])
8 G<-graph.edgelist(m)
```

```
 9 #Get the adjacency matrix
10 A<-get.adjacency(G)
11 #Choose an appropriate value for k (nearest neighbors)
12 k <- 3
13 #Call SNN_GRAPH(adjacency_matrix, k);
14 G1<-SNN_GRAPH(A,k)
15 #Plot the SNN graph
16 plot(G1)
```

In the above code, we construct the 3-SNN graph for the Graph Drawing citation graph. In the resulting graph, two vertices (papers) would be joined by an edge if those papers cited three Graph Drawing papers in common. This graph might allow us to tell whether different authors have a tendency to cite the same papers.

6.5   Bibliographic Notes

In this chapter, we have detailed two techniques that deal with in-graph proximity. Alternatively, one can consider the proximity between multiple graphs. Three ways to calculate inter-graph proximity are examining graph isomorphisms [4], graph edit distances [8], and maximum common subgraphs [14].

6.5.1   Inter-graph Proximity

As a counter to other approaches such as edge slides or edge rotations [9], isomorphisms are described mathematically with the technique of judging the distance between two graphs as the distance between the isomorphic mappings of vertices u and v. The distance between the two graphs via this method grows as the u, v mappings differ with their isomorphic translations [4].

A similar technique for calculating proximity between graphs is the idea of graph edit distance. Instead of computing the distances between pairs of vertices in isomorphic mappings, graph edit distance measures the number of edits (vertex or edge relabelings, insertions, or deletions) until the two graphs are equal. There are a variety of methods for calculating graph edit distance. A survey of several different techniques is covered in [8].

A third technique, the Maximum Common Subgraph (MCS), identifies the largest subgraph common to a pair of graphs. Intuitively, more similar graphs would have a larger common subgraph. Major applications for MCS include biology and chemistry, which often look at chemical structures for similarity. For more information on this subject, see [14] and [15].

6.5.2   In-graph Proximity

There are other algorithms like SNN that compare the structure of a single graph to determine similarity between vertices. One technique similar in concept to SNN is SimRank, in which two vertices are similar if the vertices are referenced (linked) by similar objects. To do this, vertices are paired and assigned a similarity score. The scores propagate to neighboring vertices in an iterative fashion until the similarity scores converge. See [11] for details on how these similarity scores are calculated and propagated.

6.5.3   Node Importance

We have discussed the Neumann Kernel technique and its relation to the HITS algorithm for determining the importance of a node in a graph, though there are many other algorithms for this task. One such technique, popularized by Google, is the PageRank algorithm. PageRank, which is discussed in more detail in Chapter 5, Link Analysis, essentially performs a random walk on the Web. Though PageRank doesn't explicitly define authority and hub nodes, the contributed ranks resemble the authority/hub relationship modeled in algorithms such as HITS [3]. Another algorithm, SALSA ranks websites based on a specific query. SALSA esentially performs two random walks, a forward and a backward Markov chain walk; these two walks are equivalent to the authority/hub behavior of HITS, while being lighter computationally [13].

6.6   Exercises

1. Given the term-document matrix,

$$\mathbf{X} = \begin{bmatrix} 1 & 2 & 3 \\ 4 & 5 & 6 \\ 7 & 8 & 9 \end{bmatrix},$$

    calculate:

    (a) The document correlation matrix for $\mathbf{X}$
    (b) The term correlation matrix for $\mathbf{X}$

2. Consider the graph shown in Figure 6.13:

    (a) Construct the adjacency matrix that corresponds to the graph in Figure 6.13.
    (b) List all the pairs of nodes that have at least two shared neighbors in common.

(c) Do any of the nodes share three neighbors? If so, list all the pairs that do and the neighboring nodes they have in common.

(d) Suppose node 3 is removed from the graph. Do we have any pairs of nodes that still have at least two shared neighbors in common? Justify your answer.

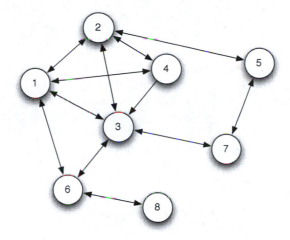

FIGURE 6.13: Example graph for Exercise 2.

3. Given the directed graph shown in Figure 6.14:

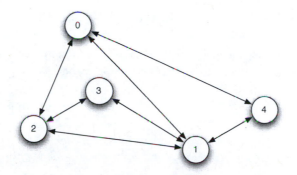

FIGURE 6.14: Example graph for Exercise 3.

(a) Give the adjacency matrix, $\mathbf{A}$, for this graph.

(b) Calculate the transpose of the adjacency matrix, $\mathbf{A^T}$.

(c) Calculate the document correlation matrix, $\mathbf{AA^T}$.

(d) Calculate the term correlation matrix, $\mathbf{A}^{\mathrm{T}}\mathbf{A}$.

(e) Calculate the maximum indegree of the graph.

(f) Calculate the maximum outdegree of the graph.

(g) Calculate the valid range for the decay factor γ in the Neumann Kernel.

(h) Verify your results using the igraph package. List the R commands used.

4. (a) Describe how the shared nearest neighbor algorithm groups vertices.

(b) Based on your answer to part a, how many total nodes are required at minimum to find a pair of nodes with n shared nearest neighbors? Explain your answer.

(c) Given the list of vertices with x and y coordinates shown below, construct an adjacency matrix of the vertices, where vertices are considered to be neighbors (adjacent) if they are within a distance of 4, using Euclidean distance. Note, the vertices should not be considered adjacent to themselves.

Node	Position	Node	Position
A	(1, 2)	F	(9, 3)
B	(4, 6)	G	(4, 1)
C	(4, 4)	H	(7, 1)
D	(5, 4)	I	(2, 7)
E	(2, 6)	J	(8, 5)

(d) Using the adjacency matrix that you have created, find and list all the pairs of nodes that have at least two shared neighbors in common.

(e) List all the pairs of nodes that have at least three shared neighbors in common.

5. (a) What does it mean for a matrix to be symmetric?

(b) Is the matrix $\mathbf{A}^{\mathrm{T}}\mathbf{A}$ symmetric for any adjacency matrix $\mathbf{A}$? Justify your answer.

(c) Is the matrix $\mathbf{A}\mathbf{A}^{\mathrm{T}}$ symmetric for any adjacency matrix $\mathbf{A}$? Justify your answer.

6. An *alpha group* is a set of vertices in which each vertex is connected to every other vertex. Figure 6.15 shows an alpha group of size 4.

(a) Suppose we are looking for pairs of vertices that share at least two neighboring nodes. How many pairs of vertices would we get for an alpha group of size 4? How many in alpha group of size 5? Size 6?

(b) Using your results from part (a), devise a function that finds how many pairs of vertices have at least two common neighbors in an alpha group of size n. (Hint: also think about alpha groups of size 3 or less.)

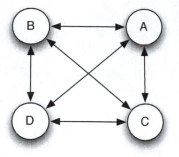

FIGURE 6.15: Example graph for Exercise 6.

7. (a) Describe how the HITS algorithm relates to the Neumann Kernel technique.

   (b) How does the decay factor γ affect the output of the Neumann Kernel algorithm?

Bibliography

[1] A. Berman and R. Plemmons. *Nonnegative Matrices in the Mathematical Sciences*. New York: Academic Press, 1979.

[2] T. Biedl and F. Brandenburg. Graph-drawing contest report. In *Proceedings of the 16th International Symposium on Graph Drawing*, pages 82–85, 2002.

[3] S. Brin and L. Page. The anatomy of a large-scale hypertextual web search engine. *Computer Networks and ISDN Systems*, 30:107–117, 1998.

[4] G. Chartrand, G. Kubicki, and M. Schultz. Graph similarity and distance in graphs. *Aequationes Mathematicae*, 55:129–145, 1998.

[5] D.J. Cook and L.B. Holder. *Mining Graph Data*. Wiley-Interscience, 2006.

[6] L. Ertoz, M. Steinbach, and V. Kumar. A new shared nearest neighbor clustering algorithm and its applications. In *Proceedings of the 1st Workshop on Clustering High Dimensional Data and Its Applications*, 2002.

[7] F. Fouss, L. Yen, A. Pirotte, and M. Saerens. An experimental investigation of graph kernels on a collaborative recommendation task. *Proceedings of the 6th International Conference on Data Mining*, pages 863–868, 2006.

[8] X. Gao, B. Xiao, D. Tao, and X. Li. A survey of graph edit distance. *Pattern Analysis & Applications*, 13:113–129, 2010.

[9] W. Goddard and H.C. Swart. Distances between graphs under edge operations. *Discrete Mathematics*, 161:121–132, 1996.

[10] T. Ito, M. Shimbo, T. Kudo, and Y. Matsumoto. Application of kernels to link analysis. In *Proceedings of the 11th ACM SIGKDD International Conference on Knowledge Discovery in Data Mining*, pages 586–592, 2005.

[11] G. Jeh and J. Widom. SimRank: A measure of structural-context similarity. In *Proceedings of the 8th ACM SIGKDD International Conference on Knowledge Discovery and Data Mining*, pages 538–543, 2002.

[12] J.S. Kandola, J. Shawe-Taylor, and N. Cristianini. Learning semantic similarity. In *Proceedings of the 16th Annual Conference on Neural Information Processing Systems*, pages 657–664, 2002.

[13] M.A. Najork. Comparing the effectiveness of HITS and SALSA. In *Proceedings of the 16th ACM Conference on Information and Knowledge Management*, pages 157–164, 2007.

[14] J.W. Raymond, E.J. Gardiner, and P. Willett. RASCAL: Calculation of graph similarity using maximum common edge subgraphs. *The Computer Journal*, 45:631–644, 2002.

[15] J.W. Raymond and P. Willett. Maximum common subgraph isomorphism algorithms for the matching of chemical structures. *Journal of Computer-Aided Molecular Design*, 16:521–533, 2002.

[16] M. Shimbo, T. Ito, D. Mochihashi, and Y. Matsumoto. On the properties of von Neumann kernels for link analysis. *Machine Learning*, 75:37–67, 2009.

7

Frequent Subgraph Mining

Brent E. Harrison, Jason C. Smith, Stephen G. Ware, Hsiao-Wei Chen, Wenbin Chen, and Anjali Khatri

North Carolina State University

CONTENTS

7.1   About Frequent Subgraph Mining

Frequent Subgraph Mining (FSM) is the process of discovering subgraphs that occur often in a database of other graphs. In this context, *often* means that the graph in question occurs more than some arbitrary *threshold* number of times.

FSM has a wide variety of applications. Graphs primarily convey structural information, so finding frequent substructures is often a reliable way to classify data that can be expressed as a graph. For example, a chemist might model a database of chemicals as graphs (where the nodes represent atoms and the edges represent bonds between atoms) and use FSM techniques to find common polyatomic ions that occur in those chemicals. The hydroxide ion is present in most acids, a fact that can be discovered by examining the frequent subgraphs of acids. See Figure 7.1 for an illustration.

FSM may also be used to find interesting features of graph-based data, such as common gene networks in two different species or recurring patterns of human interaction during the spread of an epidemic. In short, if the data has interesting structural properties, FSM can be used to highlight similar parts of that data that might reveal something about the set as a whole. Since FSM does not rely on training data, frequent subgraph mining is considered a type of *unsupervised learning*.

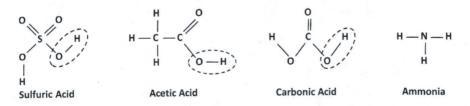

FIGURE 7.1: This database consists of four chemicals represented as graphs based on their molecular structure. The hydroxide ion is frequent because it appears in three of the four graphs. Depending on how *support* is defined, the support of hydroxide may be considered to be 0.75 or 3.

7.1.1   Anatomy of a Frequent Subgraph Mining Algorithm

All FSM techniques take as input a set of graphs (one or many), and return a set of graphs (zero, one, or many) that occur frequently in the input. All techniques share a common basic structure and have three parts:

- **Candidate generation** is the process of listing which subgraphs will be considered. It is likely that many candidates will not turn out to be frequent subgraphs, which calls for candidate pruning.

- **Candidate pruning** is the process of culling from the list of candidates any infrequent or previously checked subgraphs. This step can be very computationally expensive because checking subgraph isomorphism is NP-complete. Recall that if two graphs are isomorphic, they are structurally identical. Therefore it is necessary to remove all isomorphic graphs so that work will not be repeated. It is imperative that graph isomorphism and subgraph isomorphism be addressed in either candidate generation or candidate pruning. If this is not done, then support counts could be inaccurate because structurally identical subgraphs could be counted multiple times. The more candidates that can be removed, the better.

- **Support counting** is the process of counting how many times each of the final candidates appears in the graph database. The number of times each candidate appears determines if it is frequent or not. This step is also expensive. The set of frequent candidates is returned as output from the algorithm.

These steps do not generally happen in isolation. Usually the process is iterative, meaning that all three steps happen and then the process repeats many times. If the algorithm is running in parallel, they may happen simultaneously. These three parts are simply the conceptual phases of an FSM algorithm. When specific techniques are presented below, their various innovations will be discussed in terms of these three parts.

The most general, naïve FSM algorithm will consider every possible subgraph during candidate generation, will prune none of them, and will then perform a support count on each candidate. This procedure is prohibitively expensive to carry out for any significant dataset, so researchers have spent much effort making the process more efficient.

One simple improvement on the naïve FSM technique would be to prune candidates with the same vertices and edges. The graph made up of vertices A and B and the edge AB is the same as the graph made up of vertices B, A, and edge BA (assuming the edge is undirected). This simple step will yield considerable savings in the amount of time required to find frequent subgraphs. This step can be considered part of candidate pruning because it prevents the algorithm from considering graphs that have the same structure as one another. Most FSM innovations have come about in the candidate generation and candidate pruning processes.

In Figure 7.1, the hydroxide molecule appears 3 times, so by this definition, it has a support of 3.

These two definitions are used interchangeably in the FSM literature, so we use it interchangeably in this chapter as well.

7.1.2   History of Frequent Subgraph Mining

7.1.2.1   A priori approach

The first Frequent Subgraph Mining algorithms were based on Frequent Itemset Mining algorithms. An *itemset* is simply an unordered set of entities, such as $\{A, B, C, D\}$. Given a large number of these sets, frequent itemset mining is the process of finding sets that occur frequently. For example, given two sets $\{A, B, C, D\}$ and $\{A, B, E, F\}$, the set $\{A, B\}$ is frequent. These frequent itemset methods used the Apriori Principle to perform candidate pruning.

Definition 7.1 *Apriori Principle*
If an itemset is frequent, all of its sub-itemsets are also frequent.

These algorithms work in a breadth-first way. They join smaller frequent itemsets into larger ones, then check the frequency of those larger sets. If any subset of that larger set is infrequent, all the sets that might later be formed from that set must also be infrequent, meaning they can be pruned.

This approach was applied to graph mining, but aside from the inefficiency that Apriori-based algorithms already suffered from, graph mining proved even more difficult. Itemsets are simply an unordered group of entities, so combining $\{A, B\}$ with $\{C, D\}$ is simple: $\{A, B, C, D\}$. However, graphs contain structural data. Combining two graphs together is not as simple as combining a list of vertices and edges. Thus, the process of combining frequent graphs and checking all of their subgraphs is much more difficult than it is for itemsets. As such, Apriori-based FSM algorithms were intractable, and better alternatives had to be developed.

Since better solutions are now available, we do not present any itemset-based algorithms in this chapter. This is mentioned simply to provide a historical context.

7.1.2.2   Pattern growth approach

Modern FSM algorithms begin with a single vertex and grow the graph one edge at a time. Each time a new edge is added, a new vertex may need to be added as well. After each extension, the new graph's frequency is checked. Here is a general formulation of the pattern growth algorithm [4].

The problem with this algorithm is that a lot of work gets repeated. Many graphs which are isomorphic to one another will be generated and checked, and this is very inefficient. Most modern FSM algorithms revolve around find-

```
 1 Algorithm: Pattern_Growth(G, D, min_support, S)
   Input: a frequent graph G, a graph database D, and the minimum
          support, min_support
   Output: the set of frequent subgraphs S
 2 if G ∈ S then
 3     Return;
 4 else
 5     Insert G into S
 6 end
 7 Scan D to find all the possible ways to extend G by one edge into G';
 8 foreach G' such that support(G') ≥ min_support do
 9     Call Pattern_Growth(G', D, min_support, S);
10 end
```

Algorithm 8: A general pattern growth algorithm on which many modern FSM algorithms are based

ing ways to avoid checking graphs that are isomorphic to graphs which have already been checked.

Another nice feature of the pattern growth method is that it can be implemented in a depth-first or breadth-first fashion. Depth-first is usually chosen because it requires less memory.

7.1.3 Frequent Subgraph Mining Package for R

Included with this book is an R package for frequent subgraph mining called subgraphMining. To import this package into R, use the following code:

```
1 install.packages("subgraphMining")
```

This package contains the SUBDUE, gSpan, and SLEUTH algorithms, which are described in the following sections of this chapter. Two data sets, cslogs and metabolicInteractions, are also included. Two concrete applications of FSM techniques to these two data sets are provided later in the chapter. To load these data sets, use the following code:

```
1 # The cslogs data set
2 data(cslogs)
3 # The metabolicInteractions data
4 data(metabolicInteractions)
```

7.2   The gSpan Algorithm

One of the earliest depth-first pattern growth algorithms that is still widely
used was developed in 2002 by Xifeng Yan and Jiawei Han [13]. The gSpan
(**G**raph-based **S**ubstructure **PA**tter**N**) algorithm features an important innovation that significantly restricts the number of redundant subgraph candidates that must be examined. This algorithm was one of the first depth-first
FSM algorithms, significantly outperforming its Apriori-based predecessors,
and the parallel version of the algorithm exhibits good scalability [13].

7.2.1   gSpan Pseudocode

The general outline of gSpan is the same as the general pattern growth algorithm. The only major difference comes during the process of candidate
generation, which avoids generating subgraphs that are isomorphic to other
subgraphs already considered.

The algorithm represents graphs with a special encoding unique to gSpan
that we will call the *gSpan Encoding*. These gSpan Encodings possess a linear
order, which means that they can be ranked from smallest to largest, and
gSpan only expands graphs with the smallest encoding possible (the minimal gSpan Encoding). All graphs with non-minimal gSpan Encodings can be
safely ignored, which makes the mining process much more efficient. By only
expanding graphs with minimum gSpan Encodings through depth-first search
(DFS), gSpan avoids considering candidate subgraphs that are isomorphic to
subgraphs that have already been considered.

Since the gSpan algorithm is similar to the general pattern growth algorithm, we present it now. We focus here on describing lexicographic ordering
(line 3 of Algorithm 9), the minimum gSpan Encoding (line 2 of Algorithm 10),
and rightmost expansion (line 6 of Algorithm 10), as these are the most difficult parts of the algorithm conceptually.

Like other pattern growth algorithms, gSpan begins by considering small
subgraphs and progressively expands them. Rather than beginning with single
vertex subgraphs, gSpan begins with single edge (two vertex) subgraphs.

Each subgraph is extended one edge at a time, and the support of the
newly generated graphs is measured. If the support is greater than or equal
to *min_support*, that subgraph will be expanded further. Once it has been
extended such that its support is less than *min_support*, the algorithm back-
tracks until it has returned to a more promising subgraph, allowing gSpan to
expand graphs in a depth-first manner.

Now, let us investigate the more complex concepts that make gSpan so
novel.

---

1 **Algorithm:** gSpan(D, $min\_support$, S)

Input: a graph database D, and the minimum support, $min\_support$
Output: the set of frequent subgraphs S
2 $S \leftarrow$ all frequent one edge (two vertex) subgraphs in D
3 Sort S in lexicographic order
```
/* Make a copy of S, since S gets modified later        */
```
4 $N \leftarrow S$
5 **foreach** $n \in N$ **do**
6   Call gSpan_Expansion(D, n, $min\_support$, S)
7   Remove n from D
```
    /* n no longer needs to be considered                */
```
8 **end**
9 **return** S

Algorithm 9: The gSpan Algorithm

---

1 **Algorithm:** gSpan_Expansion(D, n, $min\_support$, S)
2 **if** $n \neq min\_gSpan\_Encoding(n)$ **then**
3   Return
4 **else**
5   Add n to S
6   **foreach** e such that e is a single edge rightmost expansion of n **do**
7   **if** $support(e) \geq min\_support$ **then**
8   Call gSpan_Expansion(D, e, $min\_support$, S)
9   **end**
10   **end**
11 **end**

Algorithm 10: The depth-first recursive candidate generation subprocedure of the gSpan algorithm

7.2.2 Novel Concepts in gSpan

7.2.2.1 gSpan Encoding

The gSpan Encodings are based on depth-first search trees. A depth-first search tree is a representation of the order in which nodes are visited when traversing a graph in a depth-first manner. A gSpan Encoding is an ordered set of edges, where the order is determined by how the edges are traversed during depth-first traversal. Note that one graph can have many different gSpan Encodings, depending on which node is chosen as the root. Figure 7.2 shows one graph and three possible DFS traversals of that graph. Table 7.1 shows the gSpan Encodings of those DFS trees.

Each edge in a gSpan Encoding is a five-tuple made up of the unique indices of the endpoints (first and second elements), the labels of these endpoints

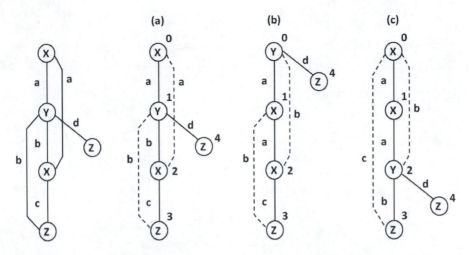

FIGURE 7.2: Possible gSpan Encodings of a sample graph (at left). The vertices are numbered according to their depth-first traversal ordering. Copyright ©IEEE. All rights reserved. Reprinted with permission, from [13]

TABLE 7.1: gSpan Encodings code for Fig. 7.2(a)-(c).

Edge	Fig. 7.2(a)	Fig. 7.2(b)	Fig. 7.2(c)
0	$(0, 1, X, a, Y)$	$(0, 1, Y, a, X)$	$(0, 1, X, a, X)$
1	$(1, 2, Y, b, X)$	$(1, 2, X, a, X)$	$(1, 2, X, a, Y)$
2	$(2, 0, X, a, X)$	$(2, 0, X, b, Y)$	$(2, 0, Y, b, X)$
3	$(2, 3, X, c, Z)$	$(2, 3, X, c, Z)$	$(2, 3, Y, b, Z)$
4	$(3, 1, Z, b, Y)$	$(3, 0, Z, b, Y)$	$(3, 0, Z, c, X)$
5	$(1, 4, Y, d, Z)$	$(0, 4, Y, d, Z)$	$(2, 4, Y, d, Z)$

(third and fifth elements, respectively), and the edge label (fourth element). The ordered collection of these edges is a gSpan Encoding. The gSpan Encoding for graph (a) in Figure 7.2 appears in the first column of Table 7.1.

7.2.2.2 Rightmost expansion

This key concept is important for candidate generation in gSpan (see line 6 of Algorithm 10).

Much like how graphs are expanded one edge at a time, it is possible to expand a gSpan Encoding by adding new five-tuples to it. However, when we add new edges, we need to make sure that the resulting gSpan Encoding still represents a valid depth-first traversal of the graph. To do this, we use a concept called *rightmost expansion*.

In a depth-first traversal, the starting node is called the *root*, and the last node is called the *rightmost node*. When considering the DFS tree (not the original graph), the shortest path from the root to the rightmost node is the *rightmost path*.

When expanding a gSpan Encoding via rightmost expansion, you may only add a new edge if one of its endpoints lies on the rightmost path. Adding edges in this way ensures that the gSpan Encoding remains valid. See Figure 7.3 for a graphical explanation.

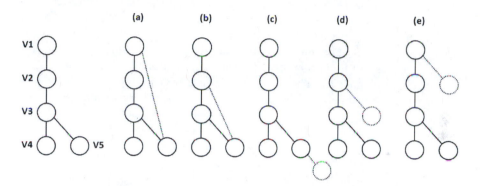

FIGURE 7.3: Graph growth: Rightmost extension to subgraphs. Copyright ©IEEE. All rights reserved. Reprinted with permission, from [13]

7.2.2.3 Lexicographic Order

This key concept is important for the initial ordering of single edge subgraphs (see line 3 of Algorithm 9). It is also important for the concept introduced in the next subsection.

The gSpan Encodings can be given a linear ordering; that is, they can be ordered from "smallest" to "largest" [13]. This ordering is based on finding edges that are common between two gSpan Encodings.

Why is this ordering important? Recall that one graph can have many different gSpan Encodings based on which node is chosen as the root of the depth-first traversal. This encoding was introduced to recognize graphs that are isomorphic to one another so that the algorithm does not waste time doing things it has already done. However, we need to ensure that the gSpan Encoding for a graph is the same no matter which vertex is the root.

7.2.2.4 Minimum gSpan Encoding

The Minimum gSpan Encoding (MgSE) is simply the smallest of all the possible gSpan Encodings (the lowest one in the lexicographic ordering). We can compare the MgSE in order to decide whether two graphs are isomorphic. Since we might have started at different places when doing the depth-first search, MgSE gives us a way to ensure that the encodings of isomorphic graphs will be the same.

In other words, one graph may have many gSpan Encodings, but it has only one Minimum gSpan Encoding, which is always the same for isomorphic graphs but different for non-isomorphic graphs. The MgSE allows gSpan to recognize when it is about to generate a subgraph that it has already considered.

MgSE is the key to candidate pruning in gSpan. This is why line 3 of Algorithm 10 returns if it encounters a gSpan Encoding that is not the minimum. When that happens, gSpan knows that either it has already found a subgraph isomorphic to this one, or that it will eventually find one isomorphic to it. In other words, gSpan only considers the subgraphs with Minimal gSpan Encodings. All others can be pruned because they are redundant (see Figure 7.4 for a graphical explanation). The use of the MgSE for candidate pruning makes gSpan much more efficient than previous Apriori-based algorithms.

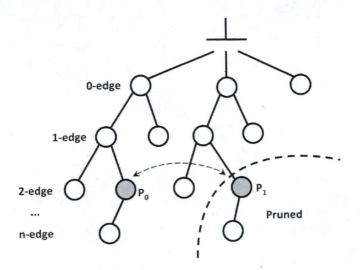

FIGURE 7.4: gSpan can avoid checking candidates that are isomorphic to ones it has already or will eventually consider. Copyright ©IEEE. All rights reserved. Reprinted with permission, from [13]

7.2.3   Complete gSpan Example

Here is an example of how gSpan mines frequent subgraphs. As shown in Figure 7.5, our input to Algorithm 9 consists of three simple graphs with labels A, B, or C on each node, and a $min\_support$ threshold of 3. First, the algorithm removes infrequent vertices and edges from the graph set. In this case, none are removed because all are frequent. Then, it finds all single edge

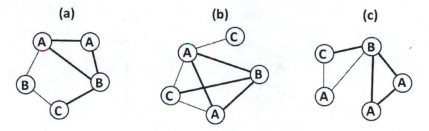

FIGURE 7.5: Example graphs on which gSpan will operate.

subgraphs (*A—A*, *A—B*, *A—C*, *B—B*, *B—C*, and *C—C*) and sorts them in lexicographic order.

If the support of any single edge subgraph is less than *min_support*, it will be eliminated. Thus, *A—C* (support=2), *B—B* (support=0), and *C—C* (support=0) are removed. The remaining frequent single edge subgraphs become the seeds to grow bigger subgraphs.

Now, Algorithm 10 begins recursively extending the one edge subgraphs found above using rightmost expansion. Line 2 is the essential pruning step because it avoids duplicate subgraphs and all their descendants to keep the mining process efficient.

Figure 7.6 shows how each subgraph is expanded and pruned. At the end of the algorithm, the frequent subgraph set is returned. In this case, three frequent subgraphs are found.

TABLE 7.2: Textual representation of the input and output for the gSpan example

	Input			Output		
(a)	(b)	(c)	(a)	(b)	(c)
v 1 A	v 1 A	v 1 C	v 1 A	v 1 A	v 1 A
v 2 A	v 2 C	v 2 A	v 2 A	v 2 A	v 2 B
v 3 B	v 3 A	v 3 A	v 3 B	v 3 B	v 3 A
v 4 C	v 4 B	v 4 A	v 4 C	v 4 C	v 4 C
v 5 B	v 5 C	v 5 B	e 1 2	e 1 2	e 1 2
e 1 2	e 1 2	e 1 2	e 2 3	e 2 3	e 2 4
e 1 5	e 1 3	e 1 5	e 3 4	e 3 4	
e 2 3	e 1 4	e 2 5	e 1 3		
e 2 5	e 2 3	e 3 4			
e 3 4	e 2 4	e 3 5			
e 4 5	e 3 4	e 4 5			

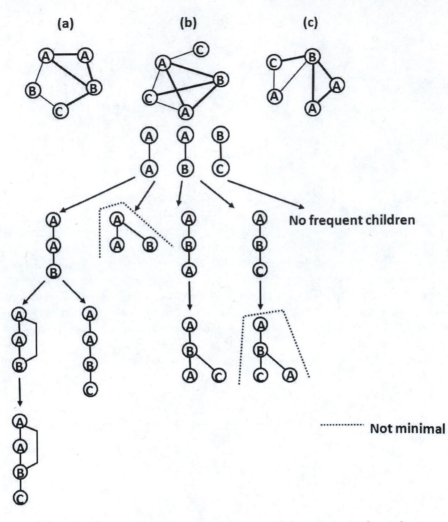

FIGURE 7.6: Example: the procedure of discovering subgraphs.

7.2.4   gSpan in R

To run gSpan in R, you will need to have the subgraphMining package installed. The gSpan implementation is written in Java, so you will need a working Java virtual machine installed in your environment. Since gSpan also uses igraph objects, you will also need the igraph R package.

```
1 # Import the subgraphMining package

2 > library(subgraphMining)
```

```
3 # Create a database of graphs.
4 # The database should be an R array of
5 # igraph objects put into list form.
6 # freq is an integer percent.  The
7 # frequency should be given as a string.
8 # Here is an example database of two ring graphs.

9 graph1 = graph.ring(5);
10 graph2 = graph.ring(6);

11 database = array(dim=2);
12 database[1] = list(graph1);
13 database[2] = list(graph2);

14 #And now we call gSpan using a support
15 #of 80%.

16 > results = gspan(database, support="80%");

17 # Examine the output, which is
18 # an array of igraph objects in
19 # list form.
20 > results

21  [[1]]
22 Vertices: 5
23 Edges: 10
24 Directed: TRUE
25 Edges:

26 [0] '1' -> '5'
27 [1] '5' -> '1'
28 [2] '2' -> '1'
29 [3] '1' -> '2'
30 [4] '3' -> '2'
31 [5] '2' -> '3'
32 [6] '4' -> '3'
33 [7] '3' -> '4'
34 [8] '5' -> '4'
35 [9] '4' -> '5'
```

Notice that the input to gSpan is a list of igraph objects and a minimum support value. The function returns the set of igraph objects corresponding to the frequent subgraphs in the input dataset. When viewing the results, R will display the graphs by showing the number of vertices, edges, and whether the graph is directed or undirected. In addition, a list of the edges is printed out in the format 'start vertex' $\rightarrow$ 'end vertex', which means that a directed edge exists between the vertices 'start vertex' and 'end vertex.'

7.3   The SUBDUE Algorithm

Exact algorithms, like gSpan and other similar algorithms, find the complete set of frequent subgraphs in a database of graphs. Even with the considerable speedup that gSpan provides, it can take a long time to run on real data. In addition, the results gathered probably contain numerous subgraphs which are frequent but uninteresting (such as all the frequent 1-vertex graphs). The application of FSM algorithms to real-world problems has prompted researchers to apply heuristics that limit the search space to only interesting subgraphs. The most widely used of these heuristic algorithms is SUBDUE [6].

The SUBDUE algorithm, originally described in 1988 by L.B. Holder [6], uses a constrained form of beam search to discover frequent subgraphs. SUBDUE reports structures based on the amount of compression they provide for the original graph (elaborated on in Section 7.3.2). If a subgraph allows for a lot of compression, it is assumed to be interesting, and therefore deserves to be further explored. This is an efficient but sometimes inexact method. SUBDUE was one of the foundational FSM systems, and it has been used and expanded for a number of different purposes. For example, SUBDUE is used in Section 11.3 to identify various types of anomalies in graph data.

7.3.1   Beam Search in SUBDUE

Using beam search to explore candidates is what makes SUBDUE so fast. Beam search is a best-first version of breadth-first search, so only the best k children are expanded at each level of the search. The rest are ignored. Here, k is called the *beam width* of the algorithm.

SUBDUE starts with all the frequent single vertex subgraphs in the database and expands them one edge at a time. There are many ways to extend any given graph, but SUBDUE only explores the best k of these.

7.3.2   Compression via Minimum Description Length

The other novel feature of SUBDUE is that it decides which subgraphs are most interesting based on the compression they provide rather than frequency alone (like most other FSM algorithms). Compression simply means representing data using a smaller number of bits, analogous to file compression technologies like zip archives. Instead of compressing files, SUBDUE compresses graphs. The best file compression programs are the ones that can shrink the files down the most. Likewise, the subgraphs that SUBDUE considers important are the ones that allow it to compress the original set of graphs into the fewest number of bits.

SUBDUE compresses graphs by replacing subgraphs with pointers. To illustrate this, consider Figure 7.7 (A). This graph has three triangles. To represent this graph, you would need 9 vertices and 11 edges. Now imagine that, instead of representing three triangles one time each, we represent one triangle three times. Represent the triangle once, and replace each instance of it in the original graph with a pointer to that one triangle, as in Figure 7.7 (B). Now the triangle has 3 vertices and 3 edges, and the original graph has only 2 edges and 3 pointers. Assuming pointers require no more bits than vertices and edges, we have now compressed the graph, as Figure 7.7 demonstrates.

TABLE 7.3: Graph Compression

Graph A	Graph B
9 vertices	3 vertices
11 edges	5 edges
0 pointers	3 pointers

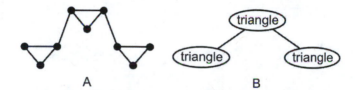

A   B

FIGURE 7.7: Graph B is a compression of graph A. Graph A has 9 vertices and 11 edges. Notice that there are three triangles in graph A. If the triangle is encoded just once, each of the three triangles can be replaced with a pointer to that single triangle, reducing the number of vertices in graph B to 3 and the number of edges to 2. Some extra space will be needed to store the representation of one triangle, but overall, graph B has a more compact representation.

To describe compression in mathematical terms, we need to introduce the concept of Minimum Description Length. All data can be represented as a string of 1's or 0's (bits). The number of bits required to represent some data is its description length. A minimum description length is simply the smallest number of bits that can be used to faithfully represent the data. In this case, our data consists of graphs, which are composed of vertices and the edges that join them.

Note that the method used to represent graphs as bits is arbitrary. Just as different programs store their data in different ways, the method used to

---

1 **Algorithm:** SUBDUE(G, D, *beam_width*, *limit*, *max_best*, S)

  Input: a graph G, a database of graphs D, the beam search width
       beam_width, and a *limit* on the depth of the search

  Output: a set of frequent subgraphs S which contains *max_best* or
       fewer subgraphs

2 *parents* $\leftarrow$ all single vertex subgraphs in D

3 *search_depth* $\leftarrow 0$

4 $S \leftarrow \emptyset$

5 **while** *search_depth* $<$ *limit* and *parents* $\neq \emptyset$ **do**

6   **foreach** *parents* **do**

7   Generate children

8   **foreach** of the *beam_width* best children **do**

9   Insert *child* into S

10   Sort S based on Description Length

11   Remove all but the best *max_best* elements of S

12   **end**

13   **end**

14   *parents* $\leftarrow$ the *beam_width* best children

15   *search_depth* $\leftarrow$ *search_depth* $+ 1$

16 **end**

17 **return** S

Algorithm 11: The SUBDUE algorithm

---

represent graphs is not important. All that matters is that the representation is binary.

> **Definition 7.2** *Description Length*
> The Description Length of a graph G is denoted $DL(G)$. The value of $DL(G)$ is the integer number of bits required to represent graph G in some binary format.

> **Definition 7.3** *Compressed Description Length*
> The Compressed Description Length of a graph G with some subgraph S is denoted $DL(G|S)$. The value of $DL(G|S)$ is the integer number of bits required to represent G after it has been compressed using S.

An ideal algorithm would always consider the minimum description length (MDL) of the database based on compression from the candidate subgraphs it is considering. However, since SUBDUE operates heuristically using beam search, the exact minimum may not be found in every case. SUBDUE seeks to minimize description length, but is not guaranteed to find the minimum.

7.3.3 SUBDUE Pseudocode

Algorithm 11 gives a pseudocode description of the SUBDUE algorithm.

The algorithm begins with the set of all one vertex subgraphs, the *original parents*. Each parent is extended in all possible ways. SUBDUE extends graphs one vertex at a time (line 7 in Algorithm 11). In other words, the set of one vertex graphs is extended into a set of two vertex graphs, and those into a set of three vertex graphs, and so on. These extended parents are called *children*.

SUBDUE then considers only the "best" *beam_width* children. The other children are ignored (see the foreach loop at line 6 in Algorithm 11). SUBDUE considers the "best" children to be ones that provide the most compression on the original database of graphs D. Formally, SUBDUE is seeking subgraphs G to minimize $DL(D|G) + DL(G)$. Note that the graphs which are being referenced by the pointers must be represented once (so that the pointers have something to point to), which is why we seek to minimize $DL(D|G) + DL(G)$ instead of simply $DL(D|G)$.

SUBDUE maintains S, a global set which holds the subgraphs that provide the overall best compression. S is what SUBDUE will eventually return. During each iteration of the foreach loop at line 6, SUBDUE checks to see if any of the new children are better candidates for S than what is currently there.

After the children are considered, they become the new parents and the process starts over. SUBDUE will only repeat this process *limit* number of times or until there is nothing left to consider. Once the outer while loop ends, S is returned and the algorithm terminates.

7.3.4 Complete SUBDUE Example

In this section, we give an example run of the SUBDUE algorithm. We will apply it to the labeled graph in Figure 7.8. Since the database of graphs that SUBDUE is attempting to compress is only a single graph, we will discover the frequent substructures of this one graph.

Before we begin describing the algorithm, we need to define a binary encoding for graphs. Rather than getting bogged down in the details of the encoding, it is enough to know how many bits are required to represent the various elements of a graph. These numbers are given in Table 7.4.

TABLE 7.4: SUBDUE Encoding Bit Sizes

Element	Bits Required
Vertex	8 bits
Edge	8 bits
Pointer	4 bits

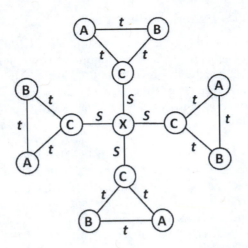

FIGURE 7.8: The example graph for SUBDUE.

The *pinwheel* graph in Figure 7.8 has 13 vertices, 16 edges, and 0 pointers. Thus, $DL(pinwheel) = 13 \cdot 8 + 16 \cdot 8 + 0 \cdot 4 = 232$ bits.

Let us look back at the pseudocode in Algorithm 11. Before the first iteration of the while loop, the *parents* list is simply all the single vertex subgraphs in the original graph. In other words, $parents = \{A, B, C, D, X\}$.

Let us consider the first iteration of the foreach loop at line 6. The first element of *parent* is A. There are two possible ways to expand A with one additional vertex: $A \overset{t}{—} B$ and $A \overset{t}{—} C$.

Consider the first way, $A \overset{t}{—} B$. This extension means replacing all instances of $A \overset{t}{—} B$ in the original graph with a pointer to a single instance. Now, $DL(pinwheel) = 5 \cdot 8 + 12 \cdot 8 + 4 \cdot 4 = 152$ bits. However, we must also consider the size of the subgraph that is being referenced by the pointers. It only needs to be included once. $DL(A \overset{t}{—} B) = 2 \cdot 8 + 1 \cdot 8 + 0 \cdot 4 = 24$ bits. So, the total description length of the pinwheel graph plus the subgraph used to compress it is 176 bits, 56 bits better than what we started with.

The algorithm then continues according to the pseudocode, progressively expanding the graphs one vertex at a time and checking which ones provide the best compression. Figure 7.9 shows the subgraphs that will be returned once SUBDUE has finished.

One important feature to note here is that subgraph (1) in Figure 7.9 will only be discovered if SUBDUE considers adding edges between existing vertices. As the traditional version of SUBDUE expands graphs one vertex at a time, it may miss certain subgraphs such as triangles. Modern implementations of SUBDUE allow it to consider these kinds of edges, meaning that when children are generated, SUBDUE might add just a new edge rather than a vertex and an edge. Unless overlap is allowed, SUBDUE will never be able to expand subgraph (2) in Figure 7.9 into subgraph (1).

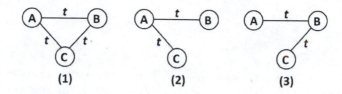

FIGURE 7.9: The frequent subgraphs discovered by SUBDUE.

7.3.5 SUBDUE in R

Included with this chapter is the subgraphMining R package, which contains the functions necessary to run the SUBDUE algorithm.

SUBDUE is written in C but has Linux-specific source code, which means it can only be compiled in a Linux environment. Compiled binaries are provided, but you may compile them with the `make` and `make install` commands if they do not run on your system.

SUBDUE uses igraph objects, so you will need the igraph R package.

An important note about the SUBDUE function is that it is run with the overlap option set to `true`, which means that overlapping subgraphs can be found.

```
1 #Import the subgraphMining package

2 > library(subgraphMining)

3 # Build your igraph object. For this example
4 # we built the graph from Figure 7.8
5 # using igraph and called it graph1.
6 # Call SUBDUE.
7 # graph1 is the igraph object to mine.

8 > results = subdue(graph1);

9 # Examine the results

10 > results

11 Vertices: 4
12 Edges: 6
13 Directed: TRUE
14 Edges:

15 [0] '2' -> '1'
16 [1] '1' -> '2'
17 [2] '1' -> '3'
```

```
18 [3]  '3' -> '1'
19 [4]  '3' -> '2'
20 [5]  '2' -> '3'
```

As with the gSpan functions, SUBDUE takes in a graph and returns and igraph representation of the set of frequent subgraphs in the graph. The igraph representation of graphs is also the same in that R will display the number of vertices, the number of edges, whether the graph is directed, and a list of the edges.

7.4 Mining Frequent Subtrees with SLEUTH

Since FSM algorithms are so computationally expensive, specific algorithms have been developed to target certain types of common graphs, such as trees. Trees encode hierarchical parent/child information and naturally represent many kinds of real-world data. XML files, such as web pages, can be considered as trees with the root node being the parent of all other nodes, which may in turn have their own children. However, the hierarchical nature of trees sometimes make them difficult to mine using traditional FSM techniques. Consider the HTML tree below:

```
<HTML>
    <HEAD>
        <TITLE> My page about puppies! </TITLE>
    </HEAD>
    <BODY>
        <H1> Puppies are amazing. </H1>
        <P> This is a photo of my puppy. Her name is <B> Blix </B>.
            <IMG src="blix.jpg" />
        </P>
        <H1> These are the things I like about puppies: </H1>
        <P>
            <UL>
                <LI>Playful</LI>
                <LI>Cute</LI>
                <LI>Warm</LI>
                <LI>Fuzzy</LI>
            </UL>
        </P>
    </BODY>
</HTML>
```

The TITLE element is a descendant of HTML, but it is not a *direct* child of HTML. In most traditional graph representations, there will be no edge connecting HTML to TITLE. For situations just such as these, the SLEUTH algorithm [14] was developed. SLEUTH can be used to mine frequent subtrees within a collection of trees. Though it is still very computationally expensive, it performs better than several of its tree mining predecessors [15] and succeeds in capturing hierarchical information that might be otherwise unavailable to general graph mining algorithms. That is, SLEUTH may be used to mine for unordered, embedded subtrees in addition to ordered and induced subtrees (definitions for all of these terms may be found in Chapter 2). This text will primarily focus on using SLEUTH to mine for frequent, labeled, unordered, embedded subtrees.

7.4.1 SLEUTH Mechanics

The intuitive and naïve approach to identifying frequently occurring subtrees among a collection of trees is to generate a list of all possible subtrees from the set of labels found within the collection and then search for each pattern, keeping a tally of their occurrences. A brute-force strategy such as this is highly inefficient, since it fails to take advantage of the fact that all subtrees of a frequent tree must themselves be frequent.

Consider a collection of trees D with a maximum tree size of k vertices, and the complete set of vertex labels of size d, then the number of potential subtrees that must be generated and examined is

$$candidates(D) = n^{n-2} \cdot d^n \tag{7.1}$$

which quickly grows to become intractably large. To illustrate, consider the numbers of potential subtrees generated for a collection of rooted trees with only 4 labels ($d = 4$) and a maximum tree size of $1, 2, \ldots, 6$ as shown in Table 7.5. Real datasets generally have a much larger set of vertex labels and tree sizes than this, so there is a need for a better alternative.

k	1	2	3	4	5	6
configurations	1	1	3	16	125	1296
labellings (d^k)	4	16	64	256	1024	4096
candidates	4	16	192	4096	128,000	5,308,416

TABLE 7.5: The number of potential labeled subtrees of a tree with up to five vertices and four labels is given by the formula in Equation 7.1. The *configurations* row indicates the number of possible node configurations for a tree of with k vertices, *labellings* indicates the number of potential label assignments for a single configuration of a tree with k vertices, and *candidates* indicate the number of potential labeled subtrees for a maximum tree size of k vertices.

7.4.1.1   Data representation

SLEUTH represents a tree collection in both horizontal and vertical formats, as seen in Figure 7.10. In the horizontal format each tree is encoded as a string of labels that follow a *preorder traversal* of the tree (see Chapter 2 for details). For unordered trees, this method forces a particular order amongst sibling nodes since siblings cannot be listed simultaneously and must be serialized in a string representation.

Horizontal Format (tree id, string encoding):

$(T_0,$ C A A $ C $ $ B C $ $ B $$)

$(T_1,$ C A $ B A $ C $ $$)

Vertical Format (tree id, scope):

A	B	C
0, [1, 3]	0, [4, 5]	0, [0, 6]
0, [2, 2]	0, [6, 6]	0, [3, 3]
1, [1, 1]	1, [2, 4]	0, [5, 5]
1, [3, 3]		1, [0, 4]
		1, [4, 4]

FIGURE 7.10:   SLEUTH Tree Database Representation. The collection of trees D is represented horizontally as (tree id, string encoding) pairs and vertically as per-label lists of (tree id, scope) pairs. The integer at each vertex gives the preorder traversal position, with 0 indicating the root, 6 indicating the rightmost descendant in T_0, and 4 indicating the rightmost descendant in T_1.

In the tree's string encoding, backtracking from a child to its parent is indicated by a symbol that is not in the list of vertex labels ($ \notin \{A, B, C\}$ in Figure 7.10). For instance, the HTML document given at the beginning of this section could be encoded as 013$$24$56$$7$589$9$9$9$$$ if the tags are represented by the integer labels 0 through 9, with the mapping given below:

0	1	2	3	4	5	6	7	8	9
↓	↓	↓	↓	↓	↓	↓	↓	↓	↓
HTML	HEAD	BODY	TITLE	H1	P	IMG	B	UL	LI

The vertical format contains one *scope-list* for each distinct label in the collection of trees. A scope-list $\mathcal{L}$ consists of (tree id, scope) pairs, which are illustrated in Figure 7.10. The *tree id* is simply an identifier for the tree in the graph database, while the *scope* of a vertex within a tree is defined by a pair of preorder traversal positions $[l, u]$, where l is the position of the vertex and u is the position of its right-most descendant. For instance, in Figure 7.10 the scope of vertex 0 with label C in tree T_0 is $[0, 6]$ since its right-most descendant is vertex 6. The (tree id, scope) pairs are sufficient for identifying which positions a single label matches within a tree. Scope-lists are necessary for efficiently computing tree frequencies, as will be shown in Section 7.4.1.3.

7.4.1.2 Candidate subtree generation

SLEUTH limits the generation of candidate subtrees by selectively extending only subtrees that are known to be frequent within the collection. That is, given a frequent subtree of size $k - 1$, a candidate tree of size k is created by attaching a child to one of the nodes in the frequent subtree. By further limiting the attachment of new vertices to only those found within the right-most path (i.e., the path from the root to the rightmost leaf in the tree), all possible *ordered*, embedded subtrees for an ordered tree can be generated [15, 1]. This method is known as *prefix-based* extension, since the candidate trees are extensions of a *prefix tree*.

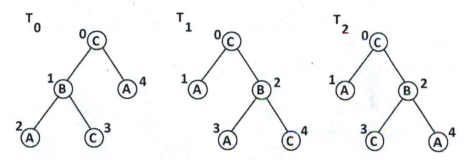

FIGURE 7.11: Label-preserving automorphisms of the same unordered tree. The integers shown represent preorder traversal positions.

For unordered trees, prefix-based extension creates a problem of redundancy, since a new candidate may belong to an *automorphism group* (see Chapter 2) from which a representative may have already been generated. One way of coping with the redundancy is to check if a generated candidate tree is in a *canonical form* (see Definition 7.4) before considering it further. With this strategy, all ordered configurations of an unordered subtree can be represented by a singular form. Consider the string encodings of the automorphic trees in Figure 7.11:

$$T_0: \text{CBA\$C\$\$A\$}$$
$$T_1: \text{CA\$BA\$C\$\$}$$
$$T_2: \text{CA\$BC\$A\$\$}$$

T_0 is not in canonical form because the sibling nodes labeled **B** and **A** appear in the wrong order. Similarly, T_2 is not in canonical form because the sibling nodes labeled **C** and **A** also appear in the wrong order. The three string encodings represent the same unordered tree, but T_1 is the canonical representation.

> **Definition 7.4** *Canonical Form*
> For the set of vertex labels $L = \{l_1, l_2, \ldots, l_d\}$ used in a tree T, let there be a linear order $\leq$ such that $l_1 \leq l_2 \leq \ldots \leq l_d$. A tree T is in **canonical form** if for each vertex $v \in T$, $L(c_i) \leq L(c_{i+1})$ for all $i \in [1, k]$, where $c_1, c_2, \ldots, c_k$ is the list of ordered children of v and $L(c_i)$ is the label of child c_i [14].

For instance, in Figure 7.11, tree T_1 is in canonical form and trees T_0 and T_2 are not (given the linear order of labels $A \leq B \leq C$).

SLEUTH generates frequent subtree candidates using an equivalence class-based extension scheme, whereby candidates of size k are created from known frequent subtrees (prefix subtrees) of size $k-1$ either through *child extension* or *cousin extension*. In both child and cousin extensions, the new vertex becomes the right-most leaf in the new subtree (and, therefore, the last vertex label in the string encoding of that tree). However, in child extension the new vertex is appended to the right-most leaf in the prefix subtree and, in cousin extension, it is appended to any other vertex in the right-most path of the prefix subtree. Any k-trees generated this way from the same $(k-1)$-tree are said to be members of the same *prefix equivalence class*, since they share the same prefix tree.

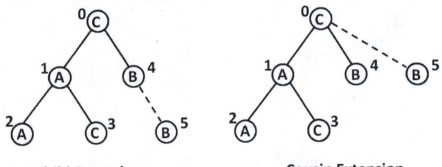

Child Extension   **Cousin Extension**

FIGURE 7.12: Child and cousin extension formed by adding a vertex with label B as a child or cousin of vertex 4, denoted P_B^4.

For a prefix tree P, let P_x^i denote the specific subtree created by attaching a new vertex with the label x to vertex i, and the class of frequent subtrees that may be generated through child and cousin extension as $[P] = \{(x, i) | P_x^i$ is frequent$\}$. Similarly, the class of frequent subtrees created by extending P_x^i with (y, j) is denoted as $[P_x^i]$. For example, in Figure 7.12, the prefix tree P_B^0

with 5 vertices is extended by affixing a new vertex labeled B to either vertex 0 (cousin extension) or to vertex 4 (child extension). The distinction between child and cousin extension is relevant to the task of frequency computation.

7.4.1.3 Support computation

Recall that a candidate subtree is considered frequent if it appears within a specified number of trees in D. If D consists of three trees, and the user-defined *threshold* is 2/3, then any candidate that is found in at least two trees is considered frequent. SLEUTH uses scope-lists (first introduced in Section 7.4.1.1) and *match-labels* to quickly determine if a candidate occurs within a tree.

Match labels map the vertices from a subtree to vertices in the containing tree, as seen in Figure 7.13, and therefore identify specific instances of a subtree within a tree. Although only one instance per tree is required to count support, all instances of a k-subtree must be uncovered so that successor $(k+1)$-subtrees can be considered.

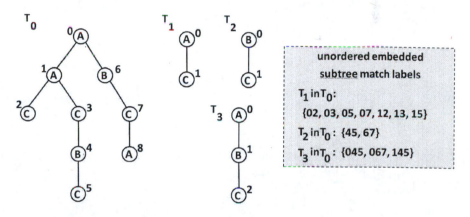

FIGURE 7.13: A match label identifies corresponding vertex positions for a subtree in its containing tree.

Scope-lists for k-subtrees with $k > 1$ consist of triples (t, m, s), where t is a tree id, m is the match label for that k-subtree, and s is a scope. The scope-lists of 1-subtrees (single labels) shown in Figure 7.10 do not have match labels since they do not originate from any prefix tree.

In both child and cousin extension SLEUTH uses scope-list joins to find instances of the candidate subtree within D. For the class $[P]$ and any two of its elements (x, i) and (y, j) it must be determined if label y occurs as either a descendant or a cousin of x. This involves checking amongst the scope-lists of the members of $[P]$ for pairs of entries with matching tree ids and match labels, where the two scopes are disjoint (cousin extension) or one scope overlaps the other (child extension). Table 7.6 shows (partial) scope-lists for tree T_0 from Figure 7.10. The scope-list for CA\$B\$ is created by joining the scope-lists of

CA\$ and CB\$. Since all entries in the lists being joined have the same tree ids and match labels, and both of the scopes in CA\$ are disjoint from both scopes in CB\$, the result is $2 \times 2 = 4$ instances of tree CA\$B\$ by cousin extension. Notice that the new match labels are formed by appending l from the $[l, u]$ scope entry to the original match label.

TABLE 7.6: Example scope-list joins for tree T_0 from Figure 7.10

A	B	C
0, [1, 3]	0, [4, 5]	0, [0, 6]
0, [2, 2]	0, [6, 6]	0, [3, 3]
		0, [5, 5]

CA\$	CB\$	CC\$
0, 0, [1, 3]	0, 0, [4, 5]	0, 0, [3, 3]
0, 0, [2, 2]	0, 0, [6, 6]	0, 0, [5, 5]

(cousin)	*(child)*
CA\$B\$	CAC\$\$
0, 01, [4, 5]	0, 01, [3, 3]
0, 01, [6, 6]	
0, 02, [4, 5]	
0, 02, [6, 6]	

7.4.2   An Example: Frequent Substructures in HTML Documents

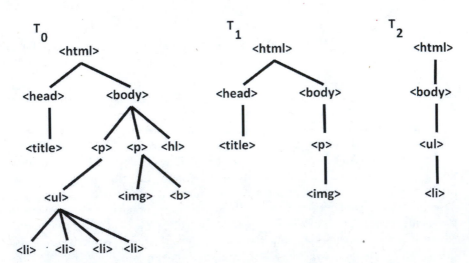

FIGURE 7.14: Example: a small collection of html documents.

Pseudocode for the SLEUTH algorithm appears in Algorithms 12 and 13. SLEUTH consists of an initialization step (Algorithm 12), and a recursively-defined operation, *Enumerate-Frequent-Subtrees* (Algorithm 13). In line 2, the frequent labels F_1 (1-subtrees) are identified. In line 3, scope lists are created for each frequent label in F_1, F_2 is populated with the frequent 2-subtrees, and their scope-lists are created.

Consider the simple collection of three HTML documents in Figure 7.14 and a *threshold* value of $\frac{2}{3}$ (meaning that SLEUTH will identify the unordered embedded subtrees that occur in at least 2 of the 3 documents). The horizontal and vertical formats for these three documents appear in Table 7.7. Notice that labels h1 (E) and b (H) are omitted from the vertical format since their support is beneath the 2/3 threshold.

TABLE 7.7: SLEUTH representation for the HTML documents in Figure 7.14

Horizontal Format:

T_0	(0, ABD$$CFIJJJ$J$$$FG$H$$E$$)
T_1	(1, ABD$$CFG$$$)
T_2	(2, ACIJ$$$)

Vertical Format

(Scope Lists):

html	head	body	title	p	img	ul	li
A	B	C	D	F	G	I	J
0,[0,13]	0,[1,2]	0,[3,13]	0,[2,2]	0,[4,9]	0,[11,11]	0,[5,9]	0,[6,6]
1,[0,5]	1,[1,2]	1,[3,5]	1,[2,2]	0,[10,12]	1,[5,5]	2,[2,3]	0,[7,7]
2,[0,3]		2,[1,3]		1,[4,5]			0,[8,8]
							0,[9,9]
							2,[3,3]

---

1 **Algorithm:** SLEUTH(D, *threshold*, S)

Input: a database of graphs D, and support boundary *threshold*
Output: S a set of frequent subtrees
2 $F_1 \leftarrow$ frequent 1-subtrees
3 $F_2 \leftarrow$ classes $[P]_1$ of frequent 2-subtrees
4 **forall the** $[P]_1 \in F_2$ **do**
5   *Enumerate-Frequent-Subtrees*($[P]_1$)
6 **end**

Algorithm 12: The SLEUTH Algorithm

```
 7 Algorithm:  Enumerate-Frequent-Subtrees([P]):
 8 foreach element (x, i) ∈ [P] do
 9     if check-canonical(P_x^i) then
10         [P_x^i] ← ∅
11         foreach element (y, j) ∈ [P] do
12             if do-child-extension then
13                 L_d ← descendant-scope-list-join((x, i), (y, j))
14
15             if do-cousin-extension then
16                 L_c ← cousin-scope-list-join((x, i), (y, j))
17
18             if child or cousin extension is frequent then
19                 Add (y, j) and/or (y, k − 1) to equivalence class [P_x^i]
20         end
21         Enumerate-Frequent-Subtrees([P_x^i])
22 end
23 SLEUTH recursive frequent subtree enumeration
```

Algorithm 13: Enumerate-Frequent-Subtrees

7.4.3   SLEUTH in R

Included with this chapter is an R package named subgraphMining.

SLEUTH is written in C++ and has a PERL component, so you will need a working installation of PERL and a C++ compiler.

If you are using a Windows XP system (or possibly other versions of Windows), pre-compiled binaries are already provided in the package.

```
 1 #Load the subgraphMining package into R

 2 > library(subgraphMining)

 3 # Call the SLEUTH algorithm.
 4 # database is an array of lists
 5 # representing trees.  See the README
 6 # in the sleuth folder for how to
 7 # encode these.
 8 # support is a float.

 9 > database = array(dim=2);
10 > database[1] = list(c(0,1,-1,2,0,-1,1,2,-1,-1,-1))
11 > database[2] = list(c(0,0,-1,2,1,2,-1,-1,0,-1,-1,1,-1))

12 > results = sleuth(database, support=.80);
```

```
13 # Examine the output, which will be
14 # encoded as trees like the input.

15 [1] "vtreeminer.exe -i input.txt -s 0.8 -o >output.g"
16 DBASE_NUM_TRANS : 2
17 DBASE_MAXITEM : 3
18 MINSUPPORT : 2 (0.8)
19 0 - 2
20 1 - 2
21 2 - 2
22 0 0  - 2
23 0 0 -1 1  - 2
24 0 0 -1 1 -1 1  - 2
25 0 0 -1 1 -1 2 - 2

26 ...

27 [1,3,3,0.001,0] [2,9,7,0,0] [3,38,11,0.001,0] [4,60,11,0,0]
28 [5,53,5,0,0] [6,16,1,0,0] [7,2,0,0,0] [SUM:181,38,0.002] 0.002
29 TIME = 0.002
30 BrachIt = 103
```

The trees used as input to SLEUTH are encoded using the horizontal format discussed previously. The resulting tree encoding begins after the "MIN-SUPPORT" text in the output. After all trees have been returned, additional statistics about the run (described further in the SLEUTH documentation) are reported.

7.5   Applications

7.5.1   Mining Metabolic Network Data with gSpan

An important area of research in the field of bioinformatics is in phenotype expression. A phenotype can be thought of as a trait that an organism possesses. For example, a well-studied phenotype in many organisms is whether it can live in extremely hot temperatures or not. Scientists are currently working on finding ways to determine whether an unknown organism will exhibit certain phenotypes. There are many different methods that are currently being researched, but the one we will focus on is the mining of metabolic networks. It is hypothesized that organisms with similar substructures in their metabolic network will exhibit similar behaviors, including phenotypes.

For this lab, you are given a dataset that consists of metabolic networks from different organisms. In each of these graphs, vertices represent enzymes and edges between vertices represent an interaction between these enzymes.

Importing and Mining the Data Set

The data set `metabolicInteractions`, which is provided with the subgraph-Mining R package, is a set of metabolic networks from several different species in graph form. Use the following R code to import and mine the data:

```
1 data(metabolicInteractions)
2 gSpan(metabolicInteractions, support="80%")
```

Discussion Questions

1. It is hypothesized that organisms with similar subgraphs in their metabolic interaction networks will exhibit similar phenotypes, therefore subgraphs with a high support are good candidates for detecting phenotype expression. Determine how many similar structures exist in the metabolic networks of all given organisms.

2. This dataset contains graphs with around 100-200 vertices and edges, which is pretty small compared to most metabolic network graphs. Given this knowledge and what you know about frequent subgraph mining, what is one potential drawback to using a frequent subgraph mining approach to finding common substructures in metabolic networks.

3. Typically, when mining metabolic networks, we are concerned with finding large subnetworks. With that in mind, re-examine the output you produced for question 1. Do you notice anything problematic or contradictory to the above statement? If you do, what are some suggestions to correct it?

Suggested Answers to Discussion Questions

1. There are 91 fragments, which means that there are 91 subgraphs that occur with a support of 100%.

2. As the size of your input graphs grows, the problem size increases exponentially, which can lead to very long run times as well as memory issues when trying to solve the subgraph isomorphism problem (which is NP-complete). Therefore, it is possible that some input datasets will cause gSpan and other frequent subgraph mining programs to run out of memory long before they arrive at an answer.

3. gSpan returns all frequent subgraphs, including all subgraphs of the maximal frequent subgraph. Since the maximal frequent subgraphs are returned, any subgraphs contained therein are unnecessary. An

example of this taken to the extreme is the single edge subgraphs that are returned. These, although possibly frequent, often give us no valuable information about the set of graphs. To solve this problem, one could simply check before returning graphs to see if they are contained within another graph that is to be returned. Another option would be to disregard smaller graphs if they are used to build larger ones.

7.5.2 Analyzing Server Logs with SLEUTH

Designing large websites is a difficult task. When you have a lot of data to organize, it can be difficult to make sure your users are able to find what they want quickly. For this reason, and for security purposes, many web servers keep a log of which pages their users visit. Web browsers usually provide a "back" button for returning to previously visited pages, so the order in which a user visits pages can be easily modeled as a tree. To transform this data into input for SLEUTH, we use integer values to represent unique page ID numbers, and -1 represents a use of the "back" button.

In this lab, you are provided with data collected from a web server log that describes the usage of many users. You will mine it for frequent patterns using the SLEUTH algorithm described earlier in the chapter in order to discover recurring patterns of use that can be used to improve the design of the website in question.

Importing and Mining the Data Set

The data set `cslogs`, which is provided with the subgraphMining R package, is real traffic information collected from a university's web servers. Use the following R code to import and mine the data:

```
1 data(cslogs)
2 sleuth(cslogs, support=.80)
```

Discussion Questions

1. Say you were going to add a "quick links" section to the home page of the website that recorded these logs. This section should provide links to the pages users most commonly visited. Which pages should you include? What is a reasonable support value to use when mining for this data? Explain your answer.

2. Now consider the results that are paths of more than one page. If these paths are usually embedded trees rather than induced trees, what might that imply about the design of the website?

3. Say you are going to add an important new page to the website and you want to put it in an accessible and logical place so that

users will notice the change. If you had access to the actual pages themselves and could analyze their content, how could you use the above data mining results to determine where the new page should go?

Suggested Answers to Discussion Questions

1. The single pages that show up in the results (frequent subgraphs of size one) are the most visited pages on the server. The most reasonable support value depends on how much space is in the "quick links." The support number used corresponds directly to the percentage of users who visited those pages. If a support of 80% is used, the single pages returned are pages that were visited by 80% of the users.

2. Suppose the path (a, b) is returned, and further suppose that it is an embedded tree. This means that many users went from a to b, but that they visited different pages on the way to b (for example, some may have used the path (a, c, d, e, b), while others used (a, x, y, z, b), etc.). This implies that the path from a to b is not clear, and that the website should be redesigned to fix this problem. Ideally, a link to b would be added to a to make the path clear.

3. First, cluster the pages based on content to determine what family the new page belongs to. Then, using the data mining results above, find other pages from its family that are frequently visited. Putting links on the most visited pages to your new page increases the chances that users will notice the new page.

7.6   Bibliographic Notes

The first Frequent Subgraph Mining algorithms, ASM (Inokuchi et al, 2000 [7]), FSG (Kuramochi and Karypis, 2001 [9]), and path-join (Vanetik et al. 2002 [11]), were derived from Apriori-based itemset mining algorithms. These methods use breadth-first search to iteratively expand smaller substructures into larger ones. Candidate pruning is performed by examining the frequency of substructures that are created by "joining" other smaller substructures; if the smaller substructures are infrequent, larger substructures containing them can also be ruled out as infrequent as well. This approach is better than the naïve approach that checks all possible substructures, but it is still computationally infeasible for large datasets. The differences in the three algorithms are that the substructures being "joined" are based on vertices, edges, and edge-disjoint paths, respectively, but these differences are fairly trivial considering the scope of the problem.

Probably the single greatest innovation in FSM techniques came about with gSpan (Yan and Han, 2002 [13]), which was able to use depth-first search to increase efficiency by several orders of magnitude [12]. The use of *Depth First Search lexicographic ordering* and *right-most tree expansion* (described earlier in the chapter) allows the algorithm to avoid generating candidate substructures that are isomorphic to one another. This technique eases the task of candidate pruning and saves a lot of time in support counting, without losing any of the accuracy of the breath-first algorithms.

Other variants on the depth-first theme include MoFa (**Mo**lecule **Fa**gment Miner, by Borgelt and Berthold, 2002 [2]), FFSM (**F**ast **F**requent **S**ubgraph **M**ining, by Huan et al. 2003 [8]), and Gaston (**G**raph **S**equence **T**ree extraction, by Nijssen and Kok, 2003 [10]). MoFa uses a fragment-local heuristic and standard isomorphism testing to remove duplicates. FFSM converts graphs into triangle matrices and uses *canonical adjacency matrices*, or *CAMs* to detect duplicates. Gaston works by generating paths first, then trees, and finally general graphs in efficient ways.

SUBDUE (by Holder, 1988 [6]) uses neither depth-first nor breadth-first search, but rather beam search. Using beam search speeds up the algorithm considerably, but it is a heuristic technique, so SUBDUE may not find all frequent subgraphs like most of its predecessors. SUBDUE is also one of the only FSM algorithms to use graph compression (rather than support) as a measure of interestingness.

SLEUTH (Zaki, 2005 [14]) is a depth-first algorithm that uses the above mentioned innovations along with the new technique of *scope list joins* (described in the chapter) to increase the speed of the support count process. Scope list joins allow SLEUTH to discover a wealth of new information about embedded trees for comparatively little extra computation, which can be done based on the data for the induced trees that other, more general algorithms are capable of finding. However, SLEUTH can only operate on trees.

Cook and Holder's textbook entitled *Mining Graph Data* provides a brief history of FSM techniques in its chapter on "Discovery of Frequent Substructures" [4]. Han et al. also provide an excellent survey paper on the topic [5]. Chi et al. have also written a very good survey paper on the subject [3].

7.7   Exercises

Answer questions 1 through 3 using Figure 7.16.

1. (a) Is graph (2) isomorphic to graph (3)?
    (b) Are graph (1) and graph (2) automorphisms?

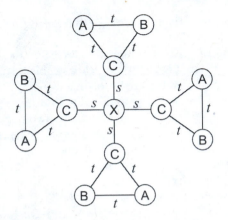

FIGURE 7.15: The pinwheel graph.

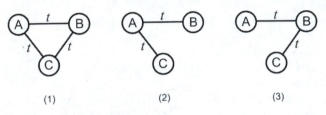

FIGURE 7.16: Frequent subgraphs discovered by SUBDUE from Figure 7.15.

    (c) Is graph (3) *frequent* if the *minimum support* is 2?
    (d) Is graph (2) induced by any of the vertices in graph (1)?

2. What is the *support* of graph (3) in Figure 7.15?

3. One interesting feature of SUBDUE is that it can be applied to
   its own results. Graphs that have been compressed can then be
   compressed again. Consider graph (1). Its current description length
   is 48 bits (based on the representation defined in the SUBDUE
   section of this chapter). See Table 7.8 for how the description length
   is calculated. How will these numbers change if you compress graph
   (1) using graph (2)? Fill in the blanks in column 2. Is it useful to
   compress graph (1) using graph (2) in this case?

Answer questions 5 through 9 using Figure 7.17.

4. Which of the following is a valid encoding for one of the edges in
   this graph?

    (a) $(0, 1, X, a, Y)$
    (b) $(1, 2, X, b, Y)$
    (c) $(0, 1, X, a, X)$
    (d) $(0, 3, X, b, Z)$

TABLE 7.8: Graph Compression

Graph (1)	Graph (1) after being compressed using graph (2)
3 vertices	— vertices
3 edges	— edges
0 pointers	— pointers
Total: 48 bits	Total: — bits

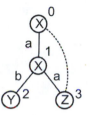

FIGURE 7.17: gSpan encodings graph.

    (e) $(1, 0, X, a, X)$

5. Aside from linking to vertex 0, what other ways can you add an edge from vertex 3 using rightmost expansion?

6. Give one graph that is isomorphic to Figure 7.17.

7. For Figure 7.17 and the graph you drew in the previous question, indicate their rightmost paths.

8. Give the full gSpan encoding for Figure 7.17.

9. Create a SLEUTH database representation of the trees shown in Figure 7.18.

10. Given the set of labels $\{X, Y, Z\}$ with the order $X \leq Y \leq Z$, and a tree T with the string encoding, XZ$YZ$$X$$, list the string encodings of all of the automorphisms of T. Which of these is the canonical form?

11. FSM algorithms are very computationally expensive because their search space is extremely large. To develop an appreciation for the efficiency of these methods, write an algorithm in pseudocode that, given some graph G with n nodes and e edges, enumerates all the subgraphs of G.

12. Give a mathematical formula for the number of undirected labeled graphs with at most n vertices, n_1 possible vertex labels, and n_2 possible edge labels, in terms of n, n_1, and n_2.

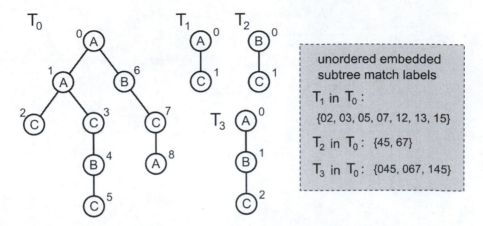

FIGURE 7.18: A match label identifies corresponding vertex positions for a subtree in its containing tree.

Bibliography

[1] T. Asai, K. Abe, S. Kawasoe, H. Sakamoto, and S. Arikawa. Efficient substructure discovery from large semi-structured data. In *Proceedings of the Second SIAM International Conference on Data Mining*, pages 158–174, 2002.

[2] C. Borgelt and M.R. Berthold. Mining molecular fragments: Finding relevant substructures of molecules. *Data Mining, IEEE International Conference on*, 0:51, 2002.

[3] Y. Chi, R.R. Muntz, S. Nijssen, and J.N. Kok. Frequent subtree mining: An overview. *Fundamenta Informaticae*, 66(1-2):161–198, 2004.

[4] D.J. Cook and L.B. Holder, editors. *Mining Graph Data*, pages 103–107. John Wiley & Sons, Inc., 2006.

[5] J. Han, H. Cheng, D. Xin, and X. Yan. Frequent pattern mining: Current status and future directions. *Data Mining and Knowledge Discovery*, 14(1), 2007.

[6] L.B. Holder. Substructure discovery in SUBDUE, 1988.

[7] A. Inokuchi, T. Washio, and H. Motoda. An apriori-based algorithm for mining frequent substructures from graph data. *Lecture Notes in Computer Science*, pages 13–23, 2000.

[8] H. Jun, W. Wang, and J. Prins. Efficient mining of frequent subgraphs

in the presence of isomorphism. In *ICDM '03: Proceedings of the Third IEEE International Conference on Data Mining*, page 549, Washington, DC, USA, 2003. IEEE Computer Society.

[9] M. Kuramochi and G. Karypis. Frequent subgraph discovery. In *Proceedings of the 2001 IEEE International Conference on Data Mining*, pages 313–320, 2001.

[10] S. Nijssen and J. N. Kok. A quickstart in frequent structure mining can make a difference. In *KDD '04: Proceedings of the Tenth ACM SIGKDD International Conference on Knowledge Discovery and Data Mining*, pages 647–652, New York, NY, USA, 2004. ACM.

[11] N. Vanetik, E. Gudes, and S.E. Shimony. Computing frequent graph patterns from semistructured data. In *Proc. of 2002 IEEE International Conference on Data Mining (ICDM)*, pages 458–465, 2002.

[12] M. Worlein, T. Meinl, I. Fischer, and M. Philippsen. A quantitative comparison of the subgraph miners MoFa, gSpan, FFSM, and Gaston. *Lecture Notes in Computer Science*, 3721:392, 2005.

[13] X. Yan and J. Han. gSpan: Graph-based substructure pattern mining. In *Proceedings of the IEEE International Conference on Data Mining*, page 721, 2002.

[14] M.J. Zaki. Efficiently mining frequent embedded unordered trees. *Fundamenta Informaticae*, 66(1-2):33–52, March/April 2005. Special issue on Advances in Mining Graphs, Trees and Sequences.

[15] M.J. Zaki. Efficiently mining frequent trees in a forest: Algorithms and applications. *IEEE Transactions on Knowledge and Data Engineering*, 17(8):1021–1035, August 2005. Special issue on Mining Biological Data.

8

Cluster Analysis

Kanchana Padmanabhan, Brent Harrison, Kevin Wilson, Michael L. Warren, Katie Bright, Justin Mosiman, Jayaram Kancherla, Hieu Phung, Benjamin Miller, and Sam Shamseldin

North Carolina State University

CONTENTS

8.1 Introduction

In Chapter 9, classification was defined as the process of assigning discrete class labels to sets of data. However, what if we do not know what these class labels should be or do not have a training set of data with known relationships? In this case, we wish to group input data together by some measure of similarity. The process of dividing the data into subsets, where each element in the same subset shares some degree of similarity, is called *clustering*, and the process of finding a structure in unlabeled data is known as *unsupervised learning*.

Definition 8.1 *Unsupervised Learning*
The process of finding relationships in sets of unlabeled or unclassified data.

Definition 8.2 *Clustering*
The process of dividing a set of input data into possibly overlapping subsets, where elements in each subset are considered related by some similarity metric.

Clustering on graphs can take two forms, similar to graph classification: *within-graph* clustering and *between-graph* clustering. Within-graph clustering clusters the vertices within an individual graph, while between-graph clustering clusters sets of graphs, each based on some measure of similarity appropriate to the problem at hand. In this chapter, we will only deal with the within-graph, graph partitioning algorithms.

Graph-based clustering techniques are extremely useful because many real-world problem domains have a natural graph representation. Social networks are one such example, where each vertex represents a user within the network, and relationships between users (such as being "friends") are represented by edges. Clustering social networks can help identify people that are not related at present but have common characteristics, such as having a similar set of relations, or edges. This information can then be used to recommend new relationships to a person. Another example of within-graph clustering is in the field of bioinformatics, where the interaction of proteins of an organism can be represented as a network. Each vertex is a protein and an edge is placed between a pair of vertices if there is evidence that suggests an interaction between them. Clustering vertices in such a graph will help identify those groups of proteins, known as "functional modules," that interact as a group to carry out some function in the cell. These clusters aid in biologists' understanding of organisms and the highly complex interactions going on between the proteins, knowledge that is particularly useful when looking at aspects such as disease causing organism's networks.

8.2 Minimum Spanning Tree Clustering

In many applications, vertex-vertex similarity can be quantified by the presence of short, high-weight paths to other vertices. These paths embody the friends of friends concept, where two vertices are similar if they are sufficiently similar to each other directly (by a high-weight edge) or indirectly, through high-weight shared neighbors and paths. Edge weights can represent similarity or distance, where low-distance means high similarity and vice versa. For example, given a set of farms and the analysis goal of identifying groups of farms with similar soil conditions, we can heuristically define the similarity of farms based on their distances from each other. Then we can construct a complete, weighted graph where each edge captures the distance between a pair of farms. However, to capture the most pertinent information from the graph, we can preprocess the graph by computing the *minimum spanning tree* of the graph.

Definition 8.3 *Spanning Tree*
A connected subgraph with no cycles that includes all vertices in the graph.

Definition 8.4 *Minimum Spanning Tree (MST)*
The spanning tree of a graph with the minimum possible sum of edge weights, if the edge weights represent distance and maximum possible sum of edge weights, if the edge weights represent similarity.

Using the minimum spanning tree has numerous benefits. It is both efficient and simple to compute and it directly captures similarity by maximizing the total weight of the resulting minimum spanning tree of the graph. Alternatively, if the edge weight represents a distance metric, then we minimize the total weight of the resulting minimum spanning tree of the graph. High similarity is synonymous with low distance and vice versa. Furthermore, the removal of an edge from a spanning tree results in the splitting of the tree into two components, each of which is a spanning tree. However, one must be careful to use it in many cases as a potentially large degree of information is thrown out as the result of edge removal.

8.2.1 Prim's Algorithm

The canonical algorithm to find a minimum spanning tree in an undirected (distance) weighted graph is Prim's algorithm. The algorithm initializes the minimum spanning tree T with an arbitrarily chosen vertex and then iteratively grows the tree until all the vertices are part of the tree. At each iteration an edge is chosen that satisfies the following two criteria: (1) exactly one of its end points is in T and (2) the edge is of minimum weight among those that satisfy (1). Algorithm 14 provides the details of the method.

As an example of using Prim's algorithm, consider the graph G in Figure 8.1 (a), with 5 vertices and 8 edges. After initialization, the resulting tree T only contains the arbitrarily chosen vertex (say, vertex 5). We now have to identify an edge that satisfies the two criteria described in the earlier paragraph. Both (4,5) and (3,5) satisfy criterion (1), but only (4,5) satisfies both criteria (Line 4) and hence is added to T (Line 5). Lines 3, 4 and 5 are executed iteratively until all the vertices in G become part of T (Line 2). When the algorithm terminates, T holds the minimum spanning tree of G (Figure 8.1 (e)). The following R code calculates the minimum spanning tree using Prim's

---

Input: A (distance) weighted, undirected graph $G = (V, E)$
Output: A graph T that represents the minimum spanning tree
1 Initialize T with a random vertex from G
2 **while** $V(T) \neq V(G)$ **do**
3    $E_T = \{(u, v) \in E(G) : u \in T \text{ or } v \in T\}$
4    $min_{edge} = (u, v) : weight(u, v) \text{ minimum in } E_T$
5   Add min_{edge} to T
6 **end**
7 **return** T

Algorithm 14: Prim's minimum spanning tree algorithm.

algorithm for the graph in Figure 8.1(d). The algorithm is implemented in the igraph package.

```
1 library(GraphClusterAnalysis,graph)
2 library(igraph,RGBL)
3 data(MST_Example)
4 G = graph.data.frame(MST_Example,directed=FALSE)
5 E(G)$weight=E(G)$V3

6 # Calculate the MST by Prim's algorithm
7 MST_PRIM = minimum.spanning.tree(G,weights=G$weight,
8           algorithm = "prim")
9 MST_PRIM
10 Vertices: 5
11 Edges: 4
12 Directed: FALSE
13 Edges:

14 [0] '1' -- '3'
15 [1] '2' -- '3'
16 [2] '3' -- '4'
17 [3] '4' -- '5'

18 # Total weight of the Minimum Spanning Tree
19 sum(E(MST_PRIM)$weight)
20 [1] 11
```

8.2.2 Identifying Clusters from MST

The minimum spanning tree, and the information contained in it (the distance associated with minimal edge weights), allows for a simple method of clustering. Since there are no cycles in the graph, the removal of any edge in

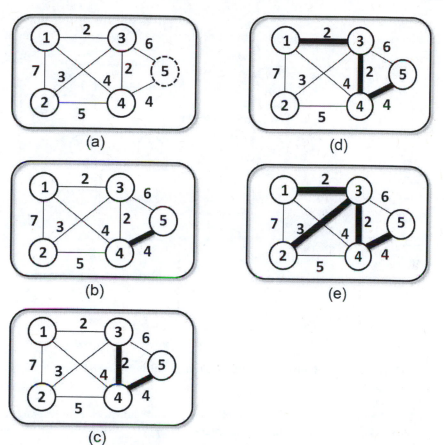

FIGURE 8.1: An example of Prim's algorithm for finding a minimum spanning tree in the graph.

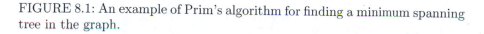

the spanning tree results in disconnecting the graph, incrementing the total number of connected components in the graph. Since each component is itself a tree, the net effect of removing $k - 1$ edges is the creation of k connected components in the resulting graph, which form the clusters [33]. For minimum spanning trees, the edges chosen are those with minimum weight (when edge weight represents distance or vice versa if edge weight represents similarity).

In order to create $k = 3$ clusters from the distance-weighted minimum spanning tree T in Figure 8.1 (e), we remove the $k - 1 = 2$ edges with the largest weight from T. As you can see in Figure 8.1 (e), we first remove edge (4,5) because it has the largest edge weight in the tree. This creates a cluster with only vertex 5 and a cluster with vertices 1, 2, 3, and 4. We then remove edge (2,3) because now it is the edge with the largest weight. The end result is the three clusters (one cluster containing only vertex 2, one cluster containing only vertex 5, and one cluster containing vertices 1, 3, and 4) (see Figure 8.2).

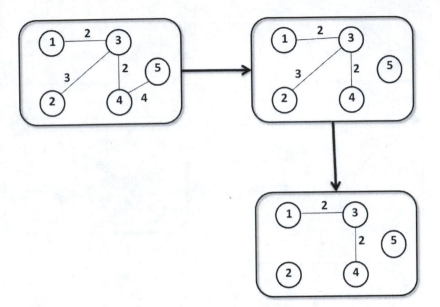

FIGURE 8.2: Clustering the minimum spanning tree in Figure 8.1.

The minimum spanning tree clustering can be performed using the k_clusterSpanningTree function included in the GraphClusterAnalysis package, which requires the igraph and graph packages.

```
 1 library(GraphClusterAnalysis,graph)
 2 library(igraph,RBGL)
 3 # Perform clustering into 3 sets using the MST
 4 OutputList = k_clusterSpanningTree(MST_PRIM,3)
 5 Clusters = OutputList[[1]]
 6 outputGraph = OutputList[[2]]
 7 # Vertices 1, 3 and 4 form a cluster,
 8 #   while vertices 2 and 5 are singleton clusters
 9 Clusters
10    VertexID ClusterID
11 1        1         0
12 2        2         1
13 3        3         0
14 4        4         0
15 5        5         2
```

8.3   Shared Nearest Neighbor Clustering

MST-based clustering defines similarity between vertices by the existence of high-weight edges and paths between vertex pairs. Removal of a possibly large number of edges results in loss of information in the resulting clusters. Therefore, a more general notion of similarity of vertex-vertex pairs can be captured through *shared nearest neighbor* (SNN) clustering, based on proximity measures of vertex pairs (see Chapter 6 on Proximity Measures). Unlike the weight-based measures, it provides a natural and robust way of preventing noise in the data set (such as the removal or addition of edges into the graph) from affecting the clustering results.

The idea behind the clustering algorithm is to place a pair of objects into the same cluster, if the number of common neighbors they share is more than some *threshold* (τ). This τ allows the user to control the degree of similarity between vertices needed to be placed in the same cluster, which can change from application to application. This form of clustering can work on both edge-weighted graphs using some proximity measure (e.g. cosine similarity) and unweighted graphs.

Jarvis-Patrick clustering is a popular within-graph, shared nearest neighbor clustering algorithm [18, 28]. The algorithm has three main steps:

1. If graph G is weighted, then preprocess G in two successive steps. In the first step all edges that fall below an input threshold ϕ are removed from G. In the second step, for each vertex only the k edges with the highest weight are retained. The new graph obtained after the two preprocessing steps is called the "nearest neighbor graph" G_{NN}. If G is unweighted, call it G_{NN}.

2. Transform G_{NN} into G_{SNN}, the "shared nearest neighbor" graph. G_{SNN} is the weighted version of the G_{NN}, where each edge weight represents the number of neighbors an adjacent vertex pair have in common.

3. Obtain the clusters by applying the threshold τ to G_{SNN}, removing all edges in G_{SNN} whose weight is $< \tau$. Then, the connected components from the resulting graph form the clusters.

Let us look at how to perform the Jarvis-Patrick clustering using R. (Figure 8.3) We require the RBGL, igraph, and GraphClusterAnalysis packages.

```
1 library(GraphClusterAnalysis,graph)
2 library(igraph,RBGL)
3 data(SNN_Example)
4 G = graph.data.frame(SNN_Example,directed=FALSE)
5 Output =  SNN_Clustering(G,3)
6 Output
```

```
 7 # The first and second columns denote
 8 #   the vertex pairs connected by an edge
 9 # The third column is the edge weight
10 #   in terms of neighbors shared
11 $'Shared Nearest Neighbor (SNN) Edge List'
12       Vertex Vertex Number of Shared Neighbors
13 [1,]      0      1                            2
14 [2,]      0      2                            2
15 [3,]      0      3                            2
16 [4,]      1      2                            2
17 [5,]      1      3                            2
18 [6,]      2      3                            3
19 [7,]      2      4                            1
20 [8,]      3      4                            1
21 # Only edge (2,3) satisfies the tau=3 criteria
22 #   and so only 2 and 3 can be placed in the same cluster
23 # All other vertices become singleton clusters
24 $'Edges from SNN that satisfy tau'
25       Vertex Vertex Number of Shared Neighbors
26 [1,]     2      3                             3
27 $Clusters
28    VertexID ClusterID
29 1         0         0
30 2         1         1
31 3         2         2
32 4         3         2
33 5         4         3
```

If the input graph G is weighted, SNN_Clustering takes an additional parameter ϕ and will preprocess the graph based on this threshold to convert to an unweighted graph.

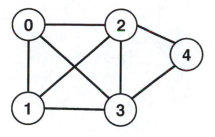

(a) The unweighted input graph G

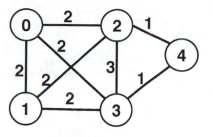

(b) The "shared nearest neighbor" graph G_{SNN}

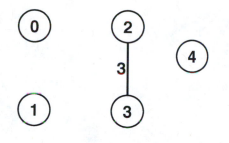

(c) The clusters resulted from the application of the Jarvis-Patrick Algorithm with $\tau=3$

FIGURE 8.3: Jarvis-Patrick clustering on unweighted graphs.

8.4 Betweenness Centrality Clustering

Another useful similarity metric between pairs of vertices is introduced in Chapter 5 on Link Analysis: the concept of betweenness centrality of a vertex. To refresh, the measure of betweenness centrality quantifies the degree to which a vertex occurs on the shortest path between all the other pairs of nodes. The graphs can be clustered by removing nodes with high betweenness centrality, under the assumption that such nodes typically separate different clusters in the graph. As a simple example involving groups of friends in a college setting, Sharon studies at both NCSU and Duke and has friends at both universities. In a social network representation, there will be a group of people from NCSU connected to Sharon and a group of people from Duke connected to Sharon. However, there may be very few direct connections between the two groups. Under such a circumstance, the betweenness centrality of Sharon will be very high and she separates the NCSU and Duke cluster in her friends list (see Figure 8.4a). Identifying vertices for clustering such as those that represent Sharon will help produce clusters with good inter-cluster similarity.

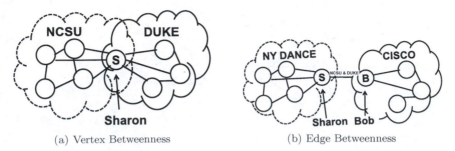

(a) Vertex Betweenness   (b) Edge Betweenness

FIGURE 8.4: Examples for vertex and edge betweenness.

Betweenness centrality can also be calculated for an edge that is defined as the degree to which an edge occurs along the shortest path between all pairs of nodes in the graph.

Definition 8.5 *Betweenness Centrality of an Edge*
Betweenness centrality ($C_b(u,v)$) for a graph G with nodes $\{s,t\} \in V(G)$ and edge $(u,v) \in E(G)$ is defined as

$$C_b(u,v) = \sum_{s \neq t} \frac{\Omega_{(u,v)}(s,t)}{\Omega(s,t)} \qquad (8.1)$$

where $\Omega(s,t)$ is the number of distinct geodesics from s to t and $\Omega_{(u,v)}(s,t)$ is the number of geodesics from s to t that pass through (u,v).

Using a similar example as before, let us consider two people, Sharon and Bob, who are in the same class in Duke and NCSU and, hence, are connected by an edge. However, Sharon is also part of the NY Dance Company and Bob works for Cisco, so the only connection between the two groups on the social network is the edge between Sharon and Bob (see Figure 8.4b). Hence, this edge will have high betweenness centrality. Clustering using this information will once again allow us to define fairly homogeneous clusters. The edge and vertex betweenness centrality formulas defined so far provide an absolute value, which likely needs to be normalized to prevent skewing based on aspects such as vertex degree. So, we can normalize the two measures as follows:

Definition 8.6 *Normalized Betweenness Centrality of a Vertex [31]*
Betweenness centrality ($C_b(v)$) for a graph G with nodes $\{s,t,v\} \in V(G)$ is defined as

$$C_b(v) = \frac{2 * (\sum_{s,t \neq v} \frac{\Omega_v(s,t)}{\Omega(s,t)})}{(|V(G)| - 1) * (|V(G)| - 2)} \qquad (8.2)$$

where $\Omega(s,t)$ is the number of distinct geodesics from s to t and $\Omega_v(s,t)$ is the number of geodesics from s to t that pass through v.

Definition 8.7 *Normalized Betweenness Centrality of an Edge [31]*
Betweenness centrality $(C_b(u,v))$ for a graph G with nodes $\{s,t\} \in V(G)$ and edge $(u,v) \in E(G)$ is defined as

$$C_b(u,v) = \frac{2*(\sum_{s \neq t} \frac{\Omega_{(u,v)}(s,t)}{\Omega(s,t)})}{(|V(G)|)*(|V(G)|-1)} \tag{8.3}$$

where $\Omega(s,t)$ is the number of distinct geodesics (see Definition in Chapter 5, Link Analysis) from s to t and $\Omega_{(u,v)}(s,t)$ is the number of geodesics from s to t that pass through *(u,v)*.

The betweenness centrality normalization for vertices is different from edges because in weighted graphs the shortest path between nodes u and v may or may not be through the edge (u,v).

Girvan and Newman [12] developed a clustering algorithm using edge betweenness centrality. The betweenness centrality of all edges is calculated, and the edge with the highest centrality is removed. The process is performed iteratively until the highest edge-betweenness centrality in the graph falls below a user-defined threshold (μ). The pseudocode is provided in Algorithm 15 ([1, 12]).

Input: A weighted or unweighted graph $G = (V, E)$
Input: Threshold μ
Output: A list of clusters

1 **while** $|E(G)| > 0$ **do**
2    $C_{u,v}$ - *betweenness centrality of edge* (u,v)
3   Calculate $C_{u,v}$ for all $(u,v) \in E(G)$
4   maxBetweennessEdge $= (x,y) : C_{x,y}$ is minimum over all (x,y) in $E(G)$
5   maxBetweennessValue $= C_{x,y}$
6   **if** $maxBetweennessValue \geq \mu$ **then**
7      $E(G) = E(G) - \{maxBetweennessEdge\}$
8   **else**
9   Break out of loop
10   **end**
11 **end**
12 **return** Connected components of modified G

Algorithm 15: Edge-betweenness centrality clustering

The edge-betweenness centrality clustering (Algorithm 15) partitions the input graph G into non-overlapping clusters (vertex sets). However, there are several real-world applications where it is necessary to obtain *overlapping clusters*. For example, if Sharon is part of both NCSU and Duke groups, then removing her entirely or putting her in just one of the groups would result in a loss of information about inter- and intragroup relationships. The algorithm

developed by Pinney and Westhead [24] uses the betweenness centrality of the
vertices in a graph, while retaining the vertices that the algorithm partitions
based on. The algorithm iteratively divides the graph at the vertex with the
maximum betweenness centrality. At the end of the algorithm, each removed
vertex v is inserted into all clusters that share at least one edge with v [30].
The pseudocode is provided in Algorithm 16.

---

1 **Algorithm:** Vertex-Betweenness Clustering(G)

  Input: A weighted or unweighted graph $G = (V, E)$
  Input: Threshold μ
  Output: A list of clusters

2 **while** $|V(G)| > 0$ **do**

3    $RemovedVertices = \{\}$

4    $G' = G$

5   C_v - *betweenness centrality of vertex* v

6   Calculate $C_v \ \forall v \in V(G)$

7    $maxBetweennessVertex = u : C_u$ minimum over all $u \in V(G)$

8    $maxBetweennessValue = C_u$

9   **if** $maxBetweennessValue \geq \mu$ **then**

10       $V(G) = V(G) - \{maxBetweennessVertex\}$

11       $E(G) = E(G) - \{(x, y) \in E(G) : x = v \text{ or } y = v\}$

12   Add $maxBetweennessVertex$ to $RemovedVertices$

13   **else**

14   Break out of loop

15   **end**

16 **end**

17 Clusters = All Connected components of G

18 **foreach** $clust \in$ Clusters **do**

19   **foreach** $k \in RemovedVertices$ **do**

20   **if** $\exists x \in clust : (x, k) \in E(G)$ **then**

21   Add k to $clust$

22   **end**

23   **end**

24 **end**

25 **return** Clusters

Algorithm 16: Vertex-betweenness centrality clustering with overlap

---

The following R example (Figure 8.5) shows edge betweenness clustering
on an undirected, unweighted graph. This example requires the GraphClusterAnalysis, graph, and RBGL package. Note that we can simply switch from
using edge betweenness to vertex betweenness by setting the *mode* parameter
of betweennessBasedClustering to **vertex**.

```
1 library(GraphClusterAnalysis,graph)
```

```
2 library(igraph,RBGL)
3 data(Betweenness_Edge_Example)
4 G = graph.data.frame(Betweenness_Edge_Example,directed=FALSE)
5 G
6 Vertices: 8
7 Edges: 9
8 Directed: FALSE
9 Edges:

10 [0] 0 -- 1
11 [1] 0 -- 3
12 [2] 1 -- 2
13 [3] 2 -- 3
14 [4] 3 -- 4
15 [5] 4 -- 5
16 [6] 4 -- 6
17 [7] 5 -- 7
18 [8] 6 -- 7
19 # Perform edge-wise betweenness centrality-based clustering
20   betweennessBasedClustering(G,mode="edge",threshold=0.2)
21 # (vertex-wise)
22 #    betweennessBasedClustering(G,mode="vertex",threshold=0.2)
23 $'Resulting Graph (G)'
24 A graphNEL graph with undirected edges
25 Number of Nodes = 8
26 Number of Edges = 8

27 $'Clusters Identified'
28 $'Clusters Identified'$'1'
29 [1] "0" "1" "2" "3"

30 $'Clusters Identified'$'2'
31 [1] "4" "5" "6" "7"
```

The edge and vertex betweenness functions by default use the normalized formulas for betweenness centrality calculation. However, we can explicitly make the function to use absolute values by setting the *normalize* parameter to FALSE. If the input graph G is weighted, the R function takes in an additional threshold parameter and will preprocess the graph based on the threshold value to convert to an unweighted graph.

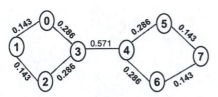

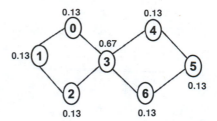

(a) Edge betweenness clustering with the initial betweenness centrality values.

(b) Vertex betweenness clustering with the initial betweenness centrality values.

FIGURE 8.5: Example normalized centrality calculations.

8.5   Highly Connected Subgraph Clustering

The connectivity within the identified cluster has not been explicitly taken into consideration in the previously discussed algorithms. Connectivity is important because it makes sure that the identified clusters are stable to a certain extent, i.e. small perturbations in the graph will not completely change the clusters obtained. This is important for applications such as recommendation systems. When using social network information to recommend movies to people, you want to identify those groups of people, where knowing the movies a few people in the group watched and rated, will help recommend the same or similar movies to the other members of the cluster. If the clusters were to keep constantly changing because a few social network links (edges) were lost or few vertices (people) left the network then the cost to collect information might end up exceeding the value gained. Highly Connected Subgraph (HCS) clustering takes connectivity explicitly into consideration during clustering. Let us define and understand a few concepts before going into the details of the algorithm.

Definition 8.8 *Cut ($Cu(G)$) of a graph G*
A set of edges whose removal disconnects a graph G.

Definition 8.9 *Minimum Edge Cut ($M_{Cu}(G)$) of graph G*
The cut with the minimum number of edges.

Definition 8.10 *Edge Connectivity ($EC(G)$) of a graph G*
The minimum number of edges whose removal will disconnect a graph G, i.e. $EC(G) = |M_{Cu}(G)|$.

Definition 8.11 *Highly Connected Subgraph S*
It is defined as a subgraph whose edge connectivity ($EC(S)$) exceeds half the number of nodes ($V(S)$), i.e., $EC(S) > \frac{V(S)}{2}$.

The HCS algorithm was proposed by Hartuv and Shamir [16] and the pseudocode is provided in Algorithm 17. The algorithm works on unweighted graphs.

Input: A weighted or unweighted graph $G = (V, E)$
Input: Threshold γ
Output: Highly connected component
1   **if** G is weighted **then**
2      $E_{remove} = \{(u, v) \in E(G) : \text{weight}(u, v) < \gamma\}$
3      $E(G) = E(G) - E_{remove}$
4   G is now taken as unweighted
5   **end**
6   Remove self-loops from G
7   $HCS(G)$

Algorithm 17: HCS clustering

Input: An unweighted graph $G = (V, E)$
Output: Highly connected component
1   *Compute the minimum cut of G,*
2   *returning the partitioned vertex sets* $\{S, V(G) - S\} = \text{MinCut(G)}$
3   **if** $EC(G) > \frac{V(G)}{2}$ **then**
4   **return** G
5   **else**
6      $HCS(S)$
7      $HCS(V(G) - S)$
8   **end**

Algorithm 18: $HCS(G)$ function

The HCS Clustering (Algorithm 17) has two preprocessing steps. The first preprocessing step removes all edges with weight less than γ and converts the resulting weighted graph to an unweighted graph. The second preprocessing step removes any self-loops that may be present in G. After these two steps, G is ready to be clustered using HCS.

The $HCS(G)$ function (Algorithm 18) first identifies the *minimum cut* of G and splits the graph G into two subgraphs S and $V(G) - S$ using the edges in the minimum cut. The algorithm returns G if it is a highly connected component; otherwise, it executes two calls to the $HCS(G)$ function with S and $V(G) - S$ as inputs, respectively. The highly connected components returned during the different recursive calls are the clusters of the graph G.

A common problem in clustering is the presence of a large number of singleton clusters. In the most extreme case, if every vertex were its own cluster, then we would essentially gain no information about the similarity between vertices. Typically, this case needs to be avoided in order to produce meaningful results, though avoiding it completely means that the clustering is not insulated against outliers. In the HCS algorithm, a heuristic called *adoption* is used to reduce the number of singletons by adding them to other existing non-singleton clusters. A singleton (x) is added to any existing non-singleton cluster C, if x has more than κ neighbors in C, where κ is a user-defined input. The adoption criterion becomes more stringent as κ increases.

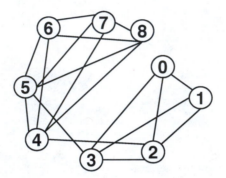

FIGURE 8.6: Unweighted graph (G) used in the HCS clustering example.

Let us now look at how to perform HCS clustering using R with an un-weighted or a weighted graph (Figure 8.6). This code requires the packages GraphClusterAnalysis, graph, and RBGL.

```
1 library(GraphClusterAnalysis,graph)
2 library(igraph,RBGL)
3 data(HCS_Example)
4 G = graph.data.frame(HCS_Example,directed=FALSE)
5 # Perform the clustering, using kappa=2 for the adoption strategy
6 HCSClustering(G,kappa=2)
7 $clusters
8 $clusters[[1]]
9 [1] "4" "5" "6" "7" "8"

10 $clusters[[2]]
11 [1] "0" "1" "2" "3"
```

If the input graph G is weighted the R function takes in an additional parameter γ and will preprocess the graph based on this threshold to convert to an unweighted graph.

8.6   Maximal Clique Enumeration

The HCS clustering algorithm discussed in the previous section outputs only those subgraphs whose connectivity is beyond a certain threshold. However, there are applications that need both a constraint on connectivity and density. An example of such an application is protein complex identification in a biological protein interaction network. This application is discussed in Section 8.8. Such networks require that the clusters found are pairwise interacting, that is, form cliques in the network. Cliques were introduced in Chapter 2, An Introduction to Graph Theory; to refresh, a *clique* is a vertex set by which each vertex pair in the set is adjacent. In other words, a clique in a graph is a complete subgraph.

However, simply identifying all cliques in the input graph will not solve all the problems. There may be several cases where one clique is completely contained within another clique and hence reporting the smaller clique becomes redundant. For instance, every graph has a single-vertex clique for every vertex in the graph, but this information is meaningless when analyzing graph structure. This redundancy can be removed by only reporting those cliques that are *maximal*.

Definition 8.12 *Maximal Clique*
A clique that is not part of a larger clique.

There are several algorithms that can enumerate all the maximal cliques in an input graph G, but the most widely-used, efficient, serial method of enumerating maximal cliques is by Bron and Kerbosch (BK) [3].

Input: A unweighted undirected graph $G = (V, E)$
Output: A list of all maximal cliques in G
1 *(Non-)maximal clique*
2 $C = \emptyset$
3 *Vertices that can be added to C to create a larger clique*
4 $P = V(G)$
5 *Vertices that would form redundant cliques if added to C*
6 $N = \emptyset$
7 $BK(C, P, N)$

Algorithm 19: Maximal clique enumeration algorithm (**BK(G)**)

The BK algorithm (Algorithms 19 and 20) uses recursion to enumerate all maximal cliques in the given input graph G. The algorithm recursively builds maximal cliques, with partial results (non-maximal cliques) represented as the set C. P is the set of vertices that can be added to C to make a larger clique. The set N is maintained to prevent the enumeration of redundant cliques. When P becomes empty we know that the set C cannot be extended

```
 1 if  P = ∅ and N = ∅ then
 2       output C as maximal clique
 3 else
 4       foreach  v ∈ P do
 5            N(v) is the set of vertices adjacent to v
 6            BK(C ∪ {v}, P ∩ N(v), N ∩ N(v))
 7            P = P − {v}
 8            N = N ∪ {v}
 9       end
10 end
```

Algorithm 20: The recursive function utilized in the **BK** algorithm (**BK(C, P, N)**)

any further and so $P = ∅$ becomes one part of the condition to check for maximality. However, by the definition of the set N, it contains vertices that are adjacent to all vertices in C. Thus if $N \neq ∅$ then any element from N can be added to C to make a larger clique, i.e. C is non-maximal. Thus $N = ∅$ becomes the second part of the condition to check for maximality. Typically, $N \neq ∅$ implies that the maximal clique $N \cup C$ will be or has been enumerated in another recursive call. Figure 8.7 provides an example to understand the general working of the maximal clique enumeration algorithm.

Allowing the graph to be clustered by using maximal clique representation provides a natural way to produce overlapping clusters without having to perform a postprocessing step. However, clique structures may not be applicable to some applications. For example, recommender systems that use the connectivity information to recommend new "potential friends." Here, cliques might represent groups where no new friend recommendations can be made.

The following R example (Figure 8.8) enumerates all the maximal cliques in a graph. The RBGL package provides the `maxClique` function that implements the BK algorithm to enumerate all the maximal cliques in the graphs.

```
 1 library(GraphClusterAnalysis,graph)
 2 library(igraph,RBGL)
 3 data(CliqueData)
 4 G = graph.data.frame(CliqueData,directed=FALSE)

 5 maximalCliqueEnumerator(G)
 6 $maxCliques
 7 $maxCliques[[1]]
 8 [1] "2" "1" "0" "3"

 9 $maxCliques[[2]]
10 [1] "2" "5" "6"
```

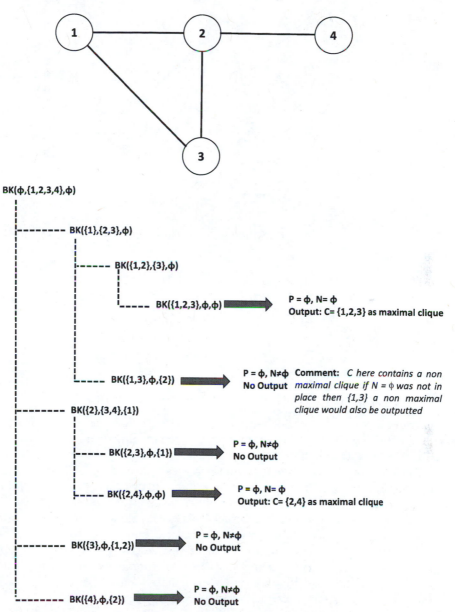

FIGURE 8.7: The BK algorithm applied on an example graph.

```
11 $maxCliques[[3]]
12 [1] "4" "0"
```

For large graphs, serial processing is too slow, since there can be a possibly exponential number of cliques in a graph (though this is rarely seen for real-

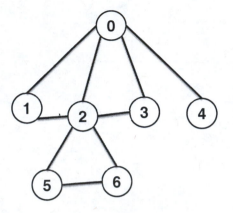

FIGURE 8.8: Graph G used in the maximal clique enumeration R example.

world graphs). For this purpose, there are parallel implementations of the BK algorithm, which split the recursive calls among many processors, developed by Schmidt et al. [26].

8.7   Clustering Vertices with Kernel k-means

k-means clustering is a widely-used vector-based clustering algorithm that can also be extended to cluster the vertices of a graph, given an appropriate definition of vertex similarity through kernel functions.

The concept of kernel functions and matrices is discussed in Chapter 4, An Introduction to Kernel Functions. To refresh, we know that we can use *within-graph* kernel functions to calculate the inner product of a pair of vertices in a user-defined feature space. The kernel function should additionally measure some structural property of the graph (i.e., vertex "similarity" to others). The results of a kernel function on each pair of vertices can be combined into a single matrix, known as the kernel matrix. The standard k-means algorithm can simply be modified to work on this calculated kernel proximity matrix and can hence cluster the vertices of the given input graph.

We begin by quickly reviewing the vector based k-means method and then go on to discuss how the method is adapted for graphs.

8.7.1   Vector-based k-means Clustering

The input to the k-means clustering algorithm is a set of data in an n-dimensional space and a value k. The algorithm picks k n-dimensional points to be the *centroids*. The algorithm then iteratively executes the following two steps:

1. Each point is assigned to the closest cluster centroid.
2. Each cluster's centroid is updated.

This process repeats until the centroids no longer change (or change minimally according to a measure of cluster quality)—a state known as *convergence*.

The ultimate goal of the k-means algorithm is to find a set of clusters $\pi_1, \pi_2, \ldots, \pi_k$ that minimize the following objective function given a set of vectors $a_1, a_2, \ldots, a_n$:

$$\sum_{c=1}^{k} \sum_{a_i \in \pi_c} \|a_i - m_c\|^2 , \qquad (8.4)$$

where $m_c = \frac{\sum_{a_i \in \pi_c} a_i}{|\pi_c|}$.

Equation 8.4 states that k-means finds a set of clusters that will minimize the distance between every point in that cluster and the *centroid* of that cluster. In the above equation, m_c represents the centroid of cluster c.

8.7.2 Graph-based k-means Clustering

The objective of the graph-based k-means is the same as the vector-based methods, i.e. to identify clusters whose within-cluster distance is minimized but the across-cluster distance is maximized. However, the notion of distance (or similarity) as noted earlier is not the same as for vectors and hence Equation 8.4 must be modified to use inner products for compatibility with kernel functions $\phi(\cdot)$.

$$\sum_{c=1}^{k} \sum_{a_i \in \pi_c} \|\phi(a_i) - m_c\|^2 , \qquad (8.5)$$

where $m_c = \frac{\sum_{a_i \in \pi_c} \phi(a_i)}{|\pi_c|}$.

We can expand the distance equation $\|\phi(a_i) - m_c\|^2$ to the following (see Chapter 4, An Introduction to Kernel Functions):

$$\phi(a_i) \cdot \phi(a_i) - \frac{2 \sum_{a_j \in \pi_c} \phi(a_i) \cdot \phi(a_j)}{|\pi_c|} + \frac{\sum_{a_j, a_l \in \pi_c} \phi(a_j) \cdot \phi(a_l)}{|\pi_c|^2}. \qquad (8.6)$$

Note that all operations that occur in the feature space defined by $\phi(\cdot)$ are inner products which we can replace with an appropriate kernel function. Given the kernel matrix $\mathbf{K}$, Equation 8.6 can be rewritten as follows:

$$\|\phi(a_i) - m_c\|^2 = \mathbf{K}_{ii} - \frac{2 \sum_{a_j \in \pi_c} \mathbf{K}_{ij}}{|\pi_c|} + \frac{\sum_{a_j, a_l \in \pi_c} \mathbf{K}_{jl}}{|\pi_c|^2} \qquad (8.7)$$

Input: The kernel matrix of graph G $\mathbf{K} = (V, E)$
Input: Number of clusters k
Input: Maximum number of iterations n_{max}
Input: Optional initial clusters $\{\pi^0\}_{c=1}^k$
Output: Clusters that represent the final partitioning of the points
$\{\pi^{final}\}_{c=1}^k$

1 **if** $\{\pi^0\}_{c=1}^k = \emptyset$ **then**
2   Initialize clusters $\pi_1^0, ..., \pi_k^0$ randomly
3   Set $n = 1$.
4 **end**
5 **foreach** $a_i \in V(G)$ **do**
6   **foreach** $c \in \pi_c^{n-1}$ **do**
7   Compute $\|\phi(a_i) - m_c\|^2$ using Equation 8.7
8   **end**
9 **end**
10 $c^*(a_i) = \underset{c}{argmin} \|\phi(a_i) - m_c\|^2$
11 Compute $\pi_c^n = \{a : c^*(a_i) = c\}$.
12 **if** not converged or $n < n_{max}$ **then**
13      $n = n + 1$
14   Go to Line 1
15 **else**
16   **return** $\{\pi_c^n\}_{c=1}^k$.
17 **end**

Algorithm 21: Kernel k-means algorithm

The pseudocode of the method is provided in Algorithm 21. If there are no initial clusters given as input, initialize $\pi_1^0, ..., \pi_l^0$ randomly. Set n, the iterator, to zero. Calculate the distance between every vertex a_i and the centroid of each cluster c obtained in the previous iteration. Using the calculated distances, for each vertex a_i, we identify the cluster c whose centroid is closest to a_i and add a_i to that cluster. If the clusters have not converged (i.e., the centroids have changed) or if $n_{max} > n$ then we move to the next iteration, otherwise, the algorithm terminates and outputs $\{\pi_c^n\}_{c=1}^k$ as the final clusters.

An R example is given below (Figure 8.9):

```
1 library(GraphClusterAnalysis,graph)
2 library(igraph,RBGL)
3 library(kernlab)
4 data(Kernel_Example)
5 G = graph.data.frame(Kernel_Example,directed=FALSE)
6 G
7 Vertices: 6
8 Edges: 9
9 Directed: FALSE
```

```
10 Edges:

11 [0] 0 -- 1
12 [1] 0 -- 3
13 [2] 1 -- 2
14 [3] 1 -- 3
15 [4] 1 -- 4
16 [5] 2 -- 3
17 [6] 2 -- 4
18 [7] 2 -- 5
19 [8] 4 -- 5


20 #Laplacian Kernel
21 lapKern = laplacedot(sigma=1)
22 F =  get.adjacency(G)
23 K =kernelMatrix(kernel=lapKern,F)
24 K
25 An object of class "kernelMatrix"
26         [,1]      [,2]      [,3]      [,4]      [,5]      [,6]
27 [1,] 1.0000000 0.1353353 0.2431167 0.1769212 0.1769212 0.1353353
28 [2,] 0.1353353 1.0000000 0.1353353 0.1769212 0.1068779 0.2431167
29 [3,] 0.2431167 0.1353353 1.0000000 0.1068779 0.1769212 0.1353353
30 [4,] 0.1769212 0.1769212 0.1068779 1.0000000 0.2431167 0.1769212
31 [5,] 0.1769212 0.1068779 0.1769212 0.2431167 1.0000000 0.1769212
32 [6,] 0.1353353 0.2431167 0.1353353 0.1769212 0.1769212 1.0000000
33 #Provide the Kernel Matrix as input
34 Clusters=kkmeans(K,centers=3)
35 Clusters
36 Spectral Clustering object of class "specc"
37  Cluster memberships:
38  3 3 2 1 1 2
39 [1] "Kernel matrix used"
40 Centers:
41         [,1]      [,2]      [,3]      [,4]      [,5]      [,6]
42 [1,] 0.1769212 0.1418996 0.1418996 0.6215584 0.6215584 0.1769212
43 [2,] 0.1892260 0.1892260 0.5676676 0.1418996 0.1769212 0.5676676
44 [3,] 0.5676676 0.5676676 0.1892260 0.1769212 0.1418996 0.1892260
45 Cluster size:
46 [1] 2 2 2
47 Within-cluster sum of squares:
48 [1] 1.571114 1.416817 1.380705
```

The k-means clustering algorithm is both easy to implement/use and fast. However, it is not without pitfalls. Poor initial *centroid* placement can lead to poor clustering, as k-means is especially prone to local minima. Different initial centroids, especially with noisy data, may produce different cluster results. A

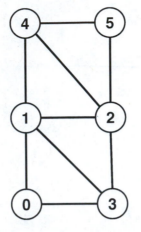

FIGURE 8.9: Graph G used in the graph-based k-means R example.

common strategy is to generate several random sets of centroids and pursue the most promising based on a predetermined measure of cluster quality, as described in Chapter 12.

Another parameter that needs to be chosen is k. There has been no real agreed-upon method to choose k. Typically an arbitrary choice is made and then adjusted based on the value obtained for the objective function. In some cases, statistical analysis [15] can be performed to arrive at a "good" value of k. In other cases, the application domain provides a way to select this parameter. For example: if a few new groups of monkeys were being clustered based on their proximity to chimpanzees or gorillas, then the natural choice of k for the algorithm is two and the chimpanzee and gorilla data are used as initial centroids.

8.8   Application

8.8.1   Protein Complexes in Biological Networks

The various functions in organism's cells are carried out by a network of interacting proteins. This network is represented as a graph where the nodes represent proteins and an edge implies that the proteins at the two ends of the edge interact in the cell. The network is called a *protein protein interaction* (PPI) network. In such networks, a biologist is interested in identifying groups of proteins that work together to realize a fairly distinct cellular function [36]. These are called *protein complexes*. Protein complexes are modeled as groups of pairwise interacting proteins [36, 11]. In graph theoretic sense, they represent cliques. All the potential protein complexes of an organism can be obtained by enumerating the maximal cliques in a organism's PPI network. We apply the maximal clique enumeration method discussed in Section 8.6 on the *Saccharomyces cerevisiae* (baker's yeast) PPI network (4,554 vertices and 15,454 edges). The network was obtained from the MIPS Database [14].

```
1 library(GraphClusterAnalysis,graph)
2 library(igraph,RBGL)
3 data(YeasPPI)
4 G = graph.data.frame(YeasPPI,directed=FALSE)
5 length(V(G))
6 [1] 4554
7 length(E(G))
8 [1] 15454
9 Potential_Protein_Complexes = maximalCliqueEnumerator(G)
10 length(Potential_Protein_Complexes$maxCliques)
11 [1] 9548
12 # Display the first 10 maximal cliques found
13  Potential_Protein_Complexes$maxCliques[1:10]
14 [[1]]
15 [1] "YJR091c" "YMR263w" "YML041c"

16 [[2]]
17 [1] "YJR091c" "YMR263w" "YNL215w"

18 [[3]]
19 [1] "YJR091c" "YMR263w" "YNL171c"

20 [[4]]
21 [1] "YJR091c" "YMR263w" "YBR231c"

22 [[5]]
23 [1] "YJR091c" "YMR263w" "YGR182c"

24 [[6]]
25 [1] "YJR091c" "YHR060w"

26 [[7]]
27 [1] "YJR091c" "YMR197c"

28 [[8]]
29 [1] "YJR091c" "YOR014w"

30 [[9]]
31 [1] "YJR091c" "YAL034w-a"
```

```
32 [[10]]
33 [1] "YJR091c" "YDR152w"
```

In this example, there were a total of 9,548 maximal cliques generated. We call them potential protein complexes because though they satisfy the structural criteria, they still need to be analyzed further to separate the maximal cliques that are actual protein complexes from maximal cliques that occurred by chance (may be due to error in data). This kind of postprocessing requires some application-specific metrics and analysis methods. One such method is the *functional enrichment* analysis, which is able to both predict the function that the complex is likely to carry out and assign a confidence score in the form of a *p*-value, quantifying the prediction. Using a cutoff like 0.05, we can then filter out any maximal cliques that are likely not protein complexes. A more detailed description of *functional enrichment* and other application-specific analysis methods and metrics are discussed in Chapter 12 on performance analysis.

8.9   How to Choose a Clustering Technique

Clustering is a powerful technique in data mining, but there is still one very important question to answer: Which clustering technique to choose. The best answer to this question is that the clustering algorithm depends largely on the domain that you are working with and the properties of the data being clustered. There are some inherent properties of the clustering algorithm that might help narrow down the choices. Two such properties are discussed below.

8.9.1   Complete vs. Partial Clustering

The complete clustering algorithm requires that every vertex belong to a cluster when the algorithm completes. For example, when clustering a group of people to be seated at different tables at a wedding, we want every person to be assigned to at least one table. However, this kind of clustering could force outliers into clusters they don't belong to. The minimum spanning tree clustering is an example of complete clustering.

Partial clustering is a type of clustering in which no vertex is required to be in a cluster, i.e., allows for singleton clusters. This type of clustering scheme ignores outliers that could skew clustering results. The maximal clique enumeration is an example of partial clustering.

8.9.2 Overlapping vs. Exclusive Clustering

Overlapping clustering methods allow vertices to belong to more than just one cluster. The advantage in using this method is that you are not forced to randomly break a tie if a vertex equally belongs to two or more clusters. In applications like recommender systems where the end-goal is identifying groups of people with similar interests, it seems natural to use an overlapping clustering scheme. The maximal clique enumeration and vertex betweenness-based centrality algorithms are examples of such techniques.

There are times, however, when overlapping clusters are simply not practical to use. For example, if we are clustering the members of a social network based on where they live, it does not make sense to allow a user to be a part of two different clusters. In this situation, it is probably best to use an exclusive clustering scheme where a datum can belong to at most one cluster. The k-means clustering is an example of the exclusive clustering scheme. However, there have been algorithms developed, known as *fuzzy k-means*, that allow for overlapping clusters.

Bibliographic Notes

Measures of centrality, as used in this chapter, can go beyond the "betweenness" of vertices and edges. For instance, Latora and Marchiori [21] use a centrality concept called *information centrality* to partition the graph. *Information centrality* is defined as the relative decrease in the average efficiency of the graph upon removal of the edge [21]. Efficiency of a pair of vertices is defined as the inverse of their distance in the graph, and average efficiency is the average of efficiency values of all distinct pairs of vertices in the graph [20].

Alternative models of clustering exist outside of the single-pass partitioning presented in this chapter. A different strategy is to generate a *tree* structure, where each node in the tree is a cluster, the root node is the full set of data, and child nodes are subsets of the parent node. This form of clustering is known as *hierarchical clustering*. Hierarchical clustering has a natural, recursive description, which is suitable for datasets such as the LinkedIn network, where a group of people may belong to different divisions and subdivisions but are part of the same company. This tree interpretation holds for the clustering methods discussed in this chapter as well, though the trees generated are only a single level, consisting of the root node and a single level of child nodes. These clustering algorithms may be generated in a top-down or bottom-up fashion. Top-down approaches begin with all the vertices in the same cluster and then recursively partition, until each vertex is in its own cluster [2, 4, 10]. Bottom-up approaches begin with each vertex in its own cluster and then iteratively merge until all vertices are part of the same cluster [6, 7, 17].

Hierarchical clustering algorithms use many of the same clustering strategies as those discussed in the chapter. For instance, apart from the Jarvis and Patrick [18] algorithm, shared nearest neighbor clustering has been adopted to fit the hierarchical clustering model [19, 13]. Furthermore, advanced metrics of shared nearest neighbors have been devised, such as the *density-based* metric [8, 9].

Classical clustering methods have also been enriched with additional descriptive information. For instance, fuzzy clustering assigns a vertex to multiple clusters, where the membership of the vertex to some clusters may carry a higher weight than others. Maximal clique enumeration [3] is a natural way of obtaining fuzzy clusters, but it may require some additional scoring metrics to quantify the member of each vertex to the clique that it is present in. Nepusz *et al.* [23] developed a fuzzy graph clustering method that models the fuzzy clustering as an optimization problem.

In a similar vein, probabilistic clustering methods, which assign probabilities for each datum to be in a particular cluster, are usually based on the random walk principle, working on the assumption that two vertices in the same cluster should be *quickly reachable* from each other [25]. Additionally, if a random walk visits a vertex belonging to a cluster, it will also likely visit several other vertices belonging to the same cluster (in succession) before moving on to a vertex in another cluster. Spielman and Teng [27] as well as van Dongen [29] discuss random walk based clustering methods.

Specialized clustering methods can also be devised depending on application-specific properties of data. For instance, a *bipartite* graph is a graph where the vertices can be split into two independent sets, such that all edges in the graph connect only vertices belonging to the two different sets. A real-world example is a graph consisting of the customers and the movies they rent. The clustering is done to vertices in a single partition based on the vertices they are connected to in the other partition. For example, two customers have similar taste if they rent the same movies. Zha *et al.* [35] propose a technique to partition bipartite graphs into clusters.

The clustering methods discussed in this chapter typically cluster all the vertices in one pass, with the global system state available. However, these approaches may run into some scalability issues when dealing with very large, dense graphs and hence *iterative* clustering methods may be required, where the vertex is initially assigned to some cluster and then later the assignments are modified to optimize some property of the clustering. Additionally, in some situations we may have to cluster the current vertex having only the knowledge of the previously seen vertices and edges. These algorithms are called *online*. Typically, the data requiring this kind of online clustering occur in a data stream. An online clustering algorithm for grouping the vertices into k clusters has been proposed by Zanghi *et al.* [34]. Sometimes, there are some incremental changes made to the graph over time, and instead of re-clustering the entire graph, the new elements are assigned to existing clusters or new clusters are formed, based on some estimation techniques. This kind of clustering is called *incremental* and Wong and Fu [32] proposed such a technique for web-page graphs.

This chapter discusses only algorithms that cluster the vertices of a single graph, however, as mentioned in the introduction, there has also been work done to cluster sets of graphs [5, 22]. The most straightforward example involves kernel k-means, where a valid between-graph kernel function allows for clustering of sets of graphs.

8.10 Exercises

1. Given the weighted graph G (weights represent distance) in Figure 8.10, calculate the minimum spanning tree of the graph. Perform the k-Spanning Tree Clustering with $k = 3$.

2. The problem of *context identification* is a critical one in the area of mobile computation. In this problem, we are given a periodic WiFi scan log, which provides information on WiFi access points accessed at various locations and observed over time. Due to the dynamic nature of wireless networks, multiple observations at the same location will not always have the same set of access points. Thus, given a set of observations, we have to identify different clusters of access points from observations. The information given is as follows, where each entry represents a set of three access points observed together. $D = \{(1,2,3),(2,3,4),(2,3,5),(1,3,4),(4,6,7),(4,7,8),(5,7,8),(6,7,8)\}$.

   Each unique integer represents a single access point. Determine the access point clusters using the SNN clustering technique for $r = 3$ and $r = 4$.

3. Which clustering technique would be best for each of the following scenarios? Justify your answers.

   a) A company wishes to perform clustering on a set of documents

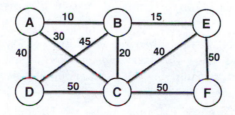

FIGURE 8.10: Graph G for Exercise 1.

based on term similarities in order to analyze them better. Since one document might fit well into two different clusters, while another might not fit well into any, the company would like each document to belong to zero or more clusters.

b) As a networking activity, a teacher wishes to assign her students to groups based on data she collected on the students' interests, so that the students in each group will have similar interests to discuss.

c) A new social networking site is trying to figure out the best algorithm to design their friend recommendation feature around, based on similar interests, similar friends, and so on.

4. In a social networking site, an automatic party invitation mechanism is being developed to invite all fans of k movie genres to a special private screening of a new indie film at a nearby theater that spans across these genres (i.e., the movie is an Action-Adventure/Comedy/Drama, and users can be defined to like one or more of these genres). The developers are tasked with identifying a clustering algorithm suited to ensure the maximum number of people with these common interests, but they also need to be able to re-use these clusters for future projects (i.e., a Drama/Romance film). Name at least three considerations they should make for the algorithm to use.

5. List a total of two advantages/disadvantages of using maximal clique representation while clustering.

6. Let *edge new-centrality* [21] be an alternative to edge-betweenness-based methods. The formula for *edge new-centrality* (NC) is as follows:

$$NC(u, v) = \frac{1}{dist(u, v)} \qquad (8.8)$$

At each iteration, the edge with the minimum NC value is removed until the minimum NC value falls above a threshold τ. Write an R code to perform clustering based on this new metric. The function should take in the graph G and τ as input (any other variables/information can be passed to the function if necessary) and return the clusters as output.

7. As discussed in the Bibliographic Notes section, maximal clique enumeration allows for fuzzy clusters. Define a function that can assign a score quantifying the membership of a vertex to a maximal clique.

8. Given the graph in Figure 8.11, use the HCS clustering algorithm to divide it into clusters (subgraphs).

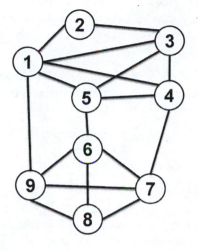

FIGURE 8.11: Graph G for Question 8.

9. Although the Jarvis-Patrick algorithm, unlike k-means, automatically determines how many clusters there are, it is still dependent on different input parameters. Discuss how Jarvis-Patrick is similar to k-means, in that the results of the clustering are dependent on the parameters.

Bibliography

[1] Ulrik Brandes. A faster algorithm for betweenness centrality. *Journal of Mathematical Sociology*, 25:163–177, 2001.

[2] Ulrik Brandes, Marco Gaertler, and Dorothea Wagner. Experiments on graph clustering algorithms. In *11th Annual European Symposium on Algorithms*, pages 568–579, 2003.

[3] Coen Bron and Joep Kerbosch. Algorithm 457: Finding all cliques of an undirected graph. *Communications of the ACM*, 16:575–577, September 1973.

[4] Thang Nguyen Bui, F. Thomson Leighton, Soma Chaudhuri, and Michael Sipser. Graph bisection algorithms with good average case behavior. *Combinatorica*, 7:171–191, 1987.

[5] Horst Bunke, P. Foggia, C. Guidobaldi, and M. Vento. Graph clustering using the weighted minimum common supergraph. In *Proceedings*

of the Fourth International Association for Pattern Recognition International Conference on Graph-based Representations in Pattern Recognition, pages 235–246, 2003.

[6] John Joseph Carrasco, Daniel C Fain, Kevin J Lang, and Leonid Zhukov. Clustering of bipartite advertiser-keyword graph. In *Proceedings of the IEEE International Conference on Data Mining*, 2003.

[7] Luca Donetti and Miguel A. Munoz. Detecting network communities: A new systematic and efficient algorithm. *Journal of Statistical Mechanics: Theory and Experiment*, 2004:P10012, 2004.

[8] Levent Ertoz, Michael Steinbach, and Vipin Kumar. A new shared nearest neighbor clustering algorithm and its applications. In *Workshop on Clustering High Dimensional Data and Its Applications at Second SIAM International Conference on Data Mining*, 2002.

[9] Levent Ertoz, Michael Steinbach, and Vipin Kumar. Finding clusters of different sizes, shapes, and densities in noisy, high dimensional data. In *Proceedings of Second SIAM International Conference on Data Mining*, 2003.

[10] Gary W. Flake, Robert E. Tarjan, and Kostas Tsioutsiouliklis. Graph clustering and minimum cut trees. *Internet Mathematics*, 1:385–408, 2004.

[11] Anne-Claude Gavin, Markus Bosche, Roland Krause, Paola Grandi, Martina Marzioch, Andreas Bauer, Jorg Schultz, Jens M. Rick, Anne-Marie Michon, Cristina-Maria Cruciat, Marita Remor, Christian Hofert, Malgorzata Schelder, Miro Brajenovic, Heinz Ruffner, Alejandro Merino, Karin Klein, Manuela Hudak, David Dickson, Tatjana Rudi, Volker Gnau, Angela Bauch, Sonja Bastuck, Bettina Huhse, Christina Leutwein, Marie-Anne Heurtier, Richard R. Copley, Angela Edelmann, Erich Querfurth, Vladimir Rybin, Gerard Drewes, Manfred Raida, Tewis Bouwmeester, Peer Bork, Bertrand Seraphin, Bernhard Kuster, Gitte Neubauer, and Giulio Superti-Furga. Functional organization of the yeast proteome by systematic analysis of protein complexes. *Nature*, 415(6868):141–147, 2002.

[12] Michelle Girvan and Mark Newman. Community structure in social and biological networks. *Proceedings of the National Academy of Sciences*, 99(12):7821–7826, 2002.

[13] Sudipto Guha, Rajeev Rastogi, and Kyuseok Shim. ROCK: A robust clustering algorithm for categorical attributes. In *Proceedings of the Fifteenth International Conference on Data Engineering*, 2000.

[14] Ulrich Güldener, Martin Münsterkötter, Matthias Oesterheld, Philipp Pagel, Andreas Ruepp, Hans-Werner Mewes, and Volker Stümpflen. MPact: The MIPS protein interaction resource on yeast. *Nucleic Acids Research*, 34(1):D436 –D441, 2005.

[15] Greg Hamerly and Charles Elkan. Learning the k in k-means. In *Proceedings of the Seventeenth Annual Conference on Neural Information Processing Systems (NIPS)*, volume 17, pages 281–288, 2003.

[16] Erez Hartuv and Ron Shamir. A clustering algorithm based on graph connectivity. *Information Processing Letters*, 76:175–181, 1999.

[17] John Hopcroft, Omar Khan, Brian Kulis, and Bart Selman. Natural communities in large linked networks. In *Proceedings of the Ninth ACM SIGKDD International Conference on Knowledge Discovery and Data Mining*, pages 541–546, 2003.

[18] Ray A. Jarvis. and Edward A. Patrick. Clustering using a similarity measure based on shared near neighbors. *IEEE Transactions on Computers*, 22:1025–1034, 1973.

[19] Gowda K. Chidananda and G. Krishna. Agglomerative clustering using the concept of mutual nearest neighbourhood. *Pattern Recognition*, 10:105–112, 1978.

[20] V. Latora and M. Marchiori. A measure of centrality based on network efficiency. *New Journal of Physics*, 9:188, 2007.

[21] Vito Latora and Massimo Marchiori. Efficient behavior of small-world networks. *Physical Review Letters*, 87:198701, 2001.

[22] Bin Luo, Richard C. Wilson, and Edwin R. Hancock. Spectral clustering of graphs. In *Proceedings of the Fourth International Association for Pattern Recognition International Conference on Graph Based Representations in Pattern Recognition*, pages 190–201, 2003.

[23] Tamas Nepusz, Andrea Petroczi, Laszlo Negyessy, and Fulop Bazso. Fuzzy communities and the concept of bridgeness in complex networks. *Physical Review E*, 77:016107, 2008.

[24] John W. Pinney and David R. Westhead. Betweenness-based decomposition methods for social and biological networks. In *Interdisciplinary Statistics and Bioinformatics*, pages 87–90. Leeds University Press, 2006.

[25] S. Schaeffer. Graph clustering. *Computer Science Review*, 1:27–64, 2007.

[26] Matthew C. Schmidt, Nagiza F. Samatova, Kevin Thomas, and Byung-Hoon Park. A scalable, parallel algorithm for maximal clique enumeration. *Journal of Parallel and Distributed Computing*, 69:417–428, 2009.

[27] Daniel A. Spielman and Shang-Hua Teng. Nearly-linear time algorithms for graph partitioning, graph sparsification, and solving linear systems. In *Proceedings of the Thirty-Sixth Annual ACM Symposium on Theory of Computing*, pages 81–90, 2004.

[28] Michael Steinbach, Levent Ertz, and Vipin Kumar. The challenges of clustering high-dimensional data. In *New Vistas in Statistical Physics: Applications in Econophysics, Bioinformatics, and Pattern Recognition*. Springer-Verlag, 2003.

[29] Stijn van Dongen. *Graph clustering by flow simulation*. PhD thesis, University of Utrecht, 2000.

[30] Jianxin Wang, Min Li, Youping Deng, and Yi Pan. Recent advances in clustering methods for protein interaction networks. *BMC Genomics*, 11(3):S10, 2010.

[31] Zhifang Wang, Anna Scaglione, and Robert J. Thomas. Electrical central-ity measures for electric power grid vulnerability analysis. In *Proceedings of the 49th IEEE Conference on Decision and Control*, pages 5792–5797, 2010.

[32] Wai-cjiu Wong and Ads Wai-chee Fu. Incremental document clustering for web page classification. In *Proceedings of the International Conference on Information Society in the 21st Century Emerging Technologies and New Challenges*, 2000.

[33] Ying Xu, Victor Olman, and Dong Xu. Minimum spanning trees for gene expression data clustering. *Genome Informatics*, 12:24–33, 2001.

[34] Hugo Zanghi, Christophe Ambroise, and Vincent Miele. Fast online graph clustering via erdos-renyi mixture. *Pattern Recognition*, 41:3592–3599, 2008.

[35] Hongyuan Zha, Xiaofeng He, Chris Ding, Horst Simon, and Ming Gu. Bipartite graph partitioning and data clustering. In *Proceedings of the Tenth International Conference on Information and Knowledge Manage-ment*, pages 25–32, 2001.

[36] Bing Zhang, Byung-Hoon Park, Tatiana Karpinets, and Nagiza F. Sama-tova. From pull-down data to protein interaction networks and complexes with biological relevance. *Bioinformatics*, 24(7):979–986, 2008.

9

Classification

Srinath Ravindran, John Jenkins, Huseyin Sencan, Jay Prakash
Goel, Saee Nirgude, Kalindi K Raichura, Suchetha M Reddy, and
Jonathan S. Tatagiri

North Carolina State University

CONTENTS

This chapter introduces several techniques for predicting properties of data
that can be represented as graphs. It describes techniques for classifying multiple graphs and for classifying individual vertices within a single graph. Most of
the chapter focuses on kernel-based classification techniques as they have been
shown to be successful in practice and are based on an implicit graph-to-vector
mapping, allowing us to use well-known numerical-vector-based classification
methods.

Classification of graph data has many applications. For example, molecular structures can be represented as graphs, and classification techniques can
be used to predict properties of molecules like its toxicity. Computer network
traffic can also be modeled this way, and we can categorize different types of
network behavior. In this chapter, a variety of approaches to graph classification and a few applications are discussed in detail. The evaluation of the
models produced by classification algorithms contains a rich set of information
and is discussed in its own chapter, Chapter 12.

Given the focus of this book on graphs, the classification methods discussed in this chapter are more specialized in nature, meaning that a number of important concepts and techniques in traditional classification are not covered. Books such as Tan et al.'s *Introduction to Data Mining* present a more complete picture [22], and we recommend a book such as theirs for a comprehensive treatment of classification that doesn't involve graph structures.

9.1   Overview of Classification

Chemists regularly work with hazardous materials, especially in the design phase when experimental chemicals are being synthesized. For them, it is important to be able to *predict* properties of new molecules. For instance, say we want to predict whether or not a given molecule is toxic, that is, *classify* the molecules. The *dependent variable* in this case is the property of being toxic, while the *independent variable* is the molecule's structural and physicochemical properties.

Performing this *classification* of molecules is a very difficult task without any prior information; we would have to rely on a combination of complex chemical interaction models, expert knowledge, and field testing. However, through data mining techniques we can make use of molecules we already know to be (non-)toxic when deciding whether a new molecule is toxic or not. That is, we can build a *model* that captures properties and relationships of the known examples and can be used to predict properties of new instances. This process is referred to as *supervised learning*.

Put into more formal language, *classification* is a predictive task in which input data is algorithmically assigned discrete values, such as toxic vs. non-toxic. These values are called *class labels*. In this chapter, we will assume *binary classification*, that is, only two classes are considered. Except for much more specialized methods, *multi-class classification* is typically performed as a simple extension or wrapper of binary classification methods. For instance, a supervised learning method could work on multiple class labels by iteratively using binary classification on a single class label vs. all other class labels, treating them as a single class. A *classifier* is presented with a set of *training examples* with known class labels. The task, then, is to build a model that can best approximate the label or target variable, using the training examples. Of course, the model built must be capable of estimating the label of examples not present in the training examples; the classifier is of no use if it can only predict known samples! Thus the aim of classifiers is to build highly accurate models that can generalize beyond the training examples.

As opposed to a predictive task such as classification, *Descriptive Tasks* are on the other side of the coin; rather than having clean-cut dependent variables, we want to partition data sets based on sometimes complex underlying relationships in data. This includes *clustering* of data by some measure of similarity (see Chapter 8), analyzing the *association* between instances of data, and *detecting anomalous features* of data (see Chapter 11).

> **Definition 9.1** *Classification*
> The task of assigning class labels in a discrete class label set Y to input instances in an input space X.

9.2 Classification of Vector Data: Support Vector Machines

While the book in general focuses on graph data structures, some of the most effective graph classification methods arise from applying kernel functions to sometimes arbitrary types to transform the problem into the classification of real-valued vectors, which is a very well-established subject. Thus, studying these classification algorithms is particularly important in the context of graph classification. By far, one of the most popular numerical-vector-based classfiers is the support vector machine (SVM), especially since it can utilize the kernel trick to capture non-linear relationships in the input vectors. Furthermore, SVMs have a very strong theoretical background in statistics and machine learning [24, 25, 26]. The following treatment of SVMs leaves out some of the finer mathematical and theoretical details; a more extensive description and tutorial on their use is provided, for example, by Burges [2].

> **Definition 9.2** *Linear Support Vector Machine*
> A binary classifier on numerical-vector data which, for input dimension d, builds a $(d-1)$-dimensional hyperplane separating the two classes.

SVMs use simple, intuitive concepts to classify vector data into one of two classes, though the mathematics behind them are more complex. Consider a distribution of two-class data on a 2-D plot, such as in Figure 9.1. Call these class labels $\{+1, -1\}$, for mathematical simplicity. Basically, we want to draw a line through the plot that puts all of the data with class $+1$ on one side of the line and data with class -1 on the other side. Then, the line is our model of the data and we can classify unknown data by determining on which side of the line the new data resides. We can perform the same for three and higher dimensions by generalizing to use a (hyper)plane, the generalization of a two-dimensional line and three-dimensional plane.

There are a number of questions that arise from this simple description. First, how do we go about choosing the line? Second, what is a good criteria to make the line fit the training examples best? And finally, what do we do if we cannot separate the data with a line? In other words, what if the classes have a non-linear relationship in the data?

The second question is the easiest to answer within a geometric context.

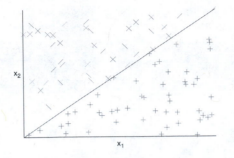

FIGURE 9.1: A binary data set which is linearly separable.

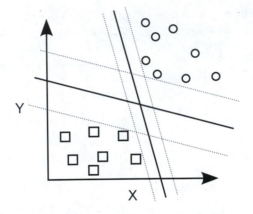

FIGURE 9.2: Two separating hyperplanes. Which one better encodes the trend of the data?

The "best" hyperplane we can find is the one that separates the input data by the largest degree (assuming that the input data is representative of the actual distribution; remember, no free lunch). That is, the plane should maximize the distance between itself and the closest points of each class. This distance is called the *margin*, and the hyperplane maximizing this distance is called the *maximum-margin hyperplane*. An example of two separating hyperplanes with different margins is shown in Figure 9.2. So, the primary goal of linear SVMs is to find the maximum-margin hyperplane for the input data. The points that belong to the hyperplane are called the *support vectors*. These points are the crux of the SVM, as one can define the hyperplane based solely on the support vectors.

The first question necessitates a formal description of the SVM formulation. Consider a real-valued set of points $X = \{\mathbf{x_1}, \mathbf{x_2}, \ldots, \mathbf{x_n}\}$ with class labels $Y = \{y_1, y_2, \ldots, y_n\}$. Each $\mathbf{x_i}$ is a real-valued vector of dimension d and, since we are focusing on binary classification, each class label y_i is of class -1 or $+1$. To encode the hyperplane, we need to know its *orientation* and its *off-*

set from the origin. To encode the orientation, we can use the *normal vector*, a vector that is perpendicular to the hyperplane. Call this vector $\mathbf{w}$, of length $\|\mathbf{w}\|$. We can encode the offset from the origin as the parameter b, where $\frac{b}{\|\mathbf{w}\|}$ is the (normalized) distance along the normal vector from the origin to the hyperplane. Therefore, any point $\mathbf{p}$ is on the hyperplane if it is a distance of 0 from the plane, in the direction of $\mathbf{w}$. In other words, $\mathbf{p}$ is on the hyperplane if the following equation holds:

$$\mathbf{w} \cdot \mathbf{p} - b = 0 \tag{9.1}$$

Now, the hyperplane described by Equation 9.1 only describes the plane in between the two sets of data. Think of expanding the plane equally along both directions of $\mathbf{w}$ until a point is hit; these planes are defined by the equations

$$\mathbf{w} \cdot \mathbf{p} - b = 1 \tag{9.2}$$
$$\mathbf{w} \cdot \mathbf{p} - b = -1 \tag{9.3}$$

The distance between the two planes is simply $\frac{2}{\|\mathbf{w}\|}$. Therefore, in order to maximize the margin, we must minimize $\|\mathbf{w}\|$. Furthermore, we wouldn't want any point within the margin, so we must add the appropriate constraint for each datum $\mathbf{x_i}$, based on Equations 9.2 and 9.3. Thanks to our choice of class labels, the equations collapse into a simple inequality:

$$y_i(\mathbf{w} \cdot \mathbf{x_i} - b) \geq 1 \ (i = 1 \ldots n) \tag{9.4}$$

The minimization of $\|\mathbf{w}\|$ involves a square root. From a mathematical point of view, that is much more difficult to contend with than a polynomial. Therefore, the expression to minimize can be transformed to $\frac{1}{2}\|\mathbf{w}\|^2$ (the $\frac{1}{2}$ is for convenience) without changing the answer. The overall optimization problem is defined as:

$$\min_{\mathbf{w},b}$$
$$\frac{1}{2}\|w\|^2$$
$$\text{subject to}$$
$$y_i(\mathbf{w} \cdot \mathbf{x_i} - b) \geq 1 \ (i = 1 \ldots n) \tag{9.5}$$

This problem is a *quadratic programming problem*. There are numerous ways of solving these programs, typically based on breaking the problem into smaller *chunks*, but we will not delve into these.

Finally, what if the data cannot be separated by a plane (the data is not *linearly separable*)? In this case, there are two methods we can use:

- Introduce *slack variables* ξ_i for each point, allowing for some classification error while adding a penalization term to the minimization problem. This is called using a *soft margin*.

- If the data can be linearly separated in some higher-dimensional space, then we can use the *dual formulation* of SVMs and transform the minimization problem to use kernel functions.

The two methods are used together to make a highly robust classifier, able to fit with a small degree of error. To use kernel functions, the minimization problem is transformed into its *dual problem*. Rather than trying to minimize the original formulation, the dual problem defines new variables based on each constraint and modifies the problem to maximize based on those variables; maximal solutions with respect to the constraint values correspond to minimal solutions in the original problem. Through the use of *Lagrange multipliers*, the constraints α_i are added into the minimization function, one for each of the n constraints in the original problem, and transformed into the following maximization function with respect to each α_i:

$$\max_\alpha$$

$$W(\alpha) = \sum_{i=1}^{n} \alpha_i - \frac{1}{2} \sum_{i,j} \alpha_i \alpha_j y_i y_j (\mathbf{x_i} \cdot \mathbf{x_j})$$

subject to

$$\alpha_i \geq 0 \ (i = 1 \dots n)$$

$$\sum_{i=1}^{n} \alpha_i y_i = 0 \tag{9.6}$$

What is nice about this formulation is that it depends only on the dot product of each pair of input data. Thus, we can replace the dot product $\mathbf{x_i} \cdot \mathbf{x_j}$ with a valid kernel function, allowing the SVM to classify data with nonlinear relationships. Even if the kernel function represents a feature space that is infinite, the dual formulation is tractable because the constraints are a function of the number of points in the algorithm.

To add the slack variables, the separating hyperplane constraints in Equation 9.4 become

$$y_i(\mathbf{w} \cdot \mathbf{x_i}) \geq 1 - \xi_i \tag{9.7}$$

and a penalization term C is added to change the minimization problem to minimizing $\mathbf{w}$ with respect to $\mathbf{w}, \xi$, and b:

$$\frac{1}{2}\|\mathbf{w}\| + C \sum_{i=1}^{n} \xi_i \tag{9.8}$$

Based on the penalization term C, points that aren't separated by the hyperplanes contribute to the overall cost, exhibited by larger values of ξ. Note that in the dual form of the problem, the slack variables disappear, reducing the computational cost of adding the slack variables into the optimization problem.

Support vector machines have a huge number of implementations across various languages; for R we use the kernlab package for SVM related operations for its simplicity. Below is an example of the `ksvm` function in the package that can be used to build a model m given the training data `train`, the class labels `labels`, and a kernel. There are a number of kernel functions provided by kernlab, but for graph data there aren't any default kernel functions available. In this case, we compute the kernel matrix for `train` and tell `ksvm` to treat it as such by passing the option "matrix" to the `kernel` argument.

```
1 m <- ksvm(trainMatrix, labels, kernel='matrix')
```

With the model m, we can now predict the class label of examples in the test data using the `predict` function in R.

```
1 predict(m, testK)
```

9.3 Classifying Graphs and Vertices

Graph classification can be investigated from two perspectives, by *graph classification* (between-graph) or *vertex classification* (within-graph). Which one is more desirable depends on the application under consideration.

> **Definition 9.3** *Graph Classification*
> The classification of individual graphs.

> **Definition 9.4** *Vertex Classification*
> The classification of individual vertices within a graph.

Whatever the type of classification task, we need to be able to capture non-trivial characteristics of graphs that would imply class membership. Furthermore, to use support vector machines as well as a wealth of other data mining methods based on numerical vectors (such as clustering in Chapter 8), we need to be able to convey and compare these characteristics through a kernel function.

We will focus on kernel methods that convey graph characteristics in terms of walks within the graph. For graph classification, we discuss the direct product kernel, introduced in Chapter 4. For vertex classification, we discuss the Laplacian kernel. However, a walk-based representation may not be effective for all kinds of graph classification tasks. Sometimes only a subset of the structures can be enough to determine the output label completely. For instance, in drug discovery, it can be determined whether a particular compound is a drug or not by just looking for the presence or absence of some substructures (i.e., molecules). However, classification based on graph substructures requires frequent subgraph mining, a known NP-hard problem. Methods to perform such mining are the subject of Chapter 7.

Although these two methods are not mutually exclusive, in general they are not applied within the same task together since they have different classification purposes. For example, graph classification is often used to classify chemical molecules. Different molecules, mapped to graph structures, may represent a type of drug or compound. Vertex classification can be used to classify individual nodes in a graph. For example, web pages on the Internet that link to each other (where a web page represents a node, and a hyperlink represents an edge) can be classified in terms of subject matter such as news, search, or social websites.

9.3.1 Graph Classification: The Direct Product Kernel

As introduced in Chapter 4, we will focus on the **direct product kernel**. The intuition behind this measure is that given two graphs, the walks between any two points within each graph will be the same in number and length if both the graphs have a similar structure. Since the kernel has already been discussed in Chapter 4, we will only provide a review of the kernel computation process.

The computation of the direct product kernel consists of four steps:

1. Compute the direct product of the pair of input graphs.

2. Compute the decay constant γ using the maximum indegree and outdegree of the direct product graph.

3. Compute the geometric series of weighted walks.

4. Sum each value in the matrix and return the resulting value.

First, the **direct product** of the two graphs is computed, denoted by $G_1 \otimes G_2$. As a reminder, the direct product of adjacency matrices $\mathbf{A}_{M \times N}$ and $\mathbf{B}_{P \times Q}$ is computed as follows:

$$\begin{bmatrix} a_{11}B & \cdots & a_{1n}B \\ \vdots & \ddots & \vdots \\ a_{m1}B & \cdots & a_{mn}B \end{bmatrix}$$

where $a\mathbf{B}$ represents the multiplication between an element of matrix $\mathbf{A}$, a, by the entire matrix $\mathbf{B}$. If the graphs are unweighted, you can think of it as a copy of $\mathbf{B}$ everywhere there is a 1 in $\mathbf{A}$, and a zero-matrix, otherwise.

Next, we want to compute the decay constant γ, using Equation 4.14 introduced in Chapter 4 and the direct product adjacency matrix $\mathbf{A}$:

$$\gamma < \frac{1}{\min(\Delta^+(\mathbf{A}), \Delta^-(\mathbf{A}))}$$

Once the decay constant is computed, we use the closed form geometric series derived in Equation 4.15 to compute and return the kernel value, given the direct product adjacency matrix $\mathbf{A}$ and decay constant γ:

$$k = \sum_{i,j} (\mathbf{I} - \gamma\mathbf{A})^{-1}$$

Algorithm 22 describes the computation of the direct product kernel and Algorithm 23 shows the computation of the decay constant.

Input: $\mathbf{A}_i$ and $\mathbf{A}_j$: the adjacency matrices for graphs G_i and G_j
Output: Kernel function value k

1 $\mathbf{A}_{ij} = \mathbf{A}_i \otimes \mathbf{A}_j$
2 Compute decay constant γ using Algorithm 23, with $\mathbf{A}_{ij}$
3 $k = \sum_{i,j}(\mathbf{I} - \gamma\mathbf{A}_{ij})^{-1}$
4 **return** k

Algorithm 22: The Direct Product Kernel

Input: $\mathbf{D}$: a $p \times p$ direct product matrix of two graphs
Output: γ: Decay constant

1 maxIndegree $= 0$
2 maxOutdegree $= 0$
3 **foreach** vertex $v_i \in$ direct product matrix $\mathbf{D}$ **do**
4   outdegree $= \sum_{j=1}^{p} \mathbf{D}_{i,j}$
5   indegree $= \sum_{j=1}^{p} \mathbf{D}_{j,i}$
6   maxIndegree $= \max(\text{indegree}, \text{maxIndegree})$
7   maxOutdegree $= \max(\text{outdegree}, \text{maxOutdegree})$
8 **end**
9 Set $\gamma < 1/min(\text{maxIndegree}, \text{maxOutdegree})$
10 **return** γ

Algorithm 23: Calculation of Decay Constant γ

In R, the kernel matrix corresponding to the desired training set of data can be generated using the `generateKernelMatrix` function. Given the computational complexity of the kernel function, this step may take some time.

```
1 trainK <- generateKernelMatrix(trainingData)
```

Once the kernel matrix is obtained for all graph pairs in the training set, the classification algorithm (i.e., kernel-based SVM) is run to generate the classification model. We use kernlab's `ksvm` function to generate our model. This uses our kernel matrix along with the class labels.

```
1 m <- ksvm(trainK, PTCLabelsSmall, kernel='matrix')
```

9.3.2   Vertex Classification: The Regularized Laplacian Kernel

Similar to the previous section, we can also classify individual vertices within a graph using a suitable kernel function. However, in this case, what are the characteristics of each vertex that we want to kernelize? If we have multiple features belonging to each vertex, then a resulting classifier could be more traditional in nature, depending on each vertex's individual features rather than the graph structure. However, for our purposes we want to use a classifier that builds a model solely on both local and global structural characteristics, with respect to each vertex.

The key intuition for the kernel function described is that vertex similarity can be approximated by comparing adjacent neighbors. For instance, a group of vertices that form a clique are much more likely to be "similar" from the application's point of view than a pair of vertices that are separated by a long path. Using neighborhood information to compare each pair of vertices utilizes the concept of *locality*; the iteration of this over all pairs and multi-hop neighborhoods (such as all vertices with a path length of 2 from the target vertex) allows us to additionally utilize *global* graph characteristics when classifying vertices.

As an example, consider the classification of web pages. Suppose we wish to classify the webpages by using the words shared among the pages. A *hypergraph* is a good representation of such data, shown in Figure 9.3.

Definition 9.5 *Hypergraph*
A generalization of a graph, where an edge can connect a subset of the vertex set. Formally, a hypergraph G is a pair $G = (V, E)$ where V is the vertex set and E is a set of non-empty subsets of V called *hyperedges* or *links*.

In our example, the hypergraph is formed by the set of web pages in our data set. Each web page is an individual vertex, and there is a hyperedge between each set of web pages that contain a common word. Naively, this would be a bad representation as connecting pages with words such as "a," "an," and "the" would likely lead to a diluting of the useful information encoded, but we do not want to delve into aspects of *natural language processing*, for which many books already exist.

The adjacency matrix is slightly different from a regular graph. Instead of each row and column representing an individual vertex, each row represents a vertex and each column an edge. The elements of the array $\mathbf{A}$, for some ordering of the vertices and edges $V = \{v_1, v_2, \ldots, v_n\}$ and $E = \{e_1, e_2, \ldots, e_m\}$, respectively, are defined as:

$$\mathbf{A}_{i,j} = \begin{cases} 1, & \text{if edge } e_j \text{ is incident on vertex } v_i \text{ in the hypergraph} \\ 0, & \text{otherwise.} \end{cases} \tag{9.9}$$

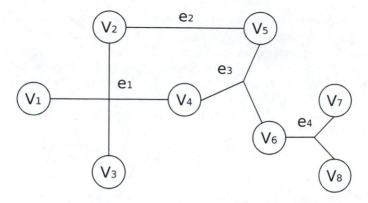

FIGURE 9.3: A example hypergraph (G).

The adjacency matrix for the graph G from Figure 9.3 is

$$
\begin{bmatrix}
1 & 0 & 0 & 0 \\
1 & 1 & 0 & 0 \\
1 & 0 & 0 & 0 \\
1 & 0 & 1 & 0 \\
0 & 1 & 1 & 0 \\
0 & 0 & 0 & 1 \\
0 & 0 & 0 & 1
\end{bmatrix}
$$

As the first step in computing the Laplacian kernel, we need to convert the hypergraph into a "similarity matrix." This can be accomplished by the product of matrix $\mathbf{A}$ and its transpose ($\mathbf{A}\mathbf{A}^\mathbf{T}$). The product $\mathbf{A}\mathbf{A}^\mathbf{T}$ eliminates the explicit edge representation as columns, and each row and column are representative of individual vertices, similar to regular graphs. Furthermore, each entry (i, j) in the matrix represents the number of common hyperedges incident on both vertices i and j; it can be thought of as a "flattening" of the hypergraph into an integer-weighted graph. So, for G, the similarity matrix is

$$
\mathbf{A}\mathbf{A}^T = \begin{bmatrix}
1 & 1 & 1 & 1 & 0 & 0 & 0 \\
1 & 2 & 1 & 1 & 1 & 0 & 0 \\
1 & 1 & 1 & 1 & 0 & 0 & 0 \\
1 & 1 & 1 & 2 & 1 & 0 & 0 \\
0 & 1 & 0 & 1 & 2 & 0 & 0 \\
0 & 0 & 0 & 0 & 0 & 1 & 1 \\
0 & 0 & 0 & 0 & 0 & 1 & 1
\end{bmatrix}
$$

This matrix is a rough encoding of vertex similarity, if vertices are similar based on locality in the graph. However, the matrix does not necessarily contain information about the degree of similarity between the vertices. For example, the similarity between vertices v_1 and v_3 ($\mathbf{A}\mathbf{A}^\mathbf{T}{}_{1,3}$) is equal to the similarity between vertices v_1 and v_2 ($\mathbf{AA^T}_{1,2}$), yet the neighborhood sets of v_1 and v_3 are the same, while v_2's neighbor set is a superset of v_1's.

To avoid these kinds of problems, we need to perform a *normalization*, or *regularization*, operation on the matrix. One way to normalize is to eliminate the effect that a high degree vertex would have on the resulting similarity scores. To do this, the weighted degree of each vertex (taking into consideration edge weights) is calculated and then divided into the base matrix. This particular transformation is called a *regularized Laplacian matrix* and is widely used in areas such as spectral graph theory, where properties of graphs are studied in terms of their eigenvalues and vectors of adjacency matrices. The target normalized Laplacian matrix for vertex set $V = \{v_1, v_2, \ldots, v_n\}$ is calculated using the following equation, using $\mathbf{AA^T}$ as the base matrix:

$$\mathbf{L}_{i,j} := \begin{cases} 1 & \text{if } i = j \text{ and } \deg(v_i) \neq 0 \\ -\dfrac{1}{\sqrt{\deg(v_i)\deg(v_j)}} & \text{if } i \neq j \text{ and } v_i \text{ is adjacent to } v_j \\ 0 & \text{otherwise.} \end{cases} \tag{9.10}$$

The resulting regularized Laplacian matrix for G is:

$$\mathbf{L} = \begin{bmatrix} 1.0 & -0.20 & -0.3 & -0.2 & 0.0 & 0.0 & 0.0 \\ -0.2 & 1.0 & -0.2 & -0.2 & -0.2 & 0.0 & 0.0 \\ -0.3 & -0.2 & 1.0 & -0.2 & 0.0 & 0.0 & 0.0 \\ -0.2 & -0.2 & -0.2 & 1.0 & -0.2 & 0.0 & 0.0 \\ 0.0 & -0.2 & 0.0 & -0.2 & 1.0 & 0.0 & 0.0 \\ 0.0 & 0.0 & 0.0 & 0.0 & 0.0 & 1.0 & -0.5 \\ 0.0 & 0.0 & 0.0 & 0.0 & 0.0 & -0.5 & 1.0 \end{bmatrix}$$

For reference, the Laplacian matrix (non-regularized) is an $n \times n$ matrix such that each (i,i) entry is the degree of vertex i and each (i,j) entry, where $i \neq j$, is -1 if the vertices are adjacent and 0, otherwise. In other words, it is the difference between the degree matrix and the adjacency matrix of a graph, where the degree matrix is defined such that all entries besides the diagonal are 0, and entries on the diagonal are vertex degrees. The regularized matrix merely divides each (i,j) entry by the square root of the product of the vertex degrees.

Now, if we look at the matrix elements, topologically different vertices are assigned different values. As in the direct product kernel, we can include multiple levels of neighborhoods (single-hop, two-hops, etc.) by using the geometric series

$$\sum_{i=1}^{\infty} \gamma^i (-\mathbf{L})^i, \tag{9.11}$$

where γ is an appropriate decay constant, working similar to the decay constant in earlier sections. In this case, since operations have already been performed on the graph, the decay constant is typically regarded as an arbitrary constant that is less than one. The infinite power series used in Equation 9.11 is analogous to measuring the walks of different lengths between given vertices. Of course, we want to be able to actually compute this summation, so the convergence of the series is used to give the regularized kernel matrix:

$$\mathbf{K} = (\mathbf{I} + \gamma\mathbf{L})^{-1}, \tag{9.12}$$

where $\mathbf{I}$ is the identity matrix. The kernel matrix $\mathbf{K}$ can now be used with a classification algorithm for predicting the class of vertices in the given dataset.

Algorithm 24 presents the computation of $\mathbf{K}$ based on the above discussion.

Input: **A**: Adjacency Matrix of Hypergraph
Output: **K**: Laplacian Kernel Matrix

1 Calculate the base matrix $\mathbf{A}\mathbf{A}^T$
2 Compute **L** using Equation 9.10
3 Choose a γ value between 0 and 1
4 Calculate Kernel Matrix $\mathbf{K} = (\mathbf{I} + \gamma\mathbf{L})^{-1}$
5 **return K**

Algorithm 24: Kernel function for vertex classification

It is straightforward to implement this algorithm in R. In the example, we assume that $\gamma = 0.5$. Given the training data, the following code returns the kernel $\mathbf{K}$.

```
1 rows = dim(trainingData)[1];
2 cols = dim(trainingData)[2];

3 # base similarity matrix and vector of vertex degrees
4 BTB <- trainingData


5 # Degree of each vertex
6 D <- diag(rowSums(BTB))

7 # regularlized Laplacian matrix
8 L <- matrix(0, rows, rows);
9 for (i in 1:rows)
10 {
11     for (j in 1:rows)
12     {
13         L[i,j] <- (D[i,j] - BTB[i,j])/sqrt(D[i,i]*D[i,j])
14     }.
15 }
```

```
16 I = diag(1,rows,rows); # The Identity matrix
17 K = solve(I + 0.5*L);  # Kernel matrix
```

The kernel computed above can now be used to train a support vector machine. The model constructed can then be used to classify unseen examples.

```
1 B <- as.matrix(graph[, 1:cols]);
2 y <- as.matrix(graph[, cols:cols+1]);

3 # Kernel matrix calculation for the vertices of a graph
4 K = generateKernelMatrixWithinGraph(B);

5 # Train the SVM to generate a model m from the data
6 m = ksvm(K, y, type="C-svc", kernel = "matrix");
```

9.4   Applications

9.4.1   Between-graph Classification: Chemical Toxicity

Molecular data can be represented as graphs, and with kernel methods can be classified using support vector machines—in this case, whether or not the molecules are toxic. In R, we will use the SVM utilities provided by the kernlab package. For the graph-based operations, we make use of the GraphClassification and iGraph packages.

First, let's load the predictive toxicology data set ("PTCData"). This dataset consists of 196 molecules, each of which has been tested positive or negative for toxicity.

```
1 # Contains the graph representation of each molecule
2 data("PTCData")
3 # Contains the class label for each molecule
4 data("PTCLabels")
```

For the purposes of this example, we will use a subset of that data to create our model.

```
1 # Sample 5 molecules to use for training
2 sTrain = sample(1:length(PTCData), 5)
3 PTCDataSmall <- PTCData[sTrain]
4 PTCLabelsSmall <- PTCLabels[sTrain]
```

To illustrate the direct product kernel, we will use as an example the dummy molecules Type-A and Type-B, shown in Figure 9.4. Let their graph representations be G_1 and G_2, respectively.

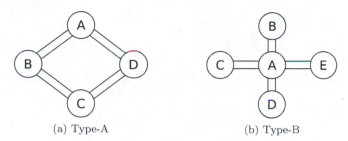

(a) Type-A   (b) Type-B

FIGURE 9.4: Two basic chemical structures.

Type-A	A	B	C	D
A	0	1	1	0
B	1	0	0	1
C	1	0	0	1
D	0	1	1	0

Type-B	A	B	C	D	E
A	0	1	1	1	1
B	1	0	0	0	0
C	1	0	0	0	0
D	1	0	0	0	0
E	1	0	0	0	0

FIGURE 9.5: Two basic chemical structures, as adjacency matrices.

The adjacency matrices for G_1 and G_2, denoted $\mathbf{A}_1$ and $\mathbf{A}_2$, respectively, are shown in Figure 9.5. The row and column labels in these matrices correspond to the node labels of their respective graphs.

The maximum indegree and outdegree of the resulting direct product of G_1 and G_2 is 8, so we must choose a decay constant that is smaller than $\frac{1}{8}$. Computing the geometric series of the direct product graph and summing each element in the matrix give us the kernel value for the pair of graphs:

$$k = \sum_{i,j}(\mathbf{I} - (\tfrac{1}{8} - \epsilon)(\mathbf{G}_1 \otimes \mathbf{G}_2)_{i,j})^{-1} = 37.33$$

Now that the model is created, we can test the model's effectiveness by labelling training examples we did not use in the classfier. Since we are using the kernelized SVM, we need to compute the kernel function between pairs of support vectors and the test data:

```
1 # Take a random sample of 2 datapoints
2 sTest = sample(1:length(PTCData), 2)
3 PTCTestData <- PTCData[sTest]

4 # Generate kernel matrix for test data
5 testK <- generateKernelMatrix(PTCTestData,PTCDataSmall)

6 # We need to extract the "support" vectors from our data
7 testK <- as.kernelMatrix(testK[,SVindex(m), drop=F])
```

Now that we have our training data, our model, and our test data, we may predict the class label of our test data.

```
1 predict(m, testK)
```

For each row, the positive value corresponds to a "+1" class label, while a negative value corresponds to a "−1" class label.

A few examples of new graphs we might want to classify are graphs based on molecules with small, local changes from known ones, such as in Figure 9.6. By following physical and chemical restrictions in the molecule modification, one can see how new molecules can be created based on old ones, and their properties predicted, in a single scientific workflow.

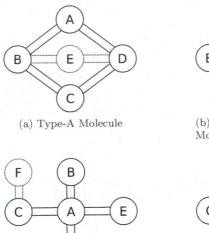

(a) Type-A Molecule

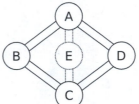

(b)   Modified   Type-A Molecule

(c) Type-B Molecule

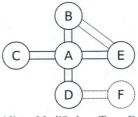

(d)   Modified   Type-B Molecule

FIGURE 9.6: Sample instances of molecule structures of different classes.

9.4.2   Within-graph Classification: Web Page Content

As an example of using the Laplacian kernel, we consider the WEBKB dataset [5], a collection of web pages from the websites of four universities. The web pages are assigned to five distinct classes according to their contents: course, faculty, student, project, and staff. The original version of the WEBKB dataset is a raw file that includes source codes of the pages and needs to be refined in order to apply data mining for information extraction.

As a preprocessing step, the webpages are first searched for the most commonly used words. There are 1,073 words that are encountered with a frequency of at least 10, which we have chosen as the pruning threshold. The refined data file is a table whose rows are the name of the web pages, and columns are the 1,073 commonly used words, using some arbitrary ordering.

If word j exists in page i then the matrix cell $\mathbf{A}_{ij} = 1$, otherwise, it is 0. By considering the web page addresses as vertices and the frequent words as hyperedges we can consider the table to be a hypergraph G. Relative to the graph in Figure 9.3, each v_i would be a web address and each e_i would be a distinct word.

To run the algorithm in R, we first need to load the data into memory by calling

```
1 data(WEBKB)
```

In order to calculate the Laplacian kernel for the WEBKB dataset, a single R function is used:

```
1 K = generateKernelMatrixWithinGraph(WEBKB)
```

This function computes the regularized Laplacian matrix and performs the summation corresponding to Equation 9.11, returning in matrix form the kernel values of each pair of vertices. Once this is computed, we can use the kernel matrix as input to the support vector machine classifier:

```
1 # a sample set is separated for testing
2 holdout <- sample(1:ncol(K), 20)
3 # model is obtained from remaining training instances
4 model=ksvm(K[-holdout,-holdout], y, kernel='matrix')
```

If the resulting model is printed out, the training process can be observed.

```
1 # Selected Class = course pages
2 OUTPUT
3 Support Vector Machine object of class "ksvm"
4 SV type: C-svc (classification) parameter : cost C = 1
5 [1] " Kernel matrix used as input."
6 Number of Support Vectors : 64
7 Training error : 0.2153846
```

Now, we have a model that can classify the training instances with the help of support vectors and we are ready to classify unseen examples. The prediction of the class labels of new data instances can be achieved using the **predict** function of the ksvm library. However, as the data is in the form of kernel matrix, we cannot directly use the **predict** function. We need to calculate the similarity of the new instances with the existing data used for training, again utilizing the kernel trick.

To find the kernel matrix between the test and training instances, the same kernel function can be used. The **predict** function requires two parameters: the model of classification and the computed kernel matrix between test and training instances.

```
1 testK <- as.kernelMatrix(K[holdout, -holdout]
2 [,SVindex(m), drop=F])
3 preds <- predict(m, testK)
4 sum(sign(preds) == sign(y[holdout])) /
5 length(holdout) # == 1 (perfect!)
```

Here we see the output class labels of the prediction phase. For the WE-BKB dataset we obtained 70% classification success within the selected classes.

```
1 #The class labels
2 > sign(preds)
3           [,1]
4  [1,]     1
5  [2,]    -1
6  [3,]     1
7  [4,]     1
8  [5,]     1
9  [6,]    -1
10 [7,]     1
11 [8,]     1
12 [9,]     1
13 [10,]   -1

14 #The percentage of correctly classified data instances
15 > sum(sign(preds) == sign(y[holdout]))/length(holdout)
16 [1] 0.7
```

9.5   Bibliographic Notes

To recall, graph classification is the process by which individual graphs or graph vertices are assigned class labels. We reviewed kernels that can be used for graphs in a graph database, and kernels that can be used for vertices in a single graph. The approach to define kernels on objects that have a natural representation as a graph is to map each graph to a set of subgraphs and measure the intersection of the two sets. However, such graph kernels cannot be computed efficiently if the mapping is required to be unique up to isomorphism. In literature, different approaches have been tried to overcome this problem. Herbrich and Graepel [9] restrict the image of the graph to paths up to a given size, and Deshpande *et al.* [7] only consider the set of connected graphs that occur frequently as subgraphs in the graph database. Diffusion kernels on graphs [13] allow for the computation of a kernel if the instance space has a graph structure. This is different from the approach in our chapter where we consider that every instance has a graph structure.

Tree kernels [4] compute the similarity of two trees based on their common subtrees. These trees are restricted to labeled trees where the label of each vertex determines the number of children of that vertex. Furthermore, a fixed order of the children of each vertex is assumed. For these restricted trees, Collins and Duffy devised an algorithm for computing the kernel with quadratic time complexity. The graph kernels described in our chapter can also be applied to trees but do not require any restriction on the set of trees. Thus, they are a more flexible, but more costly, alternative. String kernels that base the similarity of two strings on common non-contiguous substrings are strongly related to graph kernels with geometric weights. Such string kernels have been well studied [28, 15].

Methods for graph classification that do not rely on kernel methods typically work based on comparing substructures of graphs. These types of methods are the subject of Chapter 7. In particular, gBoost is a mathematical-programming-based learning method for graph data that progressively collects "informative" frequent patterns that can be used as features for subsequent classification or regression [20]. By engineering the mathematical program, it uses the same pattern search algorithm for solving both classification and regression problems. gBoost proves to be competitive or superior when compared with other state-of-the-art methods like marginalized graph kernel (MGK) [11], Gaston [12], Correlated Pattern Mining (CPM) [1], and MOLFEA [8]. It has an advantage over filter methods [1] in that it is easily extendable to a wide range of machine learning problems.

Frequent substructure mining methods such as AGM [10], Gaston [17], or gSpan [29] have been applied to enumerate frequently appearing subgraph patterns. Then, a graph is represented as a vector of binary indicators, and an existing machine learning method such as SVM [21] is applied to the vector. When L1-SVM [21] or related methods are used, one can identify a few salient substructures as well. Such an approach is commonly practiced in chemoinformatics [12]. It is called a "two step" approach, because the mining part (e.g., gSpan) and the learning part (e.g., SVM) are completely separated. However, the two step approach is considered very time and memory consuming [27]. Hence, in algorithms such as gBoost, graph mining and machine learning are "tightly integrated," which leads to a better efficiency in comparison with the naïve integration. LPBoost [6] was employed as a base algorithm and it was combined with a substructure mining algorithm. Also, compared to AdaBoost (another technique to classify graphs) [14], gBoost can build the prediction rule with fewer iterations. Hence, computationally, gBoost is competitive to AdaBoost in quality and computational costs. From the learning side, many supervised algorithms are readily described as mathematical programs [3, 19, 30]. Many of them could be easily combined with mining algorithms.

While graphs are the primary focus of this chapter and book, there are classical supervised learning techniques that are not applicable to graphs, but nevertheless important to be aware of for anyone studying data mining. Rather than graphs, these methods typically work on sets of features that tend to be discrete properties, but can additionally include numerical data.

The simplest and most intuitive of these is known as *decision trees* [16]. A *decision tree* is a tree where each node represents a comparison of some feature in the dataset (e.g. "is sex male?") and edges from nodes to children nodes represent the results of the comparison (e.g. "yes" or "no"). Leaf nodes represent class label assignments. *Decision tree induction* is the process of constructing a decision tree on a training set that best describes the data, typically based on recursively dividing the dataset on some feature based on some optimization metric, such as choosing a feature that best partitions the data by class assignment.

As opposed to classifiers that merely output the class a piece of data is expected to belong to, probabilistic methods provide a measure of expectation, through a probability measure, of class membership. This can provide a richer set of information about classification results, such as *confidence* in prediction: a high probability that an unknown piece of data belongs to some class implies a higher confidence than a class assignment with a lower probability. Bayesian belief networks encapsulate these ideas, producing a directed, acyclic graph structure used in classification, based on Bayesian inference [18]. The primary drawback is that it relies heavily on prior knowledge, as the expressivity of belief networks lies in the ability to use *conditional probability* to make network construction computationally tractable. A similar idea has been advanced by *relevance vector machines*, which shares a similar formulation with support vector machines but produces probabilistic class assignments [23].

9.6   Exercises

1. Within the realm of social networking, where nodes in graphs represent users and edges represent some sort of connection (whether the connection means the users are "friends" or share common interests), what sorts of (sub)graphs would be appropriate for between-graph labeling and classification? What about for within-graph labeling/classification?

2. To get a firmer grasp on exactly how the optimization problem in SVMs is defined, write the complete optimization problem for a data set consisting of five points in three-dimensional space. How many variables are there in the optimization problem? How many for an n-point, d-dimensional data set? What does this say about performing SVM classification on increasingly large data sets?

3. What exactly is the model produced by support vector machines? That is, once the optimization problem in Equation 9.5 has been

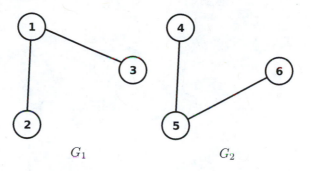

FIGURE 9.7: Graphs G_1 and G_2 in Problem 6

solved, what parameters are needed to perform the classification of unknown data? What about for the dual problem in Equation 9.6? (Hint: do you need all of the data?)

4. Think of a case where all points in a binary classification problem are support vectors in an application of SVMs (not taking into consideration kernelizations of the data). How often would cases such as the one you identified occur in real-world data?

5. The dual problem formulation allows for kernel functions to be used on the data. However, as noted in Chapter 4, some kernel functions may have an infinite feature space. Is that a problem when making the dual problem tractable? Why or why not?

6. Consider a vector of real-valued features. A *decision tree* is a classification structure where each node represents a feature of the input data and edges to children nodes represent a comparison operation against the feature for each datum. Leaf nodes represent classes. Thus, to classify a numerical vector, the tree is traversed from root node to leaf node, following edges based on the comparison between vector components and node feature, until a leaf node is reached. Assuming a binary, less-than operator at each node, against some given constant, what is the geometric interpretation of decision trees, and how does it compare to (non-kernelized) SVMs?

7. Given two graphs G_1 and G_2, shown in Figure 9.7:

    (a) Compute the direct product $D = G_1 \otimes G_2$.
    (b) Compute the maximum indegree and outdegree of D.
    (c) Compute the upper bound for γ, the decay constant.
    (d) Finally, compute the collapsed matrix in the direct product kernel (save the inversion for software, if available).

8. Provide an implementation in R of Algorithms 22 and 23. Specifically, implement the function *generateKernelMatrix* introduced in Section 9.3.1, which takes a list of input data (graphs) and computes

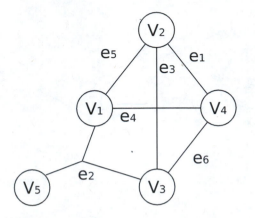

FIGURE 9.8: Hypergraph H in Problem 9.

a matrix of pairwise kernel values for each. To compute the direct product, use the R function `directProduct` discussed in Chapter 4.

9. Given hypergraph H in Figure 9.8, compute the corresponding adjacency matrix $\mathbf{A}$ and the regularized Laplacian matrix of $\mathbf{A}\mathbf{A}^T$. What is the computational complexity of this operation, given an n-vertex, m-edge graph?

Bibliography

[1] B. Bringmann, A. Zimmermann, L. De Raedt, and S. Nijssen. Don't be afraid of simpler patterns. In *10th European Conference on Principles and Practice of Knowledge Discovery in Databases (PKDD)*, pages 56–66. Springer-Verlag, 2006.

[2] C.J.C. Burges. A tutorial on support vector machines for pattern recognition. *Data Mining and Knowledge Discovery*, 2:121–167, 1998.

[3] L. Cai and T. Hofmann. Hierarchical document categorization with support vector machines. In *Proceedings of the 13th ACM International Conference on Information and Knowledge Management*, CIKM '04, pages 78–87, 2004.

[4] M. Collins and N. Duffy. Convolution kernels for natural language. In *Advances in Neural Information Processing Systems 14*, pages 625–632. MIT Press, 2001.

[5] M. Craven, D. DiPasquo, D. Freitag, A. McCallum, T. Mitchell,

K. Nigam, S. Slattery, R. Ghani, and R. Jones. CMU world-wide knowledge base WEB-KB project. `http://www.cs.cmu.edu/~webkb/`.

[6] A. Demiriz, K.P. Bennett, and J. Shawe-Taylor. Linear programming boosting via column generation. *Machine Learning*, 46:225–254, 2002.

[7] M. Deshpande, M. Kuramochi, and G. Karypis. Automated approaches for classifying structures. In *Proceedings of the 2nd ACM SIGKDD Workshop on Data Mining and Bioinformatics (BIOKDD)*, pages 11–18, 2002.

[8] C. Helma, T. Cramer, S. Cramer, and L. De Raedt. Data mining and machine learning techniques for the identification of mutagenicity inducing substructures and structure activity relationships of noncongeneric compounds. *Journal of Chemical Information and Computer Sciences*, 44:1402–1411, 2004.

[9] R. Herbrich and T. Graepel. A PAC-Bayesian margin bound for linear classifiers. *Information Theory, IEEE Transactions on*, 48(12):3140–3150, 2002.

[10] A. Inokuchi, T. Washio, and H. Motoda. An apriori-based algorithm for mining frequent substructures from graph data, 2000.

[11] H. Kashima, K. Tsuda, and A. Inokuchi. Marginalized kernels between labeled graphs. In *Proceedings of the Twentieth International Conference on Machine Learning*, pages 321–328. AAAI Press, 2003.

[12] J. Kazius, S. Nijssen, J. Kok, T. Back, and A.P. IJzerman. Substructure mining using elaborate chemical representation. *Journal of Chemical Information and Modeling*, 46(2):597–605, 2006.

[13] R.I. Kondor and J.D. Lafferty. Diffusion kernels on graphs and other discrete input spaces. In *Proceedings of the 19th International Conference on Machine Learning*, ICML '02, pages 315–322. Morgan Kaufmann, 2002.

[14] T. Kudo, E. Maeda, and Y. Matsumoto. An application of boosting to graph classification. *Advances in Neural Information Processing Systems (NIPS)*, 17:729–736, 2005.

[15] H. Lodhi, C. Saunders, J. Shawe-Taylor, N. Cristianini, and C. Watkins. Text classification using string kernels. *Journal of Machine Learning Research*, 2:419–444, 2002.

[16] S.K. Murthy. Automatic construction of decision trees from data: A multi-disciplinary survey. *Data Mining and Knowledge Discovery*, 2(4):345–389, 1998.

[17] S. Nijssen and J.N. Kok. A quickstart in frequent structure mining can make a difference. *Proceedings of the 10th ACM SIGKDD International Conference on Knowledge Discovery and Data Mining*, pages 647–652, 2004.

[18] J. Pearl. *Probabilistic Reasoning in Intelligent Systems: Networks of Plausible Inference*. Morgan Kaufmann, San Mateo, CA, 1988.

[19] G. Ratsch, S. Mika, B. Scholkopf, and K.-R. Muller. Constructing boosting algorithms from SVMs: An application to one-class classification. *IEEE Transactions on Pattern Analysis and Machine Intelligence*, 24(9):1184–1199, 2002.

[20] H. Saigo, S. Nowozin, T. Kadowaki, T. Kudo, and K. Tsuda. gBoost: A mathematical programming approach to graph classification and regression. *Machine Learning*, 75:69–89, 2009.

[21] B. Scholkopf and A.J. Smola. *Learning with Kernels: Support Vector Machines, Regularization, Optimization, and Beyond*. MIT Press, 2001.

[22] P. Tan, M. Steinbach, and V. Kumar. *Introduction to Data Mining*. Addison-Wesley Longman Publishing, 2005.

[23] M.E. Tipping and A. Smola. Sparse Bayesian learning and the relevance vector machine. *Journal of Machine Learning Research*, 1:211–244, 2001.

[24] V.N. Vapnik. *The Nature of Statistical Learning Theory*. Springer-Verlag, New York, 1995.

[25] V.N. Vapnik. *Statistical Learning Theory*. Wiley, New York, 1998.

[26] V.N. Vapnik and A.Y. Chervonenkis. *Theory of Pattern Recognition*. Nauka, Moskow, 1974.

[27] N. Wale and G. Karypis. Comparison of descriptor spaces for chemical compound retrieval and classification. *IEEE International Conference on Data Mining (ICDM)*, pages 678–689, 2006.

[28] C. Watkins. Kernels from Matching Operations. *Technical Report, Department of Computer Science, Royal Holloway, University of London*, 1999.

[29] X. Yan and J. Han. gSpan: Graph-based substructure pattern mining. *IEEE International Conference on Data Mining (IDCM)*, pages 721–724, 2002.

[30] C. Yuan and D. Casasent. A novel support vector classifier with better rejection performance. *Proceedings of the 2003 IEEE Conference on Computer Vision and Pattern Recognition (CVPR'03)*, pages 419–424, 2003.

10

Dimensionality Reduction

Madhuri R. Marri, Lakshmi Ramachandran, Pradeep Murukannaiah, Padmashree Ravindra, Amrita Paul, Da Young Lee, David Funk, Shanmugapriya Murugappan, and William Hendrix

North Carolina State University

CONTENTS

High-dimensional data, i.e., data that includes many different aspects of the objects under consideration, can be considered both a blessing and a curse [8]—a blessing because it implies a lot of information, and a curse because the data might contain a lot of irrelevant information and be tougher to analyze. High-dimensional data is known to pose a wide variety of challenges in the field of statistics. Dimensionality Reduction, or DR, is therefore employed to deal with the issue of high-dimensional data. Specifically, DR is primarily applied when there is a need to:

1. Select only relevant features from the given data (*feature selection*) or

2. Extract lower-dimensional data from the current form of the data because the current form is too difficult to analyze (*feature extraction*).

In this chapter, we focus our discussion on techniques related to *feature extraction* in the context of graphs. In the remainder of this chapter, we refer to feature extraction as DR.

The application of DR techniques to graphs primarily aims to map graphs into some low-dimensional vector space for assisting data mining tasks such as visualization. The purpose of such techniques is to extract features from graphs that preserve the relationships between them upon low-dimensional vector space representation. In this chapter, we discuss three existing techniques of DR:

1. **Multidimensional Scaling** (MDS), an unsupervised DR technique, i.e., it does not intend to preserve the class information of the data;

2. **Kernel Principal Component Analysis** (KPCA), an unsupervised DR technique that deals with non-linear projections; and

3. **Linear Discriminant Analysis** (LDA), a supervised DR technique that uses linear projection.

The first two techniques are discussed in the context of graph mining, and linear discriminant analysis is discussed to show the use of graphs for data mining tasks.

Table 10.1 presents the notations specific to this chapter.

TABLE 10.1: Notations specific to this chapter

Notation	Description
n	Number of data objects
m	Dimension of the input space
p	Dimension of the transformed space
$\mathbf{D} \in \mathbb{R}^{n \times n}$	Distance matrix between n objects, where each $d_{ij} \in \mathbb{R}$ is the distance between the ith and j^{th} data objects
$\mathbf{S} \in \mathbb{R}^{n \times n}$	Squared distance matrix; i.e., $\mathbf{S} = \mathbf{D}^2$
$\bar{s}$	Grand mean of matrix $\mathbf{S}$; the mean of all values in matrix $\mathbf{S}$
$\bar{s}_{i\bullet}$	Mean of ith row of matrix $\mathbf{S}$
$\bar{s}_{\bullet j}$	Mean of jth column of matrix $\mathbf{S}$
$\mathbf{Y} \in \mathbb{R}^{p \times n}$	Transformed matrix (after dimension reduction)
$\mathbf{GR} \in \mathbb{R}^{n \times n}$	Gramian Matrix of $\mathbf{D}$
λ_i	i^{th} eigenvalue, $1 \le i \le n$
Λ	Diagonal matrix containing the eigenvalues of $\mathbf{GR}$
$\mathbf{Z} \in \mathbb{R}^{n \times n}$	Matrix of eigenvectors of $\mathbf{GR}$
$\mathbf{GR} = \mathbf{Z}\Lambda\mathbf{Z}^{\mathbf{T}}$	Eigenvalue decomposition of $\mathbf{GR}$
$\Lambda_p \in \mathbb{R}^{p \times p}$	Diagonal matrix containing the largest p eigenvalues of $\mathbf{GR}$
$\mathbf{Z}_p \in \mathbb{R}^{n \times p}$	Eigenvector matrix containing the first p eigenvectors, where $u_i \in \mathbb{R}^n$ is the eigenvector associated with λ_i
O	Input space
$o_i \in O$	i^{th} data object in input space, $i \in \{1, \dots, n\}$
$k : O \times O \to \mathbb{R}$	Kernel function
$\mathbf{K} \in \mathbb{R}^{n \times n}$	Kernel matrix, where $k_{ij} \in \mathbb{R}$ is the kernel between objects o_i and o_j
$\mathcal{H}$	Hilbert space
$\Phi : O \to \mathcal{H}$	Mapping function that maps the objects into $\mathcal{H}$
$\mathbf{X} \in \mathbb{R}^{m \times n}$	Data matrix of all objects
C	Number of classes in the given dataset
n_c	Number of data points in class c
$\mathbf{X}_c \in \mathbb{R}^{m \times n_c}$	Data matrix of all objects in class c
μ	Vector representing the mean of the entire dataset
μ_c	Vector representing the mean of the data objects of class c
$\mathbf{S}_B \in \mathbb{R}^{m \times m}$	Between-class scatter matrix
$\mathbf{S}_W \in \mathbb{R}^{m \times m}$	Within-class scatter matrix
$\mathbf{S}_T \in \mathbb{R}^{m \times m}$	Total scatter matrix

10.1   Multidimensional Scaling

Visualization is an important requirement for graph mining applications in different disciplines, including biology, computer science, and chemistry, as well as several application domains such as social network analysis, computer network analysis, chemical bonding analysis, etc. For most of these applications, the datasets are huge, and the graph representations are non-planar in nature [22]. The dataset may contain a set of graphs, where each graph represents a single data point, or one graph, where each node in the graph represents a single data point. Multidimensional scaling (MDS) can be used to visualize graphs by representing the dataset in a two- or three-dimensional vector space in such a way that the distances (similarity/dissimilarity) between the graphs or nodes are preserved. MDS can be thought of as a way to reduce the amount of data to the point where one can visually see the relationships between the different data objects in the set.

The general objective of MDS when applied to graph data is to project the data into a space so that the relationships (similarity) between the data objects are relatively similar in both the original and transformed spaces [22]. In this chapter, we only talk about classical MDS that requires the number of dimensions we wish to map the data into and a distance or similarity matrix. We refer to classical MDS as MDS in the rest of the chapter.

For graphs, MDS can be applied directly to the distance matrix generated from the graph and can project the original data objects into a low-dimensional representation. The distance between nodes can be calculated using the shortest path algorithm, minimum spanning trees, etc.

10.1.1   Example of Using MDS in R

Imagine that you are purchasing flight tickets to travel from Raleigh to San Francisco, and you are looking for flights with the shortest travel time. Suppose you get three different options: Raleigh–New York–San Fransisco, Raleigh–Columbus–San Francisco, and Raleigh–New York–Portland–San Francisco. The graph representation of these routes (shown in Figure 10.1) is easy to visualize because it contains just a few nodes, but it may be much harder to imagine a network containing twenty of the major airports in the US and Canada. In the DRGraphMining R library provided with the book, there is a synthetically-generated matrix that represents the routes between twenty US and Canadian airports, accessed by the `airport_network_data` function. A graph representation of this network appears in Figure 10.2; clearly, it is difficult to draw conclusions from this visualization of the data. Dimensionality reduction helps us generate a two- or three-dimensional snapshot of the network, making visualization much easier. One popular algorithm used for this purpose is MDS [24].

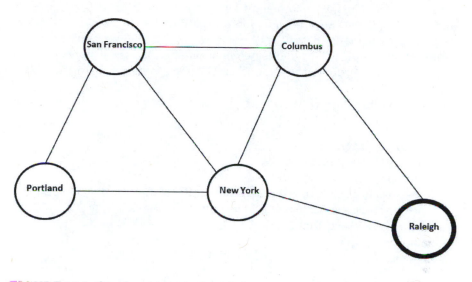

FIGURE 10.1: Graph representation of airport network with only five airports.

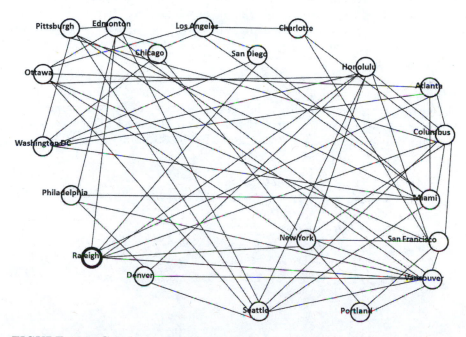

FIGURE 10.2: Graph representation of airport network with twenty different airports from the US and Canada.

In this example, we can formulate a weighted graph using nodes as airports and edges as direct paths (with no intermediate nodes) between two airports. Edge weights represent distances between two airports. The graph representation in this example will be undirected in nature because the distance between airports A and B will be the same when traveling from A to B or from B to A.

The following lines of R code can be used to generate the graphs shown in Figures 10.1 and 10.2.

```
1 library(igraph)
2 library(DRGraphMining)
3 a <- airport_network_data()
4 g <- graph.edgelist(as.matrix(a[,1:2]), directed = FALSE)
5 g <- set.edge.attribute(g, "weight", value=a[,3])
6 tkplot(g,vertex.label=V(g)$name)
7 subg <- subgraph(g, 0:4)
8 tkplot(subg,vertex.label=V(subg)$name)
```

In the data matrix, each row represents an edge in the graph along with an edge weight. This matrix represents an undirected graph where each node is an airport, and each edge represents a direct route between the airports and its distance. The edges in the matrix are passed as input to the `graph.edgelist` function in line 4 of the R code. The edge weights are then added to the graph using the `set.edge.attribute` function. Line 6 plots the graph with the names of the nodes as the vertices' labels, and line 8 plots the subgraph in Figure 10.1.

Before applying MDS, we have to first generate the distance matrix. In the following R code, the distance matrix, which is computed in line 9 by calling the `code:igraph` function from the igraph package, represents the shortest path between every pair of airports. The distance matrix is then passed as the input to the `cmdscale` function from the MASS library (line 10). A plot of the MDS output is shown in Figure 10.3.

```
9  pathsairports <- shortest.paths(g)
10 mds <- cmdscale(as.dist(pathsairports),2)
11 plot(mds,type="l")
12 namesList <- V(g)$name
13 for(i in 1:20)
14 {
15    text(mds[i,1],mds[i,2],labels=namesList[i],cex=0.6)
16 }
```

10.1.2 Overview of MDS

The objective of MDS is to find a representation of the dataset in a transformed space so that the distance between the data objects in the original

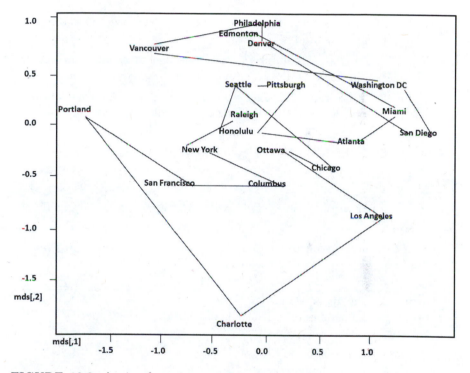

FIGURE 10.3: A visual representation of the shortest paths in the airport example graph.

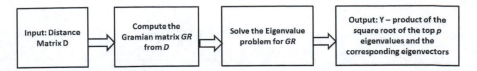

FIGURE 10.4: A high-level view of the steps involved in carrying out MDS.

space is maintained in the transformed space. MDS achieves this objective in the following steps (as shown in Figure 10.4):

1. MDS takes as input a distance matrix (of the dataset) **D** and computes its Gramian Matrix **GR**.

2. MDS then tries to minimize a *stress function* by solving the eigenvalue problem for **GR**.

3. Finally, MDS generates an output matrix **Y** as a product of the square root of the top p eigenvalues and the corresponding eigenvectors.

Essentially, the objective of MDS is to minimize the *stress function*.

Definition 10.1 *Stress*
Stress can be loosely defined as a function that represents the differences between the pairwise relationships of the objects in the transformed space relative to the original data [41].

A pseudocode description of the MDS algorithm appears in Algorithm 25. The following sections describe each of these steps in detail.

Input: D—the distance matrix
Input: p—the number of dimensions in the transformed space
Output: Y—the transformed matrix

1 Compute **S** by squaring **D**
2 Compute **GR** by double centering $-\frac{1}{2}\mathbf{S}$
3 Compute the eigenvalues Λ and eigenvectors $\mathbf{Z^T}$ from the eigenvalue decomposition of **GR**
4 Let Λ' be the p largest eigenvalues of Λ
5 Assign $\mathbf{Z}_p{}^{\mathbf{T}}$ to be the corresponding p eigenvectors from $\mathbf{Z^T}$
6 Create a diagonal matrix $\Lambda_p^{1/2}$ by assigning the diagonal values to $\sqrt{\Lambda'}$ and all other values to 0
7 Compute $\mathbf{Y} = \Lambda_p^{1/2} \cdot \mathbf{Z^T}$
8 Return **Y**

Algorithm 25: Computation of Multidimensional Scaling

10.1.3 Computation of the Gramian Matrix

Let $\mathbf{D}$ represent a symmetric distance matrix for n objects, where d_{ij} represents the distance between objects i and j. The task of MDS is to find a matrix $\mathbf{Y}$ that contains a representation of these n objects in a p-dimensional vector space of dimension p, typically two- or three-dimensional. Let $\mathbf{y}_i$ and $\mathbf{y}_j$ represent the coordinates of objects i and j in the transformed dimensional space. The stress function for MDS is defined by the squared error between the original distance d_{ij} and the distance between $\mathbf{y}_i$ and $\mathbf{y}_j$, $\|\mathbf{y}_i - \mathbf{y}_j\|$. In other words, the Gramian of $\mathbf{Y}$ should be as similar as possible to the Gramian of $\mathbf{D}$.

> **Definition 10.2** *Gramian Matrix*
> The Gramian of a set of vectors is a symmetric matrix of the inner products of the vectors [5].

The Gramian of $\mathbf{Y}$ is given by $\mathbf{Y}^{\mathbf{T}}\mathbf{Y}$ [5], and we denote the Gramian of $\mathbf{D}$ as $\mathbf{GR}$. The Gramian $\mathbf{GR}$ is calculated by *double centering* the square of the distances in $\mathbf{D}$.

Let $\mathbf{S} \in \mathbb{R}^{n \times n}$ be the square of the distance matrix $\mathbf{D}$. Since $\mathbf{D}$ is a symmetric matrix,

$$\mathbf{S} = \mathbf{D}\mathbf{D}^{\mathbf{T}}.$$

> **Definition 10.3** *Double Centering*
> Double centering is defined as the process of subtracting the mean of the rows and columns of a matrix from the elements in the row or column and adding the overall mean to all of the elements of the matrix [41]. This process will normalize the mean of every row and column to be zero.

Let $\bar{s}_{i\bullet}$ be the row mean of the matrix $\mathbf{S}$, i.e., the mean of the ith row of $\mathbf{S}$, and let $\bar{s}_{\bullet j}$ be the column mean, i.e., the mean of the jth column of matrix $\mathbf{S}$. Let $\bar{s}$ be the grand mean of the matrix $\mathbf{S}$. Then, by definition of $\mathbf{GR}$, the matrix values $\mathbf{GR}_{ij}$ are given by:

$$\mathbf{GR}_{ij} = ((-\frac{1}{2})\mathbf{S}_{ij} - \bar{s}_{i\bullet} - \bar{s}_{\bullet j} + \bar{s}) \tag{10.1}$$

We next use a numeric example to show the computation of the Gramian.

$$\mathbf{D} = \begin{bmatrix} 0 & 15 \\ 15 & 0 \end{bmatrix} \tag{10.2}$$

Therefore,

$$\mathbf{S} = \begin{bmatrix} 0 & 15 \\ 15 & 0 \end{bmatrix} \cdot \begin{bmatrix} 0 & 15 \\ 15 & 0 \end{bmatrix} \tag{10.3}$$

$$= \begin{bmatrix} 0(0) + 15(15) & 0(15) + 15(0) \\ 15(0) + 0(15) & 15(15) + 0(0) \end{bmatrix} \tag{10.4}$$

$$= \begin{bmatrix} 225 & 0 \\ 0 & 225 \end{bmatrix} \tag{10.5}$$

$$\bar{s}_{1\bullet} = 112.5, \quad \bar{s}_{2\bullet} = 112.5 \tag{10.6}$$

$$\bar{s}_{\bullet 1} = 112.5, \quad \bar{s}_{\bullet 2} = 112.5 \tag{10.7}$$

$$\bar{s} = 112.5 \tag{10.8}$$

Computing the Gramian:

$$\left(-\frac{1}{2}\right)\mathbf{S} = \left(-\frac{1}{2}\right) \begin{bmatrix} 225 & 0 \\ 0 & 225 \end{bmatrix} \tag{10.9}$$

$$= \begin{bmatrix} -112.5 & 0 \\ 0 & -112.5 \end{bmatrix} \tag{10.10}$$

$$\mathbf{GR} = \begin{bmatrix} -225 & -112.5 \\ -112.5 & -225 \end{bmatrix} \tag{10.11}$$

Lines 1 and 2 in the MDS Algorithm 25 calculate the Gramian Matrix from the input distance matrix. We now discuss how to solve the optimization problem to find the result matrix $\mathbf{Y}$.

10.1.4　Solving the Optimization Problem

Using the Gramian Matrix given by Equation 10.1, the result matrix $\mathbf{Y}$ can be determined [22] by solving the optimization problem given by:

$$\min_{\mathbf{Y} \in \mathbb{R}^{p \times n}} \left\| \mathbf{GR} - \mathbf{Y}^{\mathbf{T}}\mathbf{Y} \right\|^2 \tag{10.12}$$

Let $\mathbf{Z}\Lambda\mathbf{Z}^{\mathbf{T}}$ be the eigenvalue decomposition of $\mathbf{GR}$, where the eigenvalues are arranged in decreasing order [40]. Given this decomposition for $\mathbf{GR}$, the solution to (10.12) is given by

$$\mathbf{Y} = \Lambda_p^{1/2}\mathbf{Z}_p^{\mathbf{T}} \tag{10.13}$$

where Λ_p is a $p \times p$ matrix containing the largest p eigenvalues of Λ on its main diagonal and $\mathbf{Z}_p$ is a $p \times n$ matrix of the corresponding eigenvectors.

Line 4 of the MDS Algorithm 25 performs the eigenvalue decomposition of the Gramian $\mathbf{GR}$, and the top p eigenvalues from Λ are chosen (typically two or three). The eigenvectors corresponding to these p eigenvalues are then assigned to $\mathbf{Z}_p{}^{\mathbf{T}}$. The matrix $\Lambda_{p \times p}^{1/2}$ is constructed by taking the square root of the top p eigenvalues as shown by Line 7. The output $\mathbf{Y}$ is obtained by computing the product of $\Lambda_p^{1/2}$ and $\mathbf{Z}_p{}^{\mathbf{T}}$, as shown in Line 8 of the MDS Algorithm 25.

10.1.5 Strengths and Weaknesses

MDS is a linear mapping technique similar to principal component analysis (PCA). However, MDS requires only an input distance matrix and a value for p, as opposed to the full data set that is required for PCA defined in Section 10.2. MDS is especially useful in cases where only a distance matrix is provided and no other information is available [10]. In addition to requiring less input data, MDS can transform the data points in an arrangement that preserves their relative distances. Thus, MDS can be used to visualize graphs (and other data) in two dimensions.

There is an inherent tradeoff to reducing the dimensionality, though; some information will almost always be lost. However, it is possible to estimate how much information is being retained from the original data. By dividing the sum of the eigenvalues used by the sum of all of the eigenvalues, we can calculate the percentage of information retained. This value is called the *trace*. If the trace is high enough, then no more dimensions (or eigenvalues) need to be included. Otherwise, we can add additional eigenvalues (dimensions) until the trace improves. Adding the largest eigenvalues first allows for the highest amount of information retained.

Nonetheless, there may be situations where the eigenvalues are evenly distributed. For example, suppose our dataset contains five dimensions, with eigenvalues of $0.92, 0.84, 0.79, 0.78$, and 0.01. In this case, if we chose to use only two dimensions (eigenvalues 0.92 and 0.84), we would see a significant information loss, as the 3rd and 4th eigenvalues are also high relative to these eigenvalues. In these types of situations, MDS may produce a poor representation of the data due to the information loss.

In spite of the possible loss of information, the abilities of MDS to showcase information in a transformed space and to operate using only the distance matrix (rather than the full dataset) make it a valuable DR technique.

10.2 Kernel Principal Component Analysis

In the previous section, we described MDS and its applications. The objective of MDS is to obtain a low-dimensional vector representation of the objects, preserving inter-object distances to the best possible extent, which makes

MDS a good technique for visualization. Another important task in data analysis is to understand or identify the structural relationships inherent in the data. In order to do so, a desirable characteristic of the data is *linear separability*, the existence of a hyperplane separating data objects. In this section, we will discuss why linear separability is desirable and introduce a technique that can achieve this characteristic.

10.2.1   Example of Kernel PCA Assisting Clustering of Non–Linearly Separable Data

Consider the plots of the datasets shown in Figure 10.5. Both of these datasets have an inherent structure—the first has two distinct circular clouds, and the second has two spirals. We can load these datasets in R using the following libraries and functions.

```
1 library(DRGraphMining)
2 circles<-circlesdata()
3 plot(circles)
4 library(kernlab)
5 data(spirals)
6 plot(spirals)
```

These are two examples of non–linearly separable datasets, i.e., we cannot separate the structures (circles or spirals) in these datasets with a line (one-dimensional hyperplane). To understand why non-separable datasets are a concern, let us try an experiment where we attempt to cluster the dataset in Figure 10.5a using the k-means clustering algorithm. The clusters identified by this tool using the R code below are shown in Figure 10.6a. Clearly, k-means clustering fails to identify the actual structures in the dataset.

```
1 kmc = kmeans(circles, centers=2)
2 plot(circles, pch=kmc$cluster, col=kmc$cluster)
```

In general, identifying the structure of data becomes more complicated as the dimensionality and number of non–linearly separable structures in the data increase. To transform non–linearly separable data into linearly separable data, we introduce the kernel PCA technique. Figure 10.7 shows a plot of the dataset in Figure 10.5a after applying kernel PCA to this dataset. As we can see, the circular clouds of the original dataset are now linearly separated. The k-means clustering algorithm easily identifies the desired clusters when applied to the new dataset. Figure 10.7b, generated using the R code below, shows that the k-means algorithm can now correctly identify the two clusters.

```
1 kpc = kpca(circles, features=2)
2 plot(rotated(kpc))
3 kpc_kmc = kmeans(rotated(kpc), centers=2)
```

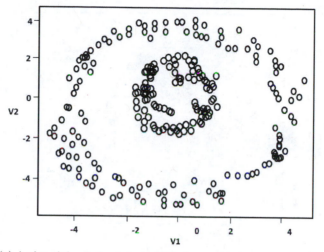

(a) A plot of the circles dataset. This dataset has two non–linearly separable circular clouds.

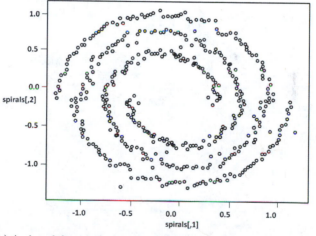

(b) A plot of the spirals dataset. This dataset has two non–linearly separable spirals.

FIGURE 10.5: Example datasets with non–linear separability. The plots are generated using R.

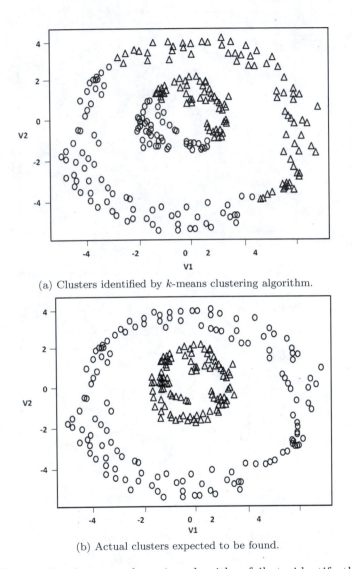

(a) Clusters identified by *k*-means clustering algorithm.

(b) Actual clusters expected to be found.

FIGURE 10.6: The *k*-means clustering algorithm fails to identify the actual clusters in the circles dataset.

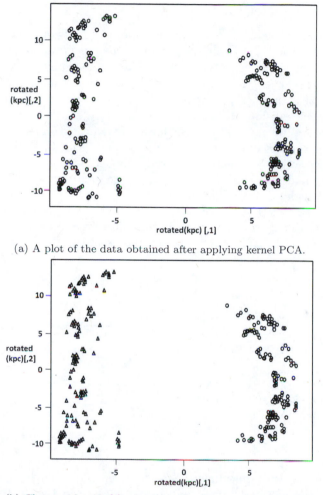

(a) A plot of the data obtained after applying kernel PCA.

(b) Clusters identified by k-means clustering on the new data.

FIGURE 10.7: The data after kernel PCA has the desired characteristic of linear separability.

```
4 plot(rotated(kpc), pch=kpc_kmc$cluster,
5 +col=kpc_kmc$cluster)
```

10.2.2 Example of Applying Kernel PCA to Separate Telephone Network Data

Suppose we are a telephone company that wants to find new customers to join our network. One way to identify potential customers might be to consider people that already make calls to existing customers in our network. For identifying new customers, it's not important what calls our existing customers make between each other, and we might not have data on telephone calls made between people outside our network.

Suppose we have used calling data for five existing customers, Alicia, Brian, Caroline, David, and Emily, to identify ten potential customers, Peter, Robert, Stephanie, Travis, Ursula, Vaughn, Wendy, Xavier, Yvonne, and Zachary. Out of these, we find that Peter through Ursula are interested in joining our network and Vaughn through Zachary are not.

We can represent the network as a *weighted bipartite graph*, where the edge weights represent the average number of minutes per week spent on the phone between two people. Numerically, we can represent this data as a matrix with 10 rows and 5 columns:

	A	B	C	D	E
P	60	120	0	0	20
R	40	0	120	80	40
S	0	0	120	120	0
T	80	80	40	40	80
U	80	120	40	0	40
V	30	90	0	0	60
W	30	0	90	60	30
X	0	0	90	90	0
Y	60	60	30	30	60
Z	60	90	30	0	30

We can use the Multidimensional Scaling technique described in Section 10.1 to visualize our data, which you can see in Figure 10.8a. The R code to generate this figure is as follows.

```
1 data=matrix(c(
2  60,120,  0,  0, 40,
3  40,  0,120, 80, 40,
4   0,  0,120,120,  0,
5  80, 80, 40, 40, 80,
6  80,120, 40,  0, 40,
7  30, 90,  0,  0, 60,
```

```
 8  30,  0, 90, 60, 30,
 9   0,  0, 90, 90,  0,
10  60, 60, 30, 30, 60,
11  60, 90, 30,  0, 30),ncol=5,byrow=TRUE)
12 mds=cmdscale(dist(data))
13 plot(mds,col=0)
14 text(mds,labels=LETTERS[c(16,18:26)],
15   col=c(rep(1,5),rep(2,5)))
```

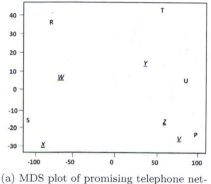

(a) MDS plot of promising telephone network customers.

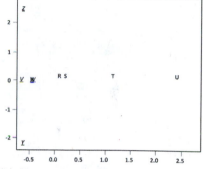

(b) Kernel PCA plot of promising telephone network customers. Customers P and R overlap, as well as customers W and X.

FIGURE 10.8: A comparison between linear (MDS) and nonlinear (kernel PCA) techniques for distinguishing between promising and not promising (underlined) customers for a telephone company.

As you can see from the figure, the division between the "promising" and "not promising" customers is not linear, but follows a circular or parabolic path. Using the kernel PCA technique, we can transform this data using the radial basis function (RBF) kernel to find a linear decision boundary (see Figure 10.8b). The R code to generate this figure is as follows:

```
16 kpc=kpca(data,features=2)
17 plot(rotated(kpc),col=0)
18 text(rotated(kpc),labels=LETTERS[c(16,18:26)],
19   col=c(rep(1,5),rep(2,5)))
```

10.2.3 Kernels

As hinted in the previous section, we are interested in transforming the data so that the interesting structures are linearly separated. To do this, we need to find a function to transform our data into a new space (usually called a

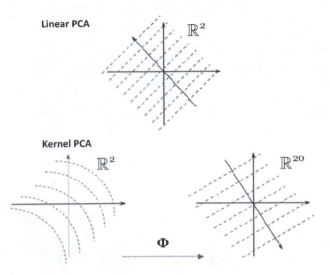

FIGURE 10.9: The figure on top depicts the principal components when linear PCA is carried out on the data. The principal component is represented by an arrow. The figure on the bottom shows the transformation of the data into a high-dimensional feature space via a transformation Φ. The "kernel trick" helps us carry out this mapping of data with the help of kernel functions. [34] Copyright @1998 Massachusetts Institute of Technology. Reprinted with permission. All rights reserved.

feature space) where the data objects are linearly separable. Two important questions we need to answer about this process are:

- how do we find such a function, and

- what is the dimensionality of the feature space?

Even if we assume that such a transformation exists, the second question still leads to concerns. The feature space may be high-dimensional, or even potentially infinite-dimensional [34]. In such cases, operating on data might be computationally intensive or impossible.

Kernels are very popular because they are simple and effectively address our questions. The following is a high-level definition of kernels (see also Chapter 4).

Definition 10.4 *Kernel*
A kernel is a real-valued function $k : O \times O \to \mathcal{H}$, where O is the original domain of the objects we are trying to transform and $\mathcal{H}$ is a Hilbert feature space with the property that there exists a mapping $\Phi : O \to \mathcal{H}$ such that $\langle \Phi(o_i), \Phi(o_j) \rangle = k(o_i, o_j)$ for all objects $o_i, o_j \in O$.

As we will describe in the later sections, kernels let us operate on the data in feature space without actually transforming individual data objects in the input space to feature space. This so-called "kernel trick" allows us to use statistical learning techniques that work well on linearly separable data to nonlinear data.

Graph Kernels

In addition to enabling us to use linear techniques on nonlinear data, another reason for the popularity of kernels is their ubiquity—kernels exist for a variety of data objects, including vectors, graphs, music, and so on. Here, we illustrate a kernel for graphs. More details on graph kernels can be obtained from Chapter 4.

Let G_1 and G_2 represent two graphs. Let G be the graph that represents the *Direct-Product* graph of G_1 and G_2.

Definition 10.5 *Direct product graph*
The direct product graph $G_1 \times G_2$ is a graph where each node represents a pair of nodes, one each from G_1 and G_2, and an edge exists between the nodes in the direct product graph if and only if the corresponding nodes in both G_1 and G_2 are adjacent [42].

Figure 10.10 shows the direct product graph of two graphs.

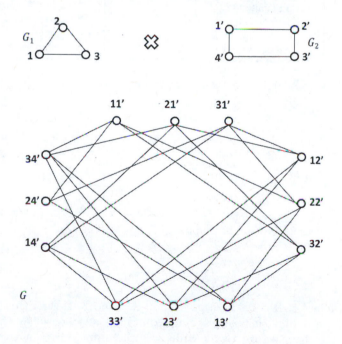

FIGURE 10.10: The *direct product* graph $G = G_1 \times G_2$, created from G_1 and G_2. [42]

The kernel function that computes the inner product (similarity) of the graphs G_1 and G_2 is given by $k(G_1, G_2)$. This value can be computed by finding the inverse of the matrix $(\mathbf{I} - \lambda \mathbf{W}_X)$ for some $\lambda > 0$, where $\mathbf{W}_X$ represents the weighted matrix of G and $\mathbf{I}$ represents the identity matrix [42].

10.2.4   Overview of Kernel PCA

As depicted in Figure 10.9, standard PCA works on the linear input space (top), whereas kernel PCA works on the linear feature space transformed from a nonlinear input space using a kernel function. As we discussed in the previous section, kernels exist for non-vector objects, too.

Once we have a kernel function, a kernel matrix can be constructed by applying the kernel function for every pair of data objects. The crux of kernel PCA is that the kernel matrix is equivalent to the Gram matrix (the matrix of inner products) of the data objects in the transformed Hilbert space [33]. Kernel PCA applies the same procedure as MDS to this "transformed Gramian," i.e., kernel PCA computes the required number of top eigenvalues and eigenvectors of the kernel matrix and uses these to produce the low-dimensional representation of the data objects. Figure 10.11 explains the steps involved in kernel PCA.

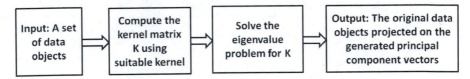

FIGURE 10.11: A high-level view of the steps involved in carrying out kernel PCA.

Algorithm 26 presents the pseudocode that performs kernel PCA on a given kernel matrix. This pseudocode represents the implementation of kernel PCA in R.

```
1 ##centering kernel matrix
2 kc <-t(t(x - colSums(x)/m) - rowSums(x)/m)+ sum(x)/m^2
3 ##t(x) computes the transpose of the matrix x

4 ##compute eigenvectors
5 res <- eigen(kc/m,symmetric=TRUE)
```

The above lines of R code correspond to lines 1 and 2 of Algorithm 26. These lines perform double centering of the kernel matrix, followed by the computation of the eigenvectors. In the code, x is the input kernel matrix, m is the number of rows in the matrix, kc is the matrix obtained after double centering the matrix x, and res is the matrix of eigenvectors.

---

1 **Algorithm:** Kernel-PCA

Input : **K**—the kernel matrix
    p—number of features in the transformed space.

Output: **PCV**—the principal components vector matrix in the feature
    space.

    ROTATED—data projected on the principal component
vectors

2 Compute **K**′ by double centering **K**

3 Compute eigenvalues Λ and eigenvectors $\mathbf{Z}^\mathbf{T}$ from eigenvalue
decomposition of **K**′

4 Compute $\mathbf{PCV} = ((\mathbf{Z}^\mathbf{T})/(\sqrt{\Lambda}))^\mathbf{T}$

5 Compute $\mathbf{ROTATED} = \mathbf{K}' \cdot \mathbf{PCV}$

Algorithm 26: Computation of kernel PCA

The principal component vectors and the original data projected on these principal components can be obtained by using the following R code. This code corresponds to lines 3 and 4 of Algorithm 26.

```
6 pcv(ret) <- t(t(res$vectors[,1:features])
7 +/sqrt(res$values[1:features]))
8 rotated(ret) <- kc %*% pcv(ret)
```

10.2.5   Strengths and Weaknesses

One of the main strengths of kernel PCA is that it can map non–linearly separable data to a high-dimensional feature space where the data becomes linearly separable by deriving low-dimensional features that incorporate higher order statistics. Cover's theorem on the separability of patterns states that non–linearly separable patterns in an input space can be transformed into linearly separable patterns with high probability if the input space is transformed nonlinearly to a high-dimensional feature space, which justifies kernel PCA [16]. Another strength of kernel PCA is that it does not require any nonlinear optimization; it is essentially no more difficult than standard PCA. Moreover, kernel PCA does not require that the number of components to be extracted be specified in advance.

One difficulty with kernel PCA is that the computation becomes prohibitive when the dataset is large. Another issue is that if the dataset changes, the whole decomposition needs to be recomputed from scratch.

10.3   Linear Discriminant Analysis

LDA is a dimension reduction technique primarily useful for supervised classification tasks. *Supervised* classification is when the class labels of the objects
in a dataset are taken into account during dimension reduction; the process
is called supervised dimension reduction [22]. Linear Discriminant Analysis
(LDA) [11] is a commonly used technique for supervised dimensional reduction or *feature extraction*. More formally, LDA aims to perform DR while
preserving as much of the class-discriminatory information as possible [45].

LDA is not specifically a graph-mining technique, though it can be applied
to kernel matrices of graphs. In the following sections, we discuss how to
represent the data in a matrix that preserves class labels, and we give the
formal definition of the LDA problem. First, though, we present an example
application of LDA for classifying data.

10.3.1   Example of LDA Assisting Classification of Data

We now show an example application of LDA. In our example, we show how
LDA can facilitate classification while preserving the class labels. Consider
the diabetes dataset in the mclust library. This dataset contains information
on patients suffering from diabetes and contains four dimensions, three independent variables and the class label of 'normal,' 'chemical,' or 'overt.' The
dataset, which contains 145 data points, is shown in Table 10.2. Our objective
in applying LDA to this dataset is to reduce its dimensionality without losing the class information of each data point. To apply LDA on this example
dataset, let us first take a quick look at how LDA works in R.

TABLE 10.2: Sample data from the diabetes dataset used in our example.
The dataset contains 145 data points and 4 dimensions, including the class
label. This dataset is distributed with the mclust package.

	class	glucose	insulin	sspg
1	normal	80	356	124
2	normal	97	289	117
3	chemical	98	478	151
4	overt	124	538	460
5	normal	90	323	240
6	chemical	110	522	325

In R, LDA can be performed using the `lda` function from the MASS package. In the most basic case, the `lda` function can be called using:

```
1 lda(formula, data)
```

where `data` is the data frame containing the data to be transformed and `formula`, in the form of `class v1+v2+...`, gives the names of the class label (`class`) and independent variables (`v1`, etc.) in `data`.

Now let us run LDA in R on our example dataset. First, load the `diabetes` dataset from the mclust package.

```
1 library(mclust)
2 data(diabetes)
```

Next, to illustrate the classification process, let's select a subset of the data to act as a training sample. We can then apply LDA on the training dataset and predict class labels for the remaining data using the model given by LDA. In the code below, `lda` is applied on 135 randomly selected data points, and all three variables in the data (`glucose`, `insulin`, and `sspg`) are used to predict the class label (`class`).

```
3 library(MASS)
4 tr<-sample(145, 135)
5 train<-diabetes[tr,]
6 res<-lda(class~.,train)
7 res
```

The lines of code above result in two linear discriminants to replace the three dimensions of the original dataset (partial output is shown below).

```
 8 Coefficients of linear discriminants:
 9                   LD1              LD2
10 glucose -0.05775897  0.010998594
11 insulin -0.01565862  0.003630055
12 sspg    -0.00755958 -0.014380665

13 Proportion of trace:
14    LD1    LD2
15 0.9722 0.0278
```

Now, we can test the ability of LDA to preserve the class label by using the results of LDA to classify the other ten data points. Basically, we use the result of `lda` as our prediction model, predict the class label of the data points not used for training, and compare the predicted class labels to the actual class labels.

```
16 test<-diabetes[-tr,]
17 ldaPred<-predict(res,test)
18 actClass<-unclass(test$class)
19 predClass<-unclass(ldaPred$class)
20 plot(ldaPred$x,pch=actClass)
21 points(ldaPred$x,pch=predClass,cex=2)
```

The results of this plot appear in Figure 10.12. In the plot, the small symbols represent the true class of the data points (circle, triangle, and plus corresponding to 'normal,' 'chemical,' and 'overt,' respectively), and the large symbols represent the predicted class. From the figure, we can see that the result of LDA is able to correctly classify all of the points. (Your result may differ due to the randomness in choosing the training set.)

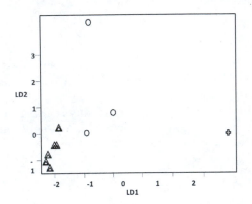

FIGURE 10.12: Experimental results for classifying `diabetes` data using the `lda` function in R. Large symbols represent the predicted class, whereas small symbols represent the actual class. The symbols are as follows: circles represent 'chemical,' triangles represent 'normal,' and pluses represent 'overt.'

10.3.2 Overview of LDA

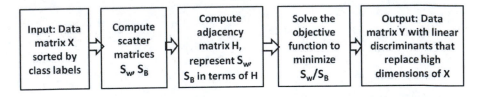

FIGURE 10.13: Overview of LDA presenting the flow of tasks in LDA.

Given an input dataset, LDA aims to project the data linearly such that the classes in the low-dimensional data are best separated (as shown in Figure 10.13). More specifically, LDA finds a linear transformation or a "discriminant function" that maximizes the ratio of between-class variance to within-class variance. The transformation seeks to rotate the axes so that when the classes are projected on the new axes, the differences between the classes are maximized, i.e., the projected means of the different classes are as far away from each other and within a particular class, all samples of that class are clustered around the projected means. Maximizing this ratio is achieved by solving a generalized eigenvalue problem.

In the following sections, we will discuss the mathematical basis for how this eigenvalue problem is formulated to find the transformation with the best between-class to within-class variance ratio [43] [22]. A pseudocode description of the LDA algorithm is given in Algorithm 27.

Input: Data set $\mathbf{X}$, with m data points with c classes.
Output: Set of eigenvectors (i.e., a matrix) $\mathbf{Y}$ of size (# of columns) p such that $p \ll m$.

1 Create $\mathbf{X}$, the data matrix
2 Sort data into c matrices $\rightarrow$ set of $\mathbf{X}_C$
3 Compute mean vectors μ, μ_c
4 Compute adjacency matrix $\mathbf{H}$
5 Compute $\overline{\mathbf{X}}$
6 Compute $\mathbf{S}_B = \overline{\mathbf{X}} \cdot \mathbf{H} \cdot \overline{\mathbf{X}}^{\mathbf{T}}$
7 Compute $\mathbf{S}_W = \overline{\mathbf{X}} \cdot (\mathbf{I} - \mathbf{H}) \cdot \overline{\mathbf{X}}^{\mathbf{T}}$
8 Solve eigenvalue problem: $\mathbf{S}_B^{1/2} \mathbf{S}_W^{-1} \mathbf{S}_B^{1/2}$
9 Let $\mathbf{Y}$ be the p most significant eigenvectors
10 Return $\mathbf{Y}$

Algorithm 27: A pseudocode description of the Linear Discriminant Analysis algorithm

10.3.3 Graph Representation of Scatter Matrices

In order to find the "optimal" transformation, it is important to represent the given data in terms of their class distributions, i.e., in *scatter matrices*.

Scatter Matrices

Scatter matrices are matrices that provide information on the distribution of a given set of data points. Let X be a dataset of n vectors $x_1, x_2, \ldots, x_n \in \mathbb{R}^m$. If we represent these vectors as columns in a matrix representation, we can form the matrix:

$$\mathbf{X} = \left[\begin{array}{cccc} \overbrace{}^{n} \\ x_{11} & x_{12} & \cdots & x_{1n} \\ x_{21} & x_{22} & \cdots & x_{2n} \\ x_{31} & x_{32} & \cdots & x_{3n} \\ x_{41} & x_{42} & \cdots & x_{4n} \\ \vdots & \vdots & \ddots & \vdots \\ x_{m1} & x_{22} & \cdots & x_{mn} \end{array}\right] \Bigg\} m \qquad (10.14)$$

Let C be the number of classes in dataset X. The data points in $\mathbf{X}$ can be ordered according to their class membership to $\mathbf{X}_1, \mathbf{X}_2, \ldots, \mathbf{X}_C$ so that $\mathbf{X}_c$ is a column matrix of all of the data points in class c. Let μ be the mean vector of the entire data set, and let μ_c be the mean vector of $\mathbf{X}_c$ for each class c. Let n_c denote the number of data points that belong to class c.

$$\mathbf{X} = \left[\begin{array}{ccccccccc} \overbrace{x_{11}^1 \quad \cdots \quad x_{1n_1}^1}^{\mathbf{X}_1} & & \cdots & & \overbrace{x_{11}^C \quad \cdots \quad x_{1n_C}^C}^{\mathbf{X}_C} \\ x_{11}^1 & \cdots & x_{1n_1}^1 & & & x_{11}^C & \cdots & x_{1n_C}^C \\ x_{21}^1 & \cdots & x_{2n_1}^1 & & \cdots & x_{21}^C & \cdots & x_{2n_C}^C \\ \vdots & \ddots & \vdots & & & \vdots & \ddots & \vdots \\ x_{m1}^1 & \cdots & x_{mn_1}^1 & & & x_{m1}^C & \cdots & x_{mn_C}^C \end{array}\right] \qquad (10.15)$$

We will illustrate these terms with a numerical example. (We will use the same example to show the computation of scatter matrices in the subsequent parts of this section). Consider a data set $\mathbf{X}$ with four data points, three features, and two classes (c_1 and c_2) such that

$$\mathbf{X} = \left[\begin{array}{cccc} \overbrace{10 \quad 7}^{c_1} & \overbrace{8 \quad 4}^{c_2} \\ 10 & 7 & 8 & 4 \\ 25 & 12 & 13 & 2 \\ 32 & 49 & 21 & 50 \end{array}\right]. \qquad (10.16)$$

If we split the matrix $\mathbf{X}$ up by class, we see that

$$\mathbf{X}_1 = \left[\begin{array}{cc} 10 & 7 \\ 25 & 12 \\ 32 & 49 \end{array}\right], \qquad (10.17)$$

$$\mathbf{X}_2 = \left[\begin{array}{cc} 8 & 4 \\ 13 & 2 \\ 21 & 50 \end{array}\right], \qquad (10.18)$$

and the corresponding mean vectors are

$$\mu_1 = \begin{bmatrix} \frac{10+7}{2} \\ \frac{25+12}{2} \\ \frac{32+49}{2} \end{bmatrix} = \begin{bmatrix} 8.5 \\ 18.5 \\ 40.5 \end{bmatrix}, \tag{10.19}$$

$$\mu_2 = \begin{bmatrix} \frac{8+4}{2} \\ \frac{13+2}{2} \\ \frac{21+50}{2} \end{bmatrix} = \begin{bmatrix} 6 \\ 7.5 \\ 35.5 \end{bmatrix}, \tag{10.20}$$

$$\mu = \begin{bmatrix} \frac{10+7+8+4}{4} \\ \frac{25+12+13+2}{4} \\ \frac{32+49+21+50}{4} \end{bmatrix} = \begin{bmatrix} 7.25 \\ 13 \\ 38 \end{bmatrix}. \tag{10.21}$$

Let us now take a look at how we compute the matrices that represent the distribution of data within and between classes. These matrices are called *within-class* and *between-class* scatter matrices, respectively.

Definition 10.6 *Within-Class Scatter Matrix*
The matrix that provides a representation of the data distribution within each class is called the *within-class scatter matrix* and is denoted by $\mathbf{S}_W$.

Definition 10.7 *Between-Class Scatter Matrix*
The matrix that provides a representation of the data distribution between classes is called the *between-class scatter matrix* and is denoted by $\mathbf{S}_B$.

The within-class scatter matrix for each class c can be calculated by

$$\mathbf{S}_W^c = \frac{1}{n_c} \sum_{\mathbf{x} \in \mathbf{X}_c} (\mathbf{x} - \mu_c)(\mathbf{x} - \mu_c)^{\mathbf{T}}, \tag{10.22}$$

and the total within-class scatter matrix is given by

$$\mathbf{S}_W = \sum_{c=1}^{C} \sum_{\mathbf{x} \in \mathbf{X}_c} (\mathbf{x} - \mu_c)(\mathbf{x} - \mu_c)^{\mathbf{T}}. \tag{10.23}$$

Similarly, the total between-class scatter matrix is

$$\mathbf{S}_B = \sum_{c=1}^{C} n_c (\mu_c - \mu)(\mu_c - \mu)^{\mathbf{T}}. \tag{10.24}$$

Figure 10.14 illustrates the scatter matrices of data with three classes, where $\mathbf{S}_{B1}$, $\mathbf{S}_{B2}$, and $\mathbf{S}_{B3}$ are the between-class scatter matrices, and $\mathbf{S}_{W1}$, $\mathbf{S}_{W2}$, and $\mathbf{S}_{W3}$ are the within-class scatter matrices. $\mathbf{S}_{B1}$, $\mathbf{S}_{B2}$, and $\mathbf{S}_{B3}$ give the distance between each class centroid and the centroid of the whole data,

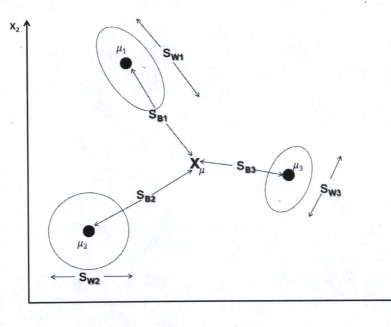

FIGURE 10.14: Within-class scatter and between-class scatter.
[research.cs.kamu.edu/prism/lectures/pr/pr_110.pdf]

whereas $\mathbf{S}_{W1}$, $\mathbf{S}_{W2}$, and $\mathbf{S}_{W3}$ give the distance of the data points to the corresponding class mean μ_c.

Let us compute the scatter matrices using our numerical example. To calculate $\mathbf{S}_W$, let us first compute $\mathbf{S}_W^c = \sum_{\mathbf{x} \in \mathbf{X}_c} (\mathbf{x} - \mu_c)(\mathbf{x} - \mu_c)^{\mathbf{T}}$ for $c = c_1$.

$$
\mathbf{S}_W^{c_1} = \left(\begin{bmatrix} 10 \\ 25 \\ 32 \end{bmatrix} - \begin{bmatrix} 8.5 \\ 18.5 \\ 40.5 \end{bmatrix} \right) \cdot \left(\begin{bmatrix} 10 \\ 25 \\ 32 \end{bmatrix} - \begin{bmatrix} 8.5 \\ 18.5 \\ 40.5 \end{bmatrix} \right)^{\mathbf{T}}
\tag{10.25}
$$

$$
+ \left(\begin{bmatrix} 7 \\ 12 \\ 49 \end{bmatrix} - \begin{bmatrix} 8.5 \\ 18.5 \\ 40.5 \end{bmatrix} \right) \cdot \left(\begin{bmatrix} 7 \\ 12 \\ 49 \end{bmatrix} - \begin{bmatrix} 8.5 \\ 18.5 \\ 40.5 \end{bmatrix} \right)^{\mathbf{T}}
\tag{10.26}
$$

$$
= \begin{bmatrix} 2.25 & 9.75 & -12.75 \\ 9.75 & 42.25 & -55.25 \\ -12.75 & -55.25 & 72.25 \end{bmatrix} + \begin{bmatrix} 2.25 & 9.75 & -12.75 \\ 9.75 & 42.25 & -55.25 \\ -12.75 & -55.25 & 72.25 \end{bmatrix}
\tag{10.27}
$$

$$
= \begin{bmatrix} 4.5 & 19.5 & -26.5 \\ 19.5 & 84.5 & -110.5 \\ -26.5 & -110.5 & 144.5 \end{bmatrix}
\tag{10.28}
$$

Similarly, we can compute $\mathbf{S}_W^{c_2}$ to be

$$\mathbf{S}_W^{c_2} = \begin{bmatrix} 8 & 22 & 58 \\ 22 & 60.5 & -159.5 \\ 58 & -159.5 & 420.5 \end{bmatrix}, \tag{10.29}$$

so the entire within-class scatter matrix $\mathbf{S}_W$ can be calculated as follows.

$$\mathbf{S}_W = \mathbf{S}_W^{c_1} + \mathbf{S}_W^{c_2} \tag{10.30}$$

$$= \begin{bmatrix} 4.5 & 19.5 & -25.5 \\ 19.5 & 84.5 & -110.5 \\ -25.5 & -110.5 & 144.5 \end{bmatrix} + \begin{bmatrix} 8 & 22 & 58 \\ 22 & 60.5 & -159.5 \\ 58 & -159.5 & 420.5 \end{bmatrix} \tag{10.31}$$

$$= \begin{bmatrix} 12.5 & 41.5 & -83.5 \\ 41.5 & 145 & -270 \\ -83.5 & -270 & 565 \end{bmatrix} \tag{10.32}$$

Now, let us compute the between-graph scatter matrix $\mathbf{S}_B$. As there are two points in both class c_1 and class c_2, $n_1 = 2$ and $n_2 = 2$. Let's first compute the scatter matrix for each class.

$$\mathbf{S}_B^{c_1} = 2 \cdot \left(\begin{bmatrix} 8.5 \\ 18.5 \\ 40.5 \end{bmatrix} - \begin{bmatrix} 7.25 \\ 13 \\ 38 \end{bmatrix} \right) \cdot \left(\begin{bmatrix} 8.5 \\ 18.5 \\ 40.5 \end{bmatrix} - \begin{bmatrix} 7.25 \\ 13 \\ 38 \end{bmatrix} \right)^{\mathbf{T}} \tag{10.33}$$

$$= \begin{bmatrix} 3.125 & 13.75 & 6.25 \\ 13.750 & 60.5 & 27.5 \\ 6.25 & 27.5 & 12.5 \end{bmatrix}. \tag{10.34}$$

$\mathbf{S}_B^{c_2}$ can be computed similarly. Consequently,

$$\mathbf{S}_B = \mathbf{S}_B^{c_1} + \mathbf{S}_B^{c_2} \tag{10.35}$$

$$= \begin{bmatrix} 3.125 & 13.75 & 6.25 \\ 13.750 & 60.5 & 27.5 \\ 6.25 & 27.5 & 12.5 \end{bmatrix} + \begin{bmatrix} 3.125 & 13.75 & 6.25 \\ 13.750 & 60.5 & 27.5 \\ 6.25 & 27.5 & 12.5 \end{bmatrix} \tag{10.36}$$

$$= \begin{bmatrix} 6.25 & 27.5 & 12.5 \\ 27.5 & 121 & 55 \\ 12.5 & 55 & 25 \end{bmatrix} \tag{10.37}$$

Let $\mathbf{S}_T$ be the total covariance matrix of $\mathbf{X}$. The formula to calculate $\mathbf{S}_T$ is:

$$\mathbf{S}_T = \sum_{x_i \in X} (x_i - \mu)(x_i - \mu)^{\mathbf{T}} \tag{10.38}$$

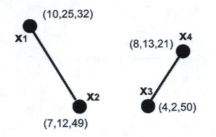

FIGURE 10.15: Graph representation of numerical example with two classes.

Conveniently, $\mathbf{S}_T$ can also be calculated by

$$\mathbf{S}_T = \mathbf{S}_B + \mathbf{S}_W. \tag{10.39}$$

In the context of our numerical example:

$$\mathbf{S}_T = \mathbf{S}_W + \mathbf{S}_B \tag{10.40}$$

$$= \begin{bmatrix} 12.5 & 41.5 & -83.5 \\ 41.5 & 145 & -270 \\ -83.5 & -270 & 565 \end{bmatrix} + \begin{bmatrix} 6.25 & 27.5 & 12.5 \\ 27.5 & 121 & 55 \\ 12.5 & 55 & 25 \end{bmatrix} \tag{10.41}$$

$$= \begin{bmatrix} 18.75 & 69 & -71 \\ 69 & 266 & -215 \\ -71 & -215 & 590 \end{bmatrix} \tag{10.42}$$

Graph Representation

Next, we represent the scatter matrices $\mathbf{S}_B$, $\mathbf{S}_W$, and $\mathbf{S}_T$ as a graph. Let G be the graph where each data point is a vertex, vertices are joined by an edge if and only if they belong to the same class, and the edge weights equal $1/n_c$, where n_c is the number of data points in class c. The resulting graph for our numerical example appears in Figure 10.15.

The graph in Figure 10.15 contains two cliques (fully connected subgraphs), representing the two classes in the data. Let $\mathbf{H}$ represent the adjacency matrix of the graph G. Reordering the vertices by class, the adjacency matrix $\mathbf{H}$ can be represented as

$$\mathbf{H} = \begin{bmatrix} \begin{bmatrix} \frac{1}{n_1} & \cdots \\ \vdots & \ddots \end{bmatrix} & [\mathbf{0}] & [\mathbf{0}] \\ [\mathbf{0}] & \begin{bmatrix} \frac{1}{n_2} & \cdots \\ \vdots & \ddots \end{bmatrix} & [\mathbf{0}] \\ [\mathbf{0}] & [\mathbf{0}] & \begin{bmatrix} \frac{1}{n_3} & \cdots \\ \vdots & \ddots \end{bmatrix} \end{bmatrix}. \tag{10.43}$$

The weighted adjacency matrix for our numerical example is shown below.

$$\mathbf{H} = \begin{bmatrix} \frac{1}{2} & \frac{1}{2} & 0 & 0 \\ \frac{1}{2} & \frac{1}{2} & 0 & 0 \\ 0 & 0 & \frac{1}{2} & \frac{1}{2} \\ 0 & 0 & \frac{1}{2} & \frac{1}{2} \end{bmatrix} \tag{10.44}$$

The advantage in using $\mathbf{H}$ as the adjacency matrix of our graph is that if we calculate the matrix $\overline{\mathbf{X}}$ by subtracting the dataset mean μ from each vector in the data matrix $\mathbf{X}$, we can represent Equation 10.24 as:

$$\mathbf{S}_B = \overline{\mathbf{X}}\mathbf{H}\overline{\mathbf{X}}^{\mathbf{T}}. \tag{10.45}$$

In our numerical example,

$$\overline{\mathbf{X}} = \begin{bmatrix} 10 & 7 & 8 & 4 \\ 25 & 12 & 13 & 2 \\ 32 & 49 & 21 & 50 \end{bmatrix} - \begin{bmatrix} 7.25 & 7.25 & 7.25 & 7.25 \\ 13 & 13 & 13 & 13 \\ 38 & 38 & 38 & 38 \end{bmatrix} \tag{10.46}$$

$$= \begin{bmatrix} 2.75 & -0.25 & 0.75 & -3.25 \\ 12 & -1 & 0 & -11 \\ -6 & 11 & -17 & 12 \end{bmatrix}, \tag{10.47}$$

and calculating the matrix product $\overline{\mathbf{X}}H\overline{\mathbf{X}}^{\mathbf{T}}$ gives us the same answer for $\mathbf{S}_B$ as calculated previously.

Similarly, $\mathbf{S}_T$ and $\mathbf{S}_W$ can be represented in terms of $\overline{\mathbf{X}}$ and $\mathbf{H}$ as

$$\mathbf{S}_T = \overline{\mathbf{X}}\overline{\mathbf{X}}^{\mathbf{T}}, \tag{10.48}$$

$$\mathbf{S}_W = \overline{\mathbf{X}}(\mathbf{I} - \mathbf{H})\overline{\mathbf{X}}^{\mathbf{T}}. \tag{10.49}$$

In the next section, we use these definitions for calculating the scatter matrices to formulate an eigenvalue problem whose answer will tell us the optimal class-preserving transformation for our data.

10.3.4 Calculating the Optimal Objective Function as an Eigenvalue Problem

In the previous section, we looked at how the scatter matrices are constructed and how they can be represented in terms of the matrix $\mathbf{H}$. In this section, we investigate how to find the optimal transformation or *objective function* for our data using these scatter matrices.

Definition 10.8 *Optimal projection.*
An optimal projection is one that *maximizes* the variance within each class while *minimizing* the variance between the classes.

Let $\mathbf{a}$ represent an optimal projection vector, and let's see what information we can tell about $\mathbf{a}$. From the previous section, we can calculate the between-class scatter matrix $\mathbf{S}_B$ as:

$$\mathbf{a}^\mathbf{T}\mathbf{S}_B\mathbf{a} = \sum_{c=1}^{C} n_c |\mathbf{a}^\mathbf{T}(\mu_c - \mu)|^2. \tag{10.50}$$

Similarly, the within-class scatter matrix can be calculated as:

$$\mathbf{a}^\mathbf{T}\mathbf{S}_W\mathbf{a} = \sum_{c=1}^{C} \sum_{\mathbf{x}_i \in \mathbf{X}_c} |\mathbf{a}^\mathbf{T}(\mathbf{x}_i - \mu_c)|^2. \tag{10.51}$$

Let r represent the ratio of the between-class scatter and the within-class scatter:

$$r = \frac{\mathbf{a}^\mathbf{T}\mathbf{S}_B\mathbf{a}}{\mathbf{a}^\mathbf{T}\mathbf{S}_W\mathbf{a}}. \tag{10.52}$$

To calculate the maximum ratio (in terms of $\mathbf{a}$), we take the partial derivative of this expression with respect to $\mathbf{a}$ and set this equal to zero:

$$\frac{\partial r}{\partial \mathbf{a}} = \frac{\mathbf{S}_B\mathbf{a}(\mathbf{a}\mathbf{S}_W\mathbf{a}) - \mathbf{S}_W\mathbf{a}(\mathbf{a}\mathbf{S}_B\mathbf{a})}{(\mathbf{a}^\mathbf{T}\mathbf{S}_W\mathbf{a})^2}, \tag{10.53}$$

$$\frac{\mathbf{S}_B\mathbf{a}(\mathbf{a}\mathbf{S}_W\mathbf{a}) - \mathbf{S}_W\mathbf{a}(\mathbf{a}\mathbf{S}_B\mathbf{a})}{(\mathbf{a}^\mathbf{T}\mathbf{S}_W\mathbf{a})^2} = 0. \tag{10.54}$$

The problem given by Equation 10.54 above is equivalent to the following eigenvalue problem:

$$\mathbf{S}_B\mathbf{a} = \lambda\mathbf{S}_W\mathbf{a} \tag{10.55}$$

$$\mathbf{S}_W^{-1}\mathbf{S}_B\mathbf{a} = \lambda\mathbf{a} \tag{10.56}$$

However, we cannot solve this eigenvalue problem because the matrix $\mathbf{S}_W^{-1}\mathbf{S}_B$ is not symmetric. In order to make the equation symmetric, we can multiply both sides of the equation by $\mathbf{S}_B^{\frac{1}{2}}$ and use the substitution $\mathbf{Y} = \mathbf{S}_B^{\frac{1}{2}}\mathbf{a}$ to get:

$$\mathbf{S}_W^{-1}\mathbf{S}_B\mathbf{a} = \lambda\mathbf{a} \tag{10.57}$$

$$\mathbf{S}_B^{\frac{1}{2}}\mathbf{S}_W^{-1}\mathbf{S}_B\mathbf{a} = \lambda\mathbf{S}_B^{\frac{1}{2}} \tag{10.58}$$

$$\mathbf{S}_B^{\frac{1}{2}}\mathbf{S}_W^{-1}\mathbf{S}_B^{\frac{1}{2}}\mathbf{Y} = \lambda\mathbf{Y} \tag{10.59}$$

Therefore, our optimal projection vectors are related to the eigenvectors of the matrix $\mathbf{S}_B^{\frac{1}{2}}\mathbf{S}_W^{-1}\mathbf{S}_B^{\frac{1}{2}}$. Thus, to find the optimal projection into p dimensions, LDA finds the top p eigenvalues and corresponding eigenvectors of this matrix.

10.3.5 Strengths and Weaknesses

LDA is most often compared to Principal Component Analysis (PCA). Both of these are dimension reduction techniques based on solving eigenvector problems, but PCA is an *unsupervised* technique [21], which means it does not take class labels into account. LDA is not only able to preserve class labels, but it also outperforms PCA when applied on large datasets [29].

The classical LDA technique finds a set of projecting vectors that best separate different classes, providing a better separation between classes in the data. In practice, LDA has been applied to many applications such as face recognition, mobile robotics, document classification, speech recognition, and multimedia information retrieval [17] [46] [47] [9].

However, classical LDA is based on two assumptions: (1) the data follows a Gaussian distribution and (2) the total scatter matrix $\mathbf{S}_T$ has an inverse [47] [20]. Because of these assumptions, classical LDA cannot be applied to real-world data in cases where these assumptions do not apply. For example, some real-world problems, such as face images, text documents, and microarray expression data, involve data where the data dimension is much larger than the number of data points. For such problems, the total scatter matrix can be singular, that is, it may not have an inverse. Classical LDA cannot be applied to these problems. There are extensions of LDA that address some of these limitations [13], but these extensions are not covered in this chapter.

10.4 Applications

10.4.1 Tumor Cell Diagnostics with MDS

In this section, we will show an example application of MDS for identifying tumor bio-markers through microarray analysis. Microarray is a technology for investigating the expression levels of thousands of genes simultaneously [37].

Computational biology and bioinformatics use microarray data to reach meaningful conclusions. For example, from DNA microarray data, researchers can identify cancer classes through the clustering of gene expression profiles. Tumors can be clustered into clinically relevant groups based on their gene expression [37].

With the help of modern biotechnologies, a large number of tumor biomarkers have been identified. Tissue microarrays are being widely used to screen protein expression patterns in a large number of patient samples. As the number of immunohistochemical markers increases, it may be possible to classify tumors based on tissue microarray results.

In particular, we focus on the problem of tumor class discovery in renal cell carcinoma tissue microarray data. Renal cell carcinoma is one of the most common types of kidney cancer in adults. We look at two main sub-problems here. One is to develop an efficient algorithm to identify clusters in the tissue microarray data, and the other is to determine if these generated clusters are biologically significant and refer to tumors. We have used the application from the work done by Tao Shi and Steve Horvath. For a better understanding of the entire application, refer to [37].

In this application, we hope to show how graph mining techniques can improve the classification of renal cell carcinoma. MDS is used in our application to visualize this improvement. For this application, we use a dataset of 366 patient samples containing staining scores for eight tumor markers (or *features*), survival time, death indicator, and class label.[1] We intend to classify these patient samples into two classes, with labels C for *clear cell* patients and label N for *non-clear cell* patients.

This application requires the following packages:

```
1 library(Hmisc)
2 library(cluster)
3 library(randomForest)
4 library(DRGraphMining)
```

A naïve approach might be to calculate Euclidean distances between patient samples and apply MDS on the resulting distance matrix, as shown in the following R code. MDS can then project this output into two dimensions (line 9).

```
5 data = read.table(file.path(package="DRGraphMining",
6 +"data","testData_366.csv"),sep=",",header=T,row.names=1)
7 datRF = data[,1:8]
8 d = dist(datRF)
9 cmd = cmdscale(d,2)
```

In the R code below, we apply Partition Around Medoid (PAM) clustering

---

[1]http://www.genetics.ucla.edu/labs/horvath/kidneypaper/RCC.htm

TABLE 10.3: Confusion matrix for clustering using Euclidean distance that indicates $38 + 5 = 43$ misclassified patients

		ClearCellStatus	
		Clear	Non-Clear
Cluster	1	278	5
	2	38	45

to this result, creating two distinct clusters in the data, which are described in Table 10.3. This *confusion matrix* is generated in lines 16 and 17) below. From the table, we can see that cluster 1 consists mostly of clear cell patients, while cluster 2 contains most of the non-clear cell patients, and a prediction based on these two clusters would incorrectly classify 43 patient samples. We also plot the MDS output (lines 12 and 13) to visualize the generated clusters. This plot appears in Figure 10.16a.

```
10 ClusterLabel = pamNew(cmd,2)
11 plot(cmd,type="n",
12 +xlab="Scale Dimension1",ylab="Scale Dimension2")
13 text(cmd,label=ifelse(data$ClearCell==1,"C","N"),
14    col=ClusterLabel)
15 ClearCellStatus=ifelse(data$ClearCell==1,
16 +"Clear","Non-Clear")
17 print(table(ClusterLabel,ClearCellStatus ))
```

Let's try a second approach to see if we can get better accuracy. This time, rather than calculating Euclidean distance between patient samples, we can use the *Random Forest* (RF) dissimilarity measure as input to MDS. Essentially, RF constructs a large set of decision trees built by selecting random subsets of the features, and the results from these trees are combined to estimate dissimilarity. Each of the decision trees is constructed using a user-specified m features out of the total M features. The trees are created by deciding which feature best discriminates between the two classes of data points, splitting the training data based on the chosen feature, and repeating this process until the data has been completely split [4].

After generating the various trees, each tree is used to classify the data points, and the similarity between two patient samples is based on the amount of agreement among the decision trees. This similarity measure forms a matrix that is positive, symmetric, and normalized to the unit interval $[0, 1]$. Then RF-dissimilarity is calculated using `RFdist` function in the randomForest package [36].

We calculate the RF dissimilarity and apply the same technique as before in the following R code. Here, we have used 2,000 forests and 80 trees. These

TABLE 10.4: Confusion matrix for clustering using RF dissimilarity measure that indicates $11 + 18 = 29$ misclassified patients

		ClearCellStatus	
		Clear	Non-Clear
RFclusterLabel	1	305	18
	2	11	32

parameter values are fairly high—reducing them may allow you to get a result faster, but it may affect the accuracy of your result, as well. The resulting clusters appear in Table 10.4, and the plot appears in Figure 10.16. In our experiment, just 29 patients were misclassified, improving the accuracy over the case of using Euclidean distance.

```
1  distRF=RFdist(datRF,mtry1=3,2000,80,addcl1=T,
2  addcl2=F,imp=T,      oob.prox1=T)
3  cmdRF=cmdscale(as.dist(distRF$cl1),2)
4  RFclusterLabel = pamNew(cmdRF,2)
5  plot(cmdRF,type="n",
6  xlab="Scale Dimension1",ylab="Scale Dimension2")
7  text(cmdRF,label=ifelse(data$ClearCell==1,"C","N"),
8       col=RFclusterLabel)
9  ClearCellStatus=ifelse(data$ClearCell==1,
10 "Clear","Non-Clear")
11 print(table(RFclusterLabel,ClearCellStatus))
```

10.4.2   Face Recognition with LDA

Face recognition is a popular area of research in the field of image analysis [15]. A major challenge in face recognition is that, even though images of people's faces contain the information required to distinguish between people, the pixels of these images can be very similar statistically [15]. Because the amount of information contained in an image is so large, Belhumeur *et al.* [2] apply the technique of LDA to reduce the dimensionality of the data while preserving the distinguishing features of the person.

   The problem of face recognition is a classification problem that takes a new image of a face and returns the identity of that person. We now illustrate the application of LDA in reducing the dimensionality of the image data used for face recognition. The dataset for this experiment is available at the University of Sheffield website.[2] The image files are in the *.pgm* file format, and some of the images from this dataset appear in Figure 10.17.

---

[2]http://www.shef.ac.uk/eee/research/iel/research/face.html

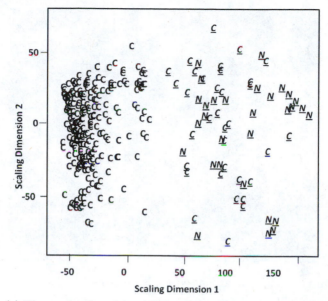

(a) The result of applying MDS and PAM clustering using Euclidean distance.

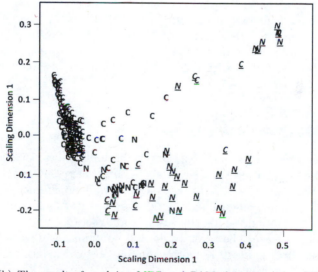

(b) The result of applying MDS and PAM clustering using RF dissimilarity measure.

FIGURE 10.16: Plot of two clusters for clear cell patients (C) and non-clear cell patients (N). The plots are generated using R.

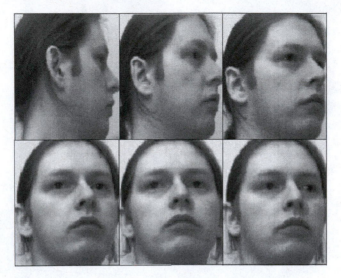

FIGURE 10.17: Sample images used to demonstrate the application of LDA for face recognition.

To apply LDA using R, we follow the procedure described by Li *et al.* [26] and use the implementation of LDA in the MASS package. Our implementation of Algorithm 28 is distributed as the `FaceRecogLDA` function in the DRGraphMining package that is available with the textbook. A sample set of images is also distributed with the package. The usage of `FaceRecogLDA` is as follows:

```
1 library(DRGraphMining)
2 FaceRecogLDA(path, trainSamplePercent)
```

Here, `path` represents the path containing the input images which are sorted into sub-folders based on their class labels. `trainSamplePercent` is the percentage of the dataset that is to be taken as training sample. A pseudocode description of the `FaceRecogLDA` function appears in Algorithm 28.

For this illustration, we use the `example` dataset distributed with the DR-GraphMining package. The `example` dataset contains a sample set of cropped images similar to Figure 10.17, corresponding to two classes, `1a` and `1e`. We set the training percentage to 80%.

```
1 result<-FaceRecogLDA("example",80)
```

The `FaceRecogLDA` function generates the model based on the training sample and validates the model by using it to predict the class labels of the images not used for building the model. The output, shown below, gives the actual and predicted classes for the testing sample.

Input: path—Folder containing images sorted into sub-folders with
     names corresponding to their class label
Input: trainSamplePercent—Percentage of the dataset to be taken as
     training sample
Output: LinearDiscriminants—the resulting linear discriminants

1 Read path folder
2 Store subfolder names as ClassLabels
3 Initialize an array of images
4 **foreach** class in ClassLabels **do**
5   Add images from directory class to image array
6 **end**
7 Randomly select trainSamplePercent percent of the images and store as
    trainingData
8 Apply LDA to trainingData
9 Return LDA result

Algorithm 28: Face Recognition using LDA

```
2 Expected:
3 1e 1e 1e 1e 1e 1e 1e 1e 1e 1a 1a 1a 1a
4 Predicted:
5 1e 1e 1e 1e 1e 1e 1e 1e 1e 1a 1a 1a 1a
```

As can be seen from the above results, our experiment using 80% of the dataset for training sample resulted in correctly predicting the 13 images in the test set.

10.5 Bibliographic Notes

To recall, dimensionality reduction is a technique for transforming high-dimensional data into a lower-dimensional vector space while preserving as much information from the original data as possible. The two main reasons for applying DR in data mining are (1) to reduce noise and extract only the important features of the data and (2) to reduce the cost of computation due to high dimensionality. DR can either be used to choose the most representative or salient features in the data (*feature selection*) or to generate novel features that best represent the data (*feature extraction*) [19].

In this chapter, we discussed dimensionality reduction in the context of feature extraction, which finds wide application in the areas where collected data is very high-dimensional, and simply selecting the dimensions is not possible or data does not have explicit dimensions, like graphs [12, 6, 7, 23, 30, 35, 43]. In the following sections, we give a broad overview of feature extraction techniques. There are a large number of papers that provide insights and solutions to various problems and the application of DR. Nevertheless, limited by space and scope, we will be covering only a small portion of the literature in the subsequent sections.

Explicit vs. Implicit

One way of classifying DR techniques is in the way the data is mapped from high-dimension space to the low-dimension space. Explicit, or *projective*, techniques produce an explicit transformation, usually a *linear* transformation, of the data from a high-dimensional to a low-dimensional space [25]. On the other hand, implicit techniques do not produce an explicit transformation into low-dimensional space, instead they try to find a low-dimensional data matrix that preserves the locality or affinity between nearby points [22]. Techniques that fall into the class of explicit DR are MDS, PCA, LDA, Locality Preserving Projections (LPP), and spectral embeddings [24, 21, 11, 18, 28], whereas Isomaps, Locally Linear Embedding (LLE), Laplacian Eigenmaps, and Maximum Variance Unfolding [32, 3, 39] fall into the category of implicit techniques.

Linear vs. Nonlinear

Another way to classify DR techniques is based on whether the techniques transform the data into a lower dimension in a linear or nonlinear fashion. In linear dimensionality reduction, a linearly separable high-dimensional input data set is transformed into a lower-dimensional space using a linear projection; however, these DR techniques are not very useful if the original data is not linearly separable to begin with. For these types of problems, *nonlinear* techniques can be used to project non–linearly separable data into a lower-dimensional coordinate system so that the resulting data is linearly separable [32].

An example application for nonlinear techniques is in data visualization; when the input data is not visually separable, nonlinear techniques can be applied to achieve an explicit separation between data points in the visualization. Linear DR techniques include PCA, MDS, LDA, Locality Preserving Projections (LPP), and spectral embeddings [24, 11, 18], while nonlinear techniques include Isomaps [31], Locally Linear Embedding (LLE) [32], and Laplacian Eigenmaps [3].

Supervised vs. Unsupervised

DR techniques can also be classified based on whether the class information of the original data is taken into account during the dimension reduction. In supervised techniques, the data is transformed according to how well the transformation preserves class identity of the data; however, class labels are not taken into account during unsupervised techniques.

Supervised DR techniques are primarily used for classification tasks in data mining, where we use a set of data with known class labels to build a predictive model for determining the class of data with an unknown class. Unsupervised techniques are used for tasks where the data does not have a class label or preserving the class label is not very important. An example task for unsupervised techniques is clustering, where we try to divide the data into groups of similar items [22]. PCA, MDS, LPP, spectral embeddings, Orthogonal Neighborhood-Preserving Projections (ONPP), Isomap, and LLE [31, 32] are all unsupervised feature extraction techniques, though some unsupervised techniques, such as Isomap, can also work in a supervised way, as with S-Isomap, which uses the class information to perform DR [14]. LDA is an example of a supervised DR technique. Supervised techniques like LDA or S-Isomap can be used in pattern classification problems like face recognition [38], whereas an unsupervised technique like MDS might be more suitable for visualization purposes or anomaly detection [1].

Summary

All DR techniques try to generate a low-dimensional projection of the original data so that most properties of the original data are preserved. All of these techniques try to optimize some type of objective function with respect to the data. This optimization is typically posed as an eigenvalue or trace optimization problem [22]. It is not uncommon that one technique may be able to be tweaked into another based on the type of data and the task at hand. For example, PCA is good at reducing dimensionality for linearly separable data with class labels, while kernel-PCA can handle non–linearly separable data [44].

Furthermore, many of these techniques are interrelated, and there have been some efforts to define a comprehensive unifying framework for these DR techniques [22]. For example, several kernel-based DR techniques are based on implicit nonlinear mappings, but applying kernel techniques to explicit mappings reveals that kernel NPP is mathematically equivalent to LLE and that kernel LPP is mathematically equivalent to Laplacian Eigenmaps [22]. Similarly, Isomap maps data points based on local neighborhood relationships, while LLE approximates an optimal mapping by using local linear surfaces [32]. As another example, spectral embedding transforms a set of graphs into vectors in eigenspace, which can then be reduced using other techniques like PCA [28].

However, even though many of these techniques are mathematically similar in nature, they can be used to assist in different data mining tasks and can be used as effective tools to deal with the burden of high-dimensional data.

10.6 Exercises

1. Which of the dimensionality reduction techniques described in this chapter is most appropriate in each of the following scenarios? Justify your answers.

   (a) We are granted license to place five gas stations in a new city, and we know the desired distances between them. We would like to determine how to place these stations in the city.

   (b) We have 400 two-dimensional vectors that we would like to cluster using k-means. The data points are in the shape of closely-spaced zigzags.

   (c) We are investigating the incidence of smoking among college students, and we have surveyed 500 college students on a range of topics, including whether they smoke or not.

   (d) We have 75 graphs we want to cluster. The graphs represent molecular structures, and we have a symmetric function that estimates how much energy it would take to convert one molecule into another.

2. Let $\mathbf{D}$ be the following data matrix.

$$\mathbf{D} = \begin{bmatrix} 0 & 12 & 34 & 7 & 9 \\ 12 & 0 & 8 & 10 & 1 \\ 34 & 8 & 0 & 16 & 2 \\ 7 & 10 & 16 & 0 & 20 \\ 9 & 1 & 2 & 20 & 0 \end{bmatrix}$$

   If you were to apply MDS to $\mathbf{D}$ using the top two eigenvalues,

   (a) What would be the dimensions of the resulting matrix?

   (b) What would be the dimensions of its Gramian Matrix? Is the dimension the same as that of the distance matrix? Why or why not?

   (c) What about the dimensions of eigenvalue and eigenvector matrices used to create $\mathbf{Y}$? What type of matrix is the eigenvalue matrix?

3. Suppose we have some data with n dimensions, and we perform kernel PCA on this data using a suitable kernel. Is the dimensionality of the data after kernel PCA necessarily less than n? Justify your answer.

4. Suppose we are applying a dataset

$$X = \{a_{11}, a_{12}, a_{13}, a_{14}, a_{21}, a_{22}, a_{23}, a_{31}, a_{32}, a_{33}, a_{34}\}$$

with three classes: $X_1 = \{a_{11}, a_{12}, a_{13}, a_{14}\}$, $X_2 = \{a_{21}, a_{22}, a_{23}\}$, and $X_3 = \{a_{31}, a_{32}, a_{33}, a_{34}\}$.

(a) If we formed a graph G_X from the dataset X, how many independent cliques would G_X contain?

(b) Calculate the weighted adjacency matrix of G_X, **H**.

(c) Draw the graph G_X.

5. Calculate the LDA class scatter matrices (between-class, within-class, and total scatter matrices) for the dataset in matrix **X** below. The dataset contains two classes, "yes" and "no."

$$\mathbf{X} = \begin{bmatrix} \overbrace{5 \quad 5 \quad 2}^{\text{yes}} & \overbrace{10 \quad 2}^{\text{no}} \\ 10 \quad 2 \quad 0 & 4 \quad 4 \end{bmatrix} \qquad (10.60)$$

6. Describe the Objective Function as it relates to MDS. Show that this function is minimized at $\mathbf{Y} = \Lambda^{1/2}\mathbf{Z}^{\mathsf{T}}$.

7. Briefly answer the following.

(a) What is the *kernel trick*?

(b) Is kernel PCA a supervised or an unsupervised technique? Justify your answer.

8. Answer the following questions.

(a) Describe the differences between LDA and PCA.

(b) Use R to find the eigenvectors of matrices **A**, **B**, and **C** below, along with their corresponding eigenvalues:

$$\mathbf{A} = \begin{bmatrix} 1 & 4 \\ 9 & 1 \end{bmatrix} \qquad (10.61)$$

$$\mathbf{B} = \begin{bmatrix} 2 & 2 & 0 \\ 2 & 1 & 1 \\ -7 & 2 & -3 \end{bmatrix} \qquad (10.62)$$

$$\mathbf{C} = \begin{bmatrix} -2 & 1 \\ -4 & 3 \end{bmatrix} \qquad (10.63)$$

9. Prove that kernel PCA is equivalent to applying standard PCA to the data transformed by the kernel by showing that solving the eigenvalue problem for the kernel matrix is equivalent to solving the eigenvalue problem for the covariance matrix in the feature space. Assume that the data in the feature space is centered.

10. Given data matrix $\mathbf{X}$ and weighted adjacency matrix $\mathbf{H}$ below, calculate all of the mean vectors $\bar{\mathbf{s}}_{i\bullet}$, $\bar{\mathbf{s}}_{\bullet j}$, and $\bar{\mathbf{s}}$, and scatter matrices $\mathbf{S}_B$, $\mathbf{S}_W$, and $\mathbf{S}_T$.

$$\mathbf{X} = \begin{bmatrix} 5 & 4 & 7 & 6 & 2 & 5 \\ 1 & 9 & 8 & 3 & 0 & 4 \end{bmatrix} \tag{10.64}$$

$$\mathbf{H} = \begin{bmatrix} \frac{1}{2} & \frac{1}{2} & 0 & 0 & 0 & 0 \\ \frac{1}{2} & \frac{1}{2} & 0 & 0 & 0 & 0 \\ 0 & 0 & 1 & 0 & 0 & 0 \\ 0 & 0 & 0 & \frac{1}{3} & \frac{1}{3} & \frac{1}{3} \\ 0 & 0 & 0 & \frac{1}{3} & \frac{1}{3} & \frac{1}{3} \\ 0 & 0 & 0 & \frac{1}{3} & \frac{1}{3} & \frac{1}{3} \end{bmatrix} \tag{10.65}$$

Bibliography

[1] Amrudin Agovic, Arindam Banerjee, Auroop Ganguly, and Vladimir Protopopescu. Anomaly Detection using Manifold Embedding and its Applications in Transportation Corridors. *Intelligent Data Analysis*, 13(3):435–455, 2009.

[2] P. N. Belhumeur, J. P. Hespanha, and D. J. Kriegman. Eigenfaces vs. Fisherfaces: Recognition Using Class Specific Linear Projection. *IEEE Transactions on Pattern Analysis and Machine Intelligence*, 19(7):711–720, August 2002.

[3] Mikhail Belkin and Partha Niyogi. Laplacian Eigenmaps for Dimensionality Reduction and Data Representation. *Neural Computation*, 15(6):1373–1396, 2003.

[4] Leo Breiman and Adele Cutler. Random Forest, 2009. http://stat-www.berkeley.edu/users/breiman/RandomForests/cc_home.htm.

[5] Mike Brookes. The Matrix Reference Manual, 2009. http://www.ee.ic.ac.uk/hp/staff/dmb/matrix/property.html\#gramian.

[6] Gerbrand Ceder, Dane Morgan, Chris Fischer, Kevin Tibbetts, and Stefano Curtarolo. Data-Mining-Driven Quantum Mechanics for the Prediction of Structure. *MRS Bulletin*, 31:981–985, 2006.

[7] Stefano Curtarolo, Dane Morgan, Kristin Persson, John Rodgers, and Gerbrand Ceder. Predicting Crystal Structures with Data Mining of Quantum Calculations. *Physical Review Letters*, 91(13), 2003.

[8] D L Donoho. High-Dimensional Data Analysis: The Curses and Blessings of Dimensionality. In *Proceedings of the 2000 Conference of American Mathematical Society Mathematical Challenges*, 2000.

[9] Kamran Etemad and Rama Chellappa. Discriminant Analysis for Recognition of Human Face Images. *Journal of Optical Society of America A*, 14:1724–1733, 1997.

[10] Alan H. Fielding. *Cluster and Classification Techniques for the Biosciences*. Cambridge University Press, 2006.

[11] R.A. Fisher. The Statistical Utilization of Multiple Measurements. *Annals of Eugenics*, 8:376–386, 1938.

[12] Imola Fodor. A Survey of Dimension Reduction Techniques. *Technical Report, Lawrence Livermore National Laboratory*, 2002.

[13] Keinosuke Fukunaga. *Introduction to Statistical Pattern Recognition*. Academic Press, 1990.

[14] Xin Geng, De-Chuan Zhan, and Zhi-Hua Zhou. Supervised Nonlinear Dimensionality Reduction for Visualization and Classification. *IEEE Transactions on Systems, Man, and Cybernetics, Part B: Cybernetics*, 35(6):1098–1107, 2005.

[15] Mislav Grgic and Kresimir Delac. Face Recognition homepage, 2009. `http://www.face-rec.org/`.

[16] S. Haykin. *Neural Networks: A Comprehensive Foundation*. Macmillan, 1994.

[17] Li He, J.M. Buenaposada, and L. Baumela. An Empirical Comparison of Graph-Based Dimensionality Reduction Algorithms on Facial Expression Recognition Tasks. In *Proceedings of the 2008 International Conference on Pattern Recognition (ICPR)*, pages 1–4, 2008.

[18] Xiaofei He and Partha Niyogi. Locality Preserving Projections. In *Proceedings of the 2004 Advances in Neural Information Processing Systems*, 2004.

[19] A. Jain and D. Zongker. Feature Selection: Evaluation, Application, and Small Sample Performance. *IEEE Transactions on Pattern Analysis and Machine Intelligence*, 19(2):153–158, 1997.

[20] Hua Yu Jie, Hua Yu, and Jie Yang. A Direct LDA Algorithm for High-Dimensional Data: With Application to Face Recognition. *Pattern Recognition*, 34:2067–2070, 2001.

[21] I. T. Jolliffe. *Principal Component Analysis*. Springer, 2002.

[22] Effrosyni Kokiopoulou, Jie Chen, and Yousef Saad. Trace Optimization and Eigenproblems in Dimension Reduction Methods. *Technical Report, University of Minnesota Supercomputing Institute*, 2009. http://www-users.cs.umn.edu/~saad/PDF/umsi-2009-31.pdf.

[23] Yehuda Koren. On Spectral Graph Drawing. In *Proceedings of the 2002 Inter Computing and Combinatorics Conference (COCOON)*, pages 496–508, 2002.

[24] Joseph B. Kruskal and Myron Wish. *Multidimensional Scaling*. Sage, 1978.

[25] John A. Lee and Michel Verleysen. *Nonlinear Dimensionality Reduction*. Springer Publishing Company, Incorporated, 2007.

[26] Yongping Li, Josef Kittler, and Jiri Matas. Effective Implementation of Linear Discriminant Analysis for Face Recognition and Verification. In *Proceedings of the 8th International Conference on Computer Analysis of Images and Patterns (CAIP 1999)*, pages 234–242, 1999.

[27] Chengjun Liu. Gabor-Based Kernel PCA with Fractional Power Polynomial Models for Face Recognition. *IEEE Transactions on Pattern Analysis and Machine Intelligence*, 26(5):572–581, 2004.

[28] Bin Luo, Richard C. Wilson, and Edwin R. Hancock. Spectral Embedding of Graphs. *Pattern Recognition*, pages 2213–2230, 2003.

[29] Aleix M. Martínez and Avinash C. Kak. PCA versus LDA. *IEEE Transactions on Pattern Analysis and Machine Intelligence*, 23(2):228–233, 2001.

[30] Andreas Noack. An Energy Model for Visual Graph Clustering. In *Proceedings of the 2003 International Symposium on Graph Drawing (GD), LNCS 2912*, pages 425–436, 2003.

[31] Bernardete Ribeiro, Armando Vieira, and João Carvalho Das Neves. Supervised Isomap with Dissimilarity Measures in Embedding Learning. In *Proceedings of the 2008 Iberoamerican Congress on Pattern Recognition*, pages 389–396, 2008.

[32] Sam T. Roweis and Lawrence K. Saul. Nonlinear Dimensionality Reduction by Locally Linear Embedding. *Science*, 290:2323–2326, 2000.

[33] Lawrence K. Saul. *Semi-Supervised Learning*. MIT Press, 2006.

[34] Bernhard Schölkopf, Alexander Smola, and Klaus-Robert Müller. Nonlinear Component Analysis as a Kernel Eigenvalue Problem. *Neural Computation*, 10(5):1299–1319, 1998.

[35] S. E. Sebastian, N. Harrison, C. D. Batista, L. Balicas, M. Jaime, P. A. Sharma, N. Kawashima, and I. R. Fisher. Dimensional Reduction at a Quantum Critical Point. *Nature*, page 441:617, 2006.

[36] T. Shi and S. Horvath. Unsupervised Learning with Random Forest Predictors. *Journal of Computational and Graphical Statistics*, 15(1):118–138, 2006.

[37] T. Shi, D. Seligson, A.S. Belldegrun, A. Palotie, and S. Horvath. Tumor Classification by Tissue Microarray Profiling: Random Forest Clustering Applied to Renal Cell Carcinoma. *Modern Pathology*, 18:547–557, 2005.

[38] Fengxi Song, David Zhang, Qinglong Chen, and Jing-Yu Yang. A Novel Supervised Dimensionality Reduction Algorithm for Online Image Recognition. In *Proceedings of the Fifth Pacific-Rim Symposium on Image and Video Technology*, volume 4319, pages 198–207, 2006.

[39] L. Song, A. J. Smola, K. Borgwardt, and A. Gretton. Colored Maximum Variance Unfolding. In *Proceedings of the 2007 Advances in Neural Information Processing Systems*, pages 1385–1392, 2007.

[40] Pang-Ning Tan, Michael Steinbach, and Vipin Kumar. *Introduction to Data Mining, (First Edition)*. Addison-Wesley Longman Publishing Co., Inc., 2005.

[41] Jengnan Tzeng1, Henry Horng-Shing Lu2, and Wen-Hsiung Li. Multidimensional Scaling for Large Genomic Data Sets. *BMC Bioinformatics*, 9(179), 2008.

[42] S. V. N. Vishwanathan, Karsten M. Borgwardt, Risi Imre Kondor, and Nicol N. Schraudolph. Graph Kernels. *Journal of Machine Learning Research*, 2008.

[43] Andrew Webb. *Statistical Pattern Recognition*. J. Wiley & sons, 2002.

[44] Kilian Q. Weinberger, Fei Sha, and Lawrence K. Saul. Learning a Kernel Matrix for Nonlinear Dimensionality Reduction. In *Proceedings of the 2004 International Conference on Machine Learning*, pages 106+, 2004.

[45] Max Welling. Fisher Linear Discriminant Analysis. `http://www.ics.uci.edu/~welling/classnotes/papers\_class/Fisher-LDA.pdf`, 2008.

[46] John (Juyang) Weng. Crescepton and SHOSLIF: Towards Comprehensive Visual Learning. In *Early Visual Learning*, eds: S.K. Nayar and T. Poggio, Oxford University Press, 1996.

[47] Jieping Ye. Least Squares Linear Discriminant Analysis. In *Proceedings of the 2007 International Conference on Machine Learning (ICML)*, pages 1087–1093, 2007.

11

Graph-based Anomaly Detection

Kanchana Padmanabhan, Zhengzhang Chen, Sriram
Lakshminarasimhan, Siddarth Shankar Ramaswamy, and Bryan
Thomas Richardson

North Carolina State University

CONTENTS

Anomaly detection is a field of study that concentrates on detecting patterns in data that do not conform to expected normal behavior [7]. Often, those anomalous patterns are referred to as *anomalies* or *outliers*. This field is of high importance because undetected anomalies can have catastrophic impacts in real life. For example, an anomalous credit card transaction may indicate credit card theft, or an anomalous traffic pattern in a computer network could mean that a hacked computer is sending out sensitive data to an unauthorized destination.

Anomaly detection in data sets represented as graphs is known as *graph-based anomaly detection*. Graph-based anomaly detection has paved the way for new approaches that not only complement the non–graph-based methods, but also provide mechanisms for handling data that cannot be easily analyzed with traditional data mining approaches [14]. For example, in fraud detection, one vertex of the graph can be a customer and other vertices can be stores, and the edges can depict the purchase history. Thus, fraud detection can be simplified to an anomalous edge (or node) detection problem.

This chapter focuses on important graph-based anomaly detection algorithms and their implementations in R. We start with a rather simple technique using the random walk theory that detects the obvious or "white crow" anomalies. Further into the chapter, we analyze the GBAD tool that has three algorithms to detect hidden or "in-disguise" anomalies that are almost similar to the normal data pattern. Finally, we discuss a very important and growing technique in the field of anomaly detection called *Tensor Analysis*, which handles complex relationships between objects such as their spatial and temporal components. We describe the strengths and weaknesses of each of these algorithms, and we discuss some sample application areas in which these techniques might be useful.

11.1 Types of Anomalies

Anomalies can be classified as one of the following types (see Figure 11.1):

Definition 11.1 *"White crow" anomaly*
A "white crow" anomaly (also called an "outlier") "is an observation that deviates so much from other observations as to arouse suspicion that it was generated by a different mechanism" [30].

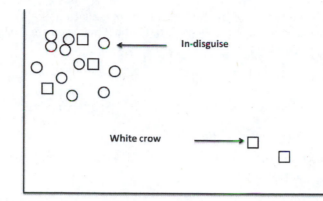

FIGURE 11.1: "White crow" and "in-disguise" anomalies.

For example, if we are analyzing the voters list and come across a person whose age is 322, we can take this as a "white crow" anomaly because the age of a voter typically lies between 18 and 100.

Definition 11.2 *"In-disguise" anomaly*
Contrary to a "white crow" anomaly, an "in-disguise" anomaly is only a minor deviation from the normal pattern.

In graphs, these anomalies are usually part of a non-anomalous substructure, or the normative pattern [14]. For example, anyone who is attempting to commit credit card fraud would not want to be caught, so he or she would want his or her activities to look as normal as possible.

Definition 11.3 *Pointwise anomaly*
Pointwise anomalies are points in time at which the observed values are significantly different than the rest of the timestamps in the time series [10]. In Figure 11.2, timestamp t^* could be considered a pointwise anomaly.

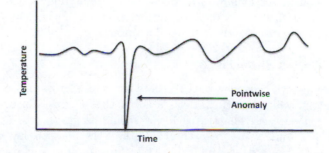

FIGURE 11.2: Example of a pointwise anomaly.

There are other types of anomalies, like contextual anomalies, collective anomalies, sub-sequence anomalies, etc., but we will focus on these three types of anomalies in this chapter.

11.2   Random Walk Algorithm

This section presents two techniques for detecting "white crow" and pointwise anomalies based on random walks.

11.2.1   Preliminaries

11.2.1.1   What is a random walk?

> **Definition 11.4** *Random walk*
> A random walk, sometimes denoted as RW, is a mathematical formalization of a graph traversal that consists of taking successive random steps [44].

Let us consider a city being modeled as a graph, where each vertex is a location and the edges are paths between these locations. If vertex A has only edges to B and to C, then a person at vertex A may go to B or C with equal probability. This concept is modeled as an algorithm using the *Markov transition matrix* that contains the probability information for which vertices can be reached from a given vertex A. The definition of the Markov transition matrix and its construction are discussed in Section 11.2.2.

In Figure 11.3, a person starting at vertex A may take one of the two paths marked with a dotted arrow, with equal probability. Sometimes, though, the different paths may not have equal probability, due to some *weight factors* assigned to the edges. For example, if edges $B \to C$ and $B \to F$ have weight factors of 1 and edge $B \to E$ has a weight factor of 2, then edge $B \to E$ would be twice as likely to be taken as either $B \to C$ or $B \to F$.

In the following sections, we will focus on understanding how random walk theory can be applied to anomaly detection in graphs formed by calculating similarity values between vector-based data points.

11.2.1.2   Cosine Similarity

Let us introduce the cosine similarity between two vectors before we go on to the random walk algorithm. Let's assume that a graph is derived from a vector-based dataset. That is, each vertex in the graph corresponds to a vector that has some value for each attribute of the dataset. Let's look at a simple example demonstrated in Table 11.1. This dataset is characterized by attributes, A, B, and C.

This data is represented as a graph in Figure 11.4, where each node corre-

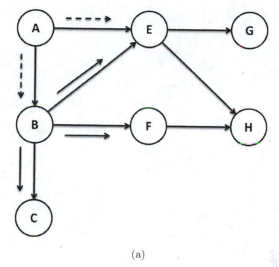

(a)

$$\begin{bmatrix} 0 & 0.5 & 0 & 0.5 & 0 & 0 & 0 \\ 0 & 0 & 0.25 & 0.5 & 0.25 & 0 & 0 \\ 0 & 0 & 1 & 0 & 0 & 0 & 0 \\ 0 & 0 & 0 & 0 & 0 & 0.8 & 0.2 \\ 0 & 0 & 0 & 0 & 0 & 0 & 1 \\ 0 & 0 & 0 & 0 & 0 & 1 & 0 \\ 0 & 0 & 0 & 0 & 0 & 0 & 1 \end{bmatrix}$$

(b)

FIGURE 11.3: Directed graph (a) and Markov transition matrix (b) for a random walk example.

sponds to a vector in the dataset. The cosine similarity between two vectors is defined as follows:

$$\cos(\mathbf{x}, \mathbf{y}) = \frac{\mathbf{x} \cdot \mathbf{y}}{\|\mathbf{x}\| \cdot \|\mathbf{y}\|} \tag{11.1}$$

The calculated cosine similarities become the edge weights of the graph. The edge weights can also be calculated in R using the cosine function in the Latent Semantic Analysis (lsa) package.

```
1 > library(lsa)
2 Loading required package: Snowball
3 Loading required package: RWeka
4 Warning messages:
5 1: package 'lsa' was built under R version 2.9.2
6 2: package 'Snowball' was built under R version 2.9.2
7 3: package 'RWeka' was built under R version 2.9.2
8 > x = c(1.2, 2.4, 3.2)
```

TABLE 11.1: Example dataset for cosine similarity

No	A	B	C
1	1.2	2.4	3.2
2	1.4	2.5	2
3	1.5	2.5	2

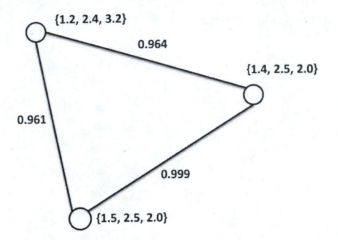

FIGURE 11.4: Cosine similarity example.

```
 9 > y = c(1.4, 2.5, 2)
10 > cosine(x, y)
11             [,1]
12 [1,]  0.9648762
```

The variables **x** and **y** in the code above correspond to the first two data points in Table 11.1, and the calculated cosine similarity will be the weight of the edge between the nodes represented by these vectors. The `cosine` function offers the following option: you represent the data points as columns of a matrix and pass the matrix to the cosine function, which will calculate the cosine similarities between every pair of columns and return the similarity matrix as output. If the dataset is very large, though, calculating the similarity between all pairs can be tedious.

```
1 > x = c(1.2,2.4,3.2)
2 > y = c(1.4,2.5,2.0)
3 > z = c(1.5,2.5,2.0)
4 > DataMatrix = cbind(x,y,z)
5 > DataMatrix
6         x    y    z
7 [1,]  1.2  1.4  1.5
```

```
 8 [2,] 2.4 2.5 2.5
 9 [3,] 3.2 2.0 2.0
10 > cosine(DataMatrix)
11           x         y         z
12 x 1.0000000 0.9648762 0.9617454
13 y 0.9648762 1.0000000 0.9996642
14 z 0.9617454 0.9996642 1.0000000
```

Here **x**, **y**, and **z** represent the three points, and the matrix in lines 11–14 contains the calculated cosine similarity values.

11.2.2   Detection of Graph Anomalies via Random Walks

We use a random walk algorithm to detect anomalies in a dataset where each data point is represented as an object with a set of attributes, like rows in a relational database. Each data point is taken as vertex of a graph, and cosine similarity between each pair of objects is calculated (using the attributes) and that value becomes the weight of the edge between the vertices. In general, we consider two vertices to be adjacent if their cosine similarity measure is non-zero. We extend this concept and find all the neighbors of a given node v_1. We apply a threshold value τ so that only pairs of nodes with similarity above τ are considered neighbors. Several other common notations used in this section appear in Table 11.2.

Using this graph, we compute a new similarity matrix (**SN**), where each value in the matrix is the number of neighbors shared between the corresponding pair of nodes [30]. For example, in Figure 11.5, A and D have two common neighbors.

TABLE 11.2: Notations for random walk on a single graph

Symbol	Description
M	Cosine similarity matrix
τ	Threshold
ϵ	Error tolerance
d	Damping factor
SN	Shared neighbors similarity matrix
S	Markov transition matrix
$\mathbf{S^T}$	Transpose of the Markov transition matrix
c	Connectivity values
$\mathbf{c}_{old}$	Previously calculated connectivity values
r	Ranking of the graph vertices based on connectivity values

The Markov transition matrix (**S**) is constructed by normalizing each value of **SN** by the sum of all elements of the corresponding row (line 5). We assign an initial connectivity value of $1/n$ to each of the n nodes v_1 to v_n, each

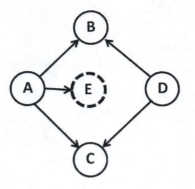

FIGURE 11.5: Vertices A and D share neighbors B and C.

---

1 **Algorithm:** Random Walk on Single Graph

Input: $\mathbf{M}$—the $n \times n$ cosine similarity matrix
Input: τ—threshold value
Input: ϵ—error tolerance value
Output: $\mathbf{r}$—outlier ranks
/* discretizing M */
2 Set $\mathbf{M}[\mathbf{I},\mathbf{J}] = 1$ if its value is greater than or equal to τ
3 Set $\mathbf{M}[\mathbf{I},\mathbf{J}] = 0$ if the value is less than τ
4 Compute the new similarity matrix $\mathbf{SN}$ of matrix $\mathbf{M}$
5 Markov transition matrix $\mathbf{S}$ is formed by normalizing $\mathbf{SN}$
6 Initialize $d \leftarrow 0.1$, $\mathbf{c}_{old} \leftarrow (1/n, 1/n, \ldots, 1/n)$, $\delta \leftarrow 0$
7 **while** $\delta < \epsilon$ **do**
8 $\quad \mathbf{c} \leftarrow [d/n \; d/n \; \ldots \; d/n]^{\mathbf{T}} + (1-d) \cdot \mathbf{S^T} \cdot \mathbf{c}_{old}$
9 $\quad \delta \leftarrow \|\mathbf{c} - \mathbf{c}_{old}\|$
10 $\quad \mathbf{c}_{old} \leftarrow \mathbf{c}$
11 **end**
12 Rank all nodes based on the corresponding values in $\mathbf{c}$ and store the rank values in $\mathbf{r}$

Algorithm 29: Pseudocode for applying the random walk technique to a single graph

having one entry in the vector $\mathbf{c}_{old}$ (line 6), and this connectivity value is then iteratively refined for every node. This technique is called the *power iteration method*.

The vector $\mathbf{c}$ is refined using the following equation:

$$\mathbf{c} = \begin{bmatrix} d/n \\ d/n \\ \vdots \\ d/n \end{bmatrix} + (1-d) \cdot \mathbf{S}^{\mathbf{T}} \cdot \mathbf{c}_{old} \qquad (11.2)$$

Here, d is a *damping factor* and $\mathbf{c}_{old}$ is the connectivity vector obtained in the previous iteration cycle. The *damping factor* is used to take into account the probability that the person may choose to stay at the same vertex. We assign a value of d/n to the probability that a person may stay on the same vertex. The second term in the sum represents the shift caused by the random transitions. If we consider having a population of people located on each vertex, taking one transition will cause this population to split up among the neighbors of the vertex according to the probabilities in the transition matrix **S**.

At the end of the random walk, the nodes are ranked based on their connectivity values (line 12). At the end of this iterative process each vertex is ranked based on its connectivity value, and the lowest-ranked nodes are considered anomalies. Anomalous vertices, which share fewer connections with other vertices, will have lower connectivity values. Conversely, if a vertex has more neighbors, then there are more paths to the vertex, and the probability to reach the vertex is higher. A pseudocode description of this algorithm appears in Algorithm 29.

The performance of this algorithm largely depends on how we fix our threshold (τ). If τ is too small, some anomalies could be misinterpreted as normal data, but if it is too large, normal data could be interpreted as anomalous. One way to pick a reasonable threshold value is to choose a value in the range $(\mu, \mu - \sigma)$, where μ is the mean and σ standard deviation of the distribution of the cosine similarity values [30].

The variable ϵ is the error tolerance value, and it can be between 0 and 1. The value of ϵ determines how many iterations occur before finalizing the connectivity **c** values.

Example 1:
Let us consider the graph in Figure 11.6. The outlier in this graph is vertex D (vertex number 4) since it has no common neighbors with any of the other vertices. Let us run our algorithm in R and verify the result.

```
1 > library(stats)
2 > library(base)
3 > library(randomWalkAnomaly)
4 ># Example 1
5 > Input = matrix(c(0,0.3,0.4,0,0.3,0,
6    0.5,0,0.4,0.5,0,0,0,0,0,0),4,4)
7 > Input
```

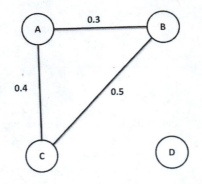

FIGURE 11.6: The random walk technique example on a single graph.

TABLE 11.3: Example 2: Vector representation of each node

Vertex	Vector
A	(1, 2, 1, 1, 2)
B	(0, 3, 1, 6, 2)
C	(2, 7, 1, 1, 1)
D	(2, 7, 4, 1, 3)
E	(2, 2, 2, 2, 2)
F	(1, 2, 3, 4, 5)
G	(6, 3, 2, 1, 4)

```
8         [,1] [,2] [,3] [,4]
9  [1,]   0.0  0.3  0.4    0
10 [2,]   0.3  0.0  0.5    0
11 [3,]   0.4  0.5  0.0    0
12 [4,]   0.0  0.0  0.0    0
13 > OutlierAnomaly(Input,0.2,0.2)
14        Vertex Connectivity_Values Ranks
15 [1,]     1              0.250       2
16 [2,]     2              0.250       2
17 [3,]     3              0.250       2
18 [4,]     4              0.025       1
```

Translating the Output: A lower connectivity value indicates a more anomalous vertex. In Figure 11.6, vertex D (4) is the most anomalous, based on the result from the R code above.

Example 2:
Let us look at another example where we know the vector representation of each vertex. Let us consider a dataset with seven data points and five attributes. The vector representation appears in Table 11.3.

Let's use R to calculate the cosine similarity values between these vertices (line 11 in the code below).

```
1 > M = data(RandomWalkExample2)
2 > M
3   A B C D E F G
4 1 1 0 2 2 2 1 6
5 2 2 3 7 7 2 2 3
6 3 1 1 1 4 2 3 2
7 4 1 6 1 1 2 4 1
8 5 2 2 1 3 2 5 4
9 >
10 > library(lsa)
11 > CosineSimilarityMatrix = cosine(as.matrix(M))
12   CosineSimilarityMatrix
13           A           B           C           D           E
14 A 1.0000000 0.7248824 0.8058230 0.9159123 0.9438798
15 B 0.7248824 1.0000000 0.5669467 0.5887124 0.7589466
16 C 0.8058230 0.5669467 1.0000000 0.9171118 0.7171372
17 D 0.9159123 0.5887124 0.9171118 1.0000000 0.8553628
18 E 0.9438798 0.7589466 0.7171372 0.8553628 1.0000000
19 F 0.8944272 0.8199778 0.5045250 0.7130221 0.9045340
20 G 0.8536101 0.4351941 0.6579517 0.7478392 0.8807710
21           F           G
22 A 0.8944272 0.8536101
23 B 0.8199778 0.4351941
24 C 0.5045250 0.6579517
25 D 0.7130221 0.7478392
26 E 0.9045340 0.8807710
27 F 1.0000000 0.6971014
28 G 0.6971014 1.0000000
29 >
30 >outlierAnomaly(CosineSimilarityMatrix,0.8,0.2)
31       Vertex connectivityValues Ranks
32 [1,]      1       0.51994038      7
33 [2,]      2       0.02045586      1
34 [3,]      3       0.05736945      2
35 [4,]      4       0.15092056      4
36 [5,]      5       0.36151334      6
37 [6,]      6       0.25666560      5
38 [7,]      7       0.07056117      3
```

The above answer (in lines 30–38) might not be immediately clear, so let us try and plot the graph to check if we have caught our anomaly. We have set our threshold to 0.8, so only those vertices with similarities higher than 0.8 will be considered neighbors. Let us modify our matrix to reflect this.

```
39 > CosineSimilarityMatrix[CosineSimilarityMatrix>=0.8]=1
40 > CosineSimilarityMatrix[CosineSimilarityMatrix<0.8]=0
41 > CosineSimilarityMatrix
42      A B C D E F G
43 A 1 0 1 1 1 1 1
44 B 0 1 0 0 0 1 0
45 C 1 0 1 1 0 0 0
46 D 1 0 1 1 1 0 0
47 E 1 0 0 1 1 1 1
48 F 1 1 0 0 1 1 0
49 G 1 0 0 0 1 0 1
```

Applying this threshold value produces the adjacency matrix for the graph. We can now use the igraph library to convert this matrix into a graph object, and we can plot the object using the `tkplot` function:

```
50 > library(igraph)
51 > GraphObject = graph.adjacency(CosineSimilarityMatrix)
52 > GraphObject
53 > tkplot(GraphObject,vertex.label = c("A","B","C","D",
54          "E","F","G"))
```

From Figure 11.7, we now clearly see that vertex "B" in our input is, in fact, the most anomalous, as calculated by our algorithm.

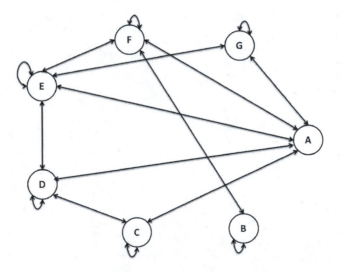

FIGURE 11.7: Output graph for the second random walk example.

11.2.3 Pointwise Anomaly Detection in Multivariate Time Series Using Random Walks

In the previous section, we found "white crow" anomalies in datasets without any temporal aspect. This section talks about an algorithm that is designed specifically to find outlier anomalies in time series data. For example, in the area of climatology, we may have graphs where the vertices represent different geographic locations, and the edges are drawn between pairs of locations with similar weather patterns over some period of time. In order to identify long-term changes in climate, a climatologist may want to find anomalies in a series of such graphs, in which each graph corresponds to a different year.

Let us first understand the concept of a *multivariate time series*. Consider a variable $X = \{x_1, x_2, \ldots, x_T\}$, where each value x_i is a real-valued (decimal) measurement taken at timestamps $1, 2, \ldots,$ and T. For example, X might represent annual rainfall or average temperature of some location across a number of years. A *multivariate time series* $D = \{X_1, X_2, \ldots, X_p\}$ is a set of p real-valued variables with measurements taken at the same timestamps.

"Multivariate time series analysis is used when one wants to model and explain the interactions and co-movements among a group of time series variables" [45]. For example, stock prices, dividends, consumption, income, interest rates, money growth, income, and inflation are all time-varying datasets related to finance. So, in the real world, D might contain the variables *Consumption* and *Income*, along with the values of these two variables at several timestamps.

For anomaly detection, one variable $Y \in D$ is taken as a *target variable*. The *target variable* is the variable whose values are to be modeled and predicted by other variables. For our example, let $Y = Consumption$ be the target variable. We call the remaining variables $X = D - Y$ the *predictor variables* [10]—*Income*, in our example. A *predictor variable* is a variable whose values will be used to predict the value of a target variable. There should only be one target variable but there can be many predictor variables [36]. The notation for terms specific to random walks on the multivariate time series appear in Table 11.4.

TABLE 11.4: Notations for applying the random walk technique to multivariate time series data (see Table 11.2 for notations on the single graph random walk technique)

Symbol	Description
$\mathbf{KX}$	Kernel matrix of predictor variables
$\mathbf{KY}$	Kernel matrix of the target variable
$\widehat{\mathbf{K}_\alpha}$	Aligned matrix

For multivariate time series, we describe *pointwise anomaly detection*, which is used to discover the timestamps at which the observed values are

significantly different than the rest of the time series [10]. To model this data
as a graph and perform anomaly detection, let us first define a similarity measure. Just like the cosine similarity we used for the single variable data, we use
the Radial Basis Function (RBF)[1] in the multivariate case. Each timestamp
is associated with a set of measurements for p variables. If we let i and j denote a pair of timestamps in the time series, the similarity measure between
timestamps i and j is defined as:

$$K(i,j) = \exp\left\{-\left(\sum_{k=1}^{p}(x_{ik} - x_{jk})^2\right)/\sigma^2\right\} \qquad (11.3)$$

Let us try and run a simple example in R to calculate this similarity matrix.

```
1 > data(KernelData)
2 > TimeSeries = as.matrix(KernelData)
3 # Columns represent timestamp
4 # Rows represent real valued variable
5 > TimeSeries
6       V1 V2 V3 V4 V5
7 [1,]  1  1  2  2  3
8 [2,]  1  5  2  2  3
9 > RBFMeasure(TimeSeries,1.414)
10          [,1]       [,2]       [,3]       [,4]       [,5]
11 [1,]  1.00000000 0.01829352 0.60643905 0.60643905 0.1352535
12 [2,]  0.01829352 1.00000000 0.08202303 0.08202303 0.1352535
13 [3,]  0.60643905 0.08202303 1.00000000 1.00000000 0.6064391
14 [4,]  0.60643905 0.08202303 1.00000000 1.00000000 0.6064391
15 [5,]  0.13525354 0.13525354 0.60643905 0.60643905 1.0000000
```

Based on this similarity measure, we can construct a nonnegative, symmetric matrix $\mathbf{K}$ to capture the pairwise similarity between every pair of
timestamps in the time series. $\mathbf{K}$ is also called a *kernel matrix*.

A pseudocode description of the random walk technique for multivariate
time series appears in Algorithm 30. The kernel matrix is constructed (line 2)
for both the predictor variables X and the target variable Y as $\mathbf{KX}$ and
$\mathbf{KY}$, respectively. Though X and Y are different variables, there will be some
dependencies among them. To capture these dependencies, we have to align
the two kernel matrices (line 3). The objective of kernel alignment is to derive
an adjusted kernel matrix $\widehat{\mathbf{K}_\alpha}$ that maximizes the correlation between the
predictor variable $\mathbf{KX}$ and the target kernel matrix $\mathbf{KY}$:

$$\max\{\langle\mathbf{K}_\alpha, \mathbf{KY}\rangle_F/(\sqrt{\langle\mathbf{K}_\alpha, \mathbf{K}_\alpha\rangle_F}\langle\mathbf{KY}, \mathbf{KY}\rangle_F)\}, \qquad (11.4)$$

---

[1] A radial basis function (RBF) is equivalent to mapping the data into an infinite-
dimensional Hilbert space; that is, we obtain kernel matrices when we apply RBF.

---

1 **Algorithm:** Random Walk on Multivariate Time Series

Input: $\mathbf{x}$—the set of predictor variables
Input: $\mathbf{y}$—the target variable
Input: d—damping factor
Input: ϵ—error tolerance value
Input: m—maximum number of iterations for algorithm
Output: $\mathbf{c}$—the connectivity values

2 Construct the kernel Matrix $\mathbf{K}$ from D using Equation 11.3

3 Obtain the aligned matrix $\widehat{\mathbf{K}_\alpha}$ using Equation 11.5

4 Construct the Markov Transition Matrix $\mathbf{S}$ by normalizing $\widehat{\mathbf{K}_\alpha}$

5 Initialize $\mathbf{c}_{old} \leftarrow (0, 0, \ldots, 0)$

6 **for** $x \in \{1, 2, \ldots, m\}$ **do**

7     $\mathbf{c} \leftarrow [d/n \; d/n \; \ldots \; d/n]^{\mathbf{T}} + (1 - d) \cdot \mathbf{S}^{\mathbf{T}} \cdot \mathbf{c}_{old}$

8     $\delta \leftarrow \|\mathbf{c} - \mathbf{c}_{old}\|$

9   **if** $\delta > \epsilon$ **then**

10   **break for**

11     $\mathbf{c}_{old} \leftarrow \mathbf{c}$

12 **end**

13

Algorithm 30: Pseudocode for applying the random walk technique to a multivariate time series

where $\langle A, B \rangle_F = \sum_{i,j} A_{ij} B_{ij}$.

$\langle A, B \rangle_F$ is known as the Frobenius product of two matrices. In R, this can be easily calculated by loading package matrixcalc and using the function `frobenius.prod` (see line 14 in the code below).

```
1 > library(matrixcalc)
2 > TempA = data(FrobeniusA)
3 > TempB = data(FrobeniusB)
4 > A = as.matrix(FrobeniusA)
5 > B = as.matrix(FrobeniusB)
6 > A
7       [,1] [,2] [,3] [,4]
8 [1,]    1  1.2  2.2  1.4
9 [2,]    1  1.0  2.0  1.0
10 > B
11       [,1] [,2] [,3] [,4]
12 [1,]  3.0  1.2  2.0    1
13 [2,]  1.2  1.0  2.1    1
14 > frobenius.prod(A,B)
15 [1] 17.64
```

The formula to calculate $\widehat{\mathbf{K}_\alpha}$ is as follows:

$$\widehat{\mathbf{K}_\alpha} = \sum \alpha_i \cdot \mathbf{v_i} \cdot \mathbf{v_i'} \tag{11.5}$$

$$\alpha_i = \lambda_i + (\langle \mathbf{v_i v_i'}, \mathbf{KY} \rangle_F)/2 \tag{11.6}$$

Here, $\mathbf{v_i}$ and λ_i are the eigenvectors and eigenvalues of $\mathbf{KX}$, respectively. Let's execute a small piece of code in R that calculates the aligned matrix.

```
1 > data(KernelPredictorSample1)
2 > data(KernelTargetSample1)
3 > X = as.matrix(KernelPredictorSample1)
4 > Y = as.matrix(KernelTargetSample1)
5 > X
6        V1 V2 V3 V4 V5
7 [1,]   1  1  2  2  3
8 [2,]   1  5  2  2  3
9 > KX = RBFMeasure(X)
10 > KY = RBFMeasure(Y)
11 > K_Aligned = matrixAlign(KX,KY)
12 > K_Aligned
13            [,1]        [,2]        [,3]        [,4]        [,5]
14 [1,] 3.50000000 0.01829352 0.60643905 0.60643905 0.1352535
15 [2,] 0.01829352 3.50000000 0.08202303 0.08202303 0.1352535
16 [3,] 0.60643905 0.08202303 3.50000000 1.00000000 0.6064391
17 [4,] 0.60643905 0.08202303 1.00000000 3.50000000 0.6064391
18 [5,] 0.13525354 0.13525354 0.60643905 0.60643905 3.5000000
```

Once the aligned $\widehat{\mathbf{K}_\alpha}$ matrix has been obtained, we normalize it to obtain the transition probability matrix $\mathbf{S}$ (line 4 in Algorithm 30). Using $\mathbf{S^T}$ as input, we perform the random walk technique using Equation 11.2. This technique will give us the connectivity values of the data points, where lower connectivity values indicate more anomalous data points.

The variable ϵ is the error tolerance value, and it can be between 0 and 1. The value of ϵ determines how many iterations occur before finalizing the connectivity $\mathbf{c}$ values. Additionally, a parameter m may be specified to limit the number of iterations that the algorithm makes. The δ value increments very slowly; hence, this m parameter is very useful when ϵ is close to 1.

This method can also be applied to identify the anomalies without the use of a target variable. For the details we refer you to the publication [11].

The *subsequence anomaly* is a second kind of anomaly that can occur in a multivariate time series.

This anomaly occurs when a segment of time of length δt is different from all other segments of length δt.

For more information on this type of anomaly we refer you to [11].

Example:
In this example, $\mathbf{X}$ is a matrix of predictor variables that has two real-valued

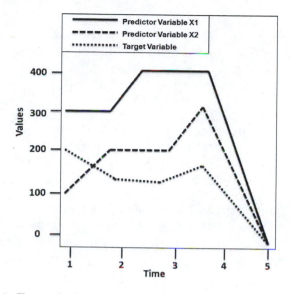

FIGURE 11.8: Example for anomaly detection in multivariate time series.

variables with measurements taken at five timestamps. **Y** contains a variable whose measurement is taken at the same five timestamps. To use the `multivariateAnomaly` function in R, we need to provide values for matrices **X** and **Y**, along with parameters that tell how many eigenvalues to use when aligning **KX** with respect to **KY** to get matrix $\widehat{\mathbf{K}_\alpha}$, the spread width to use in the RBF kernel, and (optionally) the damping factor d.

```
 1 > # X is the predictor, with two variables
 2      whose values have been measured from
 3      t1 to t5 (V1 to V5).
 4 > # Y is the target variable.
 5 > data(KernelPredictorSample2)
 6 > data(KernelTargetSample2)
 7 > X = as.matrix(KernelPredictorSample2)
 8 > Y = as.matrix(KernelTargetSample2)
 9 > X
10        V1  V2  V3  V4 V5
11 [1,] 100 200 200 300  2
12 [2,] 300 300 400 400  2
13 > Y
14        V1  V2  V3  V4 V5
15 [1,] 200 150 120 150  5
16 > # The multivariateAnomaly function takes in the target
17      and predictor matrices as input,
18 > # along with the number of eigenvalues and the spread
```

```
19      width of the RBF kernel.
20 > # Damping factor is an optional parameter
21 > RandomWalkOutput = multivariateAnomaly(X, Y, 0, 93.14, 5)
22 [1] "converged after 13 iterations"
23 > RandomWalkOutput
24      Time Stamp              Rank
25 [1,]           1 0.21857307    3
26 [2,]           2 0.27550579    5
27 [3,]           3 0.27272074    4
28 [4,]           4 0.21133942    2
29 [5,]           5 0.02186099    1
```

Translating the Output: Timestamp 5 is reported as having the lowest connectivity value, so it is the most anomalous. A graph of the matrices **X** and **Y** can be seen in Figure 11.8, and you can compare timestamp 5 to the other timestamps.

11.2.4   Strengths and Weaknesses

A key advantage of the random walk method is its simplicity. It is also easy to implement, and its efficiency can be improved by using appropriate data structures.

In addition, the random walk approach is not only well-suited for detecting uniformly scattered outliers, it is well-suited for finding small clusters of outliers [30] because it considers one data point at a time and how that data point compares with all the other data. The random walk technique determines "outlierness" from a global perspective [30]. In real-life applications like intrusion detection [25], small clusters of outliers may correspond to interesting events, such as denial-of-service or worm attacks.

However, the random walk method also has some major drawbacks. First, the performance of the random walk technique is highly dependent on the choice of similarity measure. Some similarity measures like cosine similarity are able to distinguish between normal and anomalous test data only when the anomalous data are significantly different, but they may fail to pick up minor differences.

Second, straightforward implementations of the random walk method do not scale well to large graphs, requiring quadratic space and cubic precomputation time [42].

11.3   GBAD Algorithm

In the overview section, we spoke briefly about "in-disguise" anomalies. These are anomalies that closely resemble the non-anomalous data, for example, a spy on an assignment will try to blend in with his/her surroundings and try not to attract any undue attention onto himself/herself. Another example would be a person who steals a credit card and tries to mimic normal behavior. By "normal behavior," we mean that he or she probably will not go out and buy a $20,000 piece of jewelry. "In-disguise" anomalies are such data.

When we represent any data (purchase history of credit cards) as a graph and are trying to locate anomalies, here are a few main types of anomalies we look for [14]:

- *Type 1:* An unexpected vertex or edge is present (*insertions*).
  An example would be a person buying 20 gift cards in one day.

- *Type 2:* The label on a vertex or an edge is different than expected (*modifications*).
  An example would be a person who usually buys milk in North Carolina starts buying milk in Iowa.

- *Type 3:* An expected vertex or edge is absent (*deletions*).
  An example would be a person who has been buying a cup of coffee from IHOP every other morning for 23 years is no longer doing so.

11.3.1   Minimum Description Length

A *substructure* is a connected subgraph of the overall graph. Figure 11.9 shows us a substructure. The *description length* of a graph is the number of nodes and edges required to describe a graph.

> **Definition 11.5** *Minimum Description Length (**MDL**)*
> Minimum Description Length principle is based on the insight that any regularity in a graph can be used to compress the data, i.e., to describe it using fewer symbols than the number of symbols needed to describe the data literally [21].

The MDL $M(S, G)$ of a graph G is formalized using the following equation:

$$M(S, G) = DL(G|S) + DL(S), \tag{11.7}$$

where S is the substructure used to compress G, $DL(G|S)$ is the description length of G after compressing it using S, and $DL(S)$ is the description length of S.

As seen from Figure 11.9, the link $A \rightarrow B$ occurs twice and is the most frequently occurring substructure. So, we can compress the graph G by replacing

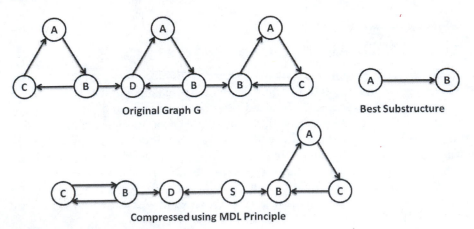

Original Graph G   Best Substructure

Compressed using MDL Principle

FIGURE 11.9: Minimum Description Length (MDL) example. © 2003 Association for Computing Machinery, Inc. Reprinted by Permission. [doi.acm.org/10.1145/95670.956831]

each occurrence of $A \rightarrow B$ by S. This will reduce the description length of graph G. When we use the most frequently occurring substructures for compression, there could be a vast difference between $DL(G)$ before compression and $DL(G)$ after compression [31].

11.3.2   How do we define an anomaly using MDL?

Using MDL, we can find the most common, or *normative*, substructures within a graph. Anomalous substructures will be substructures that are similar to the normative subgraphs but differ by some small amount.

> **Definition 11.6** *Normative*
> The term "normative" means relating to or dealing with a standard model or pattern regarded as typical. It is usually the most frequently occurring substructure.

> **Definition 11.7** *Anomalous substructure*
> A substructure S' is said to be anomalous if it is not isomorphic to the graph's normative substructure S, but is isomorphic to S within $X\%$ [14].

"Within $X\%$" means that though the anomaly is not isomorphic to the most frequently occurring substructure, if a certain percentage of the anomaly were modified, then it would be isomorphic to the normative substructure. In other words, the anomalous structure is not a direct isomorph of S, but when certain vertices and edges are added or removed, it will become an isomorph.

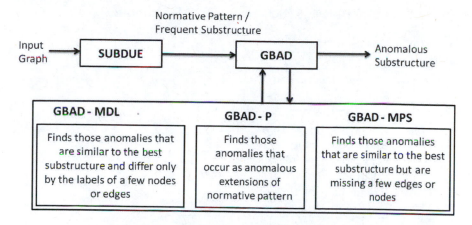

FIGURE 11.10: Overview of the GBAD system.

The variable X defines the percentage of vertices or edges that have to be changed for S' to be isomorphic to S. We use this definition so that the anomalies will be similar to a normative pattern.

11.3.3 What is GBAD all about?

GBAD [14] is a tool that implements three algorithms (see Figure 11.10), GBAD-MDL, GBAD-P, and GBAD-MPS, to detect the three types of anomalies discussed earlier. GBAD is an unsupervised approach based on the SUBDUE graph-based knowledge discovery system [21]. For more information on SUBDUE, visit `http://ailab.wsu.edu/subdue/`.

All three algorithms are based on the following four assumptions, as stated by Eberle and Holder [14]:

1. The majority of a graph consists of a normative pattern, and no more than $X\%$ of the normative pattern is altered in the case of an anomaly.

   This assumption is directly related to our definition of an anomalous substructure.

2. The graph is regular. The term *regular* implies that the data have some regular patterns of behavior. This regularity helps us distinguish between anomalies and noise.

3. Anomalies consist of one or more modifications, insertions, or deletions.

4. The normative pattern is connected.

In a real-world scenario, we can apply an approach based on MDL to data such as cargo shipments, telecommunication traffic, financial transactions, or

TABLE 11.5: Notation for GBAD algorithms

Symbol	Description
G	Graph
S	Best substructure in graph G
I	Substructure instances
$C(I, S)$	Cost to transform I
$F(I)$	Frequency of occurrence of I
AV	Anomalous value
S'	Set of extended instances of S
I'	Set of all extended instances of I
P'	Parent substructure of S
K'	Substructure instances that match P'

terrorist networks. In all cases, the data consists of a set of nodes and links that exhibit regular patterns. Certainly, graphs could contain potential anomalies across disconnected substructures, but we do not consider these types of anomalies.

Common notations for the GBAD algorithms appear in Table 11.5.

11.3.4 GBAD-MDL—Information Theoretic Approach

The GBAD-MDL algorithm uses the MDL approach to find the "best" substructure in the graph and subsequently searches for all the other substructures that look similar to the "best." By "best substructure," we mean the one that occurs most frequently and causes maximum compression in the graph using the MDL principal, i.e., the one that minimizes Equation 11.7. This algorithm finds anomalies of Type 2, modifications.

As discussed earlier, we first find the best substructure S (line 2 in Algorithm 31). We then find all substructures I (line 3) that require some cost $C(I, S)$ to match S. This step is used because when we consider data like credit card fraud, we are looking for those transactions that originated from a person who is not the owner of the card, so while looking for anomalous substructures, we don't consider exact matches, as these probably originated from the card owner. $F(I)$ is the frequency of occurrence of I. We compute the product of $C(I, S)$ and the frequency of I, $F(I)$ (line 4), and conclude that the substructures where this product is low are anomalies. We arrive at this conclusion based on two factors. The first assumption is that anomalies are rare, and the second that an anomaly will be as close to the normal data as possible, i.e., the cost to transform the anomaly to normal data will be low. A pseudocode description of the GBAD-MDL appears in Algorithm 31.

Looking at graph G in Figure 11.11, we see that $A \to B \to C \to A$ is the most frequently occurring substructure. We have two other substructures to consider.

---

1 **Algorithm:** Information Theoretic Algorithm (GBAD-MDL)
  Input: Any data modeled as a graph G
  Output: The anomalous substructures of G
2 Find the best substructure S in G that minimizes $M(S, G)$
3 Find all substructure instances I where the cost to transform I to match S, $C(I, S)$, is greater than zero
4 Calculate the "anomalous value" AV for each structure in I as the product of $C(I,\ S)$ with the frequency of I, $F(I)$
5 Output the instances of I with low AV value

Algorithm 31: Pseudocode description of the GBAD-Minimum Description Length algorithm

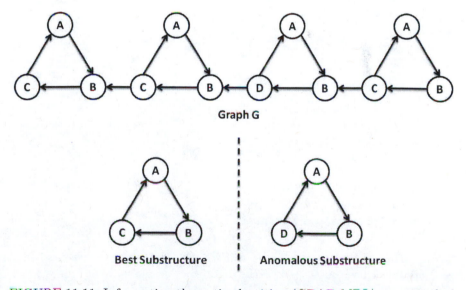

FIGURE 11.11: Information theoretic algorithm (GBAD-MDL) example. [46]

Comparing the most frequent substructures with $A \rightarrow C \rightarrow B \rightarrow A$ and $A \rightarrow B \rightarrow D \rightarrow A$, we see that $A \rightarrow C \rightarrow B \rightarrow A$ requires changes to two labels to match $A \rightarrow B \rightarrow C \rightarrow A$, and $A \rightarrow B \rightarrow D \rightarrow A$ requires only one. A cost of 1 is assigned to every vertex or edge that has to be changed. We calculate the AV values for both substructures as follows:

$$AV(I) = C(I, S) \cdot F(I)$$
$$AV(A \rightarrow C \rightarrow B \rightarrow A) = 2 \cdot 1$$
$$AV(A \rightarrow B \rightarrow D \rightarrow A) = 1 \cdot 1$$

We find that $A \rightarrow B \rightarrow D \rightarrow A$ has the lower value; hence, it is more anomalous.

Example:

We provide graph G in Figure 11.11 as input and verify that the anomalies are correctly reported.

```
1 > data(GBADExample1)
2 > G <- GBAD(GBADExample1, mps=0.8)
3 > length(G$anomalies)
4 [1] 1
5 > Anomaly <- G$anomalies[[1]]

6 > Anomaly[[1]]
7 Vertices: 3
8 Edges: 2
9 Directed: TRUE
10 Edges:

11 [0] '7' -> '8'
12 [1] '8' -> '9'

13 > V(Anomaly[[1]])
14 Vertex sequence:
15 [1] "7" "8" "9"
16 > V(Anomaly[[1]])$id
17 [1] "D" "A" "B"
18 > Anomaly$anomalous_vertex
19 [1] 1 0 0
```

Translating the Output: As we can see, the code snippet executed in R correctly identifies the $D \rightarrow A \rightarrow B$ subgraph as an anomaly in Figure 11.11.

11.3.5 GBAD-P—Probabilistic Approach

The GBAD-P algorithm again follows the basic principle of MDL by finding the "best" substructure in the graph. Now, for each occurrence of that subgraph, the *extensions* are examined. An extension can be in the form of an added vertex or an added edge. A probability of occurrence is calculated for each extension and the ones with lower probability are considered anomalous. This algorithm finds anomalies of Type 1, insertions.

To summarize, we find the most frequently occurring substructure S (line 2 in Algorithm 32). We then find all the substructure instances I that match S (line 3) and find a list of extensions I' for each element I (line 4). We create a list S' with all the extensions of S (line 5) and calculate the probability of occurrence of each extension of I' in set S', where lower probabilities correspond to more anomalous extensions. The logic behind this conclusion is that while a particular substructure may be frequent, certain anomalous extensions of it may not be frequent.

---

1 **Algorithm:** Probabilistic Algorithm (GBAD-P)

Input: Any data modeled as a graph G
Output: The anomalous substructures of G
2 Find best substructure S in G, that minimizes $M(S, G)$
3 Find all substructure instances I that match S
4 Create extended versions I' that consist of the original I with an addition of a vertex or an edge
5 Let S' be the set of all extended instances of S
6 Calculate the anomalous value $AV(I')$ by calculating the probability of occurrence of I' in S'
7 Output the substructures with low anomalous values (AV) as anomalies

---

Algorithm 32: Pseudocode description of the GBAD-P algorithm

Let us look at the following example for better understanding. Consider the graph G in Figure 11.12. Once again, let us find the best substructure. In this case, the best structure is $B \rightarrow A \rightarrow C \rightarrow B$. According to our algorithm, we now analyze the extensions of each occurrence of $B \rightarrow A \rightarrow C \rightarrow B$. We find that the substructure with an extension to C (let us refer to it as I'_1), occurs once, and the substructure with an extension to D (let us refer to it as I'_2) occurs four times. Thus, the total number of extensions of $B \rightarrow A \rightarrow C \rightarrow B$ is five. We calculate the anomalous value AV using the formula:

$$AV(I'_i) = \frac{F(I'_i)}{F(S')},\qquad(11.8)$$

where $F(I'_i)$ is the number of occurrences of substructure I'_i and $F(S')$ is the cardinality of the set of all extended instances. For our example,

$$AV(I'_1) = 1/5 \text{ and}$$
$$AV(I'_2) = 4/5.$$

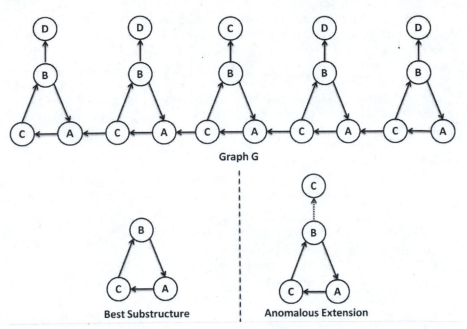

Graph G

Best Substructure   **Anomalous Extension**

FIGURE 11.12: Probabilistic algorithm (GBAD-P) example. Copyright © IEEE. All rights reserved. Reprinted with permission from [14].

So, we find that I_1' is more anomalous since the AV of I_1' is the lower of the two.

Example:
We provide graph G in Figure 11.12 as input and verify that the anomalies are correctly reported.

```
1 > library(gbad)
2 > data(GBADExample2)
3 > # prob=2 option runs GBAD-P algorithm
4 > G <- GBAD(GBADExample2, prob=2)
5 > best_substructure <- G$substructures[[1]]
6 > # best[[1]] contains the igraph object
7 > best_substructure[[1]]
8 Vertices: 3
9 Edges: 3
10 Directed: TRUE
11 Edges:

12 [0] '1' -> '2'
13 [1] '2' -> '3'
14 [2] '3' -> '1'
```

```
15 > best_substructure$value
16 [1] 1.64065
17 > best_anomaly <- G$anomalies[[1]]
18 > V(best_anomaly[[1]])$id
19 [1] "SUB_1" "C"
20 > E(best_anomaly[[1]])$label
21 [1] "e5"
```

Translating the output: The output of the code shows that the best substructure has three vertices, and the edges of the substructure are $B \rightarrow A$, $A \rightarrow C$, and $C \rightarrow B$. The output also shows that the node C connected to the best substructure is the anomaly, and C is connected to the best substructure by an edge with label $e5$.

11.3.6 GBAD-MPS (Maximum Partial Substructure) Approach

The GBAD-MPS algorithm once again uses MDL to find the best substructure S in a graph (line 2 of Algorithm 33). The parent substructure of S has the exact same structure of S with one or more nodes or edges removed. The algorithm finds the substructures that match the parent substructure of S (line 3). A cost value of 1 is associated with every additional edge or vertex that is required to make the discovered substructure match S. The structures that occur infrequently and require a lower cost to transform are considered anomalies. A pseudocode description of this algorithm appears in Algorithm 33. The algorithm finds anomalies of Type 3, deletions.

---

1 **Algorithm:** Maximum Partial Substructure (GBAD-MPS)

Input: Any data modeled as a graph G
Output: Anomalous substructures
2 Find the best substructure S in G that minimizes $M(S, G)$
3 Find the parent substructure P' of S
4 Find all instances K' that match P'
5 Calculate the anomalous value $AV(K')$ as the product of cost of transformation $C(K', S)$ and the frequency of occurrence of K', $F(K')$
6 Output the instances K' with low $AV(K')$

Algorithm 33: Pseudocode description of the GBAD-MPS algorithm

Once again, let us use an example to understand the algorithm better. Figure 11.13 depicts a graph G. The best substructure of G is shown in Figure 11.13. The structures that also match the parent structure of S are now examined ($P1$, $P2$, $P3$, and $P4$ in Figure 11.13), and the cost to transform each such structure to match S is calculated. We find that out of the four such structures in Figure 11.13, three of them already have links to C. Hence, these

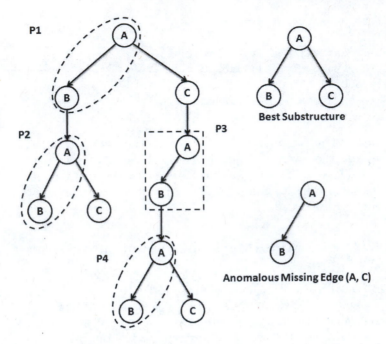

FIGURE 11.13: Graph for maximum partial structure (GBAD-MPS) example.

structures will match S without any transformation, but the structure $P3$ requires a change of one edge and one node (C) to match S, so its anomalous value AV is calculated as:

$$AV(K') = C(K', S) \cdot F(K')$$
$$= 2 \cdot 1$$

Substructures with low anomalous values (AV) are considered anomalies.

Example in R:
We provide graph G in Figure 11.13 as input and verify that the anomalies are correctly reported.

```
1 > data(GBADExample3)
2 > G <- GBAD(GBADExample3, mps=0.9)
3 > G$anomalies
4 [[1]]
5 [[1]]$graph
6 Vertices: 2
7 Edges: 1
8 Directed: TRUE
```

```
 9 Edges:
10     e
11 e [0] '7' -> '8'

12 [[1]]$anomalous_vertex
13 [1] 0 0

14 [[1]]$anomalous_edge
15 [1] 0

16 [[1]]$value
17 [1] 3

18 [[1]]$norm
19 [1] 0

20 [[1]]$iteration
21 [1] 0
```

Translating the Output: Here, GBAD has discovered an anomaly with two vertices and a directed edge between them. The edge '7' → '8' represents substructure *P*3 from our example.

A common thread in the above three algorithms is the fact that anomalies are identified by low anomalous values. You are probably asking yourself, "How low should the anomalous value be for it to be an anomaly?" This decision is based on a *threshold*. This value determines a cutoff for the anomalous value, and every substructure instance that does not meet the threshold is taken as anomalous. This threshold value is specific to the type of data being used, and in GBAD, it is a user-specified value.

11.3.7 Strengths and Weaknesses

As Eberle and Holder (the creators of GBAD) note, the GBAD algorithms are flexible enough to be implemented with a number of graph-based discovery tools, and the algorithms identify not only the anomalous patterns, but also the instances of those anomalous patterns in the data. As a disadvantage, a user would need to run all three GBAD algorithms if the type of anomaly—modification, insertion, or deletion—is not known beforehand [14].

Another significant disadvantage is the fact that threshold is a user input, so a person may have to go through a trial-and-error period to obtain an optimum threshold for a given data set.

11.4   Tensor-based Anomaly Detection Algorithm

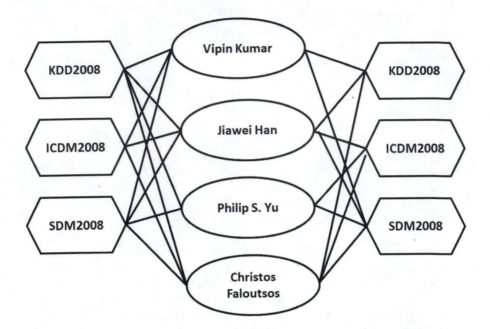

FIGURE 11.14: A simple example of DBLP data.

In the previous sections, we have described algorithms for discovering "vertex," "edge," and "subgraph" anomalies. All of these abnormal data can be represented as a two-dimensional matrix. In real-world scenarios, though, we may need to find patterns in data that contain several different types of relationships, like DBLP data on who publishes papers at which conference, with whom, and when (see Figure 11.14). Likewise, network flow data may contain information on who sends packets to whom, from what port, and when [41] (see Figure 11.15). Matrix-based tools cannot directly handle these types of relational problems.

In this section, we will introduce the concept of a *tensor*, which is a powerful tool for anomaly detection in multi-relational data. For simplicity, we will only consider third-order tensors in this chapter, although the tensor ideas can be generalized to the nth-order tensors, where $n > 3$.

11.4.1   What Is a Tensor?

A tensor is a multidimensional array. More formally, an nth-order tensor $\chi \in \mathbb{R}^{N_1 \times ... \times N_n}$ can be written as $\chi_{[N_1 \times ... \times N_n]}$, where N_i is the size of the ith

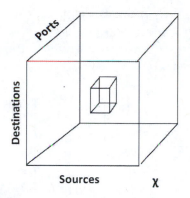

FIGURE 11.15: A third-order tensor of network flow data. [23] Copyright © 2009 Society of Industrial and Applied Mathematics. Reprinted with permission. All rights reserved.

dimension or *mode*. The *order* of a tensor, n, is the number of dimensions, also known as *ways* [23].

Based on this definition, a vector can be seen as a first-order tensor, and a matrix is a second-order tensor. A third-order tensor $\chi_{[I \times J \times K]}$ has three indices. The network flow data example mentioned in the previous section can be modeled as a third-order tensor, as shown in Figure 11.15.

Similar to using $a_{i,j}$ to denote the element of matrix $\mathbf{A}$, the elements of tensor $\chi_{[I \times J \times K]}$ can also be denoted by $X_{i,j,k}$, where $i = 1, 2, \ldots, I$, $j = 1, 2, \ldots, J$, and $k = 1, 2, \ldots, K$. For example, the element $X_{4,5,6}$ (like the highlighted cube in Figure 11.15) in the tensor of network flow data may represent the number of packets sent by source 4 to destination 5 from port 6, at a given time stamp [41].

Much how we might use A_i to represent the ith row or column of matrix $\mathbf{A}$, we adopt the convention in this chapter that X_i or $X_{(i)}$ represents the ith "frontal" slice of a third-degree tensor $\mathbf{X}$ (see Figure 11.16). That is, $\mathbf{X}_i$ is the matrix that results when we set the third dimension of $\mathbf{X}$ to be i and vary the indices of the first two dimensions. In particular, a third-order tensor $\chi_{[3 \times 4 \times 2]}$, where all elements are 1, can be written as:

$$X_1 = \begin{bmatrix} 1 & 1 & 1 & 1 \\ 1 & 1 & 1 & 1 \\ 1 & 1 & 1 & 1 \end{bmatrix},$$

$$X_2 = \begin{bmatrix} 1 & 1 & 1 & 1 \\ 1 & 1 & 1 & 1 \\ 1 & 1 & 1 & 1 \end{bmatrix}.$$

A more complicated example can be derived from the DBLP data (see Figure 11.14). The edges in Figure 11.14 indicate the authors published at least one paper in the corresponding conferences. If we use author, conference, and year as the three indices I, J, and K, respectively, and model the DBLP data as a third-order tensor, then the unweighted graph of DBLP data can be expressed as:

$$X_{2008} = \begin{bmatrix} 1 & 1 & 1 \\ 1 & 1 & 1 \\ 1 & 1 & 1 \\ 1 & 1 & 1 \end{bmatrix},$$

$$X_{2009} = \begin{bmatrix} 1 & 0 & 1 \\ 1 & 1 & 1 \\ 0 & 1 & 1 \\ 1 & 1 & 1 \end{bmatrix}.$$

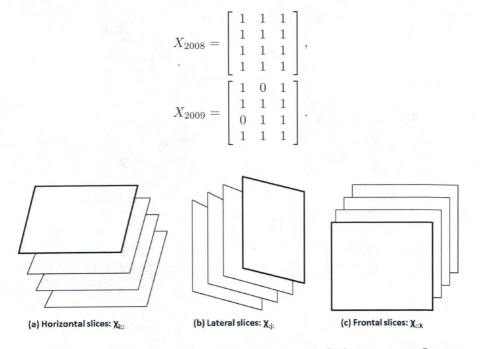

(a) Horizontal slices: $X_{i::}$ (b) Lateral slices: $X_{:j:}$ (c) Frontal slices: $X_{::k}$

FIGURE 11.16: The slices of a third-order tensor. [23] Copyright © 2009 Society of Industrial and Applied Mathematics. Reprinted with permission. All rights reserved.

How do we construct a tensor in R? One of the ways is to use the `to.tensor` function from the tensorA package. For example, the following code will construct a tensor $A_{[2 \times 2 \times 2]}$.

```
#create a tensor
> A = to.tensor(c(1,1,0,0,1,1,1,1),c(2,2,2));
#output tensor A
> A
, , 1

        I2
 I1     [,1] [,2]
  [1,]    1    0
  [2,]    1    0
```

TABLE 11.6: Table of notations for tensor-based anomaly detection

Symbol	Description
χ	Tensor
$\chi_{i_1,\ldots,i_M}$	The element of χ with index $(i_1,\ldots,i_M)$
$\mathbf{U}$	Projection matrix
ζ	Core tensor
$\mathbf{U}_i\|_{i=1}^n$	A sequence of n matrices $\mathbf{U}_1,\ldots,\mathbf{U}_n$
$U^{\mathbf{T}}$	The transpose of $\mathbf{U}$
N_i	The dimensionality of the ith mode
$\|A-B\|_F^2$	The least-squares cost between A and B

```
10 , , 2

11          I2
12 I1      [,1] [,2]
13    [1,]   1    1
14    [2,]   1    1

15 attr(,"class")
16 [1] "tensor"
```

Another simple way to construct a tensor is using the **array** function.

```
1 #create the same tensor as A
2 > B = array(c(1,1,0,0,1,1,1,1),c(2,2,2));
```

However, the other functions in tensorA package require using `to.tensor` function to construct tensors.

Notations used in this section are summarized in Table 11.6.

11.4.2 Tensor Operators

Like matrix operations including matrix inversion, matrix multiplication, matrix transposition, and so on, there are also some basic tensor operators including matricizing, mode product, and decomposition. Before we go to the tensor algorithm, it is essential to learn the following tensor operators first.

11.4.2.1 Matricizing or Unfolding

Definition 11.8 *Matricizing*
Matricizing, also known as unfolding, is the process of transforming a tensor into a matrix by reordering the elements of the tensor [23].

The mode-n matricization of a third-order tensor $\chi_{[N_1 \times N_2 \times N_3]}$ is a set of matrices obtained by adjoining the matrices formed by fixing the index n and

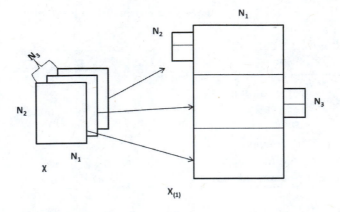

FIGURE 11.17: A third-order tensor χ is matricized along mode-1 to a matrix $\mathbf{X}_{(1)}$. © 2006 Association of Computing Machinery, Inc. Reprinted by permission [doi.acm.org/10.1145/1150402.1150445]

varying the other indices. For example, a $3 \times 4 \times 5$ tensor can be transformed into a 12×5 matrix, a 4×15 matrix, or a 3×20 matrix. The mode-n matricization of a tensor is denoted by $\mathbf{X}_{(n)}$.

Figure 11.17 shows an example of mode-1 matricization of a third-order tensor $\chi_{[N_1 \times N_2 \times N_3]}$.

More specifically, let $\chi_{[4 \times 3 \times 2]}$ be:

$$X_1 = \begin{bmatrix} 1 & 5 & 9 \\ 2 & 6 & 10 \\ 3 & 7 & 11 \\ 4 & 8 & 12 \end{bmatrix}, X_2 = \begin{bmatrix} 13 & 17 & 21 \\ 14 & 18 & 22 \\ 15 & 19 & 23 \\ 16 & 20 & 24 \end{bmatrix} \tag{11.9}$$

The three mode-1 unfoldings of $\chi_{[4 \times 3 \times 2]}$ are:

$$X_{(1)} = \begin{bmatrix} 1 & 5 & 9 & 13 & 17 & 21 \\ 2 & 6 & 10 & 14 & 18 & 22 \\ 3 & 7 & 11 & 15 & 19 & 23 \\ 4 & 8 & 12 & 16 & 20 & 24 \end{bmatrix},$$

$$X_{(2)} = \begin{bmatrix} 1 & 2 & 3 & 4 & 13 & 14 & 15 & 16 \\ 5 & 6 & 7 & 8 & 17 & 18 & 19 & 20 \\ 9 & 10 & 11 & 12 & 21 & 22 & 23 & 24 \end{bmatrix}, \text{ and}$$

$$X_{(3)} = \begin{bmatrix} 1 & 2 & 3 & 4 & 5 & 6 & 7 & 8 & 9 & 10 & 11 & 12 \\ 13 & 14 & 15 & 16 & 17 & 18 & 19 & 20 & 21 & 22 & 23 & 24 \end{bmatrix}.$$

You can use different orderings of the columns for the mode-n unfolding as long as it is consistent across related calculations. In general, the specific permutation of columns in tensor matricization is not important.

11.4.2.2 The n-mode Product

Tensor multiplication is much more complex than multiplication of matrices. Here, we consider only the tensor n-mode product, where $n \leq 3$.

Consider a third-order tensor $\chi_{[I_1 \times I_2 \times I_3]}$ and three matrices $\mathbf{U}_1 \in \mathbb{R}^{J_1 \times I_1}$, $\mathbf{U}_2 \in \mathbb{R}^{J_2 \times I_2}$, and $\mathbf{U}_3 \in \mathbb{R}^{J_3 \times I_3}$. The mode-1 product $\chi \times_1 \mathbf{U}_1$, mode-2 product $\chi \times_2 \mathbf{U}_2$, and mode-3 product $\chi \times_3 \mathbf{U}_3$ are, respectively, defined by:

$$(\chi \times_1 \mathbf{U}_1)_{(j_1 i_2 i_3)} = \sum_{i_1=1}^{I_1} x_{i_1 i_2 i_3} u_{j_1 i_1}, \forall j_1, i_2, i_3,$$

$$(\chi \times_2 \mathbf{U}_2)_{(i_1 j_2 i_3)} = \sum_{i_2=1}^{I_2} x_{i_1 i_2 i_3} u_{j_2 i_2}, \forall i_1, j_2, i_3, \text{ and}$$

$$(\chi \times_3 \mathbf{U}_3)_{(i_1 i_2 j_3)} = \sum_{i_3=1}^{I_3} x_{i_1 i_2 i_3} u_{j_3 i_3}, \forall i_1, i_2, j_3,$$

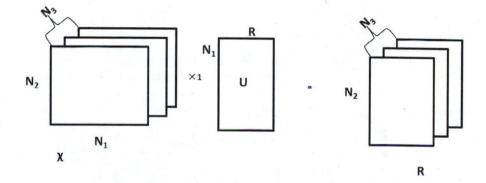

FIGURE 11.18: The third-order tensor $\chi_{[N_1 \times N_2 \times N_3]} \times_1 \mathbf{U}$ results in a new tensor in $\mathbb{R}^{R \times N_2 \times N_3}$. © 2006 Association of Computing Machinery, Inc. Reprinted by permission [doi.acm.org/10.1145/1150402.1150445]

Figure 11.18 shows an example of the third-order tensor χ mode-1 multiplied by a matrix $\mathbf{U}$. The process of χ mode-1 multiplied by $\mathbf{U}$ is equivalent to:

1. matricizing χ along mode-1,
2. performing matrix multiplication of $\mathbf{X}_{(1)}$ and $\mathbf{U}$, and
3. folding the result back as a tensor.

For example, let χ be the tensor defined in Equation 11.9 and let

$$\mathbf{U} = \begin{bmatrix} 1 & 3 & 5 \\ 2 & 4 & 6 \end{bmatrix}.$$

Then, the product $\Upsilon = \chi \times_2 \mathbf{U} \in \mathbb{R}^{4 \times 2 \times 2}$ is

$$\mathbf{Y}_1 = \begin{bmatrix} 61 & 169 \\ 70 & 178 \\ 79 & 187 \\ 88 & 196 \end{bmatrix},$$

$$\mathbf{Y}_2 = \begin{bmatrix} 76 & 220 \\ 88 & 232 \\ 100 & 244 \\ 112 & 256 \end{bmatrix}.$$

By using the `mul.tensor` function in the tensorA package, we can verify this result.

```
1 library(tensorA);
2 A=to.tensor(c(1:24),c(a1=4,a2=3,a3=2));
3 U=to.tensor(c(1:6),c(b1=2,b2=3));
4 Y=mul.tensor(A,"a2",B,"b2");
5 Y
```

11.4.2.3 The Tucker Decomposition

The Tucker decomposition is a form of higher-order principal component analysis and one of the most cited tensor decomposition methods [23]. The main objective of the Tucker decomposition is to approximate a larger tensor using a smaller tensor (called the *core tensor*) multiplied by a matrix along each mode.

Thus, in the third-order case $\chi_{[I_1 \times I_2 \times I_3]}$, we have

$$\chi \approx \zeta \times_1 \mathbf{A} \times_2 \mathbf{B} \times_3 \mathbf{C}, \tag{11.10}$$

where $\mathbf{A} \in \mathrm{R}^{J_1 \times I_1}$, $\mathbf{B} \in \mathrm{R}^{J_2 \times I_2}$, and $\mathbf{C} \in \mathrm{R}^{J_3 \times I_3}$.

Figure 11.19 shows an example of a tensor χ_i decomposed into smaller second order tensors y_i by Tucker decomposition.

The Tucker decomposition is not unique. For instance, if $\mathbf{A}$ in Equation 11.10 is post-multiplied by a square invertible matrix $\mathbf{D}$ with inverse $\mathbf{D}^{-1}$, then ζ could be replaced by $\zeta \times_1 \mathbf{D}^{-1}$ [12].

Like most dimension reduction methods, the Tucker decomposition has the potential to increase performance by reducing the number of variables in the problem, but there may be some data loss in the reconstruction of the original tensor.

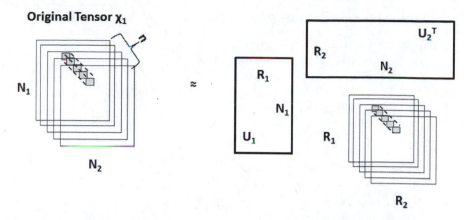

Original Tensor χ₁

Core Tensors y_i

FIGURE 11.19: The Tucker decomposition. © 2008 Association of Computing Machinery, Inc. Reprinted by permission [doi.acm.org/10.1145/1150402.1150445]

11.4.3 Tensor Analysis Algorithm

11.4.3.1 Intuition

Consider a third-order tensor $\chi \in \mathbb{R}^{N_1 \times N_2 \times N_3}$. If we could find orthogonal matrices $\mathbf{U}_1$, $\mathbf{U}_2$, and $\mathbf{U}_3$, one for each mode, we define the abnormality score of the tensor χ_j by its reconstruction error e_j [41]:

$$e_j = \left\| \chi_j - \chi_j \times_1 (\mathbf{U}_1 \mathbf{U}_1^{\mathbf{T}}) \times_2 (\mathbf{U}_2 \mathbf{U}_2^{\mathbf{T}}) \times_3 (\mathbf{U}_3 \mathbf{U}_3^{\mathbf{T}}) \right\|_F^2 .$$

Given a sequence of third-order tensors $\chi_1, \ldots, \chi_n$, if the abnormality score at time k is "enough" standard deviations away from the mean error:

$$e_k \geq mean(e_j|_{j=1}^{k}) + \beta \cdot std(e_j|_{j=1}^{k}),$$

where the value of β determines how many standard deviations is "enough," we would consider the tensor χ_k as an anomaly. In the paper [41], a value of $\beta = 2$ is used.

11.4.3.2 Tensor Analysis Algorithm

The process of the algorithm is shown in Figure 11.20. Since the algorithm processes each mode of the tensor at a time, the variance matrix of the d mode is updated as follows (see line 3 in Algorithm 34):

---

1 **Algorithm:** Tensor-based Algorithm (TensorDTA) [41]

Input : New three-way tensor—$\chi_{[N_1 \times N_2 \times N_3]}$
      Previous variance matrices—$\mathbf{C}_i|_{i=1}^3 \in \mathbb{R}^{N_i \times R_i}$
      Previous energy matrices—$\mathbf{S}_i|_{i=1}^3 \in \mathbb{R}^{R_i \times R_i}$
Output: New variance matrices—$\mathbf{C}_i|_{i=1}^3 \in \mathbb{R}^{N_i \times R_i'}$
      The rebuild tensor—$\zeta_{[N_1 \times N_2 \times N_3]}$

    `/* update every mode`   `*/`
2 **for** $d \in \{1, 2, 3\}$ **do**
3   Mode-d matricize χ as $\mathbf{X}_{(d)} \in \mathbb{R}^{(\prod_{i \neq d} N_i \times N_d)}$
4   Reconstruct variance matrix $\mathbf{C}_d \leftarrow \mathbf{U}_d S_d \mathbf{U}_d^{\mathbf{T}}$
5   Update variance matrix $\mathbf{C}_d \leftarrow \mathbf{C}_d + \mathbf{X}(d)^{\mathbf{T}} \mathbf{X}_{(d)}$
6   Diagonalize $\mathbf{C}_d = \mathbf{U}_d S_d \mathbf{U}_d^{\mathbf{T}}$
7   Compute new rank $\mathbb{R}_d$ and truncate $\mathbf{U}_d$ and $\mathbf{S}_d$
8 **end**
9 Calculate the core tensor $y = \chi \prod_{d=1}^M \times \mathbf{U}_d$
10 Compute the rebuild tensor $\zeta_{[N_1 \times N_2 \times N_3]}$

Algorithm 34: Tensor-based anomaly detection algorithm

$$\mathbf{C}_d \leftarrow \mathbf{C}_d + \mathbf{X}_{(d)}^{\mathbf{T}} \mathbf{X}_{(d)}$$

In addition, we usually do not treat every timestamp equally: more recent timestamps are more important than the past. For this, we use a forgetting factor, which changes the update step in the following way [41]:

$$\mathbf{C}_d \leftarrow \alpha \mathbf{C}_d + \mathbf{X}_{(d)}^{\mathbf{T}} \mathbf{X}_{(d)},$$

where α is a forgetting factor between 0 and 1. A value of $\alpha = 0$ disregards historical tensors, while $\alpha = 1$ treats all timestamps as equally important [41].

Examples in R

Let us consider a synthetic tensor stream $\{A, A, A, A, A, B, B, B, B\}$ as input, where A is a $2 \times 2 \times 2$ tensor

$$A_1 = \begin{bmatrix} 1 & 1 \\ 1 & 1 \end{bmatrix},$$

$$A_2 = \begin{bmatrix} 1 & 1 \\ 1 & 1 \end{bmatrix},$$

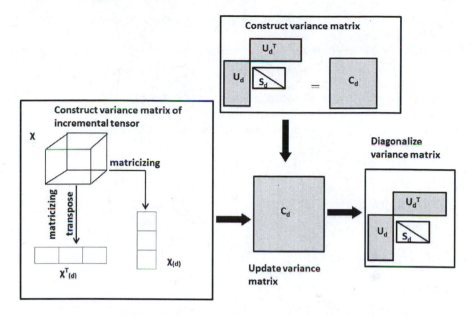

FIGURE 11.20: Outline of the tensor-based anomaly detection algorithm. © 2006 Association of Computing Machinery, Inc. Reprinted by permission [doi.acm.org/10.1145/1150402.1150445]

and B is the $2 \times 2 \times 2$ tensor

$$B_1 = \begin{bmatrix} 1 & 1 \\ 0 & 0 \end{bmatrix},$$

$$B_2 = \begin{bmatrix} 1 & 1 \\ 1 & 1 \end{bmatrix}.$$

```
1 A = array(1, c(2, 2, 2));
2 B = array(c(1, 0, 1, 0, 1, 1, 1, 1), c(2, 2, 2));
3 example = list(A, A, A, A, A, B, B, B, B);
4 err = list();

5 Xnew = example[[1]];
6 dec = TensorDTA(Xnew, R = array(c(1,1,1)), nargin = 3);
7 Cnew = dec$Cnew;
8 error = to.tensor(dec$Rebuildtensor - Xnew);
9 err[[1]] = tensorA:::norm(error)
10          / tensorA:::norm(to.tensor(Xnew));

11 #compute the reconstruction error of the tensor stream
12 for(i in 2:9)
13 {
```

```
14    #alpha is forgetting factor, the value is between 0 and 1
15    Xnew = example[[i]];
16    dec1 = TensorDTA(Xnew, R = array(c(1,1,1)), nargin = 5,
17             C = Cnew, alpha = 1);
18    Cnew = dec1$Cnew;
19    error = to.tensor(dec1$Rebuildtensor-Xnew);
20    err[[i]] = tensorA:::norm(error)
21                   / tensorA:::norm(to.tensor(Xnew));
22 }
23 #output the reconstruction error
24 err
```

The output of `err` is as follows:

```
1 example
2 [[1]]
3 [1] 2.220446e-16

4 [[2]]
5 [1] 2.220446e-16

6 [[3]]
7 [1] 2.220446e-16

8 [[4]]
9 [1] 2.220446e-16

10 [[5]]
11 [1] 2.220446e-16

12 [[6]]
13 [1] 0.4776726

14 [[7]]
15 [1] 0.4598352

16 [[8]]
17 [1] 0.4454452

18 [[9]]
19 [1] 0.4337203
```

From the output above, we can see that the sixth tensor is an anomaly, as the reconstruction error changes dramatically.

In the paper [41], Sun *et al.* applied the tensor-based anomaly detection algorithm on network flow data and found interesting patterns and outliers on the real, large dataset.

11.4.4 Strengths and Weaknesses

Numerous data mining applications, including anomaly detection, can be handled by matrix-based tools like SVD (also named PCA) and its variants and extensions, but these techniques all fall short when we want to study high-dimensional data sets, such as time-evolving traffic matrices, time-evolving datacubes, social networks with labeled edges, etc. [41].

The tensor-based approach we have described in this section is applicable to time-evolving graphs, data streams, sensor networks, and time-evolving social networks, and it can detect a wider range of anomalies than matrix-based methods [41].

11.5 Applications

In the real world, the presence of anomalies could indicate something amazingly good, like the presence of a new gene that could lead to new discoveries, or it could be extremely harmful, like the presence of malicious virus in a network. In certain applications, these anomalies can result in a huge loss of privacy, security, and financial capital. Hence, it becomes critical to identify these anomalies and take necessary action to prevent them in the future. Here, we provide two examples in which anomalies are of considerable interest.

11.5.1 Network Intrusion Detection

Anomalies in network intrusion detection are also termed "intruders." An "intruder" is an unwanted program or user trying to hack the network system. By "hack," we mean either flooding the network with data (causing an overload), getting an unauthorized look into a system, or locking up a service in such way that no one else can make use of it. Any of these types of intrusions might result in a severe disruption to the entire network. From a data mining perspective, our goal is to analyze the connection information, or *metadata*, of a network, such as the attributes listed in Table 11.7, and try to find out which data might correspond to intruders in the network.

There are four main types of attacks that can happen in a network:

1. DOS: denial-of-service
2. R2L: unauthorized access from a remote machine
3. U2R: unauthorized access using administrative or "root" privileges
4. Probing

DOS is an attack where an intruder locks up a service and disallows legitimate users from accessing it. For example, if we consider a service that can accept only a maximum of five connections, the intruder will try to occupy all five connections to prevent others from connecting to that service. *R2L* is a type of attack where an intruder will try to connect to a machine for which he or she has no authorization. Usually, a hacker will log in on this new machine and perform some other attack so that he or she cannot be traced. In *U2R*, the hacker who has some way to log into the system will try to access the administrator mode, which has unrestricted access to the system. *Probing* refers to an attempt to obtain information about a specific host on the network, usually by a system outside the network.

TABLE 11.7: Intrusion detection attributes

Attribute	Description
duration	Length of a connection
src_bytes	Number of bytes sent from source to destination
same_service	Percentage of connections to the same service
num_failed_logins	Percentage number of failed login attempts due to incorrect login data
num_file_creations	Number of files creation operations
num_access_files	Number of access file modifications
num_root	Number of "root" accesses
count	Number of connections to the same host
logged_in	Set to 1 if the user has provided a valid password for the current session

Now, the question arises as to how we can use the metadata of a network to pick up such intrusions. (Refer to Table 11.7 for a list of example metadata attributes.) To answer this question, let us consider the four types of intrusion one at a time and decide which attributes of the metadata will help detect these intrusions.

When we consider the *DOS* attack, we know that the intruder needs some way to lock up a host or service. Usually, this attack will take the form of flooding the service with innumerable requests to connect and then sending a large volume of data (number of packets) to block the communication channel. So, attributes like *duration, src_bytes*, and the *count* (in Table 11.7) become important [16].

Next, we consider the *R2L* attack. This type of attack involves an intruder trying to log in on an unauthorized system. In most cases, the intruder will not be able to log in immediately and so will have a lot of failed login attempts and a lengthy duration for the connection. Sometimes, normal users may forget their passwords and may attempt to log in multiple times, but our goal is to identify intruders who are trying to guess the login information of a system. Metadata attributes like *duration* and *num_failed_logins* can help us detect these attacks [16].

A typical *U2R* attack usually involves the hacker logging in as the administrator, creating a huge number of files, and making changes to the access control files, etc. So, if the number of file creations and the number of modifications to access files are high [2], then we most probably have our intruder. A *U2R* attack may be harder to detect than other types of intrusions, because once administrative privileges have been obtained, the intruder can easily create other administrator accounts and then enter as a legitimate user. To identify *U2R* attacks, it might be useful to consider the *num_root* attribute (refer to Table 11.7), which provides the number of "root" accesses.

While probing, an intruder outside the network will scan the network continuously and try to capture as much information as possible. Usually, the duration of connection for this intruder will last longer than usual, and the number of bytes sent by the intruder to the host will also be high. So, attributes like *duration* and *src_bytes* (refer to Table 11.7) are important [16].

For intruders, network metadata values will vary greatly from a normal communication and hence be "white crow" anomalies. We model the network metadata as a graph, where each node represents a user, with the set of parameters described in Table 11.7. We can then calculate the cosine similarity of each node with respect to all other nodes, and we should find that normal users share a higher cosine similarity than intruders. So, using our random walk on single graph algorithm (see Section 11.2.2), we can detect those users that do not fit into the norm and may possibly be intruders.

For example, let us consider a set of data where the anomaly we are looking for is a *DOS* intruder.

TABLE 11.8: Data for a *DOS* attack example

Duration	Source Bytes	Count
1	22	1
1	24	1
1	30	1
1	26	1
23	1234	4

From Table 11.8, each row is taken as a vector and assigned to one vertex in the graph, and the cosine similarity between the vectors are the edge weights. We can use this data to construct a symmetric square cosine similarity matrix with the nodes as the rows and columns. The random walk anomaly detection algorithm defined in Section 11.2.2 will take this matrix as an input and output a set of ranked connectivity values. In this output, the intruder data should be ranked much lower than regular network traffic.

```
1 > library(randomWalkAnomaly)
2 > data(Input_Data)
3 > Input_Matrix = as.matrix(Input_Data)
4 > Input_Cosine = cosineSimilarity(t(Input_Matrix))
```

```
5 > outlierAnomaly(Input_Cosine, 0.999, 0.001)
6      Vertex    connectivityValues    Ranks
7 [1,]      1              0.2150          4
8 [2,]      2              0.2150          4
9 [3,]      3              0.2075          2
10 [4,]     4              0.2075          2
11 [5,]     5              0.1550          1
```

Translating the Output: The output of the algorithm marks data point 5 as the most anomalous (rank 1). When we look at Table 11.8 we find that datapoint 5 varies significantly from the other data points in terms of the values of the attributes. We have already discussed that in a DOS attack, the attacker tries to keep the victim busy so that no other system can connect to it by sending a huge amount of data packets or making several connections to use up the maximum number of simultaneous connections a host can handle—based on these factors, data point 5 seems like a potential attacker and hence is marked as the most anomalous.

The random walk anomaly detection algorithm can also identify intruders in the KDD99 data set [2]. The KDD99 dataset has one column specifying the type of data—that is, whether the data is normal or some type of attack. We can use this information to verify the result of our algorithm.

The first type of attack we consider in the KDD99 dataset is called a "smurf," which is a type of *DOS* attack. For this problem, we then load two R libraries, lsa and randomWalkAnomaly. We first load the data set "DOS_KDD," which is a subset of the KDD99 dataset containing both normal and "smurf" data.

```
1 > data(DOS_KDD)
2 > DOS_KDD
```

```
1 > colnames(DOS_KDD)
2  [1] "duration"                "protocol_type"
3  [3] "service"                 "flag"
4  [5] "src_bytes"               "dst_bytes"
5  [7] "land"                    "wrong_fragment"
6  [9] "urgent"                  "hot"
7  [11] "num_failed_logins"      "logged_in"
8  [13] "num_compromised"        "root_shell"
9  [15] "su_attempted"           "num_root"
10 [17] "num_file_creations"     "num_shells"
11 [19] "num_access_files"       "num_outbound_cmds"
12 [21] "is_host_login"          "is_guest_login"
13 [23] "count"                  "srv_count"
14 [25] "serror_rate"            "srv_serror_rate"
15 [27] "rerror_rate"            "srv_rerror_rate"
```

```
16 [29] "same_srv_rate",                    "diff_srv_rate"
17 [31] "srv_diff_host_rate"                 "dst_host_count"
18 [33] "dst_host_srv_count"                 "dst_host_same_srv_rate"
19 [35] "dst_host_diff_srv_rate"            "dst_host_same_src_port_rate"
20 [37] "dst_host_srv_diff_host_rate"       "dst_host_serror_rate"
21 [39] "dst_host_srv_serror_rate"           "dst_host_rerror_rate"
22 [41] "dst_host_srv_rerror_rate"           "Type"
```

Once we load the data, we only use the three columns we identified earlier to predict a *DOS* attack, "duration," "src_bytes," and "count." We obtain the cosine similarity matrix for the data and pass it to the algorithm. The random walk algorithm identifies vertices 13 and 14 as the most anomalous, and when we look at the "Type" of these data points, they are indeed "smurf" *DOS* attacks.

```
1 > # We only need three columns to check for DOS attack
2 > DOS = cbind(DOS_KDD["duration"],DOS_KDD["src_bytes"],
3 >               DOS_KDD["count"],DOS_KDD["Type"])
4 > DOS
5    duration src_bytes count      Type
6 1         0       241    12 normal.
7 2         0       239     3 normal.
8 3         0       245    13 normal.
9 4         0       248    23 normal.
10 5        0       354     2 normal.
11 6        0       193     1 normal.
12 7        0       214     6 normal.
13 8        0       212     2 normal.
14 9        0       215     3 normal.
15 10       0       217     2 normal.
16 11       0       205     2 normal.
17 12       0       155     3 normal.
18 13       0      1032   316 smurf.
19 14       0      1032   511 smurf.
20 > DOS_Matrix = as.matrix(DOS[,1:3])
21 > DOS_CosineSimilarity = cosine(t(DOS_Matrix))
22 > outlierAnomaly(DOS_CosineSimilarity,0.97,0.001)
23          Vertex connectivityValues Ranks
24 [1,]        1          0.07480879     3
25 [2,]        2          0.07480879     3
26 [3,]        3          0.09377144    13
27 [4,]        4          0.09377144    13
28 [5,]        5          0.07480879     3
29 [6,]        6          0.07480879     3
30 [7,]        7          0.07480879     3
31 [8,]        8          0.07480879     3
```

32	[9,]	9	0.07480879	3
33	[10,]	10	0.07480879	3
34	[11,]	11	0.07480879	3
35	[12,]	12	0.07480879	3
36	[13,]	13	0.05169603	2
37	[14,]	14	0.01267317	1

Translating the Output: The output of the algorithm marks data points 13 and 14 as the most anomalous. When we check the class labels of those data points, we find that both of these data points have label "smurf" and correspond to real-world anomalies.

Let us look at another type of attack, the *R2L*. One type of R2L attack is the "guess password," where the attacker is trying to log in to a system he or she is not authorized to use. To apply our random walk algorithm to this problem, we first load the sample data set "R2L_KDD," another subset of KDD99. We will only use three attributes to check for this attack: "num_failed_logins," "duration," and "logged_in."

```
 1 > data(R2L_KDD)
 2 > R2L = cbind(R2L_KDD["duration"],R2L_KDD["logged_in"],
 3         R2L_KDD["num_failed_logins"],R2L_KDD["Type"])
 4 > R2L
 5     duration logged_in num_failed_logins          Type
 6 1          0         1                 0       normal.
 7 2          0         0                 0       normal.
 8 3          0         1                 0       normal.
 9 4          0         1                 0       normal.
10 5          0         1                 0       normal.
11 6          0         1                 0       normal.
12 7          0         1                 0       normal.
13 8          0         1                 0       normal.
14 9          0         1                 0       normal.
15 10         0         1                 0       normal.
16 11         1         0                 1 guess_passwd.
17 12         0         1                 0       normal.
18 13         2         0                 1 guess_passwd.
19 > R2L_Matrix = as.matrix(R2L[,1:3])
20 > R2L_CosineSimilarity = cosineSimilarity(t(R2L_Matrix))
21 >outierAnomaly(R2L_CosineSimilarity,0.1,0.001)
22         Vertex connectivityValues Ranks
23 [1,]         1       0.076923077     4
24 [2,]         2       0.007692308     1
25 [3,]         3       0.076923077     4
26 [4,]         4       0.076923077     4
27 [5,]         5       0.076923077     4
```

28	[6,]	6	0.076923077	4
29	[7,]	7	0.076923077	4
30	[8,]	8	0.076923077	4
31	[9,]	9	0.076923077	4
32	[10,]	10	0.076923077	4
33	[11,]	11	0.007692308	1
34	[12,]	12	0.076923077	4
35	[13,]	13	0.007692308	1

Translating the Output: As you can see in the code above, the random walk algorithm identifies vertices 2, 11, and 13 as anomalies, and two of these (vertices 11 and 13) correspond to *R2L* attacks. *U2R* and *Probing* can be detected similarly.

11.5.2   Fraud Detection Using Random Walks

Fraud detection has become one of the most critical applications in anomaly detection.

Definition 11.9 *Fraud*
The term "fraud" refers to an intentional deception resulting in injury to another person or deliberate trickery intended to gain an advantage [43].

Fraud detection is applicable to several important fields, including credit card fraud, insurance fraud, insider trading on the stock market, etc.

Credit card fraud happens when a person's credit or debit card gets stolen and the owner of the credit card does not notice its loss. During this time, the thief makes purchases using the stolen card. A smart thief will stay low and use the card wisely so as to not attract any undue attention to his or her transactions. From an anomaly detection perspective, our goal is to analyze the huge amounts of purchase history data and identify several common patterns. Using these patterns, we can then flag transactions that do not comply with the norm. Some fraud may be obvious, but sometimes it may differ from the norm by only a very minute amount.

Insurance fraud is an application that can lead to heavy losses for the insurance company. One of the hardest types of insurance fraud to detect is the "fraud ring." An insurance fraud ring is when several people are involved together in submitting false claims. A ring might be, for example, a couple of lawyers and their clients or possibly a doctor, a lawyer, and their clients. Members of a fraud ring are usually smart enough to keep their claim amounts small and thus fall under the radar. They accumulate huge amounts of money by filing hundreds of such small claims. From a day-to-day point of view, such claims are processed with hundreds of genuine claims and they are never noticed by the claim handlers. However, by applying anomaly detection techniques, we can analyze the claim data and start seeing patterns. For example, we might find that person A appears as the doctor whenever person B appears as the lawyer, and the number of their claims varies greatly from the typical. Such patterns, when investigated, might lead to saving the insurance company millions of dollars.

Let us look at another important area—the stock market. A person buys a stock with the intention of making a profit, and a person sells a stock either to make profit or to minimize losses. For example, consider a situation where on a certain day D, a particular stock X suddenly becomes a hot property and many people start buying it. A few days later, there is an announcement that company X has been acquired by company Y, which is one of the big stock market players in that particular field, allowing the people who bought stock X to gain a huge profit. In this situation, common sense suggests that the trading during day D did not happen by accident. In real time, there are hundreds of stocks and many such news announcements, and it is almost impossible to keep up with this flood of information and detect fraud. Using data mining techniques, though, we can come up with certain days or timestamps when the trading of a particular stock did not fit the usual pattern for that stock. The stock data at the particular timestamps can then be analyzed for fraud.

The most common fraud takes the form of insider trading. In our earlier example, insider trading is when a person who knows about the acquisition starts accumulating stocks or provides this information to someone else, giving undue advantage to the people who have this information. By law, insider trading is illegal, and detecting the fraud sooner helps to limit the damage taken by the companies involved.

Let us now take a closer look at anomaly detection in stock markets. Stock market data is collected as multivariate time series data. We are looking to find anomalous time stamps in this data that do not fit into the norm. Such anomalies can be detected using the algorithm for pointwise anomaly detection in multivariate time series (refer to Section 11.2.3).

For our application, we have used the stock prices of Nokia [22]. The multivariate time series algorithm will rank the "Dates" (timestamps) by their calculated connectivity values, where lower connectivity values correspond to more anomalous timestamps.

In stock markets, several factors affect the prices of stocks. Internal factors—news regarding the performance of a company (publishing profit results), scams, changes in the management, etc.—and external factors—favorable laws passed by the government or terrorist attacks—are a subset of a large number of factors that can affect the price of a stock on a particular day. Events like mergers or acquisitions drastically affect the stock prices in a very short span of time. Analyzing all of these factors to predict stock market anomalies is beyond the scope of this book. We will look at some of the simple attributes in this dataset that we could pass to our algorithm to identify those events that indicate potentially anomalous activity. Note, these results may not necessarily be anomalies, but are interesting enough to warrant further investigation.

The stock market dataset under consideration has seven attributes, namely date, open price, close price, high (the peak high value on that date), low (the

TABLE 11.9: Nokia stock market data attributes

Attribute	Description
Date	Time stamp
Open	Value of the stock when the stock market opened
Close	Value of the stock when the stock market closes for the day
High	Highest value a particular stock attains during the day
Low	Lowest value a particular stock attains during the day
Volume	Number of stocks traded
Adjusted Close Price	Corrected close price to include any distributions and corporate actions that occurred at any time prior to the next day's open

peak low value), volume traded, and adjusted close price, described in Table 11.9. The adjusted close price provides the closing price for the requested day, week, or month, adjusted for all applicable splits and dividend distributions. The data is adjusted using appropriate split and dividend multipliers, adhering to the Center for Research in Security Prices (CRSP) standards.

To use our algorithm for multivariate time series data, we choose 'volume' as the target series, and the attributes 'open,' 'high,' and 'close' as the predictor series. Other algorithm factors, like the auto-regression lag 'r,' spread width of the RBF kernel 'sig,' and the damping factor 'd,' can be in the range of 0–1.

```
1 > data(nokia)
2 > predictor <- as.matrix(nokia[, c(2, 3, 5)])
3 > predictor <- t(predictor)
4 > target <- as.matrix(nokia[, 6])
5 > target <- t(target)
6 > anomalies = multivariateAnomaly(predictor, target,
7 + 0, 0.1, 400, 0.1)

8 > anomalies
9       Time Stamp              Rank
10 [1,]           1 0.001731837   220
11 [2,]           2 0.001731728   200
12 [3,]           3 0.001731370   127
13 [4,]           4 0.001731518   167
14 [5,]           5 0.001732910   375
15 [6,]           6 0.001731713   195
16 [7,]           7 0.001731316   124
```

17	[8,]	8 0.001731728	201
18	[9,]	9 0.001731269	114
19	[10,]	10 0.001731145	96
20	[11,]	11 0.001733128	399
21	[12,]	12 0.001731191	102
22	[13,]	13 0.001731191	102
23	[14,]	14 0.001732288	288
24	[15,]	15 0.001732459	317
25	#*** The first 15 out of 577 rows.		

Translating the Output: The output ranks the "Dates" based on a correlation of the "open," "close," and "high" attributes with the "volume" attribute, where the lower ranked data points are possible anomalies. For example, dates when the open price, close price, and "high" price are very low but volume is high (lots of people buying or selling the stock) could be a potential anomaly. (For example, some insider information may say that the stock price will shoot up the next day because of some merger.) Such data points will be ranked lower and may need to be investigated further.

11.6 Bibliographic Notes

Detection of anomalies in graph data is an important data mining task with many potential applications. It has been studied from two perspectives—*white crow* and *in-disguise*. Anomalies classified as *white crow* are usually detected from nodes, edges or subgraphs, while *in-disguise* anomalies are now only identified from uncommon nodes or unusual patterns. These patterns can be entity alterations or substructures. A summary of the various research directions in this area is shown in Figure 11.21.

Research on *white crow* anomaly detection is mainly focused on exploring three different anomalies: anomalous nodes, edges, and subgraphs. To discover *anomalous nodes*, Moonesinghe and Tan [30] proposed a random walk–based approach that represents the dataset as a weighted, undirected graph. Similarly, a technique of random walk with restarts was used by Sun and Faloutsos [40] for relevance search in an unweighted bipartite graph, in which a vertex with a low normality score was treated as an anomaly. Hautamäki, Kärkkäinen, and Fräntiv [17] took a different approach and applied two density-based outlier detection methods to discover anomalous vertices in a *k-nearest neighbor* graph. To identify *unusual edges*, Chakrabarti [5] used the minimum descriptive length principle to group nodes and edges whose removal would best compress the graph were tagged as outliers. With the purpose of finding *abnormal subgraphs*, Noble and Cook [31] used a variant of the minimum descriptive length principle based on the SUBDUE system to identify both the anomalous substructures and subgraphs. In contrast to the

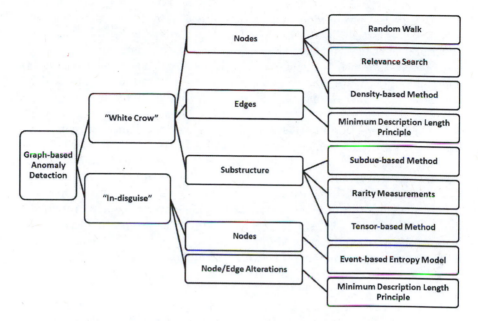

FIGURE 11.21: A summary of the various research directions in graph-based anomaly detection.

approach of Noble and Cook, Lin and Chalupsk [26] applied rarity measurements to discover *unusual linked entities* within a labeled, directed graph.

As for anomaly detection in multiple graphs, Cheng and Tan [10] provided a robust algorithm for discovery of anomalies in noisy multivariate time series data. To deal with higher-order data, the tensor-based approach discussed in our chapter was introduced by Sun, Tao, and Faloutsos [41]. Other related work on anomaly detection in multiple graphs can be found in papers written by Chan and Mahoney [6], Sun *et al.* [39], Keogh *et al.* [20], and others.

In-disguise anomalies are more difficult to detect because they are, by and large, concealed in the graph, but there are a variety of graph-based techniques proposed to detect this type of anomaly. Eberle and Holder [14] introduced the algorithms GBAD-MDL, GBAD-P, and GBAD-MPS for detecting three categories of anomalies that resemble normal behavior, including label modifications, vertex or edge insertions, and vertex or edge deletions. In addition, Shetty and Adibi [37] exploited an event-based entropy model that combines information theory with statistical techniques to discover hidden groups and prominent people in an Enron e-mail dataset. However, none of these works are focused on detecting *in-disguise* anomalies in *multiple graphs*. Recently, Chen *et al.* [9] proposed an efficient and effective algorithm for detecting community-based anomalies in evolutionary networks based on the proposed notion of graph representatives and community representatives.

Graph-based anomaly detection has been applied in many application areas. One of the most important of these areas is intrusion detection. One such system, GrIDS, is a graph-based intrusion detection system developed by Staniford-chen *et al.* [38]. Padmanabh *et al.* [32] introduced a random walk–based approach to detect outliers in wireless sensor networks. Eberle and Holder [13] focused on detecting anomalies in cargo shipments, and Noble and Cook [31] used anomaly detection techniques to discover credit card fraud.

Anomaly detection in other areas has a much longer history than graph-based anomaly detection. Related books in statistics have been written by Hawkins [18], Rousseeuw and Leroy [34], and Barnett and Lewis [3]. A general survey of anomaly detection is given by Beckman and Cook [4], as well as Chandola *et al.* [7]. An extensive survey of anomaly detection approaches from a machine learning perspective is provided by Hodge and Austin [19], and Agyemang *et al.* [1] survey different approaches from a numeric as well as symbolic data perspective. Markou and Singh [28, 29] provide an extensive review of statistical and neural network techniques for novelty detection, and Gould and Hadi [15] focus on finding outliers in multivariate data. Comparative evaluation of anomaly detection techniques for sequence data is given by Chandola, Banerjee, and Kumar [8]. While not discussed in this chapter, Shekhar *et al.* [35] introduce techniques for detecting spatial outliers. To read more about spatial outliers, see the related papers [24, 27, 33].

11.7 Exercises

1. Provide the adjacency matrix of graph G_1 in Figure 11.22. Using this information, calculate and fill in the "shared-neighbor" similarity matrix table in Table 11.10, where each cell in this matrix shows the number of shared neighbors between vertices. For example, the cell AB will contain the number of vertices adjacent to both A and B. Can you spot the anomaly by looking at this matrix? (Hint: To find the number of shared neighbors between vertices A and B, you can perform a dot product between the adjacency vectors of the vertices.)

2. (a) Using the MDL principle, compress graph G_2 in Figure 11.23 using the best one edge, two vertex substructure. Find the best one edge, two vertex substructure, and compress the resulting graph again to find the minimal graph representation. The frequency of the best substructure should be greater than one in both cases.

   (b) What is the description length of the new graph in terms of the number of vertices? Compare this result with the original

TABLE 11.10: "Shared-Neighbor" matrix for Question 1

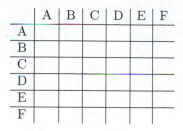

	A	B	C	D	E	F
A						
B						
C						
D						
E						
F						

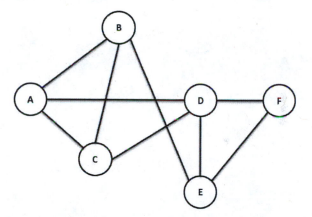

FIGURE 11.22: Graph G_1 for Question 1.

number of vertices.

(c) Using the definition that anomalies are occurrences different from the usual data, which nodes are anomalous in graph G_2?

3. The vector representations of four vertices are as follows:

$$a = \{0, 1\},$$
$$b = \{3, 4\},$$
$$c = \{1, 1\}, \text{ and}$$
$$d = \{3, 5\}.$$

Given that the formula to find cosine similarity between two vectors **x** and **y** is given by:

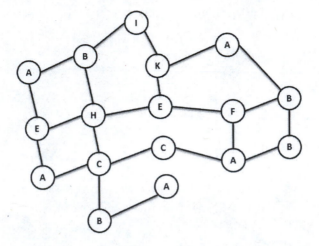

FIGURE 11.23: Graph G_2 for Question 2a.

$$cos(\mathbf{x}, \mathbf{y}) = \frac{\mathbf{x} \cdot \mathbf{y}}{\|\mathbf{x}\| \cdot \|\mathbf{y}\|},$$

calculate the cosine similarity matrix. Set the values of this matrix to be 0 on the diagonal, and discretize the matrix using a threshold value of 0.9. Draw the corresponding unweighted graph. What vertex looks most anomalous in this graph?

4. Let the values for vector $\mathbf{c}_{old}$, Markov transition matrix $\mathbf{S}$, and damping factor d be as follows:

$$\mathbf{c}_{old} = [1, 1, 2]$$

$$\mathbf{S} = \begin{bmatrix} 0 & 1 & 0 \\ 1 & 0 & 1 \\ 0 & 1 & 0 \end{bmatrix}$$

$$d = 0.25$$

Use the random walk Equation 11.11 to find the connectivity values for the vertices. Identify which of the three vertices represents an anomaly (the lowest ranked vertex).

$$\mathbf{c} = \begin{bmatrix} d/n \\ d/n \\ \vdots \\ d/n \end{bmatrix} + (1 - d) \cdot \mathbf{S}^{\mathbf{T}} \cdot \mathbf{c}_{old} \qquad (11.11)$$

5. Let the tensor $\chi_{[3\times4\times2]}$ be:

$$X_1 = \begin{bmatrix} 1 & 4 & 9 & 11 \\ 5 & 7 & 8 & 12 \\ 3 & 6 & 13 & 15 \end{bmatrix},$$

$$X_2 = \begin{bmatrix} 7 & 10 & 5 & 9 \\ 13 & 11 & 8 & 23 \\ 9 & 14 & 24 & 14 \end{bmatrix}$$

Unfold tensor $\chi_{[3\times4\times2]}$ into three mode-n matrices. Verify the result in R using the to.matrix.tensor function, available in the tensorA package.

6. Given the predictor time series X in Table 11.11, target time series Y in Table 11.12, and $\sigma = 1$, find the corresponding kernel matrices **KX** and **KY** and the weight parameters α_i. The eigenvector and eigenvalues of **KX** can be obtained using the eigen function available in the base package in R. Write a simple function in R to perform these calculations.

Find the kernel matrix using the equation:

$$\mathbf{K}(i,j) = \exp\left(-\left(\sum_{k=1}^{p}(x_{ik} - x_{jk})^2\right)/\sigma^2\right), \qquad (11.12)$$

and find the α_i values using the equation:

$$\alpha_i = \lambda_i + (\langle v_i v_i', \mathbf{KY}\rangle_F)/2, \qquad (11.13)$$

where $\langle \mathbf{A}, \mathbf{B}\rangle_F = \sum_{i,j} \mathbf{A}_{ij}\mathbf{B}_{ij}$ is the Frobenius product.

TABLE 11.11: The predictor time series X for Question 6, with variables a and b measured at times t_1, t_2, t_3, and t_4

	t_1	t_2	t_3	t_4
a	2	3	3	4
b	7	7	7	7.5

7. Apply GBAD-MDL, GBAD-P, and GBAD-MPS to graph G_3 in Figure 11.24. Using each algorithm, calculate the anomalous values and find the anomalies.

Note: For GBAD-MPS, find the best substructure with three nodes and two vertices.

TABLE 11.12: The target time series Y for Question 6, with variable c measured at times t_1, t_2, t_3, and t_4

	t_1	t_2	t_3	t_4
c	1	2	2	2

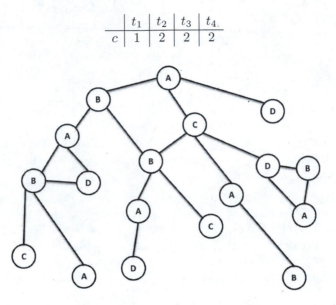

FIGURE 11.24: Graph G_3 for Question 7.

8. Let $\chi_{[3\times2\times2]}$ be given by:

$$X_1 = \begin{bmatrix} 3 & 6 \\ 4 & 7 \\ 5 & 8 \end{bmatrix},$$

$$X_2 = \begin{bmatrix} 9 & 12 \\ 10 & 13 \\ 11 & 14 \end{bmatrix},$$

and let

$$\mathbf{U}_1 = \begin{bmatrix} 1 & 3 & 5 \\ 2 & 4 & 6 \end{bmatrix},$$

$$\mathbf{U}_2 = \begin{bmatrix} 1 & 3 \\ 2 & 4 \end{bmatrix},$$

$$\mathbf{U}_3 = \begin{bmatrix} 5 & 8 \\ 6 & 9 \\ 7 & 10 \end{bmatrix}.$$

Calculate the tensor mode product $\chi \times_1 \mathbf{U}_1 \times_2 \mathbf{U}_2 \times_3 \mathbf{U}_3$ and verify your answer in R. (Hint: you can use the `mul.tensor` function available in the tensorA package.)

9. Compute the shared neighbor similarity matrix of graph G_4 in Figure 11.25. Use this adjacency matrix as input for the random walk algorithm for single graphs discussed in Section 11.2.2 to calculate the connectivity values and the corresponding rankings of the nodes. Start from line 4 in Algorithm 29. To calculate the connectivity values, use 3 iterations in place of the $\delta < \epsilon$ condition.

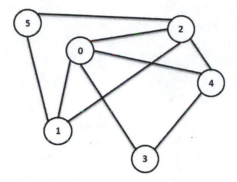

FIGURE 11.25: Graph G_4 for Question 9.

10. Let $\chi_{[2 \times 2 \times 2]}$ be:

$$X_1 = \begin{bmatrix} 9 & 10 \\ 11 & 12 \end{bmatrix},$$

$$X_2 = \begin{bmatrix} 3 & 5 \\ 6 & 7 \end{bmatrix}$$

Use the tensor decomposition algorithm to calculate the core tensor of χ and the projection matrices.

Bibliography

[1] M. Agyemang, K. Barker, and R. Alhajj. A comprehensive survey of numeric and symbolic outlier mining techniques. *Intelligent Data Analysis*, 10(6):521–538, 2006.

[2] A. Asuncion and D.J. Newman. KDD 1999 UCI machine learning repository, 2007.

[3] V. Barnett and T. Lewis. *Outliers in Statistical Data.* Wiley Series in Probability & Statistics. Wiley, West Sussex, England, 1994.

[4] R.J. Beckman and R.D. Cook. Outliers. *Technometrics,* 25(2):119–149, 1983.

[5] D. Chakrabarti. AutoPart: Parameter-free graph partitioning and outlier detection. In *Proceedings of the 8th European Conference on Principles and Practice of Knowledge Discovery in Databases,* pages 112–124, New York, NY, USA, 2004. Springer-Verlag New York, Inc.

[6] P.K. Chan and M.V. Mahoney. Modeling multiple time series for anomaly detection. In *Proceedings of the Fifth IEEE International Conference on Data Mining,* pages 90–97, Washington, DC, USA, 2005. IEEE Computer Society.

[7] V. Chandola, A. Banerjee, and V. Kumar. Anomaly detection: A survey. *ACM Computing Surveys,* 41(3):1–58, 2009.

[8] V. Chandola, V. Mithal, and V. Kumar. Comparative evaluation of anomaly detection techniques for sequence data. *Eighth IEEE International Conference on Data Mining,* pages 743–748, 2008.

[9] Z. Chen, K.A. Wilson, and *et al.* Detecting and tracking community dynamics in evolutionary networks. In *IEEE ICDM Workshop on Social Interactions Analysis and Services Providers,* pages 318–327, Washington, DC, USA, 2010. IEEE Computer Society.

[10] H. Cheng, P. Tan, C. Potter, and S. Klooster. A robust graph-based algorithm for detection and characterization of anomalies in noisy multivariate time series. In *IEEE International Conference on Data Mining Workshops,* pages 349–358, Washington, DC, USA, 2008. IEEE Computer Society.

[11] H. Cheng, P. Tan, C. Potter, and S.A. Klooster. Detection and characterization of anomalies in multivariate time series. In *SIAM International Conference on Data Mining,* pages 413–424, Philadelphia, PA, USA, 2009. SIAM.

[12] L. De Lathauwer. A survey of tensor methods. In *IEEE International Symposium on Circuits and Systems,* pages 2773–2776, Washington, DC, USA, 2009. IEEE Computer Society.

[13] W. Eberle and L. Holder. Detecting anomalies in cargo shipments using graph properties. In *Proceedings of the IEEE Intelligence and Security Informatics Conference,* New York, NY, USA, 2006. Springer.

[14] W. Eberle and L. Holder. Discovering structural anomalies in graph-based data. *Proceedings of the Seventh IEEE International Conference on Data Mining Workshops,* 393–398, 2007.

[15] W. Gould and A.S. Hadi. Identifying multivariate outliers. *Stata Technical Bulletin*, 2(11), 1993.

[16] K.K. Gupta, B. Nath, and R. Kotagiri. Layered approach using conditional random fields for intrusion detection. *IEEE Transactions on Dependable and Secure Computing*, 99(2), 5555.

[17] V. Hautamäki, I. Kärkkäinen, and P. Fränti. Outlier detection using k-Nearest neighbour graph. In *17th International Conference on Proceedings of the Pattern Recognition*, pages 430–433, Washington, DC, USA, 2004. IEEE Computer Society.

[18] D.M. Hawkins. *Identification of outliers*. Chapman and Hall, London, 1980.

[19] V.J. Hodge and J. Austin. A survey of outlier detection methodologies. *Artificial Intelligence Review*, 22:2004, 2004.

[20] E.J. Keogh, J. Lin, and A.W Fu. HOT SAX: Efficiently finding the most unusual time series subsequence. In *Fifth IEEE International Conference on Data Mining*, pages 226–233, Washington, DC, USA, 2005. IEEE Computer Society.

[21] N.S. Ketkar, L.B. Holder, and D.J. Cook. SUBDUE: compression-based frequent pattern discovery in graph data. In *OSDM '05: Proceedings of the 1st international workshop on open source data mining*, pages 71–76, New York, NY, USA, 2005. ACM.

[22] D. King and V. Vladimerou. Robust modeling of datasets with unbounded outliers. http://legend.me.uiuc.edu/~vladimer/projects/ece586ym/, 2009.

[23] T.G. Kolda and B.W. Bader. Tensor decompositions and applications. *SIAM Review*, 51(3):455–500, 2009.

[24] Y. Kou, C. Lu, and R.F. Dos Santos. Spatial Outlier Detection: A graph-based approach. In *19th IEEE International Conference on Tools with Artificial Intelligence*, pages 281–288, Washington, DC, USA, 2007. IEEE Computer Society.

[25] C. Kruegel and G. Vigna. Anomaly detection of web-based attacks. In *Proceedings of the 10th ACM conference on Computer and communications security*, pages 251–261. ACM Press, 2003.

[26] H. Chalupsky and S. Lin. Unsupervised link discovery in multi-relational data via rarity analysis. In *Proceedings of the Third IEEE International Conference on Data Mining*, pages 171–178, Washington, DC, USA, 2003. IEEE Computer Society.

[27] C. Lu, D. Chen, and Y. Kou. Multivariate spatial outlier detection. *International Journal on Artificial Intelligence Tools*, 13(4):801–812, 2004.

[28] M. Markou and S. Singh. Novelty detection: A Review—Part 1: statistical approaches. *Signal Processing*, 83(12):2481–2497, 2003.

[29] M. Markou and S. Singh. Novelty detection: A Review—Part 2: neural network based approaches. *Signal Processing*, 83(12):2499–2521, 2003.

[30] H.D.K. Moonesinghe and P. Tan. Outlier detection using random walks. In *18th IEEE International Conference on Tools with Artificial Intelligence*, pages 532–539, 2006.

[31] C.C. Noble and D.J. Cook. Graph-based anomaly detection. In *Proceedings of the ninth ACM SIGKDD International Conference on Knowledge Discovery and Data Mining*, pages 631–636, New York, NY, USA, 2003. ACM.

[32] K. Padmanabh, A. M. R. Vanteddu, S. Sen, and P. Gupta. Random walk on random graph based outlier detection in wireless sensor networks. In *3rd International Conference on Wireless Communication and Sensor Networks*, pages 45–49, Allahabad, India, 2007.

[33] F. Rasheed, P. Peng, R. Alhajj, and J.G. Rokne. Fourier transform based spatial outlier mining. In *Proceedings of the 10th International Conference on Intelligent Data Engineering and Automated Learning*, pages 317–324, Berlin, Heidelberg, 2009. Springer-Verlag.

[34] P.J. Rousseeuw and A.M. Leroy. *Robust Regression and Outlier Detection*. John Wiley & Sons, Inc., New York, NY, USA, 1987.

[35] S. Shekhar, C. Lu, and P. Zhang. Detecting graph-based spatial outliers. *Intelligent Data Analysis*, 6(5):451–468, 2002.

[36] P.H. Sherrod. Classes and types of variables. http://www.dtreg.com/vartype.htm, 2009.

[37] J. Shetty and J. Adibi. Discovering important nodes through graph entropy the case of Enron email database. In *Proceedings of the 3rd International Workshop on Link Discovery*, pages 74–81, New York, NY, USA, 2005. ACM.

[38] S. Staniford-chen, S. Cheung, and R. Crawford, *et al.* GrIDS: A graph based intrusion detection system for large networks. In *Proceedings of the 19th National Information Systems Security Conference*, pages 361–370, 1996.

[39] J. Sun, C. Faloutsos, S. Papadimitriou, and P.S. Yu. GraphScope: Parameter-free mining of large time-evolving graphs. In *Proceedings of the 13th ACM SIGKDD International Conference on Knowledge Discovery and Data Mining*, pages 687–696, New York, NY, USA, 2007. ACM.

[40] J. Sun, H. Qu, D. Chakrabarti, and C. Faloutsos. Neighborhood formation and anomaly detection in bipartite graphs. In *Proceedings of the Fifth IEEE International Conference on Data Mining*, pages 418–425, 2005.

[41] J. Sun, D. Tao, and C. Faloutsos. Beyond streams and graphs: Dynamic tensor analysis. In *Proceedings of the 12th ACM SIGKDD International Conference on Knowledge Discovery and Data Mining*, pages 374–383, New York, NY, USA, 2006. ACM.

[42] H. Tong, C. Faloutsos, and J. Pan. Fast random walk with restart and its applications. In *Proceedings of the IEEE International Conference on Data Mining*, pages 613–622, Washington, DC, USA, 2007. IEEE Computer Society.

[43] Princeton University. Princeton university "about wordnet." wordnet. <http://wordnet.princeton.edu>, 2009.

[44] Z. Yang, J. Tang, J. Zhang, J. Li, and B. Gao. Random walk through probabilistic model. In *Proceedings of the Joint International Conferences on Advances in Data and Web Management*, pages 162–173, Berlin, Heidelberg, 2009. Springer-Verlag.

[45] E. Zivot and J. Wang. *Modeling Financial Time Series with S-PLUS*. Springer-Verlag New York, Inc., New York, NY, USA, 2006.

[46] William Eberle, Lawrence B. Holder, Mining for Structural Anomalies in Graph-based Data, Internal Conference on Data Mining, 2007, 376–389.

12

Performance Metrics for Graph Mining Tasks

Kanchana Padmanabhan and John Jenkins

North Carolina State University

CONTENTS

12.1   Introduction

So far, we have detailed, discussed, and analyzed algorithms for several data mining tasks, with a focus on graphic data. Given a set of data and some mining goal (e.g. classification, clustering, etc.), we have a good idea of which algorithms to apply in order to analyze the data. However, this is only one half of the battle. The other half lies in understanding, (1) if the model or algorithm applied is (in)appropriate for the task at hand, and (2) if the model or algorithm produces usable results in the context of the problem. To help differentiate these outcomes, there are a number of well-established *performance metrics* which standardize evaluative criteria.

The task of performance measurement, unlike other areas of data mining, does not help analyze the data or the results directly. Instead, the metrics help analyze how the model or algorithm performed its intended task on the data. For example, if a model was built to perform a classification task, i.e., assign class labels to the data, performance metrics could be used to quantify various measures of model prediction accuracy.

The metrics discussed in this chapter can analyze the results of data mining models and algorithms applied to both vector and graph data. Thus, in this chapter we will utilize the generic term *points* to denote input data to a mining model or algorithm.

12.2   Supervised Learning Performance Metrics

When incorporating the use of performance metrics to evaluate supervised learning techniques (e.g. classification) on a data set, the learning process undergoes two phases before it is ready to be used to make predictions on data with unknown class labels. The first phase is called the *training phase*, where the model uses a set of data with known class labels to learn the properties of the data belonging to different classes. The second phase is called the *testing phase* where the model is used to predict the class label of a separate set of points with known class labels, to measure various forms of accuracy. To facilitate these two phases, the set of data with known class labels is partitioned into a *training set* and *test set*, respectively. The testing phase gives us an idea of how the model will work on data with unknown class labels, provided the input dataset is somewhat representative of the data to be classified. Various strategies are used for partitioning the data into test and training sets, which

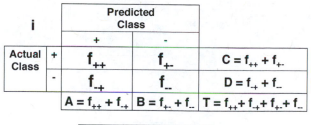

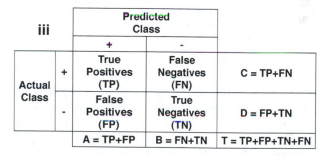

FIGURE 12.1: 2×2 confusion matrix template for model M. A number of terms are used for the entry values, which are shown in i, ii, and iii. In our text we refer to the representation in Figure i.

are discussed in Section 12.2.5. The model is typically considered to be good if most predictions made during the testing phase match the testing set's class labels. As in most data mining tasks, "most" is quantified by a threshold, based on the application domain, prior knowledge, or statistical techniques.

12.2.1 Confusion Matrices for Binary Classification

12.2.2 2×2 Confusion Matrix

Definition 12.1 *Confusion matrix [27]*
An $n \times n$ matrix, where n is the number of classes and entry (i, j) represents the number of elements with class label i, but predicted to have class label j.

Confusion matrices provide a visually appealing organization of classification

(1) Vertex ID	Actual Class	Predicted Class
1	+	+
2	+	+
3	+	+
4	+	+
5	+	-
6	-	+
7	-	+
8	-	-

(2)		Predicted Class		
		+	-	
Actual	+	4	1	C = 5
Class	-	2	1	D = 3
		A = 6	B = 2	T = 8

FIGURE 12.2: Example of a 2 × 2 confusion matrix.

results on the test set, allowing us to make a large number of observations about the model's effectiveness. A particularly important confusion matrix that we will describe in detail is the 2 × 2 matrix, describing binary classification results. The 2 × 2 matrix is shown in Figure 12.1. For simplicity, we refer to the two classes as *positive* (+) and *negative* (−). For example, if the data mining task given is to build a model to predict if the tissue sample is cancerous or not, then a cancerous tissue sample will belong to the positive class and a normal tissue sample will belong to the negative class. The four main entries of the 2 × 2 confusion matrix are described as follows:

- f_{++} or *True Positives* or *Hits* is the set of all data whose actual class and predicted class label are both +.

- f_{+-} or *False Negatives* or *Misses* is the set of all data whose actual class is + but predicted class label is −.

- f_{-+} or *False Positives* or *False Alarms* is the set of all data whose actual class is − but predicted class label is +.

- f_{--} or *True Negatives* or *Correct Rejections* is the set of all data whose actual class and predicted class label are both −.

Based on the confusion matrix, several performance metrics can be derived. This section will discuss those measures and show sample calculations using the example in Figure 12.2. Figure 12.2(1) shows the predictions of a model M when classifying the nodes of a graph $G = (V, E)$ where $|V| = 8$. Figure 12.2(2) summarizes the performance using a 2 × 2 confusion matrix.

12.2.2.1 Basic Metrics

Accuracy

Accuracy (a) [42, 19] is simply the proportion of correct predictions:

$$a = \frac{f_{++} + f_{--}}{T} \tag{12.1}$$

Accuracy measures the extent to which the model got its predictions right. An ideal model would have an accuracy of 1, i.e., actual and predicted values match on every count. The accuracy calculated using the confusion matrix in Figure 12.2 is:

$$\begin{aligned} a &= \frac{4+1}{8}, \\ &= 0.63 \end{aligned}$$

Error Rate

Error rate (ER) [42] is the converse of accuracy: the proportion of incorrect predictions. The error rate is measured as follows:

$$ER = \frac{f_{+-} + f_{-+}}{T} \tag{12.2}$$

Error rate measures the extent to which the model got its predictions wrong. An ideal model would have an error rate of 0, which means that the model has not made any incorrect predictions. The error rate calculated using the confusion matrix in Figure 12.2 is:

$$\begin{aligned} ER &= \frac{2+1}{8}, \\ &= 0.38 \end{aligned}$$

12.2.2.2 Class-specific metrics

The metrics discussed in the following section describe metrics that quantify a model's performance with respect to a specific class as opposed to a model's overall performance.

Recall

Recall is the number of input instances per class whose class label is correctly predicted by the model M. Recall quantifies the notion of *sensitivity*: How many datapoints that belong to a certain class were also predicted to belong the same class? This can take any value between 0 and 1, we ideally want it to be closer to 1. There are two specific recall measures defined for a 2×2 matrix.

True Positive Rate

The *true positive rate* (*TPR*) [42, 19], or *positive recall*, is the proportion of points predicted as positive that are correct:

$$TPR = \frac{f_{++}}{f_{++} + f_{+-}} \qquad (12.3)$$

In other words, it is the fraction of all input instances belonging to the + class that were correctly predicted to belong to the + class by model M. The true positive rate calculated using the example confusion matrix in Figure 12.2 is:

$$
\begin{aligned}
TPR &= \frac{4}{5}, \\
&= 0.80
\end{aligned}
$$

True Negative Rate

The *true negative rate* (*TNR*) [42, 19], or *negative recall*, is similarly the proportion of points predicted as negative that are correct:

$$TNR = \frac{f_{--}}{f_{-+} + f_{--}} \qquad (12.4)$$

In other words, it is the fraction of all the instances belonging to the − class that were correctly predicted to belong to the − class by M. The true negative rate calculated using the example confusion matrix in Figure 12.2 is:

$$
\begin{aligned}
TNR &= \frac{1}{3}, \\
&= 0.33
\end{aligned}
$$

Misclassification Rate

Misclassification rate is analogous to recall, being the proportion of input instances whose class label is predicted incorrectly. Ideally, we want it to be closer to 0.

False Positive Rate

The *false positive rate* (*FPR*) [42, 19] is the proportion of predicted negative values that are actually negative:

$$FPR = \frac{f_{-+}}{f_{-+} + f_{--}} \qquad (12.5)$$

In other words, it is the fraction of all the instances belonging to the − class that were misclassified as +. The false positive rate calculated using the example confusion matrix in Figure 12.2 is:

$$
\begin{aligned}
FPR &= \frac{2}{3}, \\
&= 0.67
\end{aligned}
$$

False Negative Rate

Similarly, the *false negative* (*FNR*) [42, 19] is the proportion of predicted positive values that are actually negative:

$$FNR = \frac{f_{+-}}{f_{+-} + f_{++}} \tag{12.6}$$

In other words, it is the fraction of all the instances belonging to the $+$ class that were misclassified as $-$ by M. The false negative rate calculated using the example confusion matrix in Figure 12.2 is:

$$\begin{aligned} FNR &= \frac{1}{5}, \\ &= 0.20 \end{aligned}$$

Precision

The *precision* (*P*) [42, 19] of class Y ($Y = +$ or $Y = -$) is the proportion of points classified as Y that are actually Y:

$$P^+ = \frac{f_{++}}{f_{-+} + f_{++}}, \tag{12.7}$$

$$P^- = \frac{f_{--}}{f_{+-} + f_{--}} \tag{12.8}$$

It quantifies the notion of *specificity*; How many of the points predicted as a certain class actually belong there? The precision for a positive class and a negative class calculated using the example confusion matrix in Figure 12.2 is, respectively, as follows:

$$\begin{aligned} P^+ &= \frac{4}{4+2}, \\ &= 0.67, \\ P^- &= \frac{1}{1+1}, \\ &= 0.5 \end{aligned}$$

Advanced Metrics

F-measure

F-measure (*F*) [30, 35] is the harmonic mean of precision and recall values of a class and provides a way to judge the overall performance of the model for each class. Harmonic mean is one of the Pythagorean means (along with geometric and arithmetic) and is not affected by outliers, unlike the arithmetic mean. The F-measure has a value close to 1 only when both the precision and recall are both close to 1.

$$F^+ = \frac{2 \times P^+ \times TPR}{P^+ + TPR}, \tag{12.9}$$

$$F^- = \frac{2 \times P^- \times TNR}{P^- + TNR} \tag{12.10}$$

The F-measure calculated using the example confusion matrix in Figure 12.2 is:

$$F^+ = \frac{2 \times \frac{2}{3} \times \frac{4}{5}}{\frac{2}{3} + \frac{4}{5}},$$

$$= 0.73,$$

$$F^- = \frac{2 \times \frac{1}{2} \times \frac{1}{3}}{\frac{1}{2} + \frac{1}{3}},$$

$$= 0.40$$

G-mean

The G-mean [29, 40] is the geometric mean of the positive (TPR) and negative (TNR) recall values of the two classes.

$$G\text{-mean} = \sqrt{TPR \times TNR} \tag{12.11}$$

This metric provides a way to judge the overall performance of the model because it provides equal representation for all classes. It is also a better way to quantify the performance of the model because it is less prone to the effects of the underlying class distribution of the input dataset unlike other measures like accuracy. For example, consider a dataset with 100 points, 95 of which have a positive class label and the remaining 5 have a negative class label. Predicting all points as positive will result in an accuracy value of $A = 0.95$, but in reality the model has completely missed predicting the negative class. However, the G-mean value will account for this because the TPR and TNR of the model are 1 and 0, respectively, leading to a G-mean of 0.

The G-mean calculated for the confusion matrix in Figure 12.2 is:

$$G\text{-mean} = \sqrt{\frac{4}{5} \times \frac{1}{3}},$$

$$= 0.52$$

The implementation of these measures is available as part of the Performance-Metrics package.

```
1 library(PerformanceMetrics)
2 data(M)
3 M
4      [,1] [,2]
```

```
5 [1,]    4    1
6 [2,]    2    1


7 twoCrossConfusionMatrixMetrics(M)
8 $Accuracy
9 [1] 0.625


10 $'Error Rate'
11 [1] 0.375


12 $'True Positive Rate'
13 [1] 0.8


14 $'True Negative Rate'
15 [1] 0.3333333


16 $'False Positive Rate'
17 [1] 0.6666667


18 $'False Negative Rate'
19 [1] 0.2


20 $'Precision+'
21 [1] 0.6666667


22 $'Precision'
23 [1] 0.5


24 $'F-measure+'
25 [1] 0.7272727


26 $'F-measure-'
27 [1] 0.4


28 $'G-Mean'
29 [1] 0.5163978
```

12.2.3 Multi-level Confusion Matrix

Performance metrics on 2×2 confusion matrices is an important subset for classifier evaluation, but many data mining applications work with more than two classes. For example, the cancer dataset can have three labels: two signifying two types of cancer such as acute myeloid leukemia (AML) and acute

Multi-level Confusion Matrix		Predicted Class				Marginal Sum of Actual Values
		Class 1	Class 2	----	Class N	
Actual Class	Class 1	f_{11}	f_{12}	----	f_{1N}	$\sum_{j=1}^{N} f_{1j}$
	Class 2	f_{21}	f_{22}	----	f_{2N}	$\sum_{j=1}^{N} f_{2j}$
	⋮	⋮	⋮	---	⋮	⋮
	Class N	f_{N1}	f_{N2}	----	f_{NN}	$\sum_{j=1}^{N} f_{Nj}$
Marginal Sum of Predictions		$\sum_{i=1}^{N} f_{i1}$	$\sum_{i=1}^{N} f_{i2}$	----	$\sum_{i=1}^{N} f_{iN}$	$T = \sum_{i=1}^{N} \sum_{j=1}^{N} f_{ij}$

FIGURE 12.3: Multi-level confusion matrix template.

		Predicted Class			Marginal Sum of Actual Values
		Class 1	Class 2	Class 3	
Actual Class	Class 1	2	1	1	4
	Class 2	1	2	1	4
	Class 3	1	2	3	6
Marginal Sum of Predictions		4	5	5	T = 14

FIGURE 12.4: Example of a 3×3 confusion matrix.

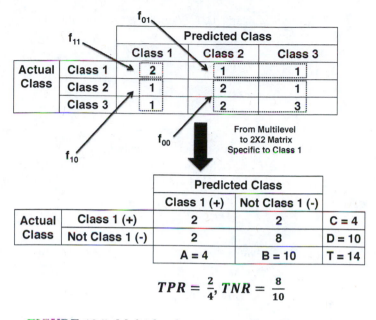

$$TPR = \frac{2}{4}, \, TNR = \frac{8}{10}$$

FIGURE 12.5: Multi-level matrix to a 2×2 conversion.

lymphoblastic leukemia (ALL), and one signifying normal tissue. In such cases, the model requires a *multi-level confusion matrix* [47, 1, 45] (see Figure 12.3).

Many of the measures discussed in the 2×2 confusion matrix, such as accuracy and *G*-mean, can be extended for confusion matrices of an arbitrary number of classes. We can also collapse the multi-level table into a 2×2 matrix for each particular class to compute other measures, such as the number of true "positives." Figure 12.5 provides an example of how to convert a multi-level matrix into a class-specific 2×2 matrix.

However, since problems utilizing multiple classes are prevalent in several application domains, such as biology and climate, measures have been developed that can be calculated for any multi-level matrix. The following measures and examples will be based on the example in Figure 12.4.

Critical Success Index

The critical success index (CSI) [45, 15], also called the *threat score*, is the proportion of the correct predictions of class L of the sum of all predicted values of L and all values of L not correctly predicted.

$$CSI^L = \frac{f_{LL}}{\sum_{i=L \text{ or } j=L} f_{ij}} \tag{12.12}$$

The CSI^{Class1} calculated using the example confusion matrix example in Figure 12.4 is:

$$CSI^{Class1} = \frac{2}{6},$$
$$= 0.33$$

Hit Rate

The hit rate (HR) [26, 45], also called the probability of detection, is the success rate of each class L. It is the ratio of the correctly predicted instances of class L to all points with class label L. This is a generalized version of the recall.

$$HR^L = \frac{f_{LL}}{\sum f_{Lj}} \qquad (12.13)$$

The HR^{Class1} calculated using the example confusion matrix in Figure 12.4 is:

$$HR^{Class1} = \frac{2}{4},$$
$$= 0.50$$

Bias

The bias (ϕ) measure [26] helps us understand whether the model is over-predicting or under-predicting a particular class. For each class L, it is the ratio of the total points with class label L to the number of points predicted as L.

$$\phi^L = \frac{\sum f_{Lj}}{\sum f_{iL}} \qquad (12.14)$$

Model under-prediction with respect to L corresponds to $\phi^L > 1$, while model over-prediction corresponds to $\phi^L < 1$. ϕ^{Class1} is:

$$\phi^{Class2} = \frac{4}{5},$$
$$= 0.8$$

The model M_2 is under-predicting $Class2$.

Mean Absolute Error

Mean Absolute Error (MAE) [24] is the average absolute difference between expected and observed values over all classes. The diagonal multi-level matrix represents the observed values for each class. The expected value is perfect classification (see Figure 12.6), where all values except the diagonal values are zero. If q_{ii} from Figure 12.6 represents the expected values for each class i and

Expected Confusion Matrix		Predicted Class			
		Class 1	Class 2	----	Class N
Actual Class	Class 1	q_{11}	0	----	0
	Class 2	0	q_{22}	----	0
	⋮	⋮	⋮	---	⋮
	Class N	0	0		q_{NN}

FIGURE 12.6: Expected confusion matrix.

Expected Confusion Matrix		Predicted Class		
		Class 1	Class 2	Class 3
Actual Class	Class 1	4	0	0
	Class 2	0	4	0
	Class 3	0	0	6

Observed Confusion Matrix		Predicted Class		
		Class 1	Class 2	Class 3
Actual Class	Class 1	2	1	1
	Class 2	1	2	1
	Class 3	1	2	3

FIGURE 12.7: An example of expected and observed confusion matrices.

f_{ii} from Figure 12.3 represents the observed value for each class i and N is the total number of classes, then the formula for MAE is given as follows:

$$MAE = \frac{1}{N} \sum_{i=1}^{N} |f_{ii} - q_{ii}| \qquad (12.15)$$

The MAE calculated using the example confusion matrix in Figure 12.7 is:

$$MAE = \frac{2+2+3}{14},$$
$$= 0.5$$

Skill Metric

The *skill metric*, as the name suggests, measures the skill or ability of a model to make correct predictions. It takes into consideration the probability of correct predictions by the model and the probability of correct predictions that could have occurred by chance, or in other words, by randomly selecting a class [46]. The concept of chance is necessary because it is important to know if the agreement between the actual and predicted value occurred due to a model's conscious decision or due to a random guess. The parameter that denotes random chance is also called the *probability of random agreement*. The term stems from the fact that the actual values and the model predictions are considered two judges, and the chance parameter quantifies the probability that the two judges placed the same point in the same class (reached an agreement) for different unrelated reasons.

Gilbert Skill Score

The *Gilbert Skill Score* (*GSS*) [45, 15], also called the equitable threat score, is similar to CSI but includes the parameter to quantify random chance. The parameter is called *chance* ($e(\omega)$) and is the product of the frequency of class prediction by the model and the number of input instances that belong to the class. The score is calculated per class. For a 2×2 matrix, it is defined as follows:

$$GSS^{L} = \frac{f_{LL} - e(\omega)}{\left(\sum_{i=\text{L or } j=\text{L}} f_{ij} \right) - e(\omega)}, \qquad (12.16)$$

$$e(\omega) = \frac{A}{T} \times C \qquad (12.17)$$

where A, C, and T are defined in Figure 12.2.

The generalized version of $e(\omega)$ that can be applied for multi-level matrices is defined as follows:

$$e(\omega) = \frac{\sum_{j=1}^{N} f_{Lj}}{T} \times \sum_{i=1}^{N} f_{iL} \qquad (12.18)$$

GSS^{Class1} of the confusion matrix example in Figure 12.4 is calculated as follows:

$$
\begin{aligned}
e(\omega) &= \frac{16}{14}, \\
&= \frac{8}{7}, \\
GSS^{Class1} &= \frac{2 - \frac{8}{7}}{6 - \frac{8}{7}}, \\
&= 0.18
\end{aligned}
$$

Pi Statistic

The Pi (π) statistic [37] takes into consideration agreements between actual and predicted classes over all classes. For a 2×2 matrix, it is calculated as follows:

$$
\pi = \frac{Agree - e(\pi)}{1 - e(\pi)}, \tag{12.19}
$$

$$
e(\pi) = \left(\frac{(A+C)}{2T}\right)^2 + \left(\frac{(B+D)}{2T}\right)^2 \tag{12.20}
$$

where A, B, C, D, and T are defined in Figure 12.2.

Agree is the proportion of times the actual and predicted values agree, or simply *Accuracy*. $e(\pi)$ represents the chance parameter. $e(\pi)$ is calculated by squaring and summing the joint proportion for each class. The *joint proportion* of each class is the sum of the marginal sum of the actual and predicted values divided by twice the total number of input instances, which denotes the two dimensions of the multi-level table (actual and predicted). The $e(\pi)$ uses an additive term to account for the collective distribution of classes across the model predictions and actual values.

The reason for including the number of dimensions in the $e(\pi)$ calculation is that π can generalize to comparing more than two dimensions as well; for example, predictions made by three models can be tabulated in a multi-level, 3-dimensional matrix. When calculating the $e(\pi)$ for this matrix, the T in the denominator is multiplied by 3.

The π of the confusion matrix example in Figure 12.2 is calculated as follows:

$$
\begin{aligned}
e(\pi) &= \left(\frac{(6+5)}{2 \times 8}\right)^2 + \left(\frac{(3+2)}{2 \times 8}\right)^2, \\
&= 0.57, \\
\pi &= \frac{0.63 - 0.57}{1 - 0.57}, \\
&= 0.14
\end{aligned}
$$

The generalized version of the $e(\pi)$ that can be applied for multi-level matrices is defined as follows:

$$e(\pi) \;=\; \sum_{k=1}^{N} \left(\frac{\sum_{j=1}^{N} f_{kj} + \sum_{i=1}^{N} f_{ik}}{2T} \right)^{2} \tag{12.21}$$

Heidke Skill Score (κ Statistic)

Cohen's Kappa (κ) statistic [5], also called the Heidke Skill Score (HSS) [20], was derived from the π statistic but the expected agreement by chance uses a multiplicative term as opposed to an additive. The multiplicative term helps account for the distribution of classes for both the actual values and model predictions. The denominator of $e(\kappa)$ does not include the dimension parameter because $e(\kappa)$ is meant for use only in a two-dimensional multi-level matrix. The κ or HSS for a 2×2 matrix is calculated as follows (see Figure 12.2 for the definition of A, B, C, D, T):

$$e(\kappa) \;=\; \frac{(A * C) + (D * B)}{T^2}, \tag{12.22}$$

$$\kappa \;=\; \frac{P_{agree} - e(\kappa)}{1 - e(\kappa)} \tag{12.23}$$

P_{agree} here is simply $(f_{--} + f_{++})/T$. The κ of the confusion matrix example in Figure 12.2 is calculated as follows:

$$\begin{aligned}
e(\kappa) &= 0.5625, \\
\kappa &= \frac{0.625 - 0.0.5625}{1 - 0.5625}, \\
\kappa &= 0.143
\end{aligned}$$

The generalized version of κ that can be applied for multi-level matrices is defined as follows. Let ac_i denote that the actual class label is i and pc_i denote that the predicted class label is i:

$$\kappa \;=\; \frac{\sum \rho(ac_i, pc_i) - \sum \rho(ac_i)\rho(pc_i)}{1 - \sum \rho(ac_i)\rho(pc_i)}, \tag{12.24}$$

$$\rho(ac_i, pc_i) \;=\; \frac{f_{ii}}{T}, \tag{12.25}$$

$$\rho(ac_i) \;=\; \frac{\sum f_{ij}}{T}, \tag{12.26}$$

$$\rho(pc_i) \;=\; \frac{\sum f_{ji}}{T} \tag{12.27}$$

A score of 1 means that the model is 100% accurate, while a score of 0 means that the model's predictions are completely random. A negative value means that the model's predictions are worse than those occurring at random.

The HSS or κ score of the confusion matrix example in Figure 12.4 is calculated as follows.

$$\kappa = \frac{(\frac{2}{14} + \frac{2}{14} + \frac{3}{14}) - (\frac{4}{14} \times \frac{4}{14} + \frac{4}{14} \times \frac{5}{14} + \frac{6}{14} \times \frac{5}{14})}{1 - (\frac{4}{14} \times \frac{4}{14} + \frac{4}{14} \times \frac{5}{14} + \frac{6}{14} \times \frac{5}{14})},$$

$$\kappa = 0.3$$

Alpha-Reliability

The alpha reliability (α) [28, 6] metric is also called the "gold standard" of skill measurements [43]. Unlike the earlier measures, it takes into consideration the amount of disagreement that occurred between the actual and predicted values (D_o) (Error rate) versus a disagreement that could have occurred due to chance (D_e). α for a 2×2 matrix is calculated as follows, where ER represents the error rate:

$$\alpha = 1 - \left(\frac{ER}{e(\alpha)} \right), \tag{12.28}$$

$$e(\alpha) = \frac{(A * C) + (D * B)}{T^2} \tag{12.29}$$

$e(\alpha)$ represents the agreement/disagreement that occurred due to chance and utilizes the same parameter as κ. $\alpha = 1$ means that the model has perfect reliability. A value of 0 indicates a random model, i.e., all the predictions that occurred were due to chance. A value of -1 indicates that disagreements that occurred are worse than those occurred by chance.

α of the confusion matrix example in Figure 12.2 is calculated as follows:

$$\alpha = 1 - \left(8 \times \frac{2+1}{(5 \times 6) + (2 \times 3)} \right),$$

$$= 1 - \left(8 \times \frac{3}{36} \right),$$

$$= 0.33$$

$e(\alpha)$, applied for multi-level matrices, is defined as follows:

$$ER = \frac{\sum_{i \neq j} f_{ij}}{T}, \tag{12.30}$$

$$e(\alpha) = \sum_{k=1}^{N} \frac{\sum_{j=1}^{N} f_{kj} \sum_{i=1}^{N} f_{ik}}{T} \tag{12.31}$$

It has been shown through various experiments and theory that a reasonable maximum value for probability by chance is 0.5 but the statistics described so far can produce probability by chance values in the range of 0 to 1 [16]. To correct for this fact, Gwet [17] introduced a new method to calculate the probability by chance. It is called $e(\gamma)$ and was defined as follows:

$$e(\gamma) \quad = \quad \beta_1(1-\beta_1) + \beta_2(1-\beta_2), \tag{12.32}$$

$$\beta_1 \quad = \quad \frac{C+A}{2 \times T}, \tag{12.33}$$

$$\beta_2 \quad = \quad \frac{B+D}{2 \times T} \tag{12.34}$$

Due to the way the confusion matrix table is constructed, we find that $\beta_1 = 1 - \beta_2$. Hence, the equation can also be rewritten as

$$e(\gamma) = 2 \times \beta_1(1-\beta_1) \tag{12.35}$$

$e(\gamma)$ of the confusion matrix in Figure 12.2 is calculated as follows:

$$\beta_1 \quad = \quad \frac{6+5}{2 \times 8},$$
$$e(\gamma) \quad = \quad 2 \times 0.69(1 - 0.69)$$
$$= \quad 0.43$$

The R implementation of these metrics is available in the PerformanceMetrics package.

```
1 library(PerformanceMetrics)
2 data(MultiLevelM)
3 MultiLevelM
4      [,1] [,2] [,3]
5 [1,]   2    1    1
6 [2,]   1    2    1
7 [3,]   1    2    3
8 multilevelConfusionMatrixMetrics(MultiLevelM)
9 $'Critical Success Index'
10 [1] 0.3333333 0.2857143 0.3750000

11 $'Hit Rate'
12 [1] 0.7142857 0.6428571 0.6428571

13 $Bias
14 [1] 1.0 0.8 1.2

15 $'Mean Absolute Error'
16 [1] 0.5

17 $'Gilbert Skill Score'
18 [1] 0.1764706 0.1025641 0.1463415

19 $'Pi Statistic'
```

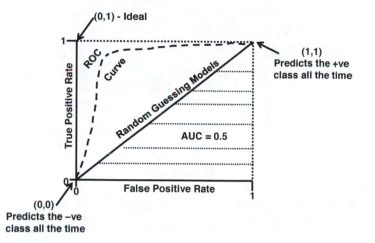

FIGURE 12.8: ROC space and curve.

```
20 [1] 0.2432432

21 $'Heidke Skill Score (kappa)'
22 [1] 0.2461538

23 $'Alpha Reliability'
24 [1] -0.4848485
```

12.2.4 Visual Metrics

Receiver Operating Characteristics

Receiver Operating Characteristics [45, 10, 42, 19, 9] (see Figure 12.8) was part of a field called "Signal Detection Theory" developed during World War II for the analysis of radar images. Radar operators had to decide whether a blip on the screen represented an enemy target, a friendly ship, or just noise. Signal detection theory measures the ability of radar receiver operators to make these important distinctions. It was adapted to judge the performance of models that perform predictive data mining.

12.2.4.1 ROC Space

Points in ROC space are built by plotting the *false positive rate* (FPR) along the horizontal axis and *true positive rate* (TPR) along the vertical axis (the true negative and false negative rates can similarly be plotted). *ROC space* is the region constrained by the four points $\{(0,0), (0,1), (1,0), (1,1)\}$, corresponding to the minimum and maximum values of both FPR and TPR. We

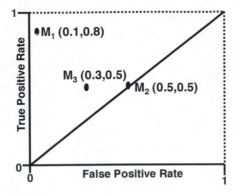

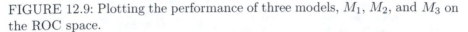

FIGURE 12.9: Plotting the performance of three models, M_1, M_2, and M_3 on the ROC space.

can judge the performance of multiple models by plotting their (FPR, TPR) values on the ROC space. The point $(0,0)$ represents a model that places all the points in the *negative class*, while point $(1,1)$ represents a model that places all the points in the *positive class*. The point $(0,1)$ denotes the ideal scenario of perfect classification. We typically want the model to lie in the upper left region of the space.

Models with (FPR, TPR) in the lower left side region of the ROC space can be termed *conservative* with respect to the positive class. The model's FP rate is low, so it makes very few mistakes but also has a low TP rate, i.e, the model does not place a datum in the positive class unless there is strong evidence. On the other hand, models with (FPR, TPR) in the upper right-hand region can be termed *liberal* with respect to the positive class. They assign more points to the *positive* class but also make a large number of misclassifications.

The line $TPR = FPR$, the diagonal across the ROC space, is termed as the *random guessing* line [10]. The model whose (FPR, TPR) lies along this line is termed to be making completely random predictions [11]. For example, a model that predicts the positive class 50% of the time has an (FPR, TPR) value of $(0.5, 0.5)$ [10]. Similarly, if the model predicts the positive class 80% percent of the time, the TPR is 0.8 but its FPR is also 0.8.

The models whose (FPR, TPR) lie below the diagonal are said to be performing worse than random. However, the ROC space separated by the diagonal is symmetric, that is, an (FPR, TPR) pair that lies below the diagonal can be negated to result in a model with an (FPR, TPR) point above the diagonal. On negation, the FPR of the original model becomes the TNR of the negated model and the TPR of the original model becomes the FNR of the negated model. The models with the (FPR, TPR) values below the diagonal are said to have learned the properties of the data correctly but are not applying them right [12].

The ROC can also be used for comparing different models that are trained and tested using the same dataset. The model whose (FPR, TPR) point is the furthest in the upper-right direction [11] is chosen. Figure 12.9 shows a ROC space with the performance of three models M_1, M_2, and M_3 on the same data plotted. We see M_1's performance occurs furthest in the upper-right direction and hence is considered the best model.

12.2.4.2 ROC Curve

There are typically two kinds of predictive models: the discrete and probabilistic. Discrete models only provide a prediction as output and the entire set of predictions can be utilized to build a confusion matrix and arrive at a single (FPR, TPR) point. The second kind provide a probability (or confidence) value as output. These models are called *probabilistic, ranking*, or *scoring classifiers*. These models can be made discrete by using a threshold of τ and considering all points with *probability* values greater than τ to belong to the positive class and the rest assigned to the negative class. This threshold τ can be varied and for each threshold we obtain a confusion matrix and thereby an (FPR, TPR) point. The set of all (FPR, TPR) points can be plotted in ROC space, and a curve is constructed using those points.

12.2.4.3 Area under the Curve

The *area under curve (AUC)* [10, 9, 42] provides a scalar value that quantifies the ROC curve. The total area in the ROC space is 1. The area under the diagonal is exactly half that space, or 0.5. We do not want the performance of any model to be less than or equal to 0.5. We can compare two predictive models by comparing the AUC values obtained on the same dataset. The model with the larger AUC is considered the better predictor.

12.2.5 Cross-validation

Cross-validation [42, 7, 47], also called rotation estimation, is a way to analyze how a predictive data mining model will perform on an unknown dataset, i.e., how well the model generalizes. One iteration of cross-validation involves dividing the data with known class labels into two non-intersecting subsets called the *training* and *validation*, or *test*, data. The training data is then utilized to build the model and the validation data is utilized to analyze the model performance.

With the *holdout* [42, 47] method, a random subset of the data, typically two-thirds of the dataset, is utilized for training, with the remaining used for testing. Then, a single round of cross-validation is performed. However, in order to avoid bias, cross-validation is performed over multiple rounds and performance metrics for each round are averaged to get the performance of the model.

There are several strategies utilized to perform this iterative cross-validation. *k-fold* validation method [42], the most common, is performed by splitting the data into k equal subsets, using $(k-1)$ sets for training and one set for testing. It is repeated until all the k subsets have had a chance to be the validation set.

A special kind of the k-fold validation is the *leave-one-out* method [42]. In this case, one single point is used for testing and the rest for training, and it is repeated until all the points have been part of the test set. It is equivalent to 1-fold validation.

Random subsampling [42] is performed by randomly splitting the data into training and test datasets. The advantage of random subsampling is that unlike k-fold cross-validation, the ratio of training to test set is not dependent on the number of iterations.

12.3   Unsupervised Learning Performance Metrics

Unsupervised learning techniques (e.g., clustering) are utilized to divide the input points into groups that share some common property. The resulting groups, also called clusters, are analyzed to quantify the overall performance of the unsupervised learning method U. The set of all clusters is denoted as $G = \{g_1, g_2, \ldots, g_W\}$ and the total number of clusters is denoted as $W = |G|$.

There are two kinds of evaluation that can take place: (1) evaluation using *prior* knowledge and (2) evaluation purely on the basis of the resulting clusters and their attributes without external knowledge. Sometimes a third evaluation can be added where a comparative analysis can be performed between two clustering algorithms, but those methods typically use metrics from the former two categories and, hence, are not discussed in a separate section.

12.3.1   Evaluation Using Prior Knowledge

One example of using *prior* knowledge to test the effectiveness of unsupervised learning methods is by considering a dataset D with known class labels, stripping the labels and providing the set as input to an unsupervised learning algorithm, U. The resulting clusters are then compared with the knowledge priors to judge the performance of U.

12.3.1.1   Contingency table

The contingency table [42] is used to evaluate unsupervised learning techniques when some *prior knowledge* about the points is available. *Prior* knowledge P includes points with known class labels or knowledge from literature that tells us which points belong together. The most common *prior* knowledge used is known class labels, and so the contingency table looks like the one in

		Cluster	
		Same Cluster	**Different Cluster**
Class	**Same Class**	u_{11}	u_{10}
	Different Class	u_{01}	u_{00}

FIGURE 12.10: Contingency table template for *prior* knowledge based evaluation.

		Cluster	
		Same Cluster	**Different Cluster**
Class	**Same Class**	9	4
	Different Class	3	12

FIGURE 12.11: Contingency table example for *prior* knowledge based evaluation.

Figure 12.10. To fill in the table, we consider every pair of non-redundant points (n points produce $(n * (n - 1))/2$ pairs). For each pair, we check which one of the four boxes it lies in. The number in each box represents the count of all the pairs that belong to that box, namely:

- The pair belongs to the same class in P and it is also placed in the same cluster by U (u_{11});

- The pair belongs to the same class in P but its points are placed in different clusters by U (u_{10});

- The paired points belong to different classes in P but they are placed in the same cluster by U (u_{01}); and

- The paired points belong to the different classes in P and they are placed in different clusters by U (u_{00}).

Similar to the confusion matrix, we ideally want u_{10} and u_{01} to be 0. The most common measures used to measure the performance of an unsupervised technique using the matching matrix are described below.

Rand Statistic

The *Rand statistic* [22, 18, 34], also called the *simple matching coefficient* [42], is a measure where both placing a pair of points with the same class label in the same cluster and placing a pair of points with different class labels in different clusters are given equal importance, i.e., it accounts for both specificity and sensitivity of the clustering. The value u_{11} accounts for sensitivity; data that should be placed together according to P and are, in fact, placed together by U. The value u_{00} accounts for specificity; data that should be separated according to P and are, in fact, not placed together by U. The formula to calculate the score is as follows:

$$Rand = \frac{u_{11} + u_{00}}{u_{11} + u_{00} + u_{10} + u_{01}} \tag{12.36}$$

The Rand statistic of the contingency matrix example in Figure 12.11 is calculated as follows:

$$\begin{aligned} Rand &= \frac{3}{4}, \\ &= 0.75 \end{aligned}$$

Jaccard Coefficient

The *Jaccard coefficient* (*JC*) [25, 42], introduced in Chapter 6 on proximity measures, can be utilized when placing a pair of points with the same class label in the same cluster is primarily important. The formula to calculate the score is as follows:

$$JC = \frac{u_{11}}{u_{11} + u_{10} + u_{01}} \tag{12.37}$$

The *JC* of the confusion matrix example in Figure 12.11 is calculated as follows:

$$\begin{aligned} JC &= \frac{9}{16}, \\ &= 0.56 \end{aligned}$$

The R implementation of these metrics is available in the PerformanceMetrics package.

```
1 library(PerformanceMetrics)
2 data(ContingencyTable)
3 ContingencyTable
4       [,1] [,2]
5 [1,]    9    4
6 [2,]    3   12

7 contingencyTableMetrics(ContingencyTable)
8 $Rand
9 [1] 0.75

10 $'Jaccard Coefficient'
11 [1] 0.5625
```

		Cluster ID			
		1	**2**	....	**W**
Class Labels	**1**	m_{11}	m_{12}	------	m_{1W}
	2	m_{21}	m_{22}	------	m_{2W}
	⋮	⋮	⋮	------	⋮
	V	m_{V1}	m_{V2}	-----	m_{VW}
Total Elements per Cluster m_j		$\sum\limits_{i=1}^{V} m_{i1}$	$\sum\limits_{i=1}^{V} m_{i2}$	......	$\sum\limits_{i=1}^{V} m_{iW}$ $T = \sum\limits_{j=1}^{W} m_j$

FIGURE 12.12: Matching matrix template for *prior* knowledge based evaluation.

		Cluster ID			
		1	**2**	**3**	
Class Labels	**1**	2	0	1	
	2	0	2	1	
m_j		2	2	2	**T = 6**

FIGURE 12.13: Matching matrix example.

12.3.1.2 Matching matrix

The matching matrix [48] (very similar to the confusion matrix) is a $V \times W$ matrix (Figure 12.12), where V is the number of class labels in P and W is the total number of resulting clusters. Each row of the matrix represents one class label and each column represents a cluster ID. Each m_{ij} entry represents the number of points from class i that are present in cluster g_j. The table is filled based on the *prior* knowledge P and clusters obtained using U. There are a number of metrics that can be used with the matching matrix.

Entropy

Entropy (E) [38, 39, 42] is the measure of impurity that is present in each cluster, i.e., it measures the extent to which a cluster contains data belonging to the same class. For each cluster g_j, the probability that the member of cluster g_j also belongs to class i is computed using the following formula:

$$p_{ij} = \frac{m_{ij}}{m_j}, \tag{12.38}$$

where m_{ij} is the number of points that belong to both class i and cluster g_j and m_j is the size of cluster g_j. Using this information the entropy (E) of each cluster is calculated as follows:

$$E_{g_j} = -\sum_{i=1}^{V} p_{ij} \log_2 p_{ij} \tag{12.39}$$

The range of values this measure E_j can take is between 0 and 1, where 0 denotes a completely homogeneous cluster. The value of $\log_2 0$ is taken as 0 for these calculations. The total entropy (TE) for the entire set of clusters is calculated as the sum of entropies of each individual cluster weighted by the number of elements in each cluster:

$$TE = \sum_{j=1}^{W} \frac{m_j}{M} E_{g_j}, \tag{12.40}$$

where M is the total number of points in the input. This similarly takes values between 0 and 1 with 0 denoting a good clustering.

The entropy calculations for the matching matrix example in Figure 12.13 are as follows:

$$
\begin{aligned}
E_1 &= 0, \\
E_2 &= 0, \\
E_3 &= 0.5, \\
TE &= 0.33
\end{aligned}
$$

The set of clusters in Figure 12.13 has a TE value of 0.33, which is close to 0 and, hence, represents the results of a good clustering algorithm.

Purity

Purity (Pu) [42] is another measure to analyze the homogeneity of the cluster with respect to the class labels. It is calculated as follows:

$$Pu_{g_j} = \max_{i=1 \text{ to } V} p_{ij} \tag{12.41}$$

This measure takes any value in the range of $1/V$ to 1, but unlike entropy, a value of 1 indicates a completely homogeneous cluster. The total purity (TPu) for the entire set of clusters is calculated as the sum of purities of each individual cluster weighted by the number of elements in each cluster.

$$TPu = \sum_{j=1}^{W} \frac{m_j}{M} Pu_{g_j} \tag{12.42}$$

The purity calculations for the matching matrix example in Figure 12.13 are as follows:

$$
\begin{aligned}
Pu_1 &= 1, \\
Pu_2 &= 1, \\
Pu_3 &= 0.5, \\
TPu &= 0.83
\end{aligned}
$$

The set of clusters in Figure 12.13 has a TPu value of 0.83, which is close to 1 and, hence, represents the results of a good clustering algorithm.

The R implementation of these metrics is also available in the PerformanceMetrics package.

```
1 library(PerformanceMetrics)
2 data(MatchingMatrix)
3 MatchingMatrix
4      [,1] [,2] [,3]
5 [1,]   2    0    1
6 [2,]   0    2    1
7 matchingMatrixMetrics(MatchingMatrix)
8 $'Entropy per cluster'
9 [1] 0 0 1

10 $'Total Entropy'
11 [1] 0.3333333

12 $'Purity per cluster'
13 [1] 1.0 1.0 0.5

14 $'Total Purity'
15 [1] 0.8333333
```

12.3.1.3 Ideal and observed matrices

Given that the number of points is T, *ideal-matrix* ($\mathbf{X}$) [42] is a $T \times T$ matrix, where each cell (i, j) has a 1 if the points i and j belong to the same class and a 0 if they belong to different classes, based on the *prior* knowledge P. The *observed-matrix* ($\mathbf{Y}$) [42] is a $T \times T$ matrix, where a cell (i, j) has a 1 if the points i and j belong to the same cluster and a 0 if they belong to different cluster. An example of these matrices is shown in Figure 12.14.

Each matrix can be wrapped into a vector by iteratively appending each row to the end of the previous row. Using these vectors, several existing similarity measures can be applied. However, there are also measures that can directly calculate the similarity of two matrices of the same rank. One such a method is discussed below.

Ideal (Based on class label) X	Data Point 1	Data Point 2	Data Point 3
Data Point 1	1	1	0
Data Point 2	1	1	0
Data Point 3	0	0	1

Observed (Based on clusters) Y	Data Point 1	Data Point 2	Data Point 3
Data Point 1	1	0	1
Data Point 2	0	1	0
Data Point 3	1	0	1

FIGURE 12.14: Example of a pair of ideal and observed matrices.

Mantel Test

The Mantel (r_M) test [31] is a statistical test of the correlation between two matrices of the same rank. The two matrices, $\mathbf{X}$ and $\mathbf{Y}$, in this case, are symmetric and, hence, it is sufficient to analyze lower or upper diagonals of each matrix; given that the size of both input matrices is $T \times T$, only $\frac{T \times (T-1)}{2}$ entries are considered. The Mantel r_M score is calculated as follows:

$$r_M(\mathbf{X}, \mathbf{Y}) = \frac{1}{n} \sum_{i=1}^{n} \sum_{j=1}^{n} \frac{x_{ij} - \overline{\mathbf{X}}}{\sigma_{\mathbf{X}}} \times \frac{y_{ij} - \overline{\mathbf{Y}}}{\sigma_{\mathbf{Y}}}, \tag{12.43}$$

$$n = \frac{T \times (T-1)}{2}, \tag{12.44}$$

where $\overline{\mathbf{X}}$ and $\sigma_{\mathbf{X}}$ denote the mean and standard deviation of the elements of $\mathbf{X}$, respectively; a similar notation holds for matrix $\mathbf{Y}$. The correlation measure takes a value between -1 and 1, where 1 represents a perfect match between the ideal and observed matrices, -1 represents a perfect mismatch between the ideal and observed matrices, and a 0 represents no relationship between the ideal and observed matrices.

12.3.2   Evaluation Using Cluster Properties and Attributes

This section describes methods and measures that can be used to analyze the performance of an unsupervised learning method solely using attributes and properties of the resulting clusters.

Cohesion and Separation

With unsupervised learning techniques, the points are often grouped based on some proximity/distance function defined over a set of attributes. The performance of the algorithm in such cases is measured both in terms of cohesion that exists within each group of nodes and the amount of separation across the groups [42]. The cohesion and separation for a set of clusters are defined as follows:

$$cohesion = \frac{\sum_{i=1}^{W} \frac{\sum_{x \in g_i, y \in g_i} proximity(x,y)}{(|g_i|)^2}}{W}, \tag{12.45}$$

$$separation = 2 \times \frac{\sum_{i=1}^{W} \sum_{j=1}^{W} \frac{\sum_{x \in g_i, y \in g_j, i \neq j} proximity(x,y)}{|g_i| \times |g_j|}}{W \times (W-1)}, \tag{12.46}$$

where $|g_i|$ denotes the number of objects in cluster g_i and *proximity* represents some proximity metric. Both cohesion and separation can take values in the range 0 to 1. We want cohesion to be closer to 1 and separation to be closer to 0 when using proximity metrics. That scenario is reversed if distance metrics are used.

Silhouette Coefficient

The silhouette coefficient (SC) [36, 42], unlike cohesion and separation, is independent of the number of clusters present. For each point d, the silhouette coefficient (SC) is calculated for each point d as follows:

$$SC(d) = \frac{\mu_{inter} - \mu_{intra}}{\max\left(\mu_{inter}, \mu_{intra}\right)}, \tag{12.47}$$

where μ_{inter} is the average distance between d and every other point not in the same cluster as d, and μ_{intra} is the average distance between d and every other node in the same cluster as d. The range is between -1 and 1, where a value closer to 1 indicates that the point has been assigned to the best possible cluster.

The average of these *per-point* coefficients provides the average SC score for the entire clustering (ASC):

$$ASC = \frac{\sum_{j=1}^{T} SC(d_j)}{T} \tag{12.48}$$

Dunn Index

The Dunn index ($Dunn$) [8] is defined as the ratio between the least inter–cluster distance and the largest intra–cluster distance. The index is defined as follows:

$$Dunn = \frac{dist_{min-inter}}{dist_{max-intra}} \tag{12.49}$$

where $dist_{min-inter}$ denotes the smallest distance between two points from different clusters, and $dist_{max-intra}$ denotes the largest distance between two points from the same cluster. The Dunn index can take a value in range 0 and ∞ and should be maximized; it is preferable to maximize the distance between clusters while minimizing the inter–cluster difference, to create a strong coupling between data points and cluster membership.

C-Index

The C-Index (χ_{index}) [23] is defined as follows:

$$\chi_{index} = \frac{K - K_{min}}{K_{max} - K_{min}} \tag{12.50}$$

where K is the sum of distances over all pairs of points from the same cluster, b is the number of those pairs, and K_{min} is the sum of the bth smallest distances over all pairs of points. K_{max} is the sum of the bth largest distances over all pairs of points. The χ_{index} can take a value in range 0 and 1 and should be minimized. We see that the numerator of χ_{index} will be closer to zero if the pairs within the same cluster are closer. The denominator is for normalization purposes.

12.4   Optimizing Metrics

Performance metrics help assess the quality of the output or quality of some model built and can also provide feedback to build better models or improve the algorithm in an iterative process. However, in some cases, the performance metric becomes part of the optimization function of the data mining algorithm and, hence, we are able to attain a balance between performance and cost (e.g., in terms of CPU time) as we run the algorithm or build the model. Two examples of such metrics are discussed below.

12.4.1   Sum of Squared Errors

Sum of squared errors (SSE) [42] is typically used in clustering algorithms to measure the quality of the clusters obtained. This parameter takes into consideration the distance between each point in a cluster to its cluster center (centroid or some other chosen representative). This value is small when points are close to their cluster center, indicating a good clustering. Similarly, a large SSE indicates a poor clustering. Thus, clustering algorithms aim to minimize SSE. During an algorithm run, if we find that the SSE of the current iteration is within acceptable limits, we may choose not to proceed with the next iteration even if the algorithm has not converged (i.e., unchanging cluster centers). For d_j, a point in cluster g_i, where m_i is the cluster center of g_i, and W, the total number of clusters, SSE is defined as follows:

$$SSE = \sum_{i=1}^{W} \sum_{d_j \in g_i} dist(m_i, d_j)^2 \qquad (12.51)$$

An alternative to the same measure can use *cohesion*, where the underlying data mining technique uses a proximity measure as opposed to a distance and, hence, the objective becomes a maximization function—maximizing the similarity between every data point and its cluster center. Thus, we may choose to stop running the algorithm when the value rises above a certain threshold. *Total cohesion* (TC) [42] is calculated as follows:

$$TC = \sum_{i=1}^{W} \sum_{d_j \in g_i} similarity(m_i, d_j) \qquad (12.52)$$

12.4.2 Preserved Variability

Preserved variability [42] is typically used in eigenvector-based dimension reduction techniques to quantify the variance preserved by the chosen dimensions. This parameter is the ratio of the sum of eigenvalues of the k out of r chosen dimensions to the sum of eigenvalues of all the dimensions. The objective of the dimension reduction technique is to maximize this parameter. The value of this parameter depends on the number of dimensions chosen: the more included, the higher the value. Choosing all the dimensions will result in the perfect score of 1. However, the idea behind dimension reduction is to reduce the number of features we have to work with. Thus, dimensions are chosen such that the preserved variability, while not 1, is within an acceptable limit (say 95%). Given that the point is represented in r dimensions ($k << r$), the eigenvalues are $\lambda_1 \geq \lambda_2 \geq \ldots \geq \lambda_{r-1} \geq \lambda_r$. The preserved variability (PV) is calculated as follows:

$$PV = \frac{\sum_{i=1}^{k} \lambda_i}{\sum_{j=1}^{r} \lambda_j} \qquad (12.53)$$

12.5 Statistical Significance Techniques

The performance metrics discussed so far in the chapter provide some score to quantify the model's performance. However, this score alone is not sufficient. In addition to the score, a confidence value for the score will add to its credibility. In this section, we discuss two methods to arrive at such a confidence value. The first is the *Monte Carlo* method, which is a more generic method to assign confidence to any score, and the second is a more specific method based on binomial experimentation that obtains a confidence interval for the error (or accuracy) of a model.

12.5.1 Monte Carlo Procedure

In data mining tasks, such as clustering, one form of validation is to calculate the pair-wise proximity (or distance) score between the points assigned to the same cluster. A high average proximity score (or low average distance) would then signify a cohesive cluster. Analyzing the proximity score alone does not say much about the cluster. For example, a cluster may have an average cosine similarity score of 0.99. At first glance, this seems like a good score, but it is possible that a randomly chosen set of points of the same size as the cluster also produces 0.99 score. What does this say about our cluster?

To answer this question, we can use the Monte Carlo procedure [32, 49] to assign a confidence (in terms of p-value) to the score obtained for a cluster. Given a cluster g with score η_g calculated using formula f, the empirical p-value for η_g is estimated by randomly sampling J (e.g., $J \approx 1,000$) subsets of size $|g|$ from the input set and calculating the score using f. Let R be the number of subsets from N that have score $\geq \eta_g$. The p-value is estimated as R/J. We can use a cutoff of, say, 0.05 (most commonly used), to filter out insignificant clusters.

The average pair-wise cosine similarity of a cluster g of size 5 is 0.85. The p-value cutoff chosen is 0.05. Through the Monte Carlo procedure, 1,000 sets ($J = 1,000$) of size 5 are randomly sampled from the input set. Let the number of random clusters with cosine similarity score greater than or equal to 0.85 be 10 ($R = 10$). The empirical p-value quantifying the significance of the score 0.85 for a cluster of size 5 is $R/J = 10/1,000 = 0.01$, which is ≤ 0.05; hence, cluster g has a significant score.

12.5.2 Confidence Interval Estimation

In predictive data mining tasks such as classification, consider an error rate associated with a model on a sample data set S from the set of data instances D. Let H be the number of instances from S that the model predicts incorrectly. Thus, the error rate for the model, ER_s, is H/S, i.e., the probability that an instance from S will be misclassified. However, ER_s may not be the true error rate ER_t, which is the probability that any random instance drawn from D will be misclassified. We need to utilize ER_s to estimate ER_t. While we cannot point out the exact value of ER_t, we can obtain an interval in which ER_t lies, called the *confidence interval*. For this purpose, the prediction task is taken as a binomial experiment that has two outcomes: a correct prediction and a wrong prediction. Assuming that S is large enough, we assume that S comes from a normal distribution. The confidence interval for ER_t [42] is estimated as follows:

$$ER_s \pm Z_l \times \sqrt{\frac{ER_s(1 - ER_s)}{|S|}}, \tag{12.54}$$

where the Z_l value comes from a standard normal distribution table pertaining to the $l\%$ area under the curve.

Let the total number of points S classified by a model M be 100 and the number of correct classifications C be 50. The error rate of the model M is $\frac{100-50}{100}$, or $\frac{1}{2}$. Given that the $l\%$ is 97.5%, the corresponding Z_l value from the standard normal distribution is 1.96. Substituting into Equation 12.54, we obtain the confidence interval ER_t of the model M as follows:

$$\frac{1}{2} \quad \pm \quad 1.96\sqrt{\frac{\frac{1}{2}(1 - \frac{1}{2})}{100}},$$

$$0.5 \quad \pm \quad 1.96 \times \frac{1}{20},$$

$$0.5 \quad \pm \quad 0.098$$

Confidence interval estimation can also be extended for unsupervised techniques, where the sample error ER_s will signify the probability that a pair of points from S will be misclustered (or misgrouped), i.e., a pair of points belonging to the same class will be placed in different clusters or a pair of points belonging to different classes will be placed in the same cluster. The true error ER_t signifies the misclustering (misgrouping) of any pair of points from D.

12.6 Model Comparison

As we have seen so far in this book and in general, there are many algorithms developed for the purpose of supervised and unsupervised learning, even for the same data mining task. The question is how to compare different models learned by different algorithms. Aside from the ROC curve, there are a number of comparison metrics, which are covered in this section.

12.6.1 Cost-based Analysis

In the metrics associated with various learning algorithms, the hits and a mistakes are treated equally, i.e., they have equal preferability when evaluating models. However, in real-world applications, certain aspects of model performance are considered more important than others. For example, if a person with cancer was diagnosed as cancer-free or vice-versa then the prediction model should be especially penalized. This penalty can be introduced in the

Cost Matrix		Predicted Class	
		+	−
Actual	+	c_{11}	c_{10}
Class	−	$_{01}$	c_{00}

FIGURE 12.15: Cost matrix template for model comparison.

Cost Matrix		Predicted Class	
		+	−
Actual	+	-20	100
Class	−	45	−10

Confusion Matrix of M_x		Predicted Class	
		+	−
Actual	+	4	1
Class	−	2	1

Confusion Matrix of M_y		Predicted Class	
		+	−
Actual	+	3	2
Class	−	2	1

FIGURE 12.16: Example of a 2×2 cost matrix.

form of a cost matrix and typically applied with contingency or confusion tables. This analysis is typically used to select one model when we have more than one choice through using different algorithms or different parameters to the learning algorithms.

Figure 12.15 shows a cost matrix. The total cost of the model, defined by the confusion matrix in Figure 12.1, is calculated by the following formula:

$$C_M = \sum_{i,j} c_{ij} \times f_{ij}, \tag{12.55}$$

where c_{ij} is the cost of classifying a datum belonging to class i into class j and f_{ij} is the number of instances where a datum belonging to class i is predicted as class j [42].

Typically, the cost associated with correct classification is a zero or less, while a misclassification is associated with a positive number. Under this circumstance, we want to minimize the cost of the model. Similarly, we can transform the problem to a maximization problem by assigning positive costs to correct classifications and assigning 0 or less costs to misclassifications.

This cost-based analysis is done to perform comparative analysis of several models trained and tested using the same dataset. The cost of each model is calculated using the same cost matrix and the model with the lowest cost is chosen. Given the cost matrix in Figure 12.16 and the confusion matrices of two models M_x and M_y, the total cost of the model M_x is a 100 and M_y is 220 and so purely on the basis of cost, M_x is a better model.

The R implementation of the cost-based analysis is available in the PerformanceMetrics package.

```
1 library(PerformanceMetrics)
2 data(Mx)
3 data(My)
4 data(CostMatrix)
5 Mx
6      [,1] [,2]
7 [1,]   4    1
8 [2,]   2    1
9 My
10      [,1] [,2]
11 [1,]   3    2
12 [2,]   2    1

13 CostMatrix
14      [,1] [,2]
15 [1,]  -20  100
16 [2,]   45  -10
17 costAnalysis(Mx,CostMatrix)
18 $'Cost Of Model'
```

₁₉ `[1]  100`

₂₀ `costAnalysis(My,CostMatrix)`
₂₁ `$'Cost Of Model'`
₂₂ `[1]  220`

A similar cost model can also be applied to the unsupervised results (contingency tables), where the cost of placing two data points belonging to the same class into the same cluster and placing two data points belonging to the different classes into the different clusters are given a zero or negative weights and the cost of placing data points belonging to two different classes into the same cluster and points of the same class into two different clusters are given positive weights. The goal is to once again minimize the associated cost.

12.6.2   Comparison of Error Rates

In predictive data mining, given two models M_1 and M_2 with error rates ER_1 and ER_2, many would reflexively choose the model with the smaller error rate. However, assuming that error rate is the most important metric to the user, this choice would only be correct if the models were trained and tested on the same datasets. If the models were obtained on two different datasets D_1 and D_2, then the first step is to identify if the two error rates are significantly different. A statistical method of determining whether the error rates are significantly different can be performed by assuming that the sizes of D_1 and D_2 are sufficiently large to warrant considering ER_1 and ER_2 to be normally distributed. The difference $diff = |ER_1 - ER_2|$ then also follows a normal distribution with true difference $diff_t$ and variance σ^2_{diff}. The variance of $diff$ is the sum of the variances of each model under the assumption that the models are independent. So the variance of $diff$ [42] is given as

$$\sigma^2_{diff} = \frac{ER_1(1 - ER_1)}{|D_1|} + \frac{ER_2(1 - ER_2)}{|D_2|} \qquad (12.56)$$

The confidence interval for the true difference $diff_t$ is calculated as

$$diff_t = diff \pm Z_l \times \sigma_{diff}, \qquad (12.57)$$

where the Z_l value comes from a standard normal distribution table pertaining to the $l\%$ area under the curve.

Let M_1 and M_2 be two models that need to be compared. The error rates for the two models are given as $ER_1 = 0.5$ and $ER_2 = 0.7$. The size of the datasets on which the error rates were obtained for M_1 and M_2 were 5 and 1,000, respectively. The $l\%$ is 97.5%. So, $diff = |ER_1 - ER_2| = 0.2$. The variance of $diff$ is calculated as follows:

$$\sigma^2_{diff} = \frac{0.5 \times 0.5}{5} + \frac{0.7 \times 0.2}{1000},$$

$$= 0.05$$

The confidence interval for the true difference $diff_t$ is given by:

$$diff_t = 0.2 \pm 1.96 \times \sqrt{0.05},$$
$$= 0.2 \pm 0.44$$

In this case, the difference is not significant since the interval 0.2 ± 0.44 contains the value 0.

12.7 Handling the Class Imbalance Problem in Supervised Learning

Class imbalance occurs when some classes are under-represented in the input dataset. The model trained on such a set may not learn to predict these classes well. One way of overcoming this problem is by a process called sampling.

Sampling is a process utilized by predictive data mining tasks to expand the training set by creating additional data-points. This is useful especially in predictive data mining tasks. Class imbalance occurs when some classes are more represented and other classes hardly have any representation.

The most common approach to solve this problem is through the use of random oversampling and random undersampling. Random undersampling randomly samples from the data belonging to the majority class and removes them [4]. Random oversampling randomly selects entities from the minority class and duplicates them. However, it has been shown [4] that random undersampling has the problem of losing important information that could help in the classification process and random oversampling could make the classifier more specific. To address this problem, SMOTE (Synthetic Minority Oversampling Technique)[3] was introduced. SMOTE generates new samples that lie in between the samples in the minority class and their nearest neighbours.

12.8 Other Issues

Model overfitting [42] occurs in a predictive model when the model has almost no training error but a large test error. This can typically occur due to several reasons: (1) the model built is too detailed with respect to the training data and, hence, it is unable to generalize for cases that it has not seen before, (2) the noise in the training data has prevented it from learning some important characteristics about the data set, and (3) there is a class imbalance, i.e., some classes have very few representatives in the training dataset. The *generalization error* should typically give us a clue if the model is overfitted.

The *generalization error* is defined as the probability that unseen data would be misclassified by the model and it is estimated using the training error. Typically, an *optimistic approach* [42] is taken, where the training error is considered as a good estimate of the model and is also considered as the generalization error. However, when overfitting occurs this is no longer a good estimate and, hence, changes are made to the *generalization error* estimate so that when model overfitting has occurred, this error value should give a clue about it.

There are two common approaches to dealing with this issue. The first method is the *pessimistic approach* [42], which takes into consideration the training error and contains a penalty term for the model complexity (since more complex models will likely also be overfitted). The second method is *reduced error pruning* [42], where the training set is divided into two smaller subsets, where one subset is used for training and the other set, known as the validation set, is used for estimating the generalization error. Reduced error pruning is used by error-prevention mechanisms such as cross-validation.

Another way to prevent overfitting is to first analyze the class distribution in the sample data and resolve issues with imbalanced classes (see Section 12.7). The second way is to analyze the data for outliers and filter them out before building the model. The third way is to follow *Occam's razor* [42], also called the *principle of parsimony*, that states that given two models with the same generalization error, the simpler one is preferable.

Missing attribute values [42] is another issue that needs to be handled in cases of real-world datasets. The main issue occurs when trying to cluster or classify data with missing attribute values. There are methods to estimate the value of the missing data; for example, the mean, median, or the most frequently occurring value for the attribute can all be used to replace the missing value. But they may still be very different from the actual value of the attribute for that specific data.

12.9   Application Domain-Specific Measures

The metrics discussed so far in the chapter have been application independent. In problems that are heavily tied to an application domain, we also want our data mining results to apply domain knowledge to validate the results. In this section, we discuss one use-case for the domain of *biology*.

For example, in Chapter 8 on Cluster Analysis, we discussed the application of the maximal clique enumeration algorithm to identify protein complexes. While the clusters identified perfectly match the formal definition of a protein complex (complete graph), we still need to perform further testing to make sure that the clusters make sense *biologically*. The easiest way is to have a domain expert look at the results and analyze them. But this would be tedious given the fact that the number of maximal cliques enumerated is typically on the order of thousands. A more feasible way would be to apply existing biological domain knowledge to computationally filter out the random/insignificant maximal cliques.

The most popular way of computationally performing *biological validation*, or assessing the results for their biological relevance, is called *functional enrichment analysis*.

Functional Enrichment Analysis

Functional enrichment analysis [2, 21] typically makes use of the hypergeometric test to analyze the clusters identified. This method works on the principle that if a set of proteins represents a protein complex, then the proteins work together to carry out a single biological function in the cell, i.e., the proteins are functionally homogeneous. In biology, there is an ontology called the *Gene Ontology (GO)*, which describes almost every possible function a protein can carry out. A term in the ontology is called a *GO* term. Each protein in an organism is associated with a set of terms from this ontology. The list of all proteins in the organism along with the associated GO terms is taken as the *population* ($\mathbb{P}$) for the hypergeometric test. The list of all proteins in the cluster with their corresponding GO terms is taken as the *sample* ($\mathbb{S}$). We now check to see if a particular GO term enriches the cluster, or if the cluster is biased toward this term. Let the GO term we are currently testing be GO_t. The proteins in the population that are annotated with GO_t are the successes in the population ($\mathbb{P}_{su}$). The proteins in the sample (cluster) that are annotated with GO_t are the successes in the sample ($\mathbb{S}_{su}$). A p-value to quantify the biological significance is calculated using the hypergeometric principle as follows:

$$p\text{-value} = \frac{\binom{|\mathbb{P}_{su}|}{|\mathbb{S}_{su}|}\binom{|\mathbb{P}|-|\mathbb{P}_{su}|}{|\mathbb{S}|-|\mathbb{S}_{su}|}}{\binom{|\mathbb{P}|}{|\mathbb{S}|}} \tag{12.58}$$

A threshold is used to determine if a p-value denotes significance or not. A typical value is 0.05, and any GO term resulting in p-value below or equal to 0.05 is said to significantly enrich the cluster.

Given a population $\mathbb{P}$ of size 20 and a GO term *GO:0008125*, the number of successes in the population for *GO:0008125* is 10 ($|\mathbb{P}_{su}| = 10$). The size of cluster (a.k.a. sample) $\mathbb{S}$ is 10 and the number of successes for *GO:0008125* in the sample is 5 ($|\mathbb{S}_{su}| = 5$). The p-value quantifying the enrichment of *GO:0008125* in $\mathbb{S}$ is calculated as follows:

$$p\text{-value} = \frac{\binom{10}{5}\binom{20-10}{10-5}}{\binom{20}{10}},$$
$$= 0.34$$

Since $0.34 > 0.05$, *GO:0008125* does not significantly enrich the given cluster $\mathbb{S}$.

Bibliographic Notes

There have been variants of the mean absolute error (MAE) that can be found in literature. The *Brier score* [46] closely resembles the mean absolute error (MAE), but with the Brier score, the difference between the predicted and observed values is squared. Other variants of the mean absolute error are *median absolute error*, *mean percentage error*, and *mean absolute percentage error* [41]. The median absolute error ($MeAE$), as the name suggests, uses the median rather than the mean to avoid the effect of outliers and skewed distributions. The mean percentage error (MPE) calculates the error rate percentage per-class label and averages over the number of class labels. The mean absolute percentage error ($MAPE$) is similar to the MPE except that the error rate that is calculated is taken as an absolute value.

The generalized version of the F-measure is called the F_β [42, 35] and uses a parameter β to examine the tradeoff between recall and precision. β can take a value between 0 and ∞. When β is closer to 0, F_β will be closer to the precision, while larger values of β move F_β closer to recall. The F-measure discussed in this chapter is called F_1, where $\beta = 1$ and precision and recall are weighted equally.

The Pierce Skill Metric [33, 46] is very similar to the Heidke Skill Score [20, 46], differing in how the chance parameter in the denominator is calculated based on the assumption that the predictions are unbiased, i.e., not influenced by the probability of the actual class information. The *odds ratio* [44] is a simple method that measures the ratio of odds of a true positive conditioned on the event occurring to the odds of a false positive conditioned on the event not occurring. The Gandin-Murphy Skill Score [46, 14, 13] is different from the other skill metrics discussed so far in that it assigns a different weight to the joint probability of the actual and predicted class labels.

The set of performance metrics discussed in this chapter is in no way comprehensive, and newer measures are being developed to improve the existing metrics in the area of data mining.

12.10 Exercises

1. Using the information provided in Table 12.1, compare the performance of models M_1 and M_2 using the metrics defined in Sec-

TABLE 12.1: Predictions by models M_1 and M_2 for Question 1

Datapoint	Actual Class	Model M_1	Model M_2
1	+	+	+
2	−	−	+
3	−	+	−
4	+	+	+
5	+	−	−
6	+	+	−
7	−	+	+
8	+	+	+

TABLE 12.2: Cost matrix for Question 2

		Predicted Class	
		Class=+	Class=−
Actual Class	Class=+	0	0
	Class=−	−145	+120

tion 12.2.2.1 *Basic Metrics*. Which model has a better performance?

2. Using the information provided in Table 12.1 and Table 12.2, perform a cost-based analysis to compare models M_1 and M_2. Which model has a better performance? What do you observe from the conclusions drawn in Question 1 and Question 2.

3. Using the information in Table 12.3 for the results of applying the maximal clique enumeration algorithm (overlapping clusters), identify which performance metric(s) can still be used to draw useful conclusions about the algorithm. Apply those metrics and provide your thoughts on the performance of the algorithm.

4. Using the information provided in Table 12.1, decide if the two

TABLE 12.3: Data for Question 3

Vertex ID	Clusters(s) Membership	Class Membership
1	1,2	+
2	1	*
3	2,3	-
4	3	*
5	2	-
6	4	+
7	4,5	*
8	3,5	+

models M_1 and M_2, have significantly different error rates (given $l\% = 98.9\%$).

5. The SNN-clustering algorithm, when applied to dataset D, produces a set of clusters G_1 of equal size, with the average entropy TE equal to 0.001 and the average purity TPu equal to 0.99. Is it safe to conclude that SNN-clustering produces a good clustering for D?

6. Can the hypergeometric test discussed in Section 12.9 be utilized to analyze the *goodness* of an unsupervised technique in the presence of *prior* class label knowledge? If yes, how?

7. Arrive at a single performance measure that utilizes accuracy, error rate, recall (both positive and negative), precision, and misclassification rates to quantify the performance of a model M that predicts only two class labels. The measure's objective function should be maximization.

8. Paddy has built a model M with 99% accurate predictions and 99.99% confidence. Paddy is developing an unsupervised algorithm U and wants to analyze its performance on a dataset D that has no *prior* knowledge associated with it. Paddy's friend Happy suggests that Paddy use M to assign class labels to the elements in D and then use that as a knowledge *prior* to analyze U's performance. In the worst case, the confidence of U's performance analysis will be 99.99%. What questions should Paddy be asking before going this route?

Bibliography

[1] T. Abudawood and P.A. Flach. Learning multi-class theories in ILP. In *Proceedings of the 20th International Conference on Inductive Logic Programming*, pages 6–13, 2011.

[2] E.I. Boyle, S. Weng, J. Gollub, H. Jin, D. Botstein, J.M. Cherry, and G. Sherlock. GO: Termfinder-open source software for accessing gene ontology information and finding significantly enriched gene ontology terms associated with a list of genes. *Bioinformatics*, 20:3710–3715, 2004.

[3] N.V. Chawla, K.W. Bowyer, L.O. Hall, and W.P. Kegelmeyer. Smote: Synthetic minority over-sampling technique. *Journal of Artificial Intelligence Research*, 16:321–357, 2002.

[4] B. Chen and J. Hu. Hierarchical multi-label classification incorporating prior information for gene function prediction. In *Proceedings of the Intelligent Systems Design and Applications*, pages 231–236, 2010.

[5] J. Cohen. A coefficient of agreement for nominal scales. *Educational and Psychological Measurement*, 20:37–46, 1960.

[6] L.J. Cronbach. Coefficient alpha and the internal structure of tests. *Psychometrika*, 16:297–334, 1951.

[7] P.A. Devijver and J. Kittler. *Pattern Recognition: A Statistical Approach.* Prentice Hall, 1982.

[8] J.C. Dunn. Well separated clusters and optimal fuzzy-partitions. *Journal of Cybernetics*, 4:95–104, 1974.

[9] T. Fawcett. ROC Graphs: Notes and Practical Considerations for Researchers. *Technical Report, HP Laboratories*, 2004.

[10] T. Fawcett. An introduction to ROC analysis. *Pattern Recognition Letters*, 27:861–874, 2006.

[11] T. Fawcett. ROC Graphs: Notes and Practical Considerations for Researchers. *Technical Report, HP Laboratories*, 2007.

[12] P. Flach. Repairing concavities in ROC curves. In *Proceedings of the Workshop on Computational Intelligence*, pages 38–44, 2003.

[13] L.S. Gandin and A.H. Murphy. Equitable skill scores for categorical forecasts. *Monthly Weather Review*, 120:361–370, 1992.

[14] J.P. Gerrity. A note on Gandin and Murphy's equitable skill score. *Monthly Weather Review*, 120:2709–2712, 1992.

[15] G. F. Gilbert. Finleys tornado predictions. *American Meteorological Journal*, 1:166–172, 1884.

[16] K. Gwet. *Handbook of Inter-rater Reliability: How to Measure the Level of Agreement Between 2 Or Multiple Raters.* STATAXIS Publishing Company, 2001.

[17] K. Gwet. Kappa statistic is not satisfactory for assessing the extent of agreement between raters. *Methods*, 1:1–5, 2002.

[18] M. Halkidi, Y. Batistakis, and M. Vazirgiannis. On clustering validation techniques. *Journal of Intelligent Information Systems*, 17:107–145, 2001.

[19] L. Hamel. Model assessment with ROC curves. In *The Encyclopedia of Data Warehousing and Mining*. Idea Group Publishers, 2008.

[20] P. Heidke. Berechnung des erfolges und der gute der windstarkvorhersagen im sturmwarnungsdienst. *Geografika Annaler*, 8:301–349, 1926.

[21] D.W. Huang, B.T. Sherman, and R.A. Lempicki. Systematic and integrative analysis of large gene lists using DAVID bioinformatics resources. *Nature Protocols*, 4:44–57, 2008.

[22] L. Hubert and P. Arabie. Comparing partitions. *Journal of Classification*, 2:193–218, 1985.

[23] L. Hubert and J. Schultz. Quadratic assignment as a general data-analysis strategy. *British Journal of Mathematical and Statistical Psychology*, 29:190–241, 1976.

[24] R.J. Hyndman and A.B. Koehler. Another look at measures of forecast accuracy. *International Journal of Forecasting*, 22:679–688, 2006.

[25] P. Jaccard. Etude comparative de la distribuition florale dans une portion des alpes et des. *Bulletin Societe Vandoise des sciences naturelles*, 37:547–579, 1901.

[26] I. Jolliffe and D. Stephenson. *Forecast Verification: A Practitioner's Guide in Atmospheric Science*. John Wiley & Sons, 2003.

[27] R. Kohavi and F. Provost. Glossary of terms. Special Issue on Applications of Machine Learning and the Knowledge Discovery Process, Machine Learning, 30:271–274, 1998.

[28] K. Krippendorff. Computing Krippendorff's Alpha Reliability. *Technical Report, University of Pennsylvania, Annenberg School for Communication*, 2007.

[29] M. Kubat, R.C. Holte, and S. Matwin. Machine learning for the detection of oil spills in satellite radar images. *Machine Learning*, 30:195–215, 1998.

[30] D.D. Lewis. A sequential algorithm for training text classifiers: Corrigendum and additional data. *Special Interest Group on Information Retrieval Forum*, 29:13–19, 1995.

[31] N. Mantel. The detection of disease clustering and a generalized regression approach. *Cancer Research*, 27:209–220, 1967.

[32] B.V. North, D. Curtis, and P.C. Sham. A note on the calculation of empirical p-values from Monte Carlo procedures. *American Journal of Human Genetics*, 71:439–441, 2002.

[33] C.S. Peirce. The numerical measure of the success of predictions. *Science*, 4:453–454, 1884.

[34] W.M. Rand. Objective criteria for the evaluation of clustering methods. *Journal of the American Statistical Association*, 66:846–850, 1971.

[35] C.J. Rijsbergen. *Information Retrieval*. Butterworth-Heinemann, 1979.

[36] P. Rousseeuw. Silhouettes: A graphical aid to the interpretation and validation of cluster analysis. *Journal of Computational and Applied Mathematics*, 20:53–65, 1987.

[37] W.A. Scott. Reliability of content analysis: The case of nominal scale coding. *Public Opinion Quarterly*, 19:321–325, 1955.

[38] C.E. Shannon. A mathematical theory of communication. *Bell System Technical Journal*, 27:379423, 1948.

[39] C.E. Shannon and W. Weaver. *The Mathematical Theory of Communication*. University of Illinois Press, 1949.

[40] Y. Sun, M.S. Kamel, and Y. Wang. Boosting for learning multiple classes with imbalanced class distribution. In *Proceedings of the 6th International Conference on Data Mining*, pages 592–602, 2006.

[41] D. Swanson, J. Tayman, and T. Bryan. MAPE-R: A rescaled measure of accuracy for cross-sectional subnational population forecasts. *Journal of Population Research*, 28:225–243, 2011.

[42] P. Tan, M. Steinbach, and V. Kumar. *Introduction to Data Mining*. Addison-Wesley Longman Publishing, 2005.

[43] J. Taylor and D. Watkinson. Indexing reliability for condition survey data. *The Conservator*, 30:49–62, 2007.

[44] A. Westergren, S. Karlsson, P. Andersson, O. Ohlsson, and I.R. Hallberg. Eating difficulties, need for assisted eating, nutritional status and pressure ulcers in patients admitted for stroke rehabilitation. *Journal of Clinical Nursing*, 10:257–269, 2001.

[45] D.S. Wilks. *Statistical Methods in the Atmospheric Sciences*. Academic Press, 2005.

[46] D.S. Wilks. *International Geophysics, Volume 100: Statistical Methods in the Atmospheric Sciences*. Academic Press, 2011.

[47] I.H. Witten, E. Frank, and M.A. Hall. *Data Mining: Practical Machine Learning Tools and Techniques*. Morgan Kaufmann Publishers, 2011.

[48] K.Y. Yeung and W.L. Ruzzo. Details of the adjusted rand index and clustering algorithms supplement to the paper "An Empirical Study on Principal Component Analysis for Clustering Gene Expression Data." *Science*, 17:763–774, 2001.

[49] B. Zhang, B.H. Park, T. Karpinets, and N.F. Samatova. From pull-down data to protein interaction networks and complexes with biological relevance. *Bioinformatics*, 24:979–986, 2008.

13

Introduction to Parallel Graph Mining

**William Hendrix, Mekha Susan Varghese, Nithya Natesan,
Kaushik Tirukarugavur Srinivasan, Vinu Balajee, and Yu Ren**
North Carolina State University

CONTENTS

This chapter introduces the reader to the world of parallel computing. We begin with a simple overview of parallel computing. Later, we explore several techniques for utilizing the power of parallel computing in R, including embarrassing parallelism, calling parallel codes from R, and implementing parallel codes in R using packages like Rmpi.

13.1 Parallel Computing Overview

Before going in depth on parallel computing, let us draw an analogy with a real-world situation. Consider a job that needs to be accomplished, where the person in charge has the liberty to entrust the job to any number of people. An intelligent manager will quickly realize that dividing the job into small chunks and assigning each to one person will help solve the problem much faster than having one worker attack the problem on his or her own. Applying the same principle to computers, it seems obvious that multiple computers working together on different parts of a large problem will oftentimes find a solution much faster than a single computer working alone.

Parallel computing offers a number of advantages [20]:

1. Solving problems faster: Parallel computing often achieves much faster results when the amount of data to be processed is huge. In these cases, the time required to process the data will be very long if the problem is solved sequentially. Consider a simple example where you are responsible for finding the name and address of a person with a particular phone number in a telephone book. The task would be a tedious one if you live in a big city and you try to find that person by yourself. You would find this person much faster if you could split the task among your friends, where each friend would choose a different letter and just look at the names beginning with that letter.

   Practical Usage:
   Weather forecasting derives a great deal of advantage from parallel computing. Meteorologists have only a few hours to come up with a 24-hour weather forecast—if the prediction can't be calculated in time, it is useless.

2. Solving larger problems: Faster computers are often increasingly difficult and costly to build, so one way of improving the performance

would be to include several relatively cheaper computers for the computation. In this way, capabilities of several computers are used to achieve performance instead of attacking problems individually.

Practical Usage:

Calculating a weather forecast for a week requires the simulation to be run for a longer time. Having multiple computers running the simulation can reduce the time required for the simulation down to what would be required for calculating a few hours of the simulation on a single computer.

3. Solving more problems: Distributing several problems of the same type across multiple processors would result in solving more instances of the problem in the same amount of time, leading to a higher *throughput* of the system.

Practical Usage:

On an airline system, many small tasks, like seat reservations and cancellations, need to be taken care of at once. By using multiple computers in parallel, more of these requests can be handled at a time.

Even though it can drastically reduce the time required to solve a problem, parallel computation might not be the right answer in every case. For example, if some of the parts of the problem depend on the solutions by other parts, some workers may need to wait for others to finish before they can work on their part. In the extreme case, each step of the problem would depend on the previous step, eliminating all of the advantage of dividing up the work!

Additionally, if a problem is very small, the task of dividing up the work into chunks may take longer than the time gained by splitting up the work. A general term for these "extra" costs incurred by parallel computation is *overhead*. To make effective use of parallel computing, we should strive to limit our overhead as much as possible and make sure that the time gained by dividing up the work will outweigh the overhead incurred. See Figure 13.1 for an overview of some of the major sources of overhead in a parallel code.

The ideal case for parallelization is a problem that can be divided into equal-sized parts that don't depend on one another. Such problems are called *embarrassingly parallel* and can be parallelized by dividing up the work among the workers, waiting for the workers to finish their jobs, and collecting the results. These problems are called *embarrassingly* parallel because they can be parallelized easily, with a minimum of overhead. Techniques for tackling embarrassingly parallel problems in R are discussed in Section 13.2.

An example of an embarrassingly parallel problem is to find the sum of a set of numbers. With a single process (worker), you would solve the problem by keeping track of a total and adding each number to this total sequentially. However, to solve this problem in parallel, you split the numbers up among

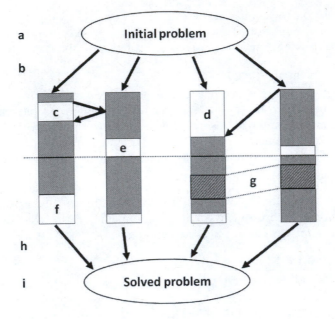

FIGURE 13.1: Some of the major sources of overhead: (a) Initialization of the parallel environment, (b) Initial data distribution, (c) Communication costs, (d) Dependencies between processes, (e) Synchronization points, (f) Workload imbalances, (g) Work duplication, (h) Final results collection, (i) Termination of the parallel environment.

the processes, let each process compute the sum for its numbers, and then add the sum from each of the processes together to get the total sum. In Figure 13.2, you can see an array of 9 integer elements being divided among 3 processes. Each of the processes performs two additions to sum their elements, and the "master" processor that collects the sums performs two more to find the total sum. Discounting the overhead of communication, this procedure could be performed in the same amount of time as four addition operations using a single process, whereas a single process would take eight additions to sum the nine integers.[1]

However, there are many different tasks where communication between the processes is imperative. As an analogy, during the construction of a building, workers performing different kinds of tasks, like plumbing, painting, or installing the electrical wiring, need to communicate with others in order to be effective (see Figure 13.3). For example, a painter shouldn't start painting in a room before the plumbing has been finished, but at the same time, having the painters do nothing until the plumbers have completed their work

---

[1]On modern computers, adding numbers is performed extremely quickly—the cost of communication here will almost certainly exceed the four addition operations saved.

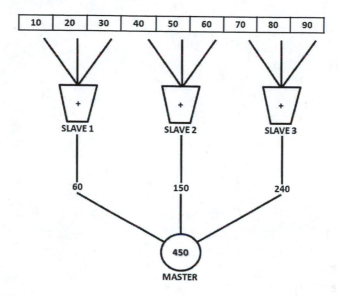

FIGURE 13.2: The diagram above explains the fundamental working principle behind the embarrassingly parallel computation. The figure illustrates a simple addition of array elements using embarrassingly parallel computing.

is a waste of resources. Getting the house finished efficiently requires communication between the two teams. *Inter-process communication* (who tells whom about what), *job scheduling* (who does what and when), and *workload balancing* (whether everyone does the same amount of work) are all important aspects to consider when parallelizing complex problems.

Fortunately, efficient parallel data mining codes exist to solve many types of commonly occurring problems. Section 13.3 discusses how to take advantage of existing codes in R.

Another type of parallel computing model that is increasingly popular is the Map-Reduce framework, originally pioneered by Google [9]. Map-Reduce splits a parallel problem into two phases, called map and reduce, where each map or reduce operation can be completed *independently*, or without any communication with the other map or reduce operations, and the only communication between the parallel workers occurs between the map and reduce phases. Map-Reduce and its R implementation are discussed further in Section 13.6.2.

Parallel computing is used to model various scientific and engineering problems. In particular, computations involving enormous amounts of data can also be solved effectively. Some examples of fields applying parallel computing are:

- Supercomputers and computer clusters use thousands of computers working in parallel. This results in computer performance in the region of teraflops (10^{12} FLoating point OPerations per second, or FLOPs). The FLOPs rat-

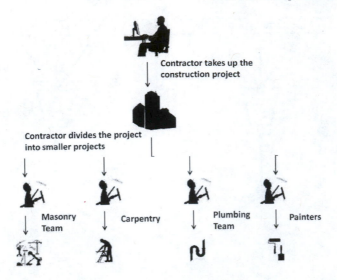

FIGURE 13.3: Division of work required to build a house.

ing is a measure of the computer's performance. Supercomputers produce and consume massive amounts of data. Supercomputers are used in tasks involving scientific calculations like weather forecasting, quantum physics, submarine tracking, weapons simulations, etc.

- Parallel computing is used in multicore architectures. Multicores consist of a number of compute cores integrated onto a single chip package. Software can be parallelized to run on many cores, resulting in significant performance gains. Multicore architectures are used in many application domains like graphics, networking, embedded computing, etc. [5, 36].

- Parallel computing is used in statistical analysis of financial markets. Large amounts of data can be studied effectively using multiple computers. Large-scale simulations can be used to predict the future movement of the markets.

- Parallelism can also be applied to semantic web search, which focuses on the meaning (or *semantics*) of queries and web page contents to return results more relevant than those based on keyword matching. A semantic-based search on the entirety of the Internet is a more challenging problem than keyword matching, and performing this search in parallel can be used to finish the search faster [6].

- In the field of bioinformatics, parallelism is used to study protein folding, in which a protein molecule formed from a chain of amino acids folds into a three-dimensional structure. Protein functions are strongly dependent on the three-dimensional structure of the protein, so if a protein doesn't fold into its intended shape, there is high chance it will be ineffective or toxic [38].

Other important uses for parallel computing include climate modeling, nuclear physics simulations, circuit design, and cryptography.

13.1.1 A Note on Parallel Graph Mining

For the sake of simplicity, most of the examples of parallel computing techniques we discuss in this chapter will be operating on matrices rather than graphs. This decision was made because the regular structure of matrices provides for more intuitive and easier-to-understand parallelization relative to graphs. However, the techniques we discuss can be directly applied to the adjacency matrix of a graph in order to solve some graph problems; e.g., calculating the eigenvalue decomposition of the adjacency matrix in parallel in order to perform spectral clustering on the graph [3]. Moreover, many of the general techniques of work division and overhead minimization described in this chapter can also be applied to parallelize graph-based algorithms that don't operate on the adjacency matrix of a graph.

13.2 Embarrassingly Parallel Computation

In general, parallel computation involves dividing up some large computation into smaller pieces, assigning these pieces to different processes, letting the processes perform the computations, and collecting the results. Sometimes, the computation we are trying to parallelize is complex, and requires the different processes to communicate between themselves to arrive at a final result. However, many tasks fall into the category of *embarrassingly parallel* computations.

Definition 13.1 *Embarrassingly parallel*
A task is said to be **embarrassingly parallel** if it can be divided into independent subtasks—that is, different parts of the task that have no dependencies on each other.

Thus, parallelizing an embarrassingly parallel problem is simply a matter of dividing up the different tasks among the available processes and collecting the results when the processes finish. See Figure 13.4 for a depiction of a typical embarrassingly parallel computation.

13.2.1 The apply Family of Functions

In R, embarrassingly parallel computations can be performed using parallel variants of the apply family of functions, which apply a specified function to

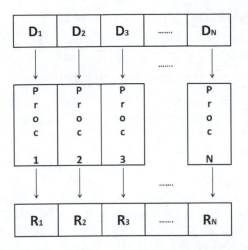

FIGURE 13.4: Basic illustration of embarrassingly parallel computation.

multiple objects. For example, the `lapply` function takes a *list* of objects and a function, applies the function to each object in the list, and returns the list of results. For example, the R code:

```
1 myList = as.list(1:100)
2 lapply(myList, sqrt)
```

generates a list of numbers from 1 to 100 (line 1) and uses the `sqrt` function in order to calculate the square root of each (line 2).

The multicore [28], pRapply [1], papply [8], and snow [26] packages all offer parallel implementations of `lapply`. We focus here on the `mclapply` method of the multicore package, but the methods of the papply and snow packages operate similarly.

The parallel methods take in several arguments in addition to those required by `lapply` that describe how the parallel environment should be set up. Due to the embarrassingly parallel nature of the `lapply` function, the result for `lapply` can be found by dividing the list elements among the processes in the parallel environment and having each process calculate the result of applying the function to the assigned list elements.

The method signature of the `mclapply` function is as follows [28]:

```
1 mclapply(X, FUNC, ..., mc.preschedule = TRUE,
2     mc.set.seed = TRUE, mc.silent = FALSE,
3     mc.cores = getOption("cores"))
```

These parameters are detailed in Table 13.1. In many cases, the default values for the parallel (mc.*) options work well.

TABLE 13.1: Parameters for `mclapply`

Parameter	Use
X	Represents a list of elements.
FUNC	The function that will be applied to each element of the list X.
...	Optional arguments to FUNC.
mc.preschedule	If set to TRUE then the computation is first divided into (at most) as many jobs are there are cores and then the jobs are started, each job possibly covering more than one value. If set to FALSE, one job is spawned for each value of X sequentially. (If used with mc.set.seed=FALSE, then random number sequences will be identical for all values.) The former is better for short computations or a large number of values of X, whereas the latter is better for jobs that have high variance of completion time and lesser values of X.
mc.set.seed	If set to TRUE, then each parallel process will set its random seed to something different than the other processes. Otherwise, all processes will start with the same (namely current) seed.
mc.silent	If set to TRUE, the output for all parallel processes spawned will be suppressed (error messages are not affected).
mc.cores	The number of cores to use, i.e., how many processes will be spawned.

13.2.2 Using `mclapply` to Solve an Embarrassingly Parallel Problem

Using the `mclapply` function to compute multiple values is often very straightforward. As an example, the R code

```
1 library(multicore)
2 myList = as.list(1:64)
3 mclapply(myList, sqrt)
```

will generate a list of numbers between 1 and 64 (line 2), and take the square root of each of these numbers, using all available compute cores. We can compare the time taken by our parallel code with the time taken by the equivalent *serial*, or single-process, code by using the commands:

```
4 system.time(lapply(myList, sqrt))
5 system.time(mclapply(myList, sqrt))
```

However, it's very likely when you run these commands that you will find that the parallel `mclapply` function isn't any faster than the `lapply` function, and may even be slower! Why is this?

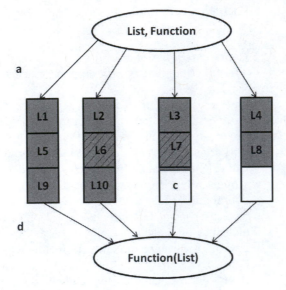

FIGURE 13.5: Some of the possible sources of overhead for the `mclapply` function: (a) Setting up the parallel environment/distributing data (spawning *threads*), (b) Duplicated work (if, say, duplicates exist in the list), (c) Unbalanced loads (from uneven distribution or unequal amounts of time required to evaluate the function on a list item), (d) Combining results/shutting down the parallel environment.

The reason is that the *overhead* of the `mclapply` function—setting up the parallel environment, distributing the work, and collecting the results— outpaces the time saved by dividing up the work. (Figure 13.5 details some of the sources of overhead for the `mclapply` function.) Since the time required to take the square root of 64 numbers is so low (0.0 seconds on the author's laptop), there are very few savings to be gained by solving the problem in parallel. So, to see an advantage for parallel computation, we need a larger, more time-consuming problem.

Though we could just consider the problem of taking the square root of more and more numbers, we may run out of memory trying to store enough numbers so that using parallel computing makes sense. So, we turn our attention now to the problem of finding the square of a matrix.

Multiplying a Matrix by Itself

Multiplying two matrices is a somewhat more complicated problem to parallelize than taking the square root of a list of numbers, but there is a parallel strategy that is pretty straightforward: if we take several rows from the left-hand matrix and multiply this by the right-hand matrix, our result will be the same as the corresponding rows in the product matrix (see Figure 13.6). The R code for calculating the square of a matrix is as follows:

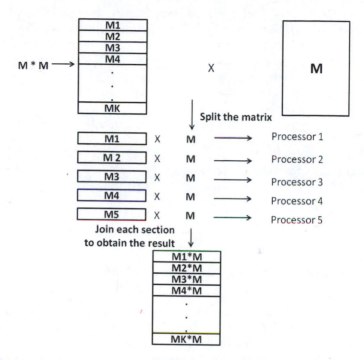

FIGURE 13.6: A simple strategy for parallel matrix multiplication.

```
1 library(multicore)
2 par.msquare = function(M, ndivs=8)
3 {
4    size = dim(M)[1] / ndivs
5    Mlist = list()
6    for (i in 1:ndivs)
7      Mlist[[i]] = M[((i - 1) * size + 1):(i * size),]
8    Mmult = mclapply(Mlist, "%*%", M)
9    Mmult = mclapply(Mmult, t)
10   return(matrix(unlist(Mmult), nrow=(dim(M)[1]), byrow=TRUE))
11 }

12 M = matrix(runif(1024 * 1024, 1, 1000), nrow=1024,
13   ncol=1024)
14 result = par.msquare(M)
```

In lines 12–13, we generate a 1024×1024 matrix filled with random numbers between 1 and 1000. We divide the rows of this matrix into eight sections of 128 rows each in lines 5–7. (The default value of `ndivs` = 8 was chosen arbitrarily: if your computer has 16 or more cores, then dividing the matrix further may produce faster results.) The `mclapply` function in line 8 multiplies each of the smaller matrices in our list by the original matrix to get the different sections of our result matrix. However, before we use the `unlist` function to reform these numbers into our result array (as in line 10), we need to take the transpose (`t`) of each of the individual matrices (line 9) so that `unlist` will put all of the values in the correct order. We can compare results of the serial and parallel versions of matrix multiplication by running:

```
15 system.time(M %*% M)
16 system.time(par.msquare(M))
17 sum(abs(M %*% M - par.msquare(M))) == 0
```

(Line 17 checks to make sure that the matrices we get from both procedures are equal.)

13.2.3 Using `mclapply` to Double Center a Matrix

Double centering refers to the act of finding the mean of each row in a matrix and subtracting the row means from the corresponding rows, then finding the column means of the resulting matrix and subtracting the column means from the corresponding columns. A diagrammatic view of our double centering strategy appears in Figure 13.7. In terms of our R code, we can think of the main operation here as taking a row or column of the matrix, finding the mean, and subtracting this mean. We will define a function `submean` to perform this operation:

```
1 submean = function(v)
2 {
3   return(v - mean(v))
4 }
```

Using this function, we can define a sequential function for double centering a matrix:

```
5 dblCenter = function(matrix)
6 {
7   if (is.matrix(matrix) == FALSE)
8     error("Argument must be a matrix")

9   nrows = dim(matrix)[1]
10   ncols = dim(matrix)[2]
```

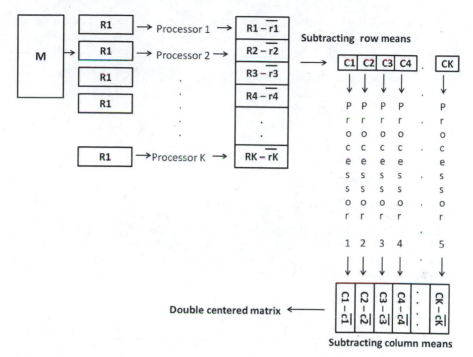

FIGURE 13.7: Strategy for parallelizing the double centering operation.

```
11   mlist = list()
12   for (i in 1:nrows)
13      mlist[[i]] = matrix[i,]

14   lapply(mlist, submean)

15   matrix = matrix(unlist(mlist), nrow=nrows, byrow=TRUE)

16   for (i in 1:ncols)
17      mlist[[i]] = matrix[,i]

18   lapply(mlist, submean)

19   return(matrix(unlist(mlist), nrow=nrows))
20  }
```

Now, to change this code to run in parallel, we simply have to change the `lapply` references in lines 13 and 20 to `mclapply`, optionally specifying the number of processes to use (with the parameter `mc.cores`).

We can test the correctness of our code by comparing the results of the
`dblCenter` function we defined with the built-in `R_dblcen` function provided
by the stats package.

```
21 M = matrix(runif(25, 1, 10), nrow=5, ncol=5)
22 sum(abs(.C(stats:::R_dblcen, M, 5, DUP = FALSE)[[1]]
23    - dblCenter(M)))
```

13.3 Calling Parallel Codes in R

In addition to taking advantage of embarrassingly parallel computations, we
can leverage the power of existing parallel codes in order to tackle larger
problems. R provides several different methods to take advantage of these
codes (see Figure 13.8 for some examples).

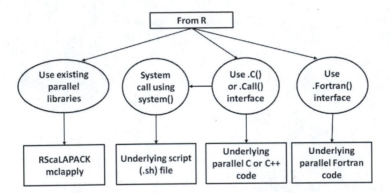

FIGURE 13.8: Some of the different ways to call parallel codes from R.

The easiest way to invoke parallel code in R is to use an R library that
has been compiled for the task. Several packages for R, including peperr [21]
and RScaLAPACK [35] provide parallel implementations of different functions
(prediction error estimation and several linear algebra functions, respectively).
Using these libraries is as simple as installing the relevant package from the
CRAN website, loading the library in R, and invoking one of the parallel
functions.

Alternately, R provides several interfaces to compiled code in other languages, such as C and Fortran. The four interfaces that R provides are:

```
1 .C(name, ..., NAOK=FALSE, DUP=TRUE, PACKAGE, ENCODING)
2 .Fortran(name,..., NAOK=FALSE,DUP=TRUE,PACKAGE,ENCODING)
3 .Call(name, ..., PACKAGE)
4 .External(name, ..., PACKAGE)
```

All four of these interfaces are used to call a function named `name` in a dynamically loaded library (.dll or .so file) that has previously been loaded with the `dyn.load` command. Due to the complexities of creating and using dynamically loaded libraries, these functions are for advanced users and will not be covered here.

13.3.1 Using RScaLAPACK to Solve Linear Algebra Problems

RScaLAPACK [35] is an R package that provides an interface to the powerful ScaLAPACK package [7]. It has functions that can parallelize intense linear algebra functions like `solve`, `eigen`, `svd`, and other common R routines. One of the functions provided by RScaLAPACK is the `sla.multiply` function, which is a parallel implementation of matrix multiplication. The signature of the `multiply` function is as follows:

```
1 sla.multiply(A, B, NPROW, NPCOL, MB, RFLAG, SPAWN)
```

A and B are obviously the matrices to be multiplied together, but what about the other parameters? `NPROW` and `NPCOL` are the number of rows and columns we split the matrix into in order to parallelize the process. For example, letting `NPROW = 2` and `NPCOL = 2` divides the matrix into four quadrants (two rows and two columns), where a different process will be responsible for calculating the result in each quadrant.[2] `MB` is the block size to use when dividing up the matrix. Without going into too much detail, `MB` should divide evenly into the size of the result matrix, and larger values may result in faster execution (or possibly out of memory errors). `SPAWN` and `RFLAG` are boolean values telling the function whether it should spawn a new process grid at the outset and whether it should release the process grid on completion. When executing the function a single time, `SPAWN = TRUE` and `RFLAG = TRUE` are perfectly appropriate; however, if you are trying to multiply several matrices together (or use any other RScaLAPACK function), it may be beneficial to spawn the process grid on only the first function and release the grid at the end. Figure 13.9 gives an overview for how matrix multiplication is divided among processes by RScaLAPACK.

As an example, the R code:

```
1 library(RScaLAPACK)
2 M1 = matrix(data=rnorm(4096), nrow=64, ncol=64)
3 M2 = matrix(data=rnorm(4096), nrow=64, ncol=64)
4 result = sla.multiply(M1, M2, 2, 2, 8, TRUE, TRUE)
```

will randomly generate two 64×64 matrices, and use four processes to multiply them together. The R code

---

[2]If four cores are available, each core will execute a single process. If only one or two cores are available, each core will execute four or two of the quadrants of the result processes.

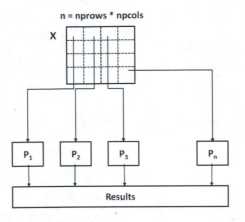

FIGURE 13.9: Work division scheme for calculating matrix multiplication in RScaLAPACK. The matrix is divided into NPROWS rows and NPCOLS columns, and the resulting blocks are distributed among the processes. Each process calculates the product for its assigned block, and the results are collected at the end.

```
5 system.time(sla.multiply(M1, M2, 2, 2, 8, TRUE, TRUE)
6 system.time(M1 %*% M2)
```

will give the amount of (elapsed) time taken by the parallel matrix multiplication versus the serial multiplication. The parallel code needs to spend time spawning the process grid, but (assuming four cores are available) the main matrix multiplication computation should finish roughly four times faster than the serial computation.

13.3.2 Using RScaLAPACK to Parallelize Dimension Reduction

In Chapter 10, we discussed how to apply the Multidimensional Scaling (MDS) technique to place vertices into Euclidean space in a meaningful way. This technique corresponds to the R function cmdscale, in the stats package, which performs a Classical (Metric) Multidimensional Scaling on a data matrix.

The major computational cost of MDS lies in the calculation of eigenvectors and eigenvalues of the processed data matrix. In the R code for cmdscale, this shows up as a pair of calls to the eigen function. Parallelizing these intensive matrix computations will reduce the running time significantly—this may be simply accomplished by using the sla.eigen function provided by RScaLAPACK. The online help for sla.eigen reveals that additional arguments have to be passed in order to execute the function in parallel. Our strategy for parallelizing cmdscale appears in Figure 13.10. In R, make the following changes in the source code of cmdscale function:

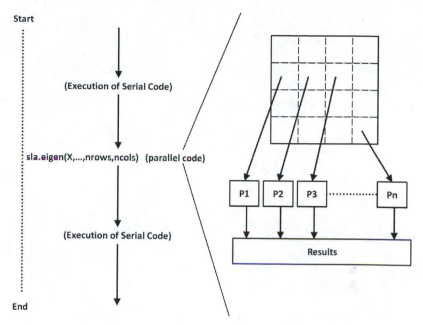

FIGURE 13.10: Basic strategy for transforming `cmdscale` to parallel `cmdscale`.

1. Use `cmdscale` or `fix(cmdscale)` to get the code for the `cmdscale` function

2. Copy and paste this code to create a new function `pcmdscale`

3. Add the parallelization arguments of `sla.eigen` to the signature of `pcmdscale`

4. Replace all instances of the serial `eigen` function calls in the code with `sla.eigen`

5. [Optional] Add an `if (require(RScaLAPACK))` statement before the call to `sla.eigen` to ensure that the RScaLAPACK library has been loaded

In the end, your code should look something like this:

```
1 pcmdscale <- function (d, k = 2, eig = FALSE,
2     add = FALSE, x.ret = FALSE, NPROWS=0,
3     NPCOLS=0, MB=48, RFLAG=1, SPAWN=1)
4 #include options for parallelization
5 {
6           ...
7   if (require("RScaLAPACK", quietly = TRUE))
8       #parallel eigen function
```

```
 9      e <- sla.eigen(Z, NPROWS, NPCOLS, MB,
10          RFLAG, SPAWN)$values
11    else
12      #serial eigen function
13      e <- eigen(Z, symmetric = FALSE,
14          only.values = TRUE)$values
15      ...
16  }
```

13.4   Creating Parallel Codes in R Using Rmpi

The Rmpi package enables the use of MPI in R. MPI, which stands for Message Passing Interface, is (as its name suggests) an interface for communication, rather than a specific software package that performs the communication [12]. In order to use the Rmpi package, you'll first need to install a software implementation of MPI, such as OpenMPI or MPICH; however, Rmpi gives full control over what actions each process is taking, allowing you to design parallel codes for arbitrarily complex algorithms.

A typical Rmpi program can be divided into three main parts: the initialization, where the parallel environment is started and all of the necessary information distributed; the main work function, which tells the different processes what work they should be doing and how they should communicate with one another; and the termination, where the results are collected and the parallel environment shuts down. We first describe how to set up and shut down the Rmpi environment and follow this with descriptions of the two different types of communication provided by Rmpi: point-to-point and collective. An overview of Rmpi is shown in Figure 13.11.

13.4.1   Initialization and Termination

There are a number of tasks that need to be accomplished before the main work of a parallel Rmpi code can begin. Like every R package, Rmpi must be loaded, with the command

```
1 library(Rmpi)
```

before it can be used. Before we can run our code or even distribute our data to the different processes, though, we need to have Rmpi start, or "spawn," the workers. Rmpi follows the "master-slave" paradigm.

The analogy of the master and slave processes is not perfect, however, as the master often participates in the main parallel work after the tasks have been divided. In Rmpi, the R slaves are started using the `mpi.spawn.Rslaves` function. For example, the code

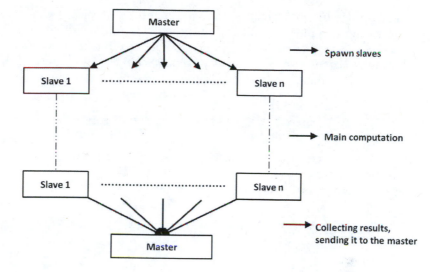

FIGURE 13.11: Overview of the three main parts of master-slave programming paradigm.

    2 `mpi.spawn.Rslaves(nslaves=3)`

will start three slave processes, which can then be assigned work for a parallel computation.

In order to keep track of which process is doing what work, each process (master and slave) is assigned a unique integer called a *process rank*. These rank IDs are assigned sequentially, with the master having a rank ID of zero (0). Rmpi provides a pair of functions to tell each process about its rank ID, as well as the number of other processes. The `mpi.comm.rank` function returns the rank ID of the current process, while the `mpi.comm.size` function returns the total number of processes running (useful when deciding how to divide a computation).

After the execution of parallel programming, the `mpi.close.Rslave` function will halt the execution of R slaves, and `mpi.exit` and `mpi.quit` functions allow us to shut down the Rmpi environment. The `mpi.exit` function will just shut down the slaves and unload the Rmpi library, whereas `mpi.quit` will also exit the R environment.

13.4.2   Initial Work Distribution

After the R slaves have been spawned, the master process needs to distribute the main work function to all of the slaves. The Rmpi `mpi.bcast.Robj2slave` function takes any R object and distributes that object to all of the R slaves. It is also notable for being one of the only methods of data distribution that does not require the slaves to coordinate receiving the data the master sends. Once

all of the data has been distributed, the `mpi.bcast.cmd` function will cause
the slaves to run a command—for our purposes, this command will usually
be a function call to a "main work" function. The `mpi.bcast.cmd` function
is interesting in that it is *asynchronous* or *non-blocking*—the master will be
able to execute R commands while the slaves are executing the command.

Definition 13.2 *Asynchronous*
An **asynchronous** function call is one that returns immediately, before its
action has necessarily completed.

In contrast, the `mpi.remote.exec` function is a *synchronous* or *blocking* call—
the master will pause until the slaves have completed the command, and the
function `mpi.remote.exec` will return the result of the given command on
each process.

Definition 13.3 *Synchronous*
A **synchronous** function call is one that returns only after its action has fully
completed.

Using just these functions, we can begin to define a rudimentary parallel
code for matrix multiplication:

```
1  par.matmult = function(A, B)
2  {
3    if (!require(Rmpi))
4      return(A %*% B)

5    if (!is.matrix(A) || !is.matrix(B))
6      error("A and B must be matrices")

7    if (dim(A)[2] != dim(B)[1])
8      error("Dimensions of matrices don't match")

9    mpi.bcast.Robj2slave(par.matmult.slave)
10   mpi.bcast.Robj2slave(A)
11   mpi.bcast.Robj2slave(B)

12   mpi.bcast.cmd(par.matmult.slave(A, B))
13   return(par.matmult.slave(A, B))
14 }

15 par.matmult.slave = function(A, B)
16 {
17   proc = mpi.comm.rank()
18   nprocs = mpi.comm.size()

19   my.cols = dim(B)[2] / nprocs
20   my.B = B[,(proc * my.cols + 1):((proc + 1) * my.cols)]
```

```
21   product = A %*% my.B
22   #add code to send all of the products back to
23   #the master process here

24   return(result)
25 }
```

Once we add some additional code near line 22 so that the slaves send their product matrices back to the master and the master reforms the multiplied matrix, we will have a fully functional code for parallel matrix multiplication. The following R code snippet will allow us to test the `par.matmult` function (once it is complete) by generating two random 1024×1024 matrices and calculating their product using four processes:

```
26 library(Rmpi)
27 mpi.spawn.Rslaves(nslaves=3)
28 m = n = k = 1024
29 A = matrix(runif(m * n, 1, 1000), ncol=k)
30 B = matrix(runif(n * k, 1, 1000), nrow=k)
31 sum(abs(par.matmult(A, B) - A %*% B))
32 system.time(par.matmult(A, B))
33 system.time(A %*% B)
34 mpi.close.Rslaves()
```

Note that, even though we distribute the matrices immediately in the code above (lines 19, 20), it may be a good idea to have the master distribute only a portion of the data initially and distribute the rest later. This strategy is especially effective if the code suffers from *load imbalance*. Load balancing is described in more detail in Section 13.5.2.

13.4.3   Point-to-point Communication

During the main parallel work of our code, we need a way for the processes to communicate with each other so that they can coordinate their efforts and combine their results. The simplest mode of communication for this purpose is *point-to-point* communication.

Definition 13.4 *Point-to-point communication*
A mode of communication where one process sends some data to another process. It involves communication between only two processes at a time.

This type of communication is in direct contrast to the master-to-slave communication of `mpi.bcast.Robj2slave`. An example for point-to-point communication is given in Figure 13.12

`mpi.send` and `mpi.recv` are the two main functions for point-to-point communication in Rmpi, and are for sending and receiving a message, respectively. Their function signatures appear below:

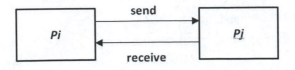

FIGURE 13.12: The figure above shows a process P_i communicating with a single process P_j.

```
1 mpi.send(x, type, dest, tag, comm = 1)
2 mpi.recv(x, type, source, tag, comm = 1, status = 0)
```

These two functions will send (receive) a character, integer, or decimal value to (from) a specific process. This small message can be annotated with a `tag` value so that the receiver can interpret different kinds of messages you might want to send. The `source` or `tag` arguments to `mpi.recv` can be specified by the `mpi.any.source` or `mpi.any.tag` functions, allowing for flexibility in where a message can be received from as well as the type of messages being sent. To use these effectively, pass a variable to `mpi.recv` as the `status` argument; when `mpi.recv` returns, passing this variable to `mpi.get.sourcetag` will return the source and tag of the received message.

One limitation of `mpi.send` and `mpi.recv` is that neither allows for sending any message other than a single character, integer, or decimal value. Rmpi provides the `mpi.send.Robj` and `mpi.recv.Robj` functions for sending larger amounts of data, which allow for the transmission of larger and more complex R objects, such as functions, vectors, data frames, and matrices.

Another critical limitation of `mpi.send` and `mpi.recv` (which is shared by `mpi.send.Robj` and `mpi.recv.Robj`) is that they are *synchronous* functions. Even though synchronous function calls may be easier to understand and use than asynchronous calls, there are some situations that make their use impractical. For instance, suppose we had two processes (running the same "main work function") that wished to exchange data. If both processes called `mpi.recv` and then `mpi.send`, neither one would send its message, and since `mpi.recv` would not complete until a message is received, the two processes would wait on each other indefinitely. Similarly, if the processes called `mpi.send` and then `mpi.recv`, neither `mpi.send` call would complete, with the same result. This type of situation, where different processes cannot continue because they are waiting on messages from each other is called *deadlock*.

Definition 13.5 *Deadlock*
Deadlock refers to a situation where the dependencies between processes form a circle, causing the processes involved to be unable to continue.

The two functions `mpi.isend` and `mpi.irecv` (or `mpi.isend.Robj`) provided by Rmpi enable asynchronous communication. Each of these functions takes an additional `request` argument over their respective synchronous counterparts. Much like the `status` argument of `mpi.recv`, passing a variable as the `request` argument will initialize it to an object that can be manipulated with other Rmpi functions. The `request` objects from the asynchronous communication functions are meant to be used with the functions `mpi.wait` and `mpi.test`. The `mpi.wait` function pauses execution until the associated `mpi.isend` or `mpi.irecv` call is complete, whereas `mpi.test` returns whether or not the communication has completed, without "blocking." Put another way, `mpi.test` is the asynchronous version of `mpi.wait`.

With these new functions, we can revisit our earlier matrix multiplication example to have the master process collect the multiplied matrices at the end. In particular, we can change the placeholder code

```
22        # add code to send all of the products back to
23        # the master process here
```

to

```
22    result = product
23    if (proc != 0)
24      mpi.send.Robj(product, dest=0, tag=0)
25    else
26      for (i in 1:(nprocs - 1))
27        result = cbind(result, mpi.recv.Robj(source=i,
28                       tag=0))
```

As a result, our code will now collect the matrix products from the slave processes and return the full product on the master processes.

However, even though our code can now successfully multiply two matrices, it's not very efficient. (You can use `system.time` to test the code for yourself.) Since each process only uses a part of the second matrix in the product, broadcasting this entire matrix to all of the processes is wasteful. A smarter strategy would be to divide up the second matrix and only send part of the matrix to each process. A modified code for this purpose is as follows:

```
1 par.matmult = function(A, B)
2 {
3   if (!require(Rmpi))
4     return(A %*% B)

5   if (!is.matrix(A) || !is.matrix(B))
6     error("A and B must be matrices")

7   if (dim(A)[2] != dim(B)[1])
8     error("Dimensions of matrices don't match")
```

```
9    b.cols = dim(B)[2]
10   mpi.bcast.Robj2slave(par.matmult.slave)
11   mpi.bcast.Robj2slave(A)
12   mpi.bcast.Robj2slave(b.cols)

13   mpi.bcast.cmd(par.matmult.slave(A, b.cols))
14   return(par.matmult.slave(A, b.cols, B))
15 }

16 par.matmult.slave = function(A, B.cols, B=NULL)
17 {
18   proc = mpi.comm.rank()
19   nprocs = mpi.comm.size()

20   my.cols = B.cols / nprocs
21   if (proc != 0)
22     my.B = mpi.recv.Robj(source=0, tag=0)
23   else
24   {
25     my.B = B[,1:my.cols]
26     for (i in 1:(nprocs - 1))
27       mpi.send.Robj(B[,(i * my.cols + 1):((i + 1)
28            * my.cols)], dest=i, tag=0)
29   }
30   product = A %*% my.B

31   result = product
32   if (proc != 0)
33     mpi.send.Robj(product, dest=0, tag=0)
34   else
35     for (i in 1:(nprocs - 1))
36       result = cbind(result, mpi.recv.Robj(source=i,
37            tag=0))

38   return(result)
39 }
```

Note the changes in lines 9, 12–14, 16, and 20–29.

Another inefficiency is that, if you look at the data distribution and collection code in lines 21–29 and 32–37, the master needs to pass out or collect a section of the matrix (serially) for all of the slave processes. A more clever strategy would be to distribute half of matrix B to process #1, then have the master and process #1 distribute half of these matrices to processes #2 and 3, etc., until all processes have received an equal-sized portion of the matrix. A sample code for distributing the matrix in this manner appears below:

```
20    if (proc == 0)
21    {
22      my.B = B
23      my.cols = dim(B)[2]
24    }

25    delta = 1
26    while (delta < nprocs)
27    {
28      src = proc - delta
29      dst = proc + delta
30      if (src < delta)
31        my.B = mpi.recv.Robj(source=src, tag=0)
32      if (dst < nprocs)
33      {
34        mpi.send.Robj(my.B[,(my.cols / 2 + 1):my.cols],
35        dest=dst,tag=0)
36        my.cols = my.cols / 2
37        my.B = B[,1:my.cols]
38      }
39      delta = delta * 2
40    }
```

For small numbers of processes, this method may not make very much difference, but as the number of processes climbs, this technique will result in distributing the matrix using fewer calls to `mpi.send.Robj` on each process. As an illustration, this method would reduce the number of function calls to `mpi.send.Robj` on a master process with 3 slaves from 3 calls (send to process #1, to #2, to #3) to 2 calls (send to #1, send to #2), but with 64 process, the improved method would take only 6 calls to `mpi.send.Robj` (send to process #1, then #2, #4, #8, #16, and finally #32) on the master processor, compared to 63 calls using our original method.

Even though we can use these two presented techniques to improve the theoretical efficiency of our matrix multiplication code, our original R code has become quite a bit more complex, and we may not even notice much of an improvement in the performance. (In particular, lines 35 and 37 in the code above create copies of the two halves of matrix `my.B`, which represents a huge source of overhead.) Fortunately, a simple solution to problems of performance and code complexity exists and is presented in the next section.

13.4.4   Collective Communication

In addition to functions that allow communication between two individual processes, Rmpi also provides functions for efficiently communicating among a group of processes.

> **Definition 13.6** *Collective communication*
> A mode of communication in which more than two processes communicate at the same time.

Much like how the sender and receiver needed to call `mpi.send` and `mpi.recv`, respectively, before a message can be passed between them, every process involved in collective communication must call the same function before the communication can take place. By default, the collective communication functions involve every process. This behavior can be changed by defining new *Communicator* objects with some of the functions provided by the Rmpi, such as `mpi.comm.spawn`, `mpi.comm.dup`, and `mpi.comm.disconnect`. In this section, though, we will focus only on communication among all processes. Rmpi provides five main functions for collective communication—one for synchronization, two for data distribution, and two for result collection.

The `mpi.barrier` function is the first and the most basic function of the collective communication. The `mpi.barrier` function causes each of the processes involved to pause its execution until all processes have called `mpi.barrier`. Calling `mpi.barrier` does not help distribute data amongst the processes, but it can be useful for separating the different parts of an algorithm and ensuring that all of the processes are synchronized.

The first function for data distribution is `mpi.bcast`. The `mpi.bcast` function, just like `mpi.bcast.Robj2slave`, takes an object that is on one process and sends a copy of that object to every processor. Unlike `mpi.bcast.Robj2slave`, `mpi.bcast` can distribute data from a slave to the master and the rest of the slaves, but it requires all of the process to call the `mpi.bcast` function. The `mpi.bcast` function itself can only broadcast a single character, integer, or decimal number, but the related function `mpi.bcast.Robj` can distribute any R object. An illustration of `mpi.bcast` is given in Figure 13.13.

For dividing a matrix or vector among processes, Rmpi provides the function `mpi.scatter`. The function signature of `mpi.scatter` is as follows:

```
1 mpi.scatter(x, type, rdata, root=0, comm=1)
```

The `root` argument specifies the rank of the process with the data to be distributed, which is passed as argument `x`. Since every process will need to call `mpi.scatter` before the data can be distributed, each process will need to specify a value for `x`; however, this value is ignored on every processor except for the `root`. This data can be a vector or matrix of characters, integers, or decimal numbers, as specified by the `type` argument. The `rdata` argument represents the variable, where the vector or matrix section will be stored.

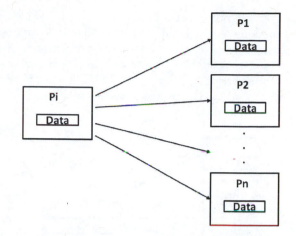

FIGURE 13.13: A basic illustration of `mpi.bcast` is shown in the above figure: process P_i sends a copy of the data to all of the other processes.

Rmpi requires that the variable be initialized to be at least as large as the data being received, which can be achieved by using the built-in `character`, `integer`, and `numeric` functions, as appropriate.

The `mpi.scatter` function is interesting in that it only allows a matrix or vector to be divided evenly. Figure 13.14 shows how `mpi.scatter` works. The `mpi.scatterv` alleviates this restriction by allowing you to pass in an integer vector (with a length equal to the number of processes and a sum equal to the data size) describing how the data should be distributed among the different processes.

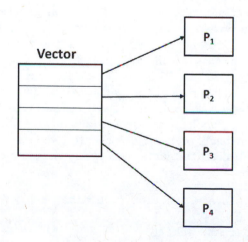

FIGURE 13.14: The above figure shows how a vector is evenly divided among four processes. Each process will receive a part of the vector.

The "inverse" of the `mpi.scatter` function is `mpi.gather`, which allows the processes to combine several small vectors or matrices of the same size into a single large vector on one process. The `mpi.allgather` function has the same effect, but distributes the combined matrix to all of the processes involved. Figure 13.15 shows how `mpi.gather` works. Similar to `mpi.scatterv`, the `mpi.gatherv` and `mpi.allgatherv` functions allow for unevenly distributed data to be combined and distributed.

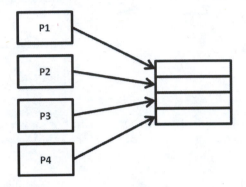

FIGURE 13.15: The above figure shows how `mpi.gather` gathers each piece of a large vector from different processes to combine into a single vector.

The last of the collective communication functions is `mpi.reduce`. The function `mpi.reduce` takes a scalar, vector, or matrix on every process and combines them together using a specified operation to form a single result. The operations that `mpi.reduce` can perform are sum, product, min, and max. Two other operations, "minloc" and "maxloc," are defined—these functions return both the minimum or maximum value as well as the index (location) of that value. The `mpi.reduce` function is restricted to operating on equal-size integer or decimal data, though the `mpi.allreduce` function does allow for the result to be propagated to all participating processes. Figure 13.16 shows how `mpi.reduce` works.

Using the `mpi.scatterv` and `mpi.gatherv` functions, we can modify our matrix multiplication code to distribute and collect our matrix results more efficiently, as well as handle matrices whose number of columns is not evenly divisible by the number of processes. In order to correctly divide the matrix B, we now need to broadcast the number of rows and columns of B. The modified code appears below:

```
1 par.matmult.slave = function(A, B.dims, B=NULL)
2 {
3     proc = mpi.comm.rank()
4     nprocs = mpi.comm.size()

5     div = floor((0:(nprocs - 1) + B.dims[2]) / nprocs)
```

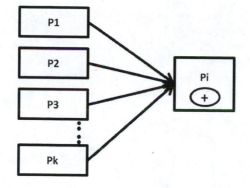

FIGURE 13.16: The above figure shows how `mpi.reduce` collects the results from each process and applies the sum operation on it in order to get the final result.

```
6          * B.dims[1]

7    my.B = matrix(numeric(div[proc + 1]), nrow=B.dims[1])
8    mpi.scatterv(B, scounts=div, rdata=my.B, type=2)
9    product = A %*% my.B

10   A.rows = dim(A)[1]
11   result = matrix(numeric(A.rows * B.dims[2]),
12       nrow=A.rows)
13   div = div / B.dims[1] * A.rows

14   mpi.gatherv(product, rcounts=div, rdata=result,
15       type=2)
16   return(result)
17 }

18 par.matmult = function(A, B)
19 {
20   if (!require(Rmpi))
21     return(A %*% B)

22   if (!is.matrix(A) || !is.matrix(B))
23     error("A and B must be matrices")

24   if (dim(A)[2] != dim(B)[1])
25     error("Dimensions of matrices don't match")

26   b.dims = dim(B)
```

```
27    mpi.bcast.Robj2slave(par.matmult.slave)
28    mpi.bcast.Robj2slave(A)
29    mpi.bcast.Robj2slave(b.dims)

30    mpi.bcast.cmd(par.matmult.slave(A, b.dims))
31    return(par.matmult.slave(A, b.dims, B))
32 }
```

13.4.5 Parallel Graph Mining Example: PageRank

The PageRank algorithm [2], originally discussed in Chapter 5, is another good candidate for using collective communication in order to divide a large problem into multiple processes. As you'll recall, PageRank is a technique that was originally developed to estimate the importance of web pages using the link structure of the Internet. Essentially, web pages get a high PageRank score by being linked to by other pages with a high PageRank score. The most straightforward way to calculate PageRank is to assume that all web pages have equal rank and have each page "distribute" its PageRank score to each linked web page, iterating until the PageRank scores converge. In particular, the algorithm terminates when the difference before and after updating the PageRank value for every web page is less than ϵ for some small value of ϵ.

The update function for PageRank appears below:

$$\mathbf{pr}_{t+1} = d \cdot \mathbf{pr}_t \cdot \mathcal{M} + \frac{1-d}{N} \cdot \mathbf{1}, \tag{13.1}$$

where $\mathbf{pr}$ is a vector representing the PageRank of the N web pages, d is a constant value (usually 0.85), and $\mathcal{M}$ is a matrix such that

$$\mathcal{M}[i,j] = \begin{cases} 0, & \text{if } O[i] > 0 \text{ and there is no link from page } i \text{ to } j \\ 1/O[i], & \text{if } O[i] > 0 \text{ and there is a link from page } i \text{ to } j \\ 1/N, & \text{if } O[i] = 0 \end{cases},$$

where $O[i]$ represents the total number of outbound links from web page i.

To implement PageRank in R, we take in the adjacency matrix of a directed graph, normalize each column to have a sum of 1, initialize the PageRank values to be equal, and iteratively apply Equation 13.1, until the PageRank values do not change significantly. The R code appears below:

```
1 pagerank = function(A, d=0.85, eps=0.001)
2 {
3    if (!is.matrix(A) || dim(A)[1] != dim(A)[2])
4    {
5       print("A must be a square matrix!")
```

```
6      return(0)
7    }

8    N = dim(A)[1]
9    Anorm = sweep(A, 1, rowSums(A), '/')
10   Anorm[is.nan(Anorm)] = 1 / N

11   PR = rep(1/N, N)
12   converged = FALSE

13   while (!converged)
14   {
15     tPR = d * PR %*% Anorm + (1 - d) / N
16     if (max(abs(PR - tPR)) <= eps)
17       converged = TRUE
18     PR = tPR
19   }

20   return(PR)
21 }
```

To parallelize this code, we can divide the update to the PR vector (in line 15) so that each process only calculates the PageRank (PR) value for a portion of the total number of web pages. Because this update function depends on the normalized adjacency matrix Anorm, each process would only need the corresponding columns of Anorm to update the PR values; however, each process needs all of the PageRank values to calculate its updated PR values. Thus, we can use mpi.scatterv to divide up the Anorm matrix before the while loop in line 13, and we collect the results in PR vector on the master process using mpi.allgatherv after the update. We could further improve the algorithm by parallelizing the computation of the normalized adjacency matrix (lines 9–10), but we don't present that optimization due to its complexity. The resulting parallel R code appears below:

```
1 par.pagerank.slave=function(A=NULL,d=0.85,eps=0.001,N=0)
2 {
3    rank=mpi.comm.rank()
4    nprocs=mpi.comm.size()
5    if (!is.null(A))
6      N = dim(A)[1]

7    if (rank == 0)
8    {
9      A = sweep(A, 1, rowSums(A), '/')
10     A[is.nan(A)] = 1 / N
11   }
```

```
12   split.vec = N * (1 + floor((N - 1:nprocs) / nprocs))
13   myCols = split.vec[rank + 1] / N
14   myA=rep(0, myCols * N)

15   mpi.scatterv(A, split.vec, 2, myA)
16   myA=matrix(myA, ncol=myCols)

17   mpi.bcast(d, 2)
18   mpi.bcast(eps, 2)

19   lastPR = rep(1 / N, N)
20   PR = lastPR[1:N]

21   converged = 0
22   split.vec = split.vec / N
23   while (converged == 0)
24   {
25     myPR = d * PR %*% myA + (1 - d) / N
26     mpi.allgatherv(myPR, 2, PR, split.vec)
27     if (max(abs(PR - lastPR)) <= eps)
28       converged = 1

29     lastPR = PR
30   }

31   return(PR)
32 }

33 par.pagerank = function(A, d=0.85, eps=0.001)
34 {
35   if (!require(Rmpi))
36     return(pagerank(A, d, eps))

37   if (!is.matrix(A) || dim(A)[1] != dim(A)[2])
38     error("A must be a square matrix")
39   rows=dim(A)[1]

40   mpi.bcast.Robj2slave(par.pagerank.slave)
41   mpi.bcast.Robj2slave(rows)

42   mpi.bcast.cmd(par.pagerank.slave(N=rows))
43   return(par.pagerank.slave(A=A, d=d, eps=eps))
44 }
```

13.5   Practical Issues in Parallel Programming

One of the main goals of parallel computing is to achieve faster execution time while processing large amounts of data [32]. However, we may not always achieve the faster execution time we seek due to several possible sources of overhead. Parallel overhead can be defined as the extra amount of work done by the parallel program that is not done by the serial program. The main sources of parallel overhead include [17, 19]:

1. **Communication costs**

    Parallel computation that requires communication clearly qualifies as a source of overhead, since a serial computation does not need to communicate with itself. While communication often drastically reduces the amount of redundant computation performed by the parallel processes, time spent on communication is time not spent solving the problem. While embarrassingly parallel computations do not require inter-process communications at all, many parallel computations including those performed by RScaLAPACK use them to coordinate tasks.

2. **Redundant computation**

    Another source of overhead in parallel programming is extra or redundant computations. This situation occurs because the different processes work independently and may end up performing the same computations as other processes. Often, the amount of redundant computation can be reduced by communicating between processes. In some cases, though, the communication cost to eliminate all redundant computations exceeds the amount of time saved, necessitating a compromise.

3. **Idle processes**

    Idle time refers to the situation where one or more processes wait for results from other processes. This situation may arise when there are dependencies between the parallel tasks (as when one process needs results from another before it is able to continue its computation) or *load imbalance*, where one or more processes finish before others. While task dependencies are often problem-specific and not addressable in a general way, the issue of load imbalance is covered in detail in Section 13.5.2, Load Balancing.

13.5.1   Measuring Scalability

Even though practitioners are very interested in how well various algorithms adapt to larger and larger numbers of compute cores, there is no single, universally accepted test for determining the *scalability* of parallel codes.

> **Definition 13.7** *Scalability*
> **Scalability** refers specifically to the capability of a parallel algorithm to take advantage of more computers while limiting overhead to a small fraction of the overall computing time.

The primary goal of measuring scalability is to determine how efficiently a parallel algorithm exploits the parallel processing capabilities of parallel hardware [37]. The performance increase of using parallel computation is limited by the available hardware, i.e., by the number of physical machines or cores available. Hardware limitations are often temporary, though, as newer, cheaper, and more powerful computers are constantly being developed. On the other hand, performance limitations that are intrinsic to the parallel algorithm are much more difficult to circumvent, so being able to estimate the number of computers or cores that an algorithm can effectively utilize is an important question. Evaluating the amount of time taken by a parallel code as more and more processes are added allows us to make predictions as to how well a parallel code will scale. Scalability results allow us to predict how well a parallel code will perform on a large-scale system, as well as how many processes we can apply to a problem before the additional overhead introduced outweighs the amount of time saved.

In this section, we discuss the concepts of strong and weak scaling in parallel computing and provide examples to illustrate these concepts.

13.5.1.1   Strong scaling

Current trends in computing seem to be moving towards multicore systems with an ever-increasing number of cores. However, as the number of cores on a system trends upwards, the power of each individual core may well trend downwards. Cores that are less powerful individually mean that algorithms or codes that do not scale to larger numbers of processes may not perform well on future systems [10]. Measuring the *strong scaling* of a parallel code is a way of testing how the code will be able to adapt to a larger number of processes.

Strong scaling is a measure of the speedup achieved by increasing the number of processes that are applied to the exact same problem. The term *speedup*, when applied to → used to solve parallel computing, refers to how many times faster a code runs in parallel than it runs serially. Mathematically, speedup is defined by the equation

$$\text{Speedup} = \frac{t_s}{t_p},$$

where t_p is the amount of time taken by the parallel algorithm and t_s is the amount of time taken by the serial algorithm. *Ideal* or *linear speedup* describes a situation where the amount of time taken by the algorithm is inversely proportional to the number of processes involved—that is, having twice as many processes halves the time required, having four times as many quarters the time required, etc. Ideal speedup is the case where all computers or cores are fully utilized—that is, all of the machines are performing useful work, all of the time.

> **Definition 13.8** *Processor utilization*
> The **processor utilization** of a parallel code is a measure of what percentage of the computers time is being spent on useful work.

A good example to explain strong scaling is the matrix multiplication code `par.msquare`, which was presented in Section 13.2.2. The code for `par.msquare` also appears below:

```
1 par.msquare = function(M, ndivs=8)
2 {
3   size = dim(M)[1] / ndivs
4   Mlist = list()
5   for (i in 1:ndivs)
6     Mlist[[i]] = M[((i - 1) * size + 1):(i * size),]
7   Mmult = mclapply(Mlist, "%*%", M)
8   Mmult = mclapply(Mmult, t)
9   return(matrix(unlist(Mmult),
10          nrow=(dim(M)[1]), byrow=TRUE))
11 }
```

Strong scaling of the `par.msquare` function can be tested by generating a matrix and calculating the square of the matrix using more and more processes, like the code:

```
12 M = matrix(runif(1024*1024,1,1000),nrow=1024,ncol=1024)
13 system.time(M %*% M)
14 system.time(par.msquare(M, ndivs=1))
15 system.time(par.msquare(M, ndivs=2))
16 system.time(par.msquare(M, ndivs=4))
17 system.time(par.msquare(M, ndivs=8))
18 system.time(par.msquare(M, ndivs=16))
```

Running this code on an 8-core machine resulted in the timing and speedup results reported in Figure 13.17. As expected, the serial run (line 13 above) finished faster than a run using the parallel code with one process. This result is a natural consequence of the overhead introduced by the parallel algorithm, such as setting the parallel environment, dividing the matrix, distributing the data, and collecting and reforming the multiplied matrix at the end. However, as the number of processes used is increased to 2, 4, 6, 8 and 16, the time

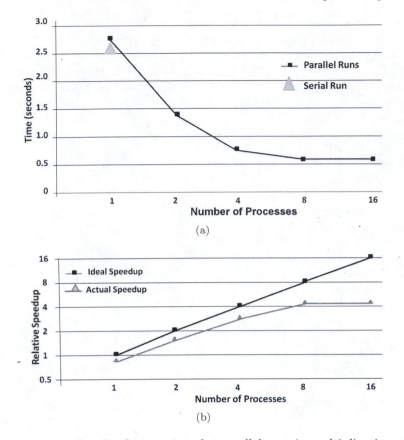

(a)

(b)

FIGURE 13.17: Results for running the parallel matrix multiplication code. Graph (a) shows the amount of time taken by the serial and parallel codes, and graph (b) shows the relative speedup for the different numbers of processes. The runs were performed on an 8-core machine, resulting in little or no speedup at the 16-process level.

required to solve the problem decreases relative to the serial run. Though the figure shows that the scaling in our runs was not quite ideal (doubling the number of processes causes the algorithm to take a bit more than half the amount of time), the results do show good scaling up to 8 cores, which was the limit of the hardware on our testing machine.

13.5.1.2   Weak scaling

In contrast to strong scaling, *weak scaling* is a measurement of the speedup achieved by a parallel code as both the number of processes and the size of the problem under consideration are increased. The goal of weak scaling is to determine how much the overhead increases with larger numbers of processes as the amount of work done by each process remains the same. As larger problems tend to be more easily divided into parallel tasks, a good strong scaling result is harder to achieve than a good result with weak scaling. In an ideal case for weak scaling, the amount of time taken to solve the problem will remain constant (a flat line) as the problem size and number of processes are increased [10].

Since the number of arithmetic operations involved in taking the square of a matrix increases much faster than the size of the matrix involved, matrix multiplication serves as a poor example for weak scaling.

13.5.2   Load Balancing

One of the key issues facing parallel computing professionals is the issue of load balancing.

> **Definition 13.9** *Load balancing*
> Load balancing is a general term for techniques used to distribute a workload across all the participating processes so that each process has the same amount of work to complete.

When a load is unbalanced, the processes with lighter loads will be idle while the process(s) with the heaviest load are still finishing their computations. Since the total time taken by the parallel algorithm is determined by the heaviest load, having unbalanced loads will result in poor performance relative to the number of processes used (see Figure 13.18 for examples of balanced and unbalanced workloads).

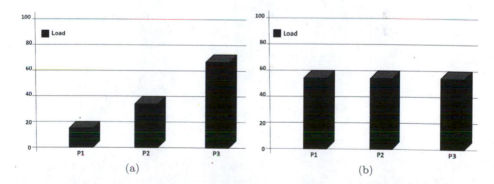

FIGURE 13.18: Sample unbalanced (a) and balanced (b) workload distributions. In (a), the parallel algorithm would be limited by the time it takes process 3 to finish, whereas in (b), all of the processes would finish at the same time, resulting in faster overall computation.

We can simulate the effects of load balancing in R by using multiple calls to the `Sys.sleep` function to represent a workload. `Sys.sleep` is an R function that pauses the execution of code for a given amount of time, which represents the amount of time required by a process to complete a given task or set of tasks. We can demonstrate the beneficial effects of load balancing by creating two lists of numbers representing balanced and unbalanced workloads and applying the `Sys.sleep` function to these artificial "workloads" with `mclapply`. An example R code for producing balanced and unbalanced lists of numbers appears below, and the timing results for one run of this code appear in Figure 13.19. As the two lists generated by the code (v and v2), have the same sum, the serial `lapply` function calls (lines 4 and 5) take exactly the same amount of time. The parallel `mclapply` function call with the unbalanced distribution (line 6) takes nearly twice as long as the `mclapply` call using the even distribution (line 7).

```
1 library(multicore)
2 v = runif(16, 1, 10) * .04
3 v2 = rep(mean(v), 16)
4 system.time(lapply(as.list(v), Sys.sleep))
5 system.time(lapply(as.list(v2), Sys.sleep))
6 system.time(mclapply(as.list(v), Sys.sleep))
7 system.time(mclapply(as.list(v2), Sys.sleep))
```

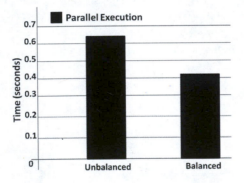

FIGURE 13.19: Simulation results for solving a problem with an unbalanced vs. a balanced load.

Various factors need to be taken into account when attempting to balance the load. One such factor is the speed of the individual computers. In the case where the computers run at different speeds, the faster machines will always finish their workloads "ahead of schedule" relative to the slower machines. In this case, any attempt to assign loads without considering the different speeds won't be effective. Another factor to consider is the time required for individual tasks. In some applications, the amount of time required to solve a problem may vary based on the data in question. A third possible factor is whether the problem would benefit from assigning some processes to coordinate different tasks such as inter-process communication or file accesses, a strategy often pursued in grid computing [18].

There are two types of load balancing—static and dynamic [29]. In static load balancing, each process is assigned a workload at the outset of the computation by an appropriate load balancing algorithm. Static load balancing works best when the amount of time taken by each part of the computation can be estimated accurately, and all of the process run at the same speed [29].

Dynamic load balancing, in contrast, involves having the processes communicate during the computation and redistribute their workloads as necessary. A simple strategy for dynamic load balancing is to maintain a single, centralized "stack" of work, which each process draws from as they run out of work [29]. An alternative is to have the different processes communicate to rebalance their workloads as the computation progresses. This strategy can be implemented in one of two ways: a "push model," where a process with a large workload passes some of its workload to processes with smaller workloads, or a "pull model" (also called "work stealing"), where a process with little or no work takes work from a process with a larger workload [25]. Dynamic load balancing is useful when the workload cannot be divided evenly, when the time needed to compute a task may be unknown, or where the machines may be running at different speeds [29].

13.6 Bibliographic Notes

Several different researchers have contributed to the growing body of literature and packages on parallel and high-performance computing in R. These parallel approaches can be divided broadly into implicit methods, where the work of parallelization is hidden from the user, and explicit methods, where the user can parallelize their own code.

13.6.1 Explicit Parallelism

Explicit parallelism is a feature of a programming language where the programmer explicitly specifies what parts need to be executed independently as parallel tasks. The snow and snowfall packages enable users to use explicit parallel programming in R. The snow package is meant for simple parallel computing in R [15]. It can be tailored to suit any parallel application resulting in fewer bugs [26]. Meanwhile, snowfall is a package that enhances the usability of snow. The snowfall package includes features for error handling, saving intermediate results, and switching from parallel to sequential processing [15].

13.6.2   Implicit Parallelism

The mapReduce package provides implicit parallelism in R that gives a model
for processing and producing large data sets [34]. The mapReduce framework
is made up of two functions, namely, map and reduce. The map function takes
a $(key, value)$-pair and transforms it into a different $(key', value')$-pair. The
reduce function takes all of the values with the same key and performs some
operation to combine them into an output value [22]. The mapReduce parallel
programming model hides the details of parallelization, load balancing and
optimization from the user and leaves these details for the runtime machine
to handle [9].

The hive library provides an interface to Hadoop [14], a popular open-
source implementation of mapReduce capable of accelerating problems on a
very large scale. Though Hadoop is a powerful software package capable of
scaling to large systems, the use of this software is an advanced topic beyond
the scope of this book.[3] Here, we focus our attention on the mapReduce
package, which is simpler to use and requires no software external to R.

The `mapReduce` function provided by the mapReduce library in R operates
similarly to the mapReduce framework described previously, though it differs
in its details. The syntax for the `mapReduce` function is as follows:

```
1 mapReduce(map, ..., data, apply=sapply)
```

where **data** is a data frame or list containing the data to be processed, and
potentially the $(key', value')$ pairs from the map operation; **map** specifies how
to calculate the key' values (or which field to use) from **data**; **apply** gives the
function from the **apply** family (such as **sapply**, **lapply**, or **mc.lapply**) that
will be used in the computation; and the remaining arguments give the results
to be computed in the reduce phase. Note that in this function, parallelism
comes from the use of parallel **apply** functions, so you would need to use a
function like **papply** or **mc.lapply** to see an improvement in performance.

In the following example, we use the **mapReduce** function to count the
number of appearances of each word in a string.

```
2 str="apples bananas oranges apples
3       apples plums oranges bananas"
4 str=unlist(strsplit(str, " "))
5 df=data.frame(key=str, value=1)
6 mapReduce(key, count=sum(value), data=df)
```

In the example, we construct a data frame with two fields, **key** and **value**
(line 5). Initially, the **key** field holds all of the words in our string, and the
value field stores the number 1 for each of the words. When performing the
mapReduce (line 6), the reduce phase will collect all of the values associated
with each key, and report a **count**, which is the sum of all of the values for

---

[3]Interested readers may read more about Hadoop at the Hadoop website [14].

each key. As all of the values are set to be 1, this sum will represent the number of times the word appears in the original string. The example code is serial, but if we passed a parallel `apply` function like `papply` as a parameter to `mapReduce` in line 6, each of the sums could be computed in parallel.

13.6.3 Applications

While some R packages are written to allow R users to write their own parallel codes, others are designed to implement parallel codes for a specific application. The pvclust package is used to calculate the support for a hierarchical clustering in the data. This assessment is based on the quantity, called the P value, which is computed via (parallel) multiscale bootstrap resampling [27]. The pvclust package computes two variants of P, the Approximately Unbiased (AU) value and Bootstrap Probability (BP) value. The AU value is more commonly used because it is a better approximation to BP value. The resulting value of P for each cluster lies between 0 to 1, and this value indicates how strongly the cluster is supported by the data.

13.6.4 Grid-based Computing in R

The gridR and multiR packages provide as a basis for grid-based computing in R to enable faster computations in a grid environment. The gridR package provides an interface for sharing functions and variables among different machines. The gridR toolkit consists of the gridR environment, the gridR Services, and the gridR Client. The gridR Client is implemented as an R package and can request service from gridR Services, which can be implemented as either a grid- or web-based service [30, 31]. The multiR package can also be leveraged to perform grid-based computations in R. It is implemented as a client interface for use in R and extends the `apply` family of functions, similar to snow and gridR. One advantage of the multiR package is that it is independent of hardware or software systems and does not require the installation of additional software [13].

13.6.5 Integration with Existing Parallel Systems

In addition to tools that allow users to specify their own parallel jobs, there are a few R packages that allow integration with existing high-performance computing environments. Examples of these packages include the Rlsf and Rsge packages [24], which implement parallel versions of the `apply` function that allow integration with the LSF and SGE job queuing systems, respectively.

R has also successfully been used with the Condor [16] computing environment [33]. Unlike most high-performance computing environments, Condor is focused on achieving high *throughput*, or total amount of work completed, rather than high *performance*, or quickly finishing individual jobs. This integration is achieved by writing the code to be executed into files, and scheduling R jobs through Condor that will execute the given "script."

13.6.5.1   Parallel performance gains using graphical processing units (GPUs)

An exciting possibility for low-cost high performance computing is the use of Graphical Processing Units (GPUs) to perform computationally intensive tasks. GPUs are highly specialized hardware that can provide high throughput on codes with a high degree of parallelism, modest memory requirements, and few branching conditions (if statements) [23]. In practice, the gputools package for R [4] hides the complexities of employing sophisticated GPU hardware and provides a straightforward interface for performing various statistical operations.

For example, the R code

```
1 library(gputools)
2 M = matrix(rnorm(1024 * 1024), nrow=1024, ncol=1024)
3 Minv = gpuSolve(M)
```

will generate a random 1024×1024 matrix with entries distributed normally around 0 and calculate the inverse of the random matrix using the GPU. (Since the matrix in the code above is generated randomly, it may not have an inverse in every case.)

13.7   Exercises

1. Ray tracing is a method used in computer graphics for producing visual images by tracing the path of light through pixels. Ray tracing is a point sampling algorithm. Is ray tracing an example of an embarrassingly parallel problem?

2. Review the online documentation for the mclapply function. For the following problems, should you set preschedule to TRUE or FALSE? Justify your answer.

   (a) Calculating the product of a list of decimal numbers.

   (b) Calculating the prime factorization of a list of large numbers.

3. **Claim:** Using mclapply does not always reduce your time to perform computation and in some cases it is better to use lapply than mclapply.

   Do you agree with this claim or not? Justify your choice.

4. Produce R code that takes an integer n and an integer matrix `mat` of size n × n and computes and displays the sum of each column in the matrix using `mclapply`.

5. Modify your code from problem 4 to calculate the sum of every other number in each column, starting with the first (i.e., if n equals six, add the first, third, and fifth numbers in each column together).

6. (a) Using the `sample` function in R (with `size = 1000`), write a function for estimating the probability that at least two people will have the same birthday in a group of n people, for some integer n [11].

   (b) Write a parallel code that estimates this probability for n from 1 to 100.

7. Write a function to generate a parabola centered at the origin with a focus point at $(0, a)$, where a is a non-zero real number. Then using the `mclapply` and `integrate` functions, write a parallel R code to compute the area under the parabola in the range $[-b, b]$, where $-b$ and b are integers.

8. Explore the functions in the RScaLAPACK library. Pick a function to find:

   (a) The inverse of a matrix of size 10 × 10.
   (b) The inverse of a matrix of size 1024 × 1024.

   Compare the amount of time taken to run both of these functions. What do you see? Can you provide an explanation for the results?

9. Using the Rmpi package, write a parallel R code that calculates the maximum value of a given vector `vec`.

10. Using the Rmpi package, write a parallel R code that applies a cumulative sum to a vector `vec`. Your solution should pass no more than $\lceil \log_2(n) \rceil$ messages per processor (not counting the initial data distribution), where n is the number of slaves spawned.

Bibliography

[1] P. Breimyer, W. Hendrix, G. Kora, and N. F. Samatova. pR: Lightweight, easy-to-use middleware to plugin parallel analytical computing with R. In *The 2009 International Conference on Information and Knowledge Engineering (IKE'09)*, 2009.

[2] Sergey Brin and Lawrence Page. The anatomy of a large-scale hypertextual web search engine. In *Computer Networks and ISDN Systems*, pages 107–117, 1998.

[3] Dongbo Bu, Yi Zhao, Lun Cai, Hong Xue, Xiaopeng Zhu, Hongchao Lu, Jingfen Zhang, Shiwei Sun, Lunjiang Ling, Nan Zhang, Guojie Li, and Runsheng Chen. Topological structure analysis of the protein-protein interaction network in budding yeast. *Nucleic Acids Research*, 31(9):2443–2450, 2003.

[4] J. Buckner, M. Dai, B. Athey, S. Watson, and F. Meng. Enabling GPU computing in the R statistical environment. In *Bioinformatics Open Source Conference*, 2009.

[5] Lei Chai, Qi Gao, and D. K. Panda. Understanding the impact of multi-core architecture in cluster computing: A case study with intel dual-core system. In *Cluster Computing and the Grid, 2007. CCGRID 2007. Seventh IEEE International Symposium on*, pages 471–478, May 2007.

[6] Hsinchun Chen, Bruce Schatz, Tobun Ng, Joanne Martinez, Amy Kirchhoff, and Chienting Lin. A parallel computing approach to creating engineering concept spaces for semantic retrieval: The Illinois Digital Library Initiative Project. *IEEE Transactions on Pattern Analysis and Machine Intelligence*, 18(8):771–782, 1996.

[7] J. Choi, J. Demmel, I. Dhillon, J. Dongarra, S. Ostrouchov, A. Petitet, K. Stanley, D. Walker, and R. C. Whaley. ScaLAPACK: A portable linear algebra library for distributed memory computers – design issues and performance. *Computer Physics Communications*, 97(1–2):1–15, 1996. High-Performance Computing in Science.

[8] D. Currie. papply: Parallel apply function using MPI, 2005.

[9] Jeffrey Dean and Sanjay Ghemawat. MapReduce: Simplified data processing on large clusters. *Commun. ACM*, 51(1):107–113, 2008.

[10] J. Dongarra, D. Gannon, G. Fox, and K. Kennedy. The impact of multicore on computational science software. *CTWatch Quarterly*, 3:3–10, 2007.

[11] Manuel J. A. Eugster. Parallel computing with R tutorial, 2009.

[12] William Gropp, Ewing Lusk, Nathan Doss, and Anthony Skjellum. High-performance, portable implementation of the MPI Message Passing Interface Standard. *Parallel Computing*, 22(6):789–828, 1996.

[13] Daniel J Grose. Distributed computing using the multiR package.

[14] Hadoop. http://hadoop.apache.org.

[15] Jochen Knaus, Christine Porzelius, Harald Binder, and Guido Schwarzer. Easier parallel computing in R with snowfall and sfCluster. *The R Journal*, 1(1), 2009.

[16] Michael Litzkow, Miron Livny, and Matthew Mutka. Condor: A hunter of idle workstations. In *Proceedings of the 8th International Conference of Distributed Computing Systems*, June 1988.

[17] S. M. Mahjoudi. Parallel computing explained: Parallel code tuning, 2009.

[18] B. Otero, J. M. Cela, R. M. Badia, and J. Labarta. Data distribution strategies for domain decomposition applications in grid environments. In *6th International Conference on Algorithms and Architectures for Parallel Processing, ICA3PP*, pages 214–224, 2005.

[19] P. S. Pacheco. *Parallel Programming with MPI*. Morgan Kaufmann Publishers Inc., San Francisco, CA, 1996.

[20] Dana Petcu. Parallel computers.

[21] C. Prozelius, H. Binder, and M. Schumacher. Parallelized prediction error estimation for evaluation of high-dimensional models. *Bioinformatics*, 25(6):827–829, 2009.

[22] C. Ranger, R. Raghuraman, A. Penmetsa, G. Bradski, and C. Kozyrakis. Evaluating MapReduce for multi-core and multiprocessor systems. In *High Performance Computer Architecture, 2007. HPCA 2007. IEEE 13th International Symposium on*, pages 13–24, Feb. 2007.

[23] S. Ryoo, C. I. Rodrigues, S. S. Baghsorkhi, S. S. Stone, D. B. Kirk, and W. W. Hwu. Optimization principles and application performance evaluation of a multithreaded GPU using CUDA. In *13th ACM SIGPLAN Symposium on Principles and Practice of Parallel Programming*, pages 73–82. ACM Press, 2009.

[24] M. Schmidberger, M. Morgan, D. Eddelbuettel, H. Yao, L. Tierney, and U. Mansmann. State of the art in parallel computing with R. *Journal of Statistical Software*, 31(1), 2009.

[25] M. C. Schmidt, N. F. Samatova, K. Thomas, and B.-H. Park. A scalable, parallel algorithm for maximal clique enumeration. *Journal of Parallel and Distributed Computing*, 69(4):417–428, 2009.

[26] W Schroder-Preikschat, P. O. Alexandre Navaux, and A. A. Medeiros. SNOW: A parallel programming environment for clusters of workstations.

[27] R. Suzuki and H. Shimodaira. Pvclust an R package for assessing the uncertainty in hierarchical clustering. *Bioinformatics*, 22(12):1540–1542, 2006.

[28] Simon Urbanek. Package "multicore." http://www.rforge.net/src/contrib/Documentation/multicore.pdf, 2009.

[29] J. Urbanic. Parallel computing: Overview. http://www.psc.edu/training/TCD_Sep04/Parallel_Computing_Overview.ppt.

[30] D. Wegener, D. Hecker, C. Korner, M. May, and M. Mock. Parallelization of R-programs with GridR in a GPS-trajectory mining application. In *1st Ubiquitous Knowledge Discovery Workshop (UKD)*, 2008.

[31] Dennis Wegener, Thierry Sengstag, Stellios Sfakianakis, Stefan Ruping, and Anthony Assi. GridR: An R-based tool for scientific data analysis in grid environments. *Journal of Future Generation Computer Systems*, 25(4):481–488, 2009.

[32] D. A. Wood and M. D. Hill. Cost-effective parallel computing. *Computer*, 28(2):69–72, 1995.

[33] Xianhong Xie. Running long R jobs with Condor DAG. *R News*, 5(2):13–15, November 2005.

[34] Hung-chih Yang, Ali Dasdan, Ruey-Lung Hsiao, and D. Stott Parker. Map-reduce-merge: Simplified relational data processing on large clusters. In *SIGMOD '07: Proceedings of the 2007 ACM SIGMOD International Conference on Management of Data*, pages 1029–1040, New York, NY, USA, 2007. ACM.

[35] S. Yoginath, N. F. Samatova, D. Bauer, G. Kora, G. Fann, and A. Geist. RScaLAPACK: High performance parallel statistical computing with R and ScaLAPACK. In *Proc. 18th Int'l Conf. on Parallel and Distributed Computing Systems*, pages 61–67, September 2005.

[36] M. J. Zaki, M. Ogihara, S. Parthasarathy, and W. Li. Parallel data mining for association rules on shared-memory multi-processors. In *Supercomputing '96: Proceedings of the 1996 ACM/IEEE conference on Supercomputing (CDROM)*, page 43, Washington, DC, USA, 1996. IEEE Computer Society.

[37] X. D. Zhang, Y. Yan, and K. Q. He. Latency metric: An experimental method for measuring and evaluating parallel program and architecture scalability. *Journal of Parallel and Distributed Computing*, 22(3):392–410, 1994.

[38] Albert Y. Zomaya. *Parallel Computing for Bioinformatics and Computational Biology*, Wiley Series on Parallel and Distributed Computing. Wiley-Interscience, 2005.

Index